In Continuing & Grateful M...
BOY SOLDIERS
KILLED IN BELGIU...

by Paul Foster, FRSA

Published by Minutecircle Services Limited

ISBN 978-1-908345-21-9

"If any ask us why we died

Tell them, because our fathers lied."

Rudyard Kipling

Designed, typeset and published by Minutecircle Services Limited, 12 Conqueror Court, Sittingbourne, Kent ME10 5BH.

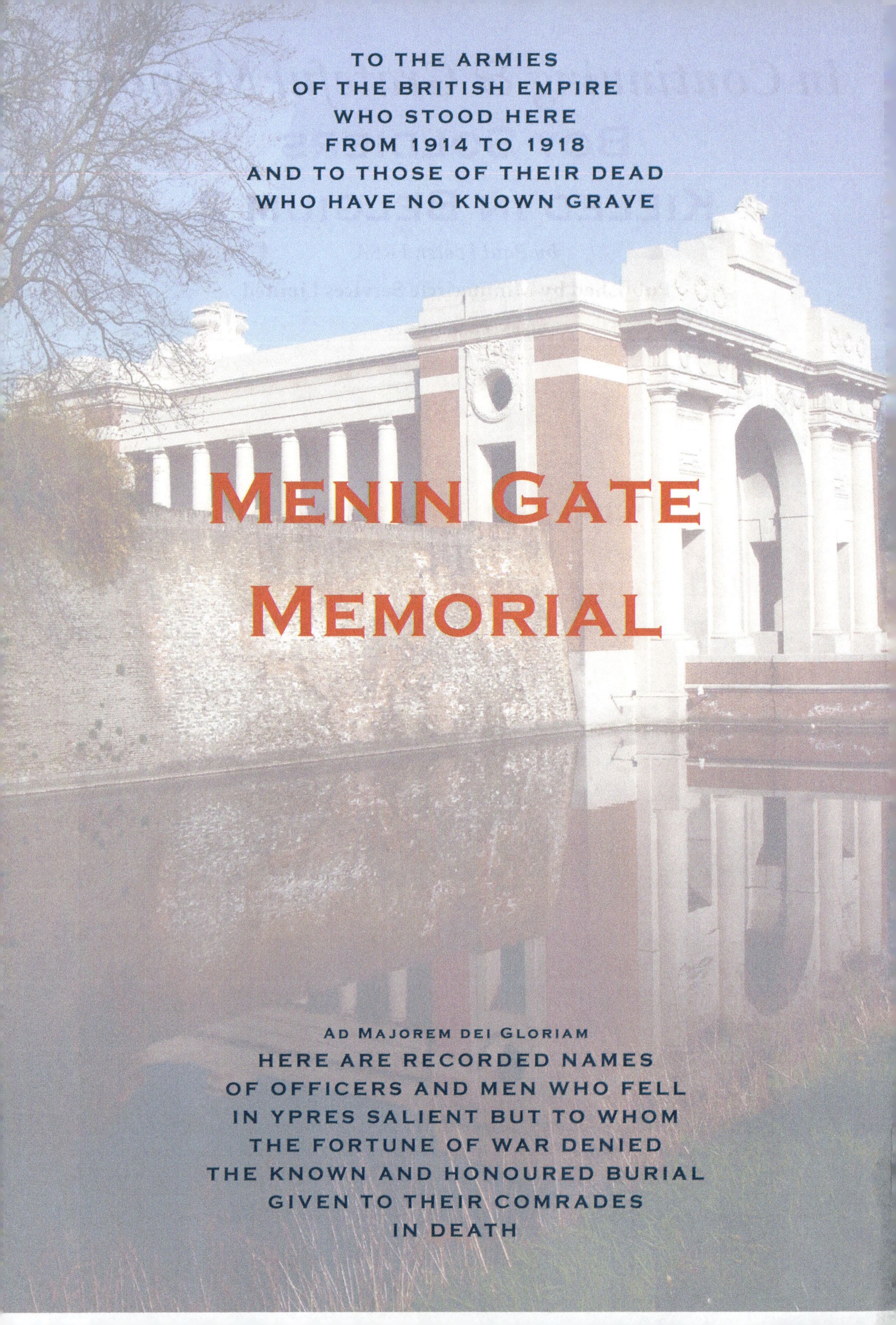

TO THE ARMIES
OF THE BRITISH EMPIRE
WHO STOOD HERE
FROM 1914 TO 1918
AND TO THOSE OF THEIR DEAD
WHO HAVE NO KNOWN GRAVE

Menin Gate
Memorial

Ad Majorem dei Gloriam
HERE ARE RECORDED NAMES
OF OFFICERS AND MEN WHO FELL
IN YPRES SALIENT BUT TO WHOM
THE FORTUNE OF WAR DENIED
THE KNOWN AND HONOURED BURIAL
GIVEN TO THEIR COMRADES
IN DEATH

The book is dedicated to Bob and Myra Sargison my good friends who have

provided me with considerable support during the writing of my books.

PREFACE

For many years I have visited the battlefields of the First World War spending considerable time wandering around the cemeteries and memorials that dot the landscape. Every grave in a cemetery, or a name carved on a memorial, records the supreme sacrifice made by an individual. The raison d'être for producing the series of books is to pay tribute to the memory of all those who served in the war particularly to those who made the ultimate sacrifice. They are, in so many ways, anonymous — some are remembered but too many are now forgotten with the passage of time. Compiling the book has been a labour of love and provided me with considerable satisfaction. It has been fascinating conducting the research as I have learned so much and appreciate even more the bravery of the young boys who wanted to serve the King and Country. They come from a world and a society that is now long departed, the war itself changed the world landscape, Empires fell and society changed.

Nearly eight hundred young boys who eagerly volunteered gave their lives in Belgium before they were old enough to enlist or to serve at the front. There are nearly three hundred and fifty young men commemorated on the Menin Gate Memorial. A sister publication, Boy Soldiers Killed in Belgium 1, covers four hundred and fifty cameos of boys buried in the cemeteries of Belgium, for details of the book please see page 191. There were very many more boys who are not recorded in the books as their real age at the time of their death has not yet come to light. Many under age boys served and survived the war, sadly they are not remembered in the books. I have included a selection of officers aged only 18 to illustrate how young so many of the officers were who came straight from school to command troops on the Western Front. Only a handful of the boys included in the book gave their real age, the majority lied about their date of birth. The recruiting officers turned a blind eye to many who were allowed to 'slip through', as it was clear they wanted to serve. It must also be remembered that many of the parents could have demanded to have their boys returned to the family but they did not, others did their best to stop them from enlisting but failed.

When I began the research for the book I thought that the majority of the boys would have slipped through in the initial stages of the war when the 'blind eye' was to the fore. It was surprising therefore, to see how many were able to enlist in the latter stages of the war when stricter controls were supposedly enforced.

It is a magnificent compliment and tribute to the boys of The Empire with their love of their own and the home country together with their King, George V, that so many volunteered from Australia, Canada, New Zealand, South Africa and India. The ties to the mother country were wonderfully strong and they wanted to serve when they had no requirement to do so — all were volunteers. Today, with the ubiquitous, ghastly, political correctness and revisionist drivel, we sadly forget or ignore the spirit of our 'cousins' spread across the world that were spawned at a time of Empire, an Empire that did far more good than harm. Troops of all religions, races and colours came together under one King and one flag with an enthusiasm to support one cause. Let us not forget what they believed in and what they were fighting for too.

For each individual I have written a cameo that includes information relating to their family background, education, employment and interests which is followed by their service during the war. An extensive range of source material has been used to compile the publication from contemporary books, family records to the internet. For some individuals the information was relatively easy to access, for others it has been a case of following one clue after another, then finally putting the pieces together like a jig-saw — however incomplete! The quotes included in the text are as they were originally produced, irrespective of the spelling that was used at the time or errors included. I have not interrupted the flow of the text by continuously adding [sic]. The books are illustrated with contemporary illustrations produced during the war coupled with original photographs and postcards. The captions are mine and are not necessarily those that were used when the illustration or photograph was originally reproduced but the cartoons retain their original captions. I have drawn or reproduced maps throughout the text that I hope will assist in the comprehension of the battles and actions undertaken.

www.remembering1418.com

Email: remembering@btinternet.com

Post: In Continuing & Grateful Memory, c/o 15 Cress Way, Faversham, Kent ME13 7NH.

Paul Foster, FRSA

CONTENTS

	Page
Preface	4
Name Index	6-11
The Menin Gate Memorial	12-17
The Architect, Sir Reginald Blomfield	14
The Cameos	18-187
'In Continuing & Grateful Memory' — The Menin Gate	188
'In Continuing & Grateful Memory' — The Ploegsteert Sector	189
'In Continuing & Grateful Memory' — From Ypres to Zillebeke via Hooge	190
'In Continuing & Grateful Memory' — Boy Soldiers Killed In Belgium 1	191
'I Was There' Series	192-195
IC&GM Tours	196

NAME INDEX

Name	Rank	Date of Death	Regiment	Panel	Awards	Page
Alker, R	Private	24.5.15	Lancashire Fusiliers	Panel 33		18
Allen, W	Private	29.4.15	The Royal Hampshire Regiment	Panel 35		18
Anderson, J S	Private	2.5.15	Middlesex Regiment	Panel 49		18-19
Angus, A	Private	1.11.14	London Regiment (London Scottish)	Panel 54		19-20
Archer-Shee, G	Lieutenant	31.10.14	South Staffordshire Regiment	Panel 35		20-21
'The Winslow Boy'						
Arkinstall, J	Rifleman	25.4.15	Monmouthshire Regiment	Panel 50		21
Ashdown, H R	Rifleman	12.10.15	King's Royal Rifle Corps	Panel 53		21-22
Askew, O G	Private	14.5.15	Essex Yeomanry	Panel 5		22-23
Ashley, A R	Private	27.4.15	East Surrey Regiment	Panel 34		24
Averill, J J	Private	5.8.15	North Staffordshire Regiment	Panel 55		25
Avila, L F	Rifleman	4.12.14	London Regiment (Queen Victoria's Rifles)	Panel 54		25
Bailey, J R	Rifleman	6.7.15	Rifle Brigade	Panel 46		25-26
Ball, W	Private	27.12.15	West Yorkshire Regiment (Prince of Wales's Own)	Panel 21		26
Barr, H	Private	2.5.15	East Yorkshire Regiment	Panel 21		26-27
Beaton, H B	Private	14.6.16	Canadian Infantry (Central Ontario Regiment)	Panel 30		27-28
Beattie, R	Private	26.4.15	Northumberland Fusiliers	Panel 12		28
Berube, M	Private	3.6.16	Canadian Infantry	Panel 30		28-29
Binning, J	Corporal	26.4.15	Northumberland Fusiliers	Panel 12		29
Birch, S H	Lance Corporal	22.2.15	Queen's (Royal West Kent Regiment)	Panel 45		29
Bird, W	Rifleman	18.1.16	Rifle Brigade	Panel 46		30
Blackwell, S	Private	8.5.15	King's Own Yorkshire Light Infantry	Panel 47		30
Blay, K	Private	25.9.15	Oxford and Bucks Light Infantry	Panel 39		30-31
Blaymire, S	Private	30.3.15	York and Lancaster Regiment	Panel 55		31
Blissett, H F	Private	20.4.15	East Surrey Regiment	Panel 34		31
Bolton, T	Private	27.4.15	King's Own (Royal Lancaster Regiment)	Panel 12		31
Bowen, R E	Rifleman	14.8.17	King's Royal Rifle Corps	Panel 53		31-32
Boyder, W G	Private	10.4.18	South African Infantry	Panel 15		32
Boyle, J	Private	24.4.15	Canadian Infantry (British Columbia Regiment)	Panel 24		32-33
Bradley, C E	Private	10.11.17	Canadian Infantry (Manitoba Regiment)	Panel 24		33
Bradley, J	Private	31.10.14	The Loyal North Lancashire Regiment	Panel 43		34
Brand, J	Private	27.3.16	Royal Scots Fusiliers	Panel 19		35
Bridges, W	Private	25.9.15	Suffolk Regiment	Panel 21		35
Briggs, W	Private	25.5.15	Suffolk Regiment	Panel 21		35
Brophy, P P	Lance Corporal	16.6.17	Leinster Regiment	Panel 44		36-37
Bryant, J B	Private	26.9.17	Australian Infantry, AIF	Panel 29		38
Buchan, T	Private	5.3.16	Royal Scots	Panel 11		38-39
Bulleid, G E	Private	22.4.15	Canadian Infantry (Eastern Ontario Regiment)	Panel 18		39
Bunce, F G	Private	10.6.17	Cheshire Regiment	Panel 22		39
Burden, C B	Private	31.7.17	Queen's Own (Royal West Kent Regiment)	Panel 45		39-40
Burden, H F	Private	21.7.15	Northumberland Fusiliers	Panel 60		40-41
Burlace, P	Private	12.8.15	Leinster Regiment	Panel 44		41-42
Burton, A E	Private	20.4.15	East Surrey Regiment	Panel 34		42-44
Cairns, J	Private	16.4.15	Argyll and Sutherland Highlanders	Panel 42		44
Cameron, A	Private	15.12.14	King's Own Scottish Borderers	Panel 22		44
Cameron, H D	Private	21.4.15	Canadian Infantry (Quebec Regiment)	Panel 24		45
Capey, E	Private	17.2.16	Royal Welsh Fusiliers	Panel 22		46
Carr, J W	Private	2.6.16	5th Canadian Mounted Rifles (Quebec Regiment)	Panel 32		46-47
Cassell, L C	Private	1.8.17	Worcestershire Regiment	Panel 34		47
Cassells, J	Private	17.6.15	South Lancashire Regiment	Panel 37		47
Cathcart, G	Private	23.4.15	King's Own (Royal Lancaster Regiment)	Panel 12		48
Cathcart, J	Private	4.5.15	King's Own (Royal Lancaster Regiment)	Panel 12		48-49
Cattell, C H C	Private	14.5.15	Essex Yeomanry	Panel 5		50
Cawtheray, W	Private	4.10.15	King's Own Yorkshire Light Infantry	Panel 47		50-51
Chambers, A N	Private	25.5.15	Cheshire Regiment	Panel 22		51
Chandler, R	Private	26.4.15	The Royal Hampshire Regiment	Panel 35		51-52
Clarke, A P	Private	20.9.17	South African Infantry	Panel 15		52
Clipston, R	Private	9.5.15	East Surrey Regiment	Panel 34		52
Coles, L	Private	16.6.15	Lincolnshire Regiment	Panel 21		52
Collins, T G	Private	3.5.15	The Buffs (East Kent Regiment)	Panel 14		53
Colman, E A	Rifleman	6.1.16	Rifle Brigade	Panel 48		53
Compton, J H	Private	25.4.15	East Surrey Regiment	Panel 34		53-54

Name	Rank	Date of Death	Regiment	Panel	Awards	Page
Connolly, J A	Lance Corporal	25.9.15	Royal Irish Rifles	Panel 40		54
Constantine, C	Private	2.3.16	King's Own (Royal Lancaster Regiment)	Panel 12		54-55
Cooper, A L	Private	5.8.15	Oxford and Bucks Light Infantry	Panel 39		55
Cooper, F	Private	31.10.17	5th Battalion Canadian Mounted Rifles	Panel 32		55-56
Cooper, J	Private	25.9.15	Gordon Highlanders	Panel 38		56
Cosgrove, A	Private	27.3.16	Northumberland Fusiliers	Panel 12		57
Coshall, J H	Private	18.4.15	Queen's Own (Royal West Kent Regiment)	Panel 45		57-58
Cowling, R	Private	2.3.15	Suffolk Regiment	Panel 21		58
Crook, J R	Private	19.8.16	Canadian Infantry (Quebec Regiment)	Panel 28		58-59
Crosby, K B	Private	11.4.16	Canadian Infantry (Quebec Regiment)	Panel 26		59
Crossman, G	Private	24.5.15	Royal Fusiliers	Panel 8		59
Cruickshank, J S	Private	25.9.15	Gordon Highlanders	Panel 38		60
Crust, F C	Private	8.2.16	Queen's Own (Royal West Kent Regiment)	Panel 45		60
Cunningham, W	Rifleman	7.6.17	London Regiment (Post Office Rifles)	Panel 54		60-61
Cunnison, T	Private	11.11.14	Black Watch (Royal Highlanders)	Panel 37		61
Currey, H H	Private	31.7.15	Duke of Cornwall's Light Infantry	Panel 20		61
Curtis, R J	Private	25.9.15	Oxford and Bucks Light Infantry	Panel 39		62
Dalton, J	Private	13.5.15	Royal Irish Fusiliers	Panel 42		62
Davies, J	Private	25.5.15	Welsh Regiment	Panel 37		62
Davies, W	Private	9.8.15	King's Shropshire Light Infantry	Panel 49		62-63
Davis, W G	Rifleman	30.7.15	King's Royal Rifle Corps	Panel 53		63
Dewhurst, I	Private	2.3.16	King's Own (Royal Lancaster Regiment)	Panel 12		63
Dix, P W	Private	20.9.17	South African Infantry	Panel 15		63
Domeney, O T	Private	7.6.17	Australian Infantry, AIF	Panel 25		64
Domleo, S H	Private	10.4.18	South African Infantry	Panel 15		64
Donnachie, W	Private	12.11.15	Highland Light Infantry	Panel 38		64-65
Dowse, H	Private	19.4.15	Bedfordshire Regiment	Panel 33		65
Duchart, J	Private	25.4.15	Argyll and Sutherland Highlanders	Panel 44		65-66
Duffy, J	Rifleman	30.7.15	King's Royal Rifle Corps	Panel 53		66
Dunlop, J B	Private	2.6.16	Canadian Infantry (Alberta Regiment)	Panel 30		66
Dunn, G A	Private	1.11.14	Oxford and Bucks Light Infantry	Panel 39		67-68
Dunn, W H	Lance Corporal	14.3.15	Duke of Cornwall's Light Infantry	Panel 20		68
Edge, N V	Private	19.4.15	East Surrey Regiment	Panel 34		69
Edwards, J	Private	18.11.14	King's Own Scottish Borderers	Panel 22		69
Espie, D	Private	24.10.14	Royal Scots Fusiliers	Panel 19		69
Farrell, M	Private	14.4.15	King's Own (Royal Lancaster Regiment)	Panel 12		70
Faulkner, W A	Private	29.7.17	Worcestershire Regiment	Panel 34		70
Felton, W	Private	14.2.16	Machine Gun Corps (Infantry)	Panel 56		70
Ferens, A P	Private	26.4.15	Durham Light Infantry	Panel 36		70
Ferguson, J A R	Lieutenant	9.5.15	Royal Sussex Regiment	Panel 20		71-72
Fido, F L	Private	25.5.15	Welsh Regiment	Panel 37		72
Fillingham, J J	Private	9.8.15	York and Lancaster Regiment	Panel 55		72
Fletcher, J	Private	5.2.15	King's Own (Royal Lancaster Regiment)	Panel 12		72-73
Flin, F S	Private	13.6.16	Canadian Infantry (Quebec Regiment)	Panel 17		73
Floyd, J	Private	29.6.15	East Lancashire Regiment	Panel 34		73
Ford, W H	Private	31.7.15	Duke of Cornwall's Light Infantry	Panel 20		73
Forest, H S	Gunner	25.4.15	Canadian Field Artillery	Panel 10		73-74
Forsyth, G	Private	12.5.15	Cameron Highlanders	Panel 38		74
Forsyth-Ingram, J L	Private	11.4.18	South African Infantry	Panels 16		74
Fox, N	Private	5.5.15	Duke of Wellington's (West Riding Regiment)	Panel 20		74-75
Francis, W M	Private	29.9.15	Middlesex Regiment	Panel 51		75
Gale, B P	Private	25.9.15	Oxford and Bucks Light Infantry	Panel 39		76
Gaynor, F	Private	29.2.16	Durham Light Infantry	Panel 36		76
Gibbons, P A	Rifleman	10.5.15	Rifle Brigade	Panel 48		76
Gillard, J	Private	2.3.16	King's Own (Royal Lancaster Regiment)	Panel 12		76
Godbehere, W	Private	8.5.15	York and Lancaster Regiment	Panel 55		77
Gough, J	Private	29.12.14	Royal Scots	Panel 11		77
Goulden, F	Private	16.6.15	Wiltshire Regiment	Panel 53		77
Graham, D L	Private	13.1.15	Gordon Highlanders	Panel 38		77
Graham, H	Private	14.12.14	Gordon Highlanders	Panel 38		77-78
Grant, J	Private	10.5.15	Cameron Highlanders	Panel 38		78
Grice, H	Private	27.4.15	King's Own (Royal Lancaster Regiment)	Panel 12		78

Name	Rank	Date of Death	Regiment	Panel	Awards	Page
Grinham, W J	Private	30.10.14	Yorkshire Regiment	Panel 33		78-80
Gunnell, A E	Private	14.11.14	South Wales Borderers	Panel 22		80
Gutteridge, A J	Lance Corporal	2.3.15	Royal Fusiliers	Panel 6		80-81
Hall, E H	Private	8.5.15	Middlesex Regiment	Panel 51		81
Hall, W	Rifleman	1.8.15	Rifle Brigade	Panel 48		81
Hanson, F	Private	9.7.17	London Regiment	Panels 54		81-82
Harford, H T	Private	26.5.15	Norfolk Regiment	Panel 4		82
Harris, J H	Private	6.5.15	Royal Irish Regiment	Panel 33		82
Harrison, C J	Private	2.6.16	5th Canadian Mounted Rifles Battalion	Panel 32		82
Hart, G	Private	27.6.15	South Lancashire Regiment	Panel 37		83
Harvey, G B P	Private	7.8.17	Royal Fusiliers	Panel 8		83-84
Harwood, C W	Private	25.5.15	The Buffs (East Kent Regiment)	Panel 14		84
Hawes, W E	Private	25.5.15	Suffolk Regiment	Panel 21		84
Hawtin, J	Rifleman	6.7.15	King's Royal Rifle Corps	Panel 53		84
Hay, J S	Private	12.12.14	King's Own Scottish Borderers	Panel 22		84
Hayhurst, H	Private	31.7.17	Royal Berkshire Regiment	Panel 45		84
Haynes, C H	Private	3.6.16	Canadian Infantry	Panel 24		85-87
Healy, M J	Private	4.6.17	Connaught Rangers	Panel 42		87-88
Henry, H A	Private	18.6.16	Canadian Infantry (New Brunswick Regiment)	Panel 26		88
Hill, H	Private	3.5.15	Royal Fusiliers	Panel 8		89
Hills, R B	Sapper	7.2.18	Australian Engineers	Panel 7		89-90
Hilson, A R	Rifleman	10.5.15	King's Royal Rifle Corps	Panel 53		90
Hindley, H	Private	25.9.15	King's Shropshire Light Infantry	Panel 49		90-91
Hirst, H	Private	8.5.15	King's Own Yorkshire Light Infantry	Panel 47		91
Hives, A	Private	26.4.15	Royal Fusiliers	Panel 6		91
Holborow, W E	Private	10.5.15	Gloucestershire Regiment	Panel 22		91
Hollows, H	Rifleman	10.5.15	King's Royal Rifle Corps	Panel 53		92
Holohan, A	Private	9.5.15	Royal Dublin Fusiliers	Panel 46		92
Hollom, J E	Rifleman	30.7.15	King's Royal Rifle Corps	Panel 53		92
Hood, G	Private	28.4.15	Duke of Cornwall's Light Infantry	Panel 20		92-93
Hornsey, F A	Private	12.4.18	South African Infantry	Panel 15		93
Howard, F	Private	24.5.15	Northumberland Fusiliers	Panel 12		93
Hudson, E	Rifleman	16.6.15	Royal Irish Rifles	Panel 40		93-94
Hunter, A	Private	26.4.15	Durham Light Infantry	Panel 36		94
Hurley, T	Private	7.5.15	Monmouthshire Regiment	Panel 50		94
Huxtable, A H E	Rifleman	6.8.15	King's Royal Rifle Corps	Panel 53		94-95
Inglis, R	Private	27.5.15	Royal Scots	Panel 11		95
Jacob, A	Private	29.9.15	Middlesex Regiment	Panel 51		95
James, G	Private	2.5.15	Monmouthshire Regiment	Panel 50		95
James, W J	Private	31.7.17	Royal Welsh Fusiliers	Panel 22		95-96
Jarrold, G	Private	29.9.15	Middlesex Regiment	Panel 51		96
Jeffs, W A	Private	14.12.14	Gordon Highlanders	Panel 38		97
Johnson, C T	Private	13.5.15	Essex Regiment	Panel 39		97
Johnson, R	Private	8.5.15	King's Own (Royal Lancaster Regiment)	Panel 12		97
Johnson, W H	Private	2.6.16	4th Canadian Mounted Rifles (Central Ontario Regiment)	Panel 32		97-98
Jones, A G	Private	26.5.15	King's Shropshire Light Infantry	Panel 49		98
Jones, E C V	Private	25.5.15	Welsh Regiment	Panel 37		98-101
Jones, E H	Rifleman	10.2.15	London Regiment (The Rangers)	Panel 54		102
Jones, W E	Private	14.5.15	Essex Yeomanry	Panel 5		102
Judd, A	Private	16.12.14	East Surrey Regiment	Panel 34		102
Kelly, E R	2nd Lieutenant	7.7.15	Border Regiment	Panel 35		102
Kennedy, J R	Private	2.6.16	4th Canadian Mounted Rifles Battalion	Panel 32		103-104
Kidd, T	Private	3.5.15	East Yorkshire Regiment	Panel 31		104
Kiernan, J	Rifleman	28.1.16	King's Royal Rifle Corps	Panel 53		105
Kitcherside, A G	Rifleman	31.10.16	King's Royal Rifle Corps	Panel 53		105
Klagge, W R	Rifleman	8.5.15	London Regiment (The Rangers)	Panel 54		105-106
Lake, E	Rifleman	10.5.15	Rifle Brigade	Panel 48		106-107
Lally, F	Private	8.11.14	Duke of Wellington's (West Riding Regiment)	Panel 59		107
Lamb, A A	Private	24.4.15	East Yorkshire Regiment	Panel 31		107
Lambert, P H	Private	13.6.16	Canadian Infantry (Central Ontario Regiment)	Panel 18	MM	107-108
Lane, C H	Private	6.11.14	Welsh Regiment	Panel 37		108-110

Name	Rank	Date of Death	Regiment	Panel	Awards	Page
Lane, E F	Private	6.6.15	Wiltshire Regiment	Panel 53		110
Lear, W	Private	26.4.15	Devonshire Regiment	Panel 21		110
Ledwidge, F	Private	24.5.15	Royal Dublin Fusiliers	Panel 46		110
Lennon, T	Private	23.5.15	Royal Dublin Fusiliers	Panel 46		110
Liddell, T	Private	25.4.15	Durham Light Infantry	Panel 36		110
Lilley, W G	Private	24.5.15	Royal Warwickshire Regiment	Panel 8		111
Little, A	Private	18.11.14	The King's (Liverpool Regiment)	Panel 4		111-112
Llewellyn, A G	Lance Corporal	12.11.14	Coldstream Guards	Panel 11		112-113
Lloyd, H	Private	25.5.15	Welsh Regiment	Panel 37		113
Macauslan, W T	Private	25.9.15	Gordon Highlanders	Panel 38		113
Macdonald, K	Private	3.6.16	Canadian Infantry	Panel 24		113-114
Maddock, T H	Private	13.5.15	Leicestershire Yeomanry	Panel 5		114
Maguire, P	Rifleman	10.8.17	Royal Irish Rifles	Panel 40		114
Mahoney, M	Private	10.5.15	Royal Dublin Fusiliers	Panel 46		114-115
Malcolm, P	Private	8.5.15	Argyll and Sutherland Highlanders	Panel 44		115
Manning, T W	Private	20.7.15	Middlesex Regiment	Panel 51		115
Marks, E	Private	7.6.17	Australian Infantry, AIF	Panel 25		115-116
Martin, C	Private	11.11.14	Cameron Highlanders	Panel 38		116
Mcaughtrie, W	Private	21.7.15	Gordon Highlanders	Panel 38		116
McClelland, J	Rifleman	6.8.17	Royal Irish Rifles	Panel 40		116
Mcgarva, T H	Private	21.7.17	Cameronians (Scottish Rifles)	Panel 22		117
Mcguinness, J	Private	24.5.15	Royal Dublin Fusiliers	Panel 46		117
McLellan, A	Private	21.4.16	Durham Light Infantry	Panel 38		117
Mcleod, K	Private	29.10.14	Cameron Highlanders	Panel 38		117
Mcleod, N	Private	11.11.14	Cameron Highlanders	Panel 38		118
Mcloughlin, T	Private	31.7.17	East Lancashire Regiment	Panel 34		118
McManus, H J	Private	7.10.15	Somerset Light Infantry	Panel 21		118-119
Mcmath, N C	Private	6.6.16	Canadian Infantry	Panel 28		119
McStravick, J	Private	25.4.15	Royal Irish Fusiliers	Panel 42		119-120
Mead, H	Private	13.11.14	Dorsetshire Regiment	Panel 37		120
Menoch, J	Private	10.5.15	Argyll and Sutherland Highlanders	Panel 44		120-121
Meredith, R L	Private	7.6.17	Australian Infantry, AIF	Panel 27		121-122
Millar, R	Rifleman	9.5.15	Royal Irish Rifles	Panel 40		122
Miller, H	Private	31.10.14	Connaught Rangers	Panel 42		122-124
Mills, G H	Private	5.7.15	Dorsetshire Regiment	Panel 37		124
Milton, C R	Private	27.4.15	Somerset Light Infantry	Panel 21		124-125
Mogford, J	Private	8.5.15	Monmouthshire Regiment	Panel 50		125
Molloy, E J S	Private	4.10.17	Australian Infantry, AIF	Panel 7		125-126
Morgan, J B	Private	3.5.15	Royal Scots	Panel 11		126
Morris, H G	2nd Lieutenant	23.5.15	Duke of Cornwall's Light Infantry	Panel 58		127
Morrison, W	Private	26.4.15	Northumberland Fusiliers	Panel 8		128
Morton, A	Private	7.6.17	Lincolnshire Regiment	Panel 21		128
Mott, W C	Rifleman	15.3.15	Rifle Brigade	Panel 48		128
Mountcastle, G A	Private	30.6.15	Lincolnshire Regiment	Panel 21		128
Nash, F L	Rifleman	24.5.15	London Regiment (The Rangers)	Panel 54		129
Nicholls, J	Private	14.6.16	Canadian Infantry	Panel 24		129
Norcott, C C	Private	11.2.16	Oxford and Bucks Light Infantry	Panel 39		129
Norton, J A	Private	8.5.15	Monmouthshire Regiment	Panel 50		129-130
Oakes, T A V	Private	18.4.15	Queen's Own (Royal West Kent Regiment)	Panel 45		130
Oliver, R	Private	8.5.15	Northumberland Fusiliers	Panel 8		130
Over, E C	Private	22.5.15	Royal Fusiliers	Panel 6		130-131
Owen, C A	Private	13.6.16	Canadian Infantry	Panel 28		131-132
Page, H K	Private	12.10.17	Australian Infantry, AIF	Panel 27		132
Parsons, J	Private	26.9.15	Somerset Light Infantry	Panel 21		132
Pasfield, J	Private	31.7.17	Northamptonshire Regiment	Panel 45		132-133
Patterson, A	Private	16.6.15	Lincolnshire Regiment	Panel 21		133
Peacock, J E	Private	6.11.17	Canadian Infantry	Panel 26		133-134
Pearce, A	Lance Corporal	29.4.15	Cheshire Regiment	Panel 19		134
Peffers, J J	Private	20.9.17	South African Infantry	Panel 16		135
Perry, A R	Private	1.10.17	Australian Infantry, AIF	Panel 25		135
Petchey, E J	Private	13.5.15	Essex Yeomanry	Panel 5		136
Phelps, C	Private	8.5.15	King's Own (Royal Lancaster Regiment)	Panel 12		136

Name	Rank	Date of Death	Regiment	Panel	Awards	Page
Platt, T	Rifleman	25.9.15	Rifle Brigade	Panel 48		136
Powell, W B	Private	4.11.15	Bedfordshire Regiment	Panel 33		136-137
Preece, L	Private	3.8.15	King's Shropshire Light Infantry	Panel 49		137
Presant, B A	Private	26.4.15	Canadian Infantry (Quebec Regiment)	Panel 24		137
Price, P	Rifleman	30.7.15	Rifle Brigade	Panel 48		137-138
Pulsford, F T	Rifleman	21.4.15	London Regiment (The Rangers)	Panel 54		138
Purnell, T	Lance Corporal	20.4.15	Gloucestershire Regiment	Panel 22		139
Quincey, G F	Private	13.11.14	Worcestershire Regiment	Panel 34		139-140
Quinn, B T	Rifleman	25.9.15	Rifle Brigade	Panel 48		140-141
Radford, H	Private	7.5.15	King's Own Yorkshire Light Infantry	Panel 47		141
Read, E	Private	24.4.15	Suffolk Regiment	Panel 21		141
Read, W	Private	14.11.14	Dorsetshire Regiment	Panel 37		141
Redman, J	Private	31.7.17	Royal Scots Fusiliers	Panel 19		141-142
Reeves, H	Private	10.5.15	Gloucestershire Regiment	Panel 34		142
Reid, L T S	Private	1.11.14	London Regiment (London Scottish)	Panel 54		142
Renshaw, V	Lance Corporal	7.5.15	King's Own Yorkshire Light Infantry	Panel 47		142-143
Rhodes, R	Private	8.5.15	York and Lancaster Regiment	Panel 55		144
Richmond, H J	Private	25.4.15	Argyll and Sutherland Highlanders	Panel 44		144
Roberts, J	Private	1.11.14	Lincolnshire Regiment	Panel 21		144
Robertshaw, G W	Private	24.2.15	Duke of Wellington's (West Riding Regiment)	Panel 20		144
Robichaud, J C V	Private	15.11.17	Canadian Infantry	Panel 28		144-146
Robins, H T	Private	27.4.15	Somerset Light Infantry	Panel 21		146-147
Rose, O	Private	30.4.15	Middlesex Regiment	Panel 51		147
Ross, D A C	Rifleman	25.9.15	Rifle Brigade	Panel 48		147-148
Ross, F A O	Private	20.9.17	Australian Infantry, AIF	Panel 17		148
Rostron, J	Private	25.5.15	King's Shropshire Light Infantry	Panel 49		149
Rushbrooke, T E	Rifleman	30.7.15	Rifle Brigade	Panel 48		149-151
Russell, J	Private	9.5.15	Cameron Highlanders	Panel 38		151
Sadler, J A	Private	25.9.15	Oxford and Bucks Light Infantry	Panel 39		151
Sampson, T	Rifleman	4.1.16	Rifle Brigade	Panel 48		151
Sangster, H	Private	14.11.15	Royal Scots	Panel 11		151-152
Saunders, G A	Private	1.8.17	Cameronians (Scottish Rifles)	Panel 22		152-153
Savoie, F	Private	2.6.16	Canadian Infantry (Quebec Regiment)	Panel 24		153-154
Scott, D	Private	9.5.15	East Surrey Regiment	Panel 34		154-155
Sellers, J H	2nd Lieutenant	24.5.15	Northumberland Fusiliers	Panel 12		155
Shaw, H	Private	9.8.15	East Yorkshire Regiment	Panel 31		155-156
Sheehy, J	Private	10.11.14	Royal Munster Fusiliers	Panel 44		156
Slater, E J	Private	21.1.15	Duke of Wellington's (West Riding Regiment)	Panel 20		156
Slattery, H W	Private	27.5.15	The Buffs (East Kent Regiment)	Panel 12		156-158
Smith, H G	Private	24.4.15	Middlesex Regiment	Panel 51		158
Smith, J	Private	2.3.16	Northumberland Fusiliers	Panel 8		158-159
Smith, J I	Private	7.11.17	Canadian Infantry (Quebec Regiment)	Panel 24		159-160
Smith, L V	Private	16.11.14	Cheshire Regiment	Panel 19		160
Smith, R B	Private	2.6.16	4th Canadian Mounted Rifles Battalion	Panel 32		160-161
Smith, W	Private	13.5.15	Leicestershire Yeomanry	Panel 5		161
Smullen, J	Private	24.5.15	Royal Dublin Fusiliers	Panel 46		161-162
Speer, H J	Lance Serjeant	22.11.15	King's Royal Rifle Corps	Panel 53		162
Spence, H R	Private	9.6.17	Machine Gun Corps (Infantry)	Panel 56		162-163
Spencer, S W	Private	9.5.15	East Surrey Regiment	Panel 34		163
Stainer, A E E	Rifleman	13.5.15	Rifle Brigade	Panel 50		163-164
Steel, E T	Private	8.5.15	Royal Fusiliers	Panel 6		164
Stewart, T	Rifleman	25.9.15	Royal Irish Rifles	Panel 40		164
Stewart, W D	Private	31.10.17	Royal Canadian Regiment	Panel 10		164
Stiff, C W	Private	6.5.15	Monmouthshire Regiment	Panel 50		165
Stobbart, M	Private	16.6.15	Northumberland Fusiliers	Panel 8		165
Stoddart, W A	Private	2.6.16	5th Canadian Mounted Rifles Battalion	Panel 32		166
Stratton, G R	Gunner	3.6.16	Canadian Field Artillery	Panel 10		166
Stringfellow, V M	Private	27.9.17	Australian Infantry, AIF	Panel 17		166-168
Sturman, J A	Private	31.12.15	The Buffs (East Kent Regiment)	Panel 12		168
Sutherland, C A	Private	9.5.15	Argyll and Sutherland Highlanders	Panel 44		169
Sutherland, F S	Private	20.9.17	South African Infantry	Panel 16A		169
Suttie, K W	Private	19.4.16	Canadian Infantry	Panel 28		169-170
Taylor, F C	Rifleman	8.5.15	Monmouthshire Regiment	Panel 50		170

Name	Rank	Date of Death	Regiment	Panel	Awards	Page
Taylor, N	Private	15.11.17	Canadian Infantry	Panel 28		170-172
Thomson, H C	Private	2.5.15	Canadian Infantry	Panel 18		172-173
Thorpe, G T	Private	26.4.15	Yorkshire Regiment	Panel 33		173
Thurston, S C	Trooper	13.5.15	Royal Horse Guards	Panel 3		174
Tricker, W E	Private	6.11.17	Canadian Infantry	Panel 18		174-176
Turner, F P	Rifleman	8.5.15	London Regiment (The Rangers)	Panel 54		176
Turner, L	Rifleman	30.7.15	Rifle Brigade	Panel 50		176
Turner, P	Private	25.5.15	Welsh Regiment	Panel 37		176
Turner, W	Private	25.4.15	Middlesex Regiment	Panel 51		176
Uglow, W E T	Rifleman	1.1.15	London Regiment (Queen Victoria's Rifles)	Panel 54		176-177
Usher, F G	Lance Corporal	20.9.17	Australian Machine Gun Corps	Panel 31		177-178
Vickery, G W	Private	16.2.16	London Regiment (Royal Fusiliers)	Panel 52		178
Waller, R P	Private	16.5.15	Durham Light Infantry	Panel 38		178-179
Walton, C W	Private	16.6.15	Lincolnshire Regiment	Panel 21		179
Warwick, L	Private	8.5.15	King's Own (Royal Lancaster Regiment)	Panel 12		179
Watt, G	Private	27.4.15	Highland Light Infantry	Panel 38		179
Webb, W D	Private	26.4.15	Royal Fusiliers	Panel 6		179-180
Wedgwood, A	Private	25.9.15	Royal Scots Fusiliers	Panel 19		180
Wellbelove, H C	Private	7.11.14	Gloucestershire Regiment	Panel 34		180-182
Weston, G	Rifleman	21.5.17	King's Royal Rifle Corps	Panel 53		182
White, E G	Private	12.3.15	Wiltshire Regiment	Panel 53		182
White, L C	Private	2.6.16	Canadian Infantry	Panel 28		182
Widmer, E	Private	2.5.15	Dorsetshire Regiment	Panel 37		182-184
Williams, C F	Private	22.6.15	Wiltshire Regiment	Panel 53		184
Williams, F P	Private	27.4.15	The King's (Liverpool Regiment)	Panel 4		184
Wilson, H E	Private	2.6.16	Canadian Machine Gun Corps	Panel 32		184-185
Wilson, R C	Private	11.6.15	London Regiment (Royal Fusiliers)	Panel 52		185
Winn, J	Private	26.4.15	Durham Light Infantry	Panel 38		185
Winnan, J C	Private	23.4.15	Duke of Cornwall's Light Infantry	Panel 20		185
Wood, E	Private	2.6.16	4th Canadian Mounted Rifles (Central Ontario Regiment)	Panel 32		185-186
Woodcock, J	Private	9.11.15	Duke of Wellington's (West Riding Regiment)	Panel 20		186
Wright, P A	Private	13.6.16	Canadian Infantry	Panel 24		186-187
Yeoman, A J	Private	21.9.15	Worcestershire Regiment	Panel 34		187
Young, A W	Private	2.6.16	Canadian Infantry (Alberta Regiment)	Panel 30		187

FOR FREEDOM

Menin Gate Memorial

Panel Numbers quoted at the end of each entry relate to the panels dedicated to the Regiment with which the casualty served. In some instances, where a casualty is recorded as attached to another Regiment, his name may appear within their Regimental Panels. Please refer to the on-site Memorial Register Introduction. The Addenda Panel lists those service personnel whose details are awaiting addition to the Regimental Panels. All odd panel numbers are on the North side of the road and even numbers are located on the South side of the road.

Steps on either side of the memorial leading to the rear of the memorial, make wheelchair access to the rear impossible. There is however, a slope at the side of the memorial which gives wheelchair users some access but due to the incline, it may not be possible to ascend/descend unaided.

The Menin Gate is one of four memorials to the missing in Belgian Flanders which cover the area known as the Ypres Salient. Broadly speaking, the Salient stretched from Langemarck in the north to the northern edge in Ploegsteert Wood in the south, but it varied in area and shape throughout the war.

The Salient was formed during the First Battle of Ypres in October and November 1914, when a small British Expeditionary Force succeeded in securing the town before the onset of winter, pushing the German forces back to the Passchendaele Ridge. The Second Battle of Ypres began in April 1915 when the Germans released poison gas into the Allied lines north of Ypres. This was the first time gas had been used by either side and the violence of the attack forced an Allied withdrawal and a shortening of the line of defence.

There was little more significant activity on this front until 1917, when in the Third Battle of Ypres an offensive was mounted by Commonwealth forces to divert German attention from a weakened French front further south. The initial attempt in June to dislodge the Germans from the Messines Ridge was a complete success, but the main assault north-eastward, which began at the end of July, quickly became a dogged struggle against determined opposition and the rapidly deteriorating weather. The campaign finally came to a close in November with the capture of Passchendaele.

The German offensive of March 1918 met with some initial success, but was eventually checked and repulsed in a combined effort by the Allies in September.

The battles of the Ypres Salient claimed many lives on both sides and it quickly became clear that the commemoration of members of the Commonwealth forces with no known grave would have to be divided between several different sites.

The site of the Menin Gate was chosen because of the hundreds of thousands of men who passed through it on their way to the battlefields. It commemorates casualties from the forces of Australia, Canada, India, South Africa and United Kingdom who died in the Salient. In the case of United Kingdom casualties, only those prior Thursday 16th August 1917 (with some exceptions). United Kingdom and New Zealand servicemen who died after that date are named on the memorial at Tyne Cot, a site which marks the furthest point reached by Commonwealth forces in Belgium until nearly the end of the war. New Zealand casualties that died prior to Thursday 16th August 1917 are commemorated on memorials at Buttes New British Cemetery and Messines Ridge British Cemetery.

The Menin Gate Memorial now bears the names of more than 54,000 officers and men whose graves are not known. The memorial, designed by Sir Reginald Blomfield with sculpture by Sir William Reid-Dick, was unveiled by Lord Plumer on Sunday 24th July 1927.

No of Identified Casualties: 54,405

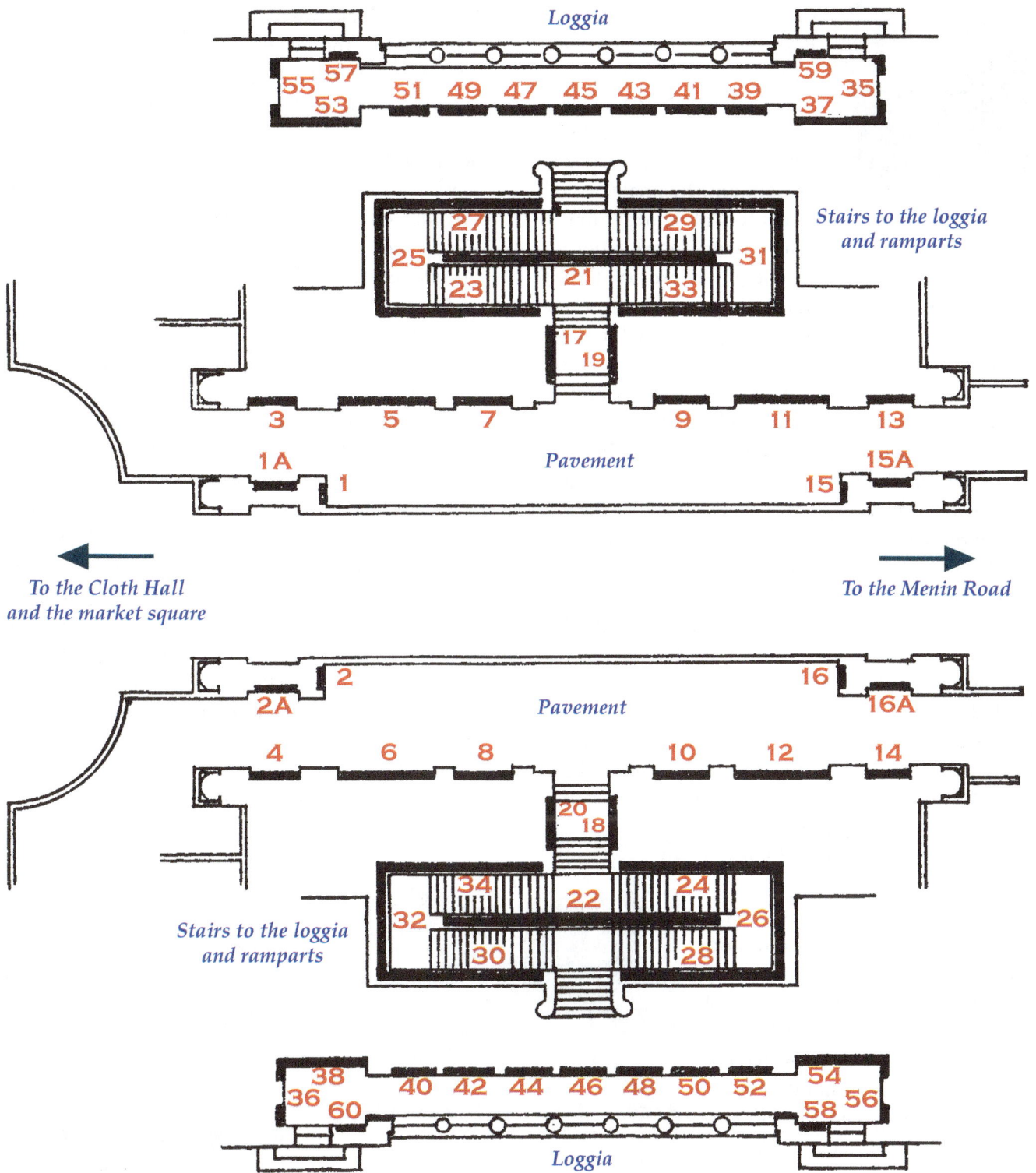

Loggia

55 57 51 49 47 45 43 41 39 59 35
53 37

27 29
25 31
23 21 33

17
19

Stairs to the loggia
and ramparts

3 5 7 9 11 13

1A 15A
1 Pavement 15

← To the Cloth Hall
and the market square

To the Menin Road →

2 16
2A 16A
Pavement

4 6 8 10 12 14

20
18

34 24
32 22 26
30 28

Stairs to the loggia
and ramparts

38 54
40 42 44 46 48 50 52
36 60 58 56

Loggia

THE ARCHITECT

SIR REGINALD THEODORE BLOMFIELD

Sir Reginald Blomfield

Reginald Theodore Blomfield was born on Saturday 20th December 1856, third son of the Reverend George Blomfield, Rector of Aldington, Kent, and Mrs Isabella Blomfield (daughter of Right Reverend Charles James Blomfield, DD, Bishop of London). Reginald was educated at Haileybury School (with an exhibition) and went up to Exeter College, Oxford, (with a scholarship) where he studied the classics.

Following Oxford, and prior to being articled to his uncle, Sir Arthur Blomfield, ARA, Reginald spent a year travelling in Europe. From late 1881 he began his career in architecture and also began studying at the Royal Academy School where he won a number of prizes. Reginald's early work under his uncle included designs for war memorials at Marlborough College and Shrewsbury School (for many of their sons he would later help design their final resting places in the cemeteries or on the memorials of the First World War). In 1884 Reginald established his own architectural firm at 17 Southampton Street, London, where he specialised in the renovation of country houses (including Chequers) plus the design and construction of new ones. Reginald was a popular and successful architect, however, the changes brought about by the First World War ended such grandiose projects that were the fashion in profusion during the late Victorian and Edwardian Britain.

At the conclusion of the First World War a number of famous architects, including Reginald, were commissioned to design the memorials and cemeteries that now dot the line of the Western Front: perhaps the most famous being the Menin Gate which he designed. Reginald also designed the Cross of Sacrifice that is placed in the majority of Commonwealth War Graves cemeteries throughout the world.

Reginald was a Fellow of the Royal Institute of British Architects (President from 1912 to 1914), a member of the Royal Academy (Royal Gold Medal winner in 1913), an Honorary Fellow of Exeter College, Oxford, and LittD of Liverpool University. He held honorary memberships of the American Academy of Arts and Letters, the National Academy of Design of America and Vice President of the Royal Historical Society. Reginald was knighted in 1919 and was created Chevalier of the Legion of Honour, Officer of the Orders of the Crown and of Leopold I; and Leopold II of Belgium. He held memberships of the Athenæum and The Arts.

Reginald Blomfield's publications include: *The Formal Garden in England (1892); A History of Renaissance Architecture in England (1897); A Short History of Renaissance Architecture in England (1900); Studies in Architecture (1906); The Mistress Art (1908); A History of French Architecture 1491-1661 (1911); Architectural Drawing and Draughtsmen (1912): History of French Architecture 1661-1774 (1920); The Touchstone of Architecture (1925); Byways, Leaves from an Architect's Note-book (1929); Memoirs of an Architect (1932); Modernismus (1934); Six Architects (1935); Sebastien le Prestre de Vauban (1938); Life of R Norman Shaw (1940)*

Reginald married Frances, daughter of Henry Burns, in 1886, and they had two sons and a daughter. They lived at Point Hill, Playden, Sussex, at 51 Frognal, Hampstead, London, and 1 New Court, Temple, London EC4. Reginald died at 51 Frognal, Hampstead, on Sunday 27th December 1942, a week after his 86th birthday. Sir Reginald Reid-Dick, with whom he had worked with on the Menin Gate, produced a bronze bust in his memory that is exhibited in the National Portrait Gallery.

Reginald left an estate of £112,057 5s 9d.

... the plans for the iconic Menin Gate (courtesy of the CWGC)

THE CONSTRUCTION OF THE MENIN GATE

(Photographs courtesy of the CWGC)

THE INAUGURATION OF THE MENIN GATE, SUNDAY 24TH JULY 1927

The inauguration of the Menin Gate took place on Sunday 24th July 1927. Various dates were decided upon but one postponement after another occurred. Despite the importance and the symbolism the Menin Gate held for 'The Armies of the British Empire', it was not possible for either HM King George V or Field Marshal Earl Haig to attend the inauguration so Field Marshal Lord Plumer was asked to officiate. Elaborate preparations were made for the inauguration, with invitations being sent around the world inviting the great and the good to Ypres on Sunday 27th July 1927.

Promptly at 9.30am HM King Albert of Belgium arrived at the Hôtel de Ville in a motorcade accompanied by the Compte de Broqueville, the Belgian Minister of National Defence. The King was presented to Field Marshal Lord Plumer, The Right Honourable Sir Laming Worthington-Evans, GBE, MP, the British Secretary State for War; Baron Janssens de Bisthoven, Governor of West Flanders; Mr Sobry, Deputy Mayor of Ypres; the French Generals de Lisle and Boye; a selection of Ambassadors and a large number of local mayors and dignitaries from West Flanders.

King Albert led the possession, with Lord Plumer on his left and the British Ambassador to his right, from the town square along the narrow road to the Menin Gate that was lined by Les Diables Noirs (Belgian Cyclist Carabiniers). They marched under the Menin Gate to the strains of 'Brabançonne' and took position on the causeway beyond and then the ceremony began. The band of the 1st Battalion The York and Lancaster Regiment played the hymn 'O God our help in ages past' that was sung with gusto. The Archbishop of Canterbury had composed a special prayer for the occasion that was read by The Right Reverend Bishop Gwynne, DD, CMG, CBE, who had been Deputy Chaplain General to the British Armies in France and Flanders from 1914 to 1920.

Lord Plumer turned towards the Menin Gate that had an enormous Union Jack covering the dedication on top of the Memorial with the Belgian and French flags on either side. He pressed an button that released the flags to unveil the Memorial and finished his address with: *"To the glory of God and to the memory of those whose names are inscribed heron I unveil this memorial in the names of the Father and of the Son and the Holy Ghost."* His Majesty King Albert of Belgium took the podium and thanked Lord Plumer and, in fluent English, addressed the massed crowd. Bishop Gwynne delivered the dedication of the Memorial before

leading everyone in the hymn, *'For all the Saints'*.
The Right Reverend Dr John Simms, DD, CB, CMG, KHC, MP, who had been the Principal Chaplain to the British Armies in France and Flanders from 1914 to 1920, read three prayers that was followed by the singing of *'Now thank we all our God'*. The Right Reverend Bishop Keatinge, Roman Catholic Bishop in Ordinary of the British Army and Royal Air Force, led everyone in further prayer before silence fell as the 2nd Battalion of The Somerset Light Infantry sounded the *'Last Post'*. From high above the assembled audience, on top of the Menin Gate, the pipers from 1st Battalion Scots Guards then played *'Flowers of the Forest'* that was followed by one minute's silence. Reveille broke through the intense silence and the service ended with the playing of the Belgian and British national anthems. As the last strains of *'God Save The King'* floated away on the warm breeze King Albert moved forward to lay a large wreath of scarlet enthrones and pink roses on behalf of a grateful Belgian nation. Lord Plumer followed and placed a wreath on behalf of HM King George V. Representatives then placed their tributes on the Memorial on behalf of the British Dominions, the British Army, Navy and Air Force, the Belgian and French armed services, local Belgian towns and villages, followed by wreaths from the families and people attending the opening.

Those who attended the Official Opening were given a small medal on a ribbon as a memento. Travelling abroad in the 1920s was not commonplace for the majority so considerable assistance had to be provided, see *'Individual and Organised Pilgrimages'* below. In the month that followed the opening over twenty-three thousand people signed the Visitors Book. Today it remains a site of pilgrimage for so many from every corner of the world.

When the Menin Gate was completed, with its 54,405 names, less than one hundred errors were discovered, the majority being minor spelling errors. In recent years more and more of the missing have been found and identified as new roads are constructed and the towns and villages expanded. Many of those who are listed on the Menin Gate as 'missing' have now been given a named grave. The majority remain to be recovered and placed in a grave but they all remain *'Known Unto God'*.

(The photographs overleaf illustrates the inauguration.)

Field Marshal Lord Plumer ...

... many deep, the spectators watch the ceremony

... HM King Albert

... shortly before the wreath laying

The speeches are made in front of the dignitaries ...

... local dignitaries wait to lay their tributes

... the crowds stretched out along the mote ...

... some of the tributes laid on the Menin Gate

(Photographs courtesy of the CWGC)

4995 PRIVATE ROBERT ALKER
2nd Battalion Lancashire Fusiliers
Died on Monday 24th May 1915, aged 17
Commemorated on Panel 33.

Robert was born and raised in Blackrod, Chorley, Lancashire, only son of Joseph and Margery Alker. Following his education, Robert was employed as a plater.

He enlisted in Horwich, Lancashire, and gave his elder sister as his next of kin, Alice Hatton, of 185 New Street, Blackrod. Robert went out to France on Saturday 15th May 1915 and joined the Battalion whilst they were taking part in The Second Battle of Ypres.

On his first visit to the front line Robert was killed in action but his body was lost on the battlefield.

He is commemorated on Blackrod War Memorial.

11742 PRIVATE WILLIAM ALLEN
1st Battalion Hampshire Regiment
Died on Thursday 29th April 1915, aged 16
Commemorated on Panel 35.

William was born in Fenchingfield, Norfolk, the son of Alfred and Hannah Allen, of 23 Peckford Place, Brixton, London. He was educated locally.

He enlisted in Brixton and went out to France with a draft, joining the Battalion on Wednesday 21st April 1915. During the early evening of Thursday 22nd urgent communications were received at Battalion Headquarters: the Germans had launched a gas attack against the French line to the north of Ypres, the Battalion was told to prepare to reinforce the line at a moment's notice. Despite the distance from the raging battle, the sound of the artillery blazing away could be clearly heard by William and his comrades. At noon on Saturday 24th he entrained in Bailleul for Poperinghe. As the train rattled its way along William heard the sound of battle grow consistently louder and he was able to witness, in the distance, the smoke and fire pouring high into the air. Upon arrival in Poperinghe the smell of chlorine floated in the air and the sight of the French colonial troops staggering into the town dying in agony in front of him was not an encouraging or pleasant experience. To make matters worse William arrived in the pouring rain. Much to the relief of everyone, billets were provided south of the town, thus escaping a night out in the rain. Early on Sunday 25th William marched to St Jan then a short time later to Wieltje. Colonel Hicks was ordered to take the Battalion into the line between 'Berlin Wood' and St Julien that was achieved despite heavy artillery fire. No guides were available, the ground was unknown

to the officers who were sent out to reconnoitre as best they could. An officer wrote of the Colonel: *"… he rose to the occasion as few men would. The odds against him were overwhelming. We should have been justified in retiring to the Zonnebeke ridge where trenches existed."* William moved into his allotted position and started to dig furiously that lasted throughout the night to create something of a trench that would provide cover. The ground was soft that assisted the work and the men found some disused trenches that were made use of. As dawn rose a heavy mist hung over the area providing more time for digging and preparation. In the mist a patrol was heard who claimed to be Royal Fusiliers: it was a German patrol that was soon dealt with! On another part of their line the Germans attacked that claimed a number of casualties before they were repulsed. By 7.00am the mist lifted and as soon as it was clear the Germans opened their artillery on their line. The German infantry advanced expecting to take the lines with ease, however, they were repulsed. The newly dug trenches provided only sufficient room to stand, moving around was difficult and sending back the wounded more so. For the next two days the Battalion came under sustained artillery fire and constant attack. On Thursday 29th it was decided to straighten the line (to make it more defensible) between 'Sanctuary Wood', east of Hooge, to Frezenberg and up to 'Mouse Trap Farm'. The Battalion was detailed to remain at the front totally exposed whilst providing cover as the line was straightened. William was killed as the Germans poured fire on the Battalion during the retirement.

L/15162 PRIVATE JAMES SYDNEY ANDERSON
'C' Company, 3rd Battalion Middlesex Regiment
Died on Sunday 2nd May 1915, aged 17
Commemorated on Panel 49.

James was born at home, second son of William Reginald and Helen Louisa Anderson, of 13 Leverett Street, Chelsea, London. He was raised and educated in Chelsea with his sisters, Helen, Florence, and Bertha, and brothers William, Reginald and Cyril.

James volunteered in Chelsea and was sent out to France with a draft on Wednesday 17th March 1915 to join the Battalion whilst they were serving at Rossignol where the Battalion was on call to relieve the line at St Eloi — the call never came.

The Battalion was sent to Zonnebeke on Saturday 10th April before moving to St Jan on Wednesday 21st. The next day James was ordered to dig a new line to the north of the village. At 9.30pm Colonel Ernest

Stephenson received orders to send two Companies to assist guarding the pontoon bridge across the Canal — he sent Major Neale with 'B' and 'D' Companies. 'A' and 'C' Companies were sent to join up with the French troops, but at dawn on Friday 23rd they met the Canadian troops who had held on in face of the gas attack. At 6.20am James was led forward and the Battalion went with the Canadians to entrench seven hundred yards in front of the German line. They were stretched out in the open under heavy artillery fire and gas continued to drift across into their positions. Major Neale was ordered to advance with his men over open ground but took very heavy losses. Colonel Stephenson had to organise reinforcements that was particularly difficult as the majority of 'A' Company had been wiped out. Colonel Stephenson went up to the line and was mortally wounded. His Adjutant, Captain Kitchin, carried him to a shell hole, some one hundred and fifty yards to the rear where he died, his last words being: *"Die hard, boys, die hard".* (Colonel Stephenson is also commemorated on the Menin Gate.) James finally got some respite from fighting during the last few days of April. The enemy laid down a heavy barrage on Saturday 1st May across the sector from Gravenstafel to *Ernest Stephenson* Zonnebeke and during the bombardment James was killed.

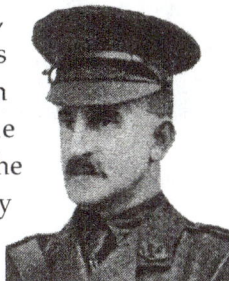

3085 PRIVATE ARCHIBALD ANGUS
1st/14th Battalion London Regiment
(London Scottish)
Died on Sunday 1st November 1914, aged 17
Commemorated on Panel 54.

Angus was born in Coronel, Chile, on Wednesday 7th April 1897, son of David and Mary Wilson Angus, of 9 Muswell Road, London, N10. He was educated at Edinburgh Academy from 1908 to 1914 where he was the Pipe Major in the OTC.
At the outbreak of war Archibald volunteered and was sent for training. Colonel George Alexander Malcolm led the Battalion to Watford Station where they entrained to Southampton. Archibald sailed to Le Havre on *SS Winifredian* on Tuesday 15th September 1914 and was given a heros welcome when he marched through the town. The Battalion was ordered to Villeneuve St Georges where they were split up and sent on a series of different duties including one company sent to guard Field Marshal Sir John French at his Headquarters in La Fère-en-Tardonenois.

Colonel Malcolm collected his Battalion together in St Omer between Sunday 25th and Wednesday 28th October. A large number of motorised omnibuses collected the Battalion at 5.00pm on Thursday 29th and drove them to Ypres where they arrived at 3.00am the next morning. He was able to marvel at the medieval splendour of the old town for a few hours before an artillery barrage woke everyone. Archibald paraded in front of the Cloth Hall then marched out through

... the centre of Ypres shortly before the war

the Menin Gate and along the Menin Road to *'White Château'*, General Sir Douglas Haig's Headquarters. The Battalion halted whilst Colonel Malcolm went into Headquarters to discuss plans with General Haig before pressing on to the woods near Hooge, soon to be named *'Sanctuary Wood'*. Archibald was able to get his pack off and have some rest. Colonel Malcolm was ordered to take his Battalion to Hooge Château where he met General Munro who came out to inspect the parade. With the situation around Gheluvelt calming down the Battalion was not required in the sector but were deployed to the south. Archibald marched back along the Menin Road and into Ypres once again where he embussed. The fleet trundled out of the town via the Lille Gate and were forced to slow down by refugees fleeing the fighting as they arrived in St Eloi. Archibald got some sleep in a local barn at Wytschaete before being awoken at midnight. He paraded on the road and as he waited to march off a column of the Scots Greys and some French Cuirassiers rode by. The Greys gave the London Scottish a great cheer that was reciprocated. Colonel Malcolm spoke with General Gough and told him of the Battalion: *"... had been travelling the whole of the previous night and marching and counter-marching during the day, and it would be advisable to given them some rest."* Archibald was able to get some rest until 8.00am on Sunday 31st then marched with a full pack along the pavé to Wytschaete that was being evacuated with locals milling about. With every step south they went closer to the sound of the guns and shells were bursting along the road. Archibald was sent into reserve at 'Enfer Road', close to the windmill on the heights, where he lay low as he came under heavy shellfire throughout the day. During the hours of darkness he began to dig in furiously and at 9.00am the enemy mounted an attack. The relatively fresh German troops were full of enthusiasm being led forward by a number of bands play martial music including 'Deutschland, Deutschland, über Alles' — this was curbed when Archibald and the Battalion opened rapid fire on them. An artillery duel began with the windmill being hit and bursting into flames, the whole sky was ablaze as the houses and farms were consumed in the inferno. Despite their hard efforts the pressure on the Battalion was too much. Large numbers were killed by shellfire but the majority died in fierce close combat. How young Archibald met his fate is unknown.

General Edmund Allenby wrote to General Sir Douglas Haig: *"I wish to tell you how magnificent the London Scottish have behaved. In discipline and tactical efficiency they have been up to he standard of the best Regular Troops. Last night they took their place in the trenches after a hard day of marching and fighting, as I had not enough strength to keep them in reserve. In the small hours of the morning, my front was broken and the brunt of the attack came on that section, held by the London Scottish. Not a man left his trench, until the trenches were overrun by the enemy. They made a great fight, and accounted for hundreds of Germans. The losses were I fear very great, but their staunchness enabled us to maintain the important position at Wytschaete, until the arrival of reinforcements. The Cavalry Corps and the Army owe them a debt of great gratitude. I regret deeply the loss of so many brave men."*

Generals Allenby and Haig

... German soldiers march to entrain to the front

'THE WIMSLOW BOY'
LIEUTENANT GEORGE ARCHER-SHEE
3rd Battalion South Staffordshire Regiment
Died on Saturday 31st October 1914, aged 19
Commemorated on Panel 35.

George Archer-Shee

George as a cadet at Osbourne with his father

George was the only son of Mr and Mrs Martin Archer-Shee, of Woodchester, Gloucestershire, his father was a bank official. He was educated at Hodder Preparatory School followed by Stonyhurst College. He left for the Royal Naval College, Osborne, in 1908. Whilst there he was accused of stealing a five shilling postal order from one of his classmates. George was expelled from Osborne on a charge of theft, however he was accepted back at Stonyhurst. The story became the subject of Terence Rattigan's play 'The Winslow Boy'. Terence Rattigan gave his reasons for writing the play: *"The drama of injustice and of a little man's dedication to setting things right, seemed to have more pathos and validity just because it involved an inconsequential individual."* Sir Edward Carson (the famous Ulster Unionist politician and barrister who had prosecuted Oscar Wilde) represented George for a nominal fee only — notwithstanding that George was a Roman Catholic. HM King Edward VII received the Petition and signed the document *"Let Right Be Done"* that allowed proceedings to continue. On Tuesday 26th July 1910 the trial commenced, after four days the defence collapsed and members of the jury clambered into the Court to shake the hands of George and his family. George was totally vindicated and awarded £7,120 in damages (a very large sum of money at the time), he also received an apology from Mr McKenna, the First Lord of the Admiralty. The matter was discussed in the House of Commons with Austen Chamberlain, Arthur Balfour and Lord Charles Beresford, amongst many others, speaking in the debate (the full record of the debate can be read in 'Hansard').

George was gazetted in May 1913 and promoted to Lieutenant in February 1914.

George joined the 1st Battalion at camp at Lyndhurst after it had returned to Southampton from Pietermaritzburg, South Africa, in mid-September 1914. He left with his men for Zeebrugge on Tuesday 6th October to assist with the defence of Antwerp. By the time they arrived Antwerp was being evacuated with the Belgian and French armies falling back towards Ghent. The Staffordshires were ordered to march to Ypres and upon arrival were sent along the Menin Road to take part in the town's defence. George was killed in action at Klein Zillebeke during the Battle of Gheluvelt.

Colonel Ovens, CMG, wrote: *"He was a most promising young officer, and in the short time he was in the 1st Bn. The South Staffordshire Regt. he earned the love and respect of both officers and men, and by his bravery and example contributed largely to the success of the battalion in the actions near Ypres."*

One of his fellow officers wrote: *"It seems that during the retirement of the Division he was in charge of a platoon in an exposed portion of the line; other units of other corps, it seems, had received orders to retire, but the order had not reached him. Someone, it is said, pointed out to him that the units on each side of him were retiring; he replied that he did not care what they did, but not one of his men was to retire till he gave them order to do so, and so they held on against great odds.*

Later a message seems to have reached him, for he gave the order to the men to retire as best they could. He, it is said, was the last to retire, and a man, since killed, reported that he looked round and saw him lying face downwards on the ground, motionless, as though killed instantly, his head towards the enemy. He earned the highest opinions of his brother officers, and his loss is most keenly felt by all who knew him.

He was such a charming and interesting young fellow, and had seen such a lot of the world for his years, that he was a most pleasant companion at all times and made many friends."

In Digby Stuart College, Roehampton, a white memorial tablet was erected in his memory with the inscription: *"George Archer-Shee, Lieut. S. Staff. Regt. 1st Batt. S.R. Killed near Ypres, Oct. 31. 1914, aged 19."*

George is also is commemorated on the o

1801 RIFLEMAN JAMES ARKINSTALL
1st Battalion Monmouthshire Regiment
Died on Sunday 25th April 1915, aged 17
Commemorated on Panel 50.

James was born at home, second son of William and Mary Ellen Arkinstall, of 5 Jones's Terrace, Bassalleg, Monmouthshire. He was educated locally with his elder brother, Owen, and younger sisters Agnes and Hazel.

He volunteered and was sent for training in Bury St Edmunds, Suffolk, followed by Cambridge. James left with the Battalion from Southampton for Le Havre on Saturday 13th February 1915. He entrained for final training in northern France near Bailleul.

James began tours of duty without being involved in any particular action until the opening of The Second Battle of Ypres on Thursday 22nd April. Whilst defending the line and mounting a series counter-attacks James was killed.

R/8375 RIFLEMAN HERBERT REGINALD WILLIAM ASHDOWN
8th Battalion King's Royal Rifle Corps
Died on Tuesday 12th October 1915, aged 17
Commemorated on Panel 53.

Herbert was born at home, eldest son and child of Bryan Mark and Henrietta Sarah Ashdown, of 30 Randolph Road, Gillingham, Kent. He was educated locally as were his younger siblings, Mary, Raymond and Benjamin.

Herbert volunteered in Chatham, Kent, and was sent for training that was completed in Bordon and Aldershot, both in Hampshire. The Battalion arrived in Boulogne on Wednesday 19th May 1915 under the command of Lieutenant Colonel H Green. Herbert entrained for Watten in northern France to continue training. From Friday 28th he was attached to the North and South Staffordshires for practical experience in the front line on the French-Belgian border.

The Battalion undertook their first tour of duty at St Eloi on Monday 7th June that was a particularly grim and unhealthy sector. Herbert was moved to the Hooge sector where a mine was blown on Saturday 17th July under the German lines. It was fully expected that the enemy would retaliate in some way and for the 8th Battalion it would be their first major action. Herbert had completed a tour of duty in front of Hooge and was relieved late on Thursday 29th to a camp in Vlamertinghe. He arrived tired and looking forward to a good sleep. Herbert had hardly had more than an hour on his bed before he was roused and ordered to parade when the Germans attacked Hooge on Friday 30th July where flammenwerfer (flame throwers or liquid fire) was used for the first time. The attack on Hooge had started and the Battalion was needed to help hold the line.

The Official History records: *"Rumours of German retaliation, by an attack along the Menin Road, were current on the 26th, but it did not take place until the morning of the 30th, and then against the Hooge sector, held by the 41st*

Brigade (Brigadier-General O. S. W. Nugent), of the 14th Division (Major-General V. Couper), which had taken over the sector a week before.

The 8th Rifle Brigade (Lieut.-Colonel R. C. Maclachlan) held the front at the Hooge crater, with the 7th K.R.R.C. (Lieut.-Colonel G. A. P. Rennie) on its right. The crater itself was untenable, owing to constant trench-mortaring and 'strafing', and the trenches, dry but dilapidated beyond measure, ran up to the lip on either side, with no definite connection round the

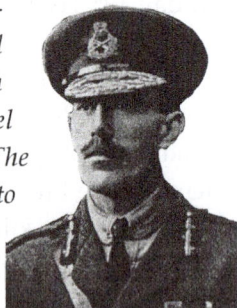

Colonel, later General Rennie

crater. The sector had an evil reputation for being subject to incessant sniping and bombing, besides trench-mortaring and shellfire; but on the night of the 29th/30th, when the two battalions took over from the very tired and worn 7th Rifle Brigade and 8th K.R.R.C., there was ominous silence. No notice was taken by the enemy of the noise inseparable from a relief, and even a few bombs thrown by the new-comers into the German trenches — in places only 15 feet away — provoked no reply. Half an hour before dawn the trench garrison stood to arms, and there was still complete quiet. Then at 3.15 a.m., with dramatic suddenness, came the carefully planned German stroke. The site of the stables of the château was blown up, whilst a sudden hissing sound was heard by the two companies of the 8th Rifle Brigade on either side of the crater, and a bright crimson glare over the crater turned the whole scene red. Jets of flame, as if from a line of powerful hoses, spraying fire instead of water, shot across the front trenches of the Rifle Brigade, and a thick black cloud formed. It was the first attack on the British with liquid fire. At the same time fire of every other kind was opened: trench-mortar bombs and hand-grenades deluged the front trenches, machine-gun and shrapnel bullets swept the two communication trenches and the 300 yards of open ground between the front and support lines in Sanctuary and Zouave Woods; high-explosive shells rained on these Woods, whilst the ramparts of Ypres and all exits from the town were bombarded anew.

The surprise was complete, and would probably have led to an entry even at the strongest part of the line. Most of the 8th Rifle Brigade in the front trenches were overwhelmed, the rest fell back gradually over the fire-swept open ground to the support line. The enemy did not follow: he at once set about consolidating the trenches he had secured, and trying to increase his gain by attacking the 7th K.R.R.C. in front, flank, and rear. There was desperate trench fighting, in which parties again brought up Flammenwerfer, but rapid fire was turned on to them at 20 yards range, and the attempt to use them broke down. In the end, however, after several counter-attacks, all but a small sector of the K.R.R.C. trenches were lost.

The 42nd Brigade, on the left of the 41st, was not affected, and the 1/8th Sherwood Foresters (the left of the 46th Division) on the right, though attacked, managed to maintain its position. With the help of brigade reinforcements the new line on the edge of the woods was held, and at 11.30 a.m., by order from the VI Corps, Major-General V. Couper made arrangements for an assault at 2.45 p.m. to recover the lost ground. It was to be carried out by both 41st and 42nd Brigades (Brigadier-Generals O. S. W. Nugent and C. J. Markham) after three-quarters of an hour's bombardment by the divisional artillery and No. 2 Group Heavy Artillery Reserve — feeble indeed after the German tornado, but still, serving to encourage the assault — the 46th Division on the right and the 6th Division on the left co-operating by fire. The attack northwards of the 41st Brigade, with the 6th Duke of Cornwall's Light Infantry of the 43rd Brigade (Brigadier-General G.

Generals Couper and Nugent

Cockburn) attached, failed, not a man getting within 150 yards of the Germans; but the attack eastwards by the 9th K.R.R.C. of the 42nd Brigade succeeded in regaining part of the lost trenches."

He continued to serve in the sector until, whilst in action at the front line, Herbert was hit and mortally wounded.

1055 PRIVATE OXLEY GORDON ASKEW
Essex Yeomanry
Died on Friday 14th May 1915, aged 17
Commemorated on Panel 5.

Gordon was born at home, second son of Abraham Arthur and Elizabeth Askew, of 48, Mill Road, Maldon, Essex. He had an elder sister May, and brother George, with younger siblings Hilda, Arthur and Phyllis. Gordon was educated locally.

He volunteered in Maldon. Lieutenant Colonel Ned Deacon sent out telegrams to all his officers on Friday 7th August 1914, it contained one word: *"Mobilise"*. (The Colonel was killed on Thursday 13th May 1915 and is commemorated on the Menin Gate.) The Essex Yeomanry mobilised at Ipswich where they were also billeted as part

Ned Deacon

Henry Hodgson

of the Eastern Mounted Brigade under Brigadier General Henry West Hodgson, CVO.

Gordon moved billets to Melton where he paraded with the Regiment for an inspection on Tuesday 10th November by HM King George V and two days later the Colonel received the orders for taking his men to France. The Regiment entrained on Sunday 29th November at Woodbridge, Suffolk, for Southampton to embark for Le Havre. Upon arrival they marched into a muddy camp. After the men were settled down the officers were invited for a dinner by Colonel Harry Cooper, CMG, Vice Chairman of the Essex County Territorial Force Association, who was based in the town.

Gordon entrained for St Omer on Thursday 3rd December and was greeted by snow, sleet and rain as he marched to Wardrecques. After a week of further training Gordon marched through Hazebrouck to Grand Sec Bois. Three days later the Regiment got close to the front line when they went into support at Loker during an attack on Wytschaete but did not see any action.

Gordon was ordered to stand to on Wednesday 27th January 1915, the Kaiser's birthday, as it was thought an attack would be launched but it did not materialise. In the afternoon Gordon paraded for inspection by Field Marshal Sir John French who was accompanied by HRH The Prince of Wales. The next day Gordon moved his billet to Mount Croquet. However, before the Regiment left Grand Sec Bois a farewell dinner for the officers was held with the local dignitaries where Colonel Deacon thanked the local population for their kindness to all ranks and their help since the Regiment had been based in their village.

The Regiment went to Ypres on Wednesday 3rd February by motor omnibus, via Hazebrouck, Steenvoorde, Poperinghe and Vlamertinghe. They were billeted in a school along the Menin Road. Major Hill took 'A' Squadron into the line immediately where some of the German lines were only twelve yards apart. Whilst billeted in the school some of the men constructed a periscope made from an old down pipe. It was over twenty foot long and when finished it was camouflaged with bark to look like a tree. It was taken into the line where it was a popular and useful addition for them and those who followed them in the line.

The Battle of Neuve Chapelle commenced and the Essex Yeomanry was ordered to stand to: however, they were not called upon to go into the line. A few days later HRH Prince Arthur of Connaught organised a Brigade Marathon that the Yeomanry won, Colonel Deacon was presented with a silver cup by the Prince. Orders were received by Colonel Deacon on Friday 23rd April to move into the Salient. The next day Gordon marched to a camp near Vlamertinghe. He was then sent to Brielen, arriving at 7.30pm on Wednesday 5th May. He helped to dig trenches along the Yser Canal that was completed by 1.30am — they had dug under light emanating from Ypres that was in flames. The Yeomanry returned to their old billets at Mount Croquet on Friday 7th. Gordon was taken to construct a communication trench near Potijze on Wednesday 12th. With his comrades they managed to undertake the majority of the work as digging could only take place under the cover of darkness and even then heavy machine gun and rifle fire poured down on them.

At 4.00am on Thursday 13th a German preliminary barrage commenced; Gordon was in the support trenches on the northeastern edge of the gardens of Potijze Château. By 9.00am the line was beginning to give way and retirement was the only option. At lunchtime Colonel Deacon received orders to move forward and the Regiment were to relieve the Blues and 10th Hussars who had been able to move forward. Colonel Deacon, together with the squadron leaders, met Brigadier General Charles Bulkeley Johnson, in his Brigade Headquarters in the château gardens. (General Bulkeley Johnson was killed on Wednesday 11th April 1917 and is buried in Gouy-en-Artois Communal Cemetery Extension). It was agreed that a counter-attack would be mounted at 2.15pm. Colonel Deacon sent Major Buxton with two scouts to report to Lieutenant Colonel Robert Shearman of the 10th Hussars (who was killed on Saturday 15th May 1915 and is buried in Vlamertinghe Military Cemetery) that the men were coming up on his right flank. As the Yeomanry advanced, at the point of the bayonet, they were being mown down. Lieutenant Colonel Shearman ordered them to halt and lay down, which they did. Shortly afterward the Germans were seen leaving their post and retiring so the Yeomanry advanced at speed but took heavy casualties. During the attack Gordon was killed but his body was never found.

Charles Bulkeley Johnson

Robert Shearman

11002 PRIVATE
ALBERT RICHARD ASHLEY
2nd Battalion East Surrey Regiment
Died on Tuesday 27th April 1915, aged 15
Commemorated on Panel 34.

Albert was born in Worth, Sussex, on Monday 15th May 1899, second son of Minnie Ford (formerly Ashley) of 1 Putland Terrace, Denton, Newhaven, Sussex, and the late James William Ashley. He had an elder brother, Robert, and a younger brother, Harry. Albert was educated locally.

Albert enlisted on Wednesday 11th November 1914 in Melton, Surrey, and sent for training.

At 7.30am on Sunday 14th February the Battalion was ordered to march to Brigade Headquarters at Trois Rois. In the afternoon they were ordered to retake some lost trenches close to 'Triangular Wood', the plan of attack was put together by Major Gilbert-Cooper. The advance went well and they reached 'Upper Oosthoek Farm' without loss when the Germans opened up with heavy fire causing a number of casualties. The last three hundred yards of the attack was over open fields and the thick clay helped cause many of the casualties due to the men having to wade knee-deep through the slime. Their slow progress made them easy targets for the German defenders. The attack had to be called off and only two officers and twenty-five men returned unwounded. The Battalion was relieved and sent for rest and reorganisation. They needed drafts of men to return the Battalion to full strength.

Albert joined his new comrades whilst they were in camp with a draft on Saturday 6th March 1915. Following a tour of duty the Battalion marched to Loker on Tuesday 16th March where eight days of training and rest followed. Major Lawrence Le Fleming recorded: *"… a good deal of stiff drill as a battalion, in addition to practising the attack, physical training, bayonet work, etc."*

The Battalion was inspected by General James Haldane on Wednesday 31st March who also distributed medal ribbons to a number of officers and men. The next day they were back in the line at St Eloi where they remained in the trenches until the night of Saturday 3rd April when they were relieved. After only twenty-four hours rest Albert marched to Ypres and into the line at Château Rosenthal where he remained until the next day. General Sir Horace Smith-Dorrien

James Haldane

inspected the Battalion at Vlamertinghe on Thursday 8th when he complimented them on their turnout. Albert was ordered back into the line on Saturday 10th and marched along the cobbled road to Ypres, now badly damaged by shell fire. In front of the Cloth Hall comrades of the 1st Battalion were marching out of the line — each Battalion cheered and called out messages to their family and friends. The Battalion took position in front of Broodseinde and were greeted by increased artillery fire. Intelligence and reconnaissance reports told of German mining activity. Major Lawrence Le Fleming visited the trenches at 6.00pm and gave advice to the officers and men about how to deal with mining. He was visiting every Company and was severely wounded when he was sniped (he was eventually killed on Thursday 21st March 1918 and is commemorated on Pozières Memorial). Albert and his comrades were heavily shelled on Tuesday 13th so it was with great relief to all that they were taken out of the line the next day to billets in St Jan. At midnight on Friday 23rd the Germans, building on their gas attack north of the line, commenced an attack on the Battalion's central section. Albert was ordered to rapid fire, supported by the Battalion machine-guns, and the German attack was successfully repulsed. At 1.00pm the next day a further attack was launched along the whole line they 'tasted' their first experience of gas. An artillery bombardment continued throughout the day as did the counter-attacks, with some repulsed at the point of the bayonet.

The Brigade Commander wrote: *"The 2nd East Surrey have fought with great gallantry all day — much heavy fighting — parapets blown to bits — and men partially asphyxiated. Our losses are heavy, but the enemy's greater."* Brigadier General Archibald Chapman sent a message to the 2nd Battalion: *"General Bulfin wishes you to know that the conduct of the Royal Fusiliers and East Surrey Regt. has gained the greatest praise of the Commander-in-Chief in the field. He looks to them with confidence to hang on to their position with determination until the present phase of operations admits of their relief. All look to your battalions to save the situation for the British in Belgium and to enable a victory to be won."*

Albert was wounded in both hands on Sunday 25th — his thumbs heavily bandaged but he remained in the line. During the morning of Tuesday 27th he was with a party from the Battalion that assisted in driving the Germans from a position they had captured. Sadly Albert was killed, together with thirteen others and a further nineteen wounded. One of Albert's comrades reported finding his young body in a trench; Albert was identified by his bandaged thumbs and buried where he died. In the ensuing battles the grave was lost.

2467 PRIVATE JOHN JAMES AVERILL
1st/5th Battalion North Staffordshire Regiment
Died on Thursday 5th August 1915, aged 15
Commemorated on Panel 55.

John was born in Penkhull, Staffordshire, eldest son of Ambrose and Phoebe Averill, of 4 Cartledge Street, Hartshill, Stoke-on-Trent, Staffordshire. His father served in the war and survived. John had siblings Florence, Ambrose and Sydney.

He enlisted in Stoke-on-Trent and was sent for training in Luton, Bedfordshire, followed by Bishop's Stortford, Hertfordshire. John marched out of the barracks with the Battalion and entrained to Southampton. He sailed to Le Havre where he landed in France on Thursday 4th March 1915 and was sent for training in northern France before taking the line at the beginning of April in front of Messines. The weather was particularly dreadful, the rain was pouring down and flooding the trenches. A number of gum boots were issued amongst the men that were some assistance in helping avert trench foot. The Battalion remained in the Messines to Wulverghem sector until the end of June. Whilst on a tour of duty John was mortally wounded in action.

Colonel J H Knight wrote a letter of consolation and appreciation to John's mother.

John Averill

2181 RIFLEMAN
LEONARD FREDERICK AVILA
1st/9th Battalion London Regiment
(Queen Victoria's Rifles)
Died on Friday 4th December 1914, aged 17
Commemorated on Panel 54.

Leonard was born at home, eldest son of the late William Henry and Annie Maria Avila, of West Norwood, London. He was educated at Alleyn's Elementary School.

He volunteered at the outbreak of war and sent for training. He went out to France on Wednesday 4th November 1914, for Leonard's story and that of the Battalion, see Rifleman William Uglow.

S/11631 RIFLEMAN
JOSEPH ROBERT BAILEY
1st Battalion Rifle Brigade
Died on Tuesday 6th July 1915, aged 17
Commemorated on Panel 46.

Joseph was born in Stepney, London, second son of Frederick and Elizabeth Bailey, of 3 Tomlin's Terrace, Limehouse, London. He had an elder brother, Frederick, and two younger siblings, George and Helen. Joseph was educated locally.

He enlisted in Canning Town, London, and allocated to the West Riding Regiment with the service number 15611 before transferring to the Rifle Brigade. Joseph went out to France on Tuesday 22nd June 1915 to join the Battalion in the field with a draft when they were serving in the Salient. The Battalion had suffered badly during the Second Battle of Ypres and was in much need of reinforcements.

Joseph joined his new comrades whilst they were in camp following a tour of duty on the Yser Canal near Boesinghe. The Second Battle of Ypres had significantly altered the front line and in the sector the front line had been captured by the enemy. A communication trench from the old front line to the second line had gained the name 'International Trench' as at one end were the British and the Germans at the other. A single barricade separated the opposing forces. As was normal, the Germans occupied the high ground behind the front line that they had comprehensively strengthened by fortified farmhouse and outbuildings. They had quite a command of the field of fire in the sector. It was decided that a minor action in the sector would be mounted to capture 'International Trench' then move forward to take the surrounding area.

Whilst planning for the attack Joseph remained on tours of duty and fatigues before preparing to take part. General Henry Fuller Maitland Wilson, the Divisional Commander wrote in a letter to the Corps Commander: *"I have every confidence that the operation if undertaken will succeed — but it will probably be at a loss heavier to ourselves than the Germans, and, if it is undertaken entirely with the object of improving the tactical situation on my left flank, it does not appear to me the best method of attaining the object."* Not the most ringing of endorsements, and if shared with the men would hardly have filled them with confidence for the attack. The attack would take place at 6.00am on Tuesday 6th July, Joseph moved forward into the front line and waited for the whistles to be blown that would signal the attack. He clambered over the parapet into No Man's Land, Joseph had to cover less that fifty yards to reach the German line. The enemy machine gunners opened fire in great numbers, their infantry began rapid fire and the artillery shells were bursting one after another. Joseph ran into the maelstrom and like all of his officers and so many of his comrades he was cut down and killed.

18031 PRIVATE WILFRED BALL
10th Battalion West Yorkshire Regiment
(Prince of Wales's Own)
Died on Monday 27th December 1915, aged 17
Commemorated on Panel 21.

Wilfred Ball

Wilfred was born at home, second son of Mrs Sarah Ball, of 3 Caroline Street, Newport, Monmouthshire.

He volunteered in Bath and sent for training. Wilfred went out to Boulogne with the Battalion on Tuesday 13th July 1915. He disembarked the next morning and entrained at 3.30pm bound for Lumbres. He paraded outside the station at 10.00pm then marched to billets in Ouve-Wirquin. After three days of rest Wilfred marched to Arques and rested overnight, then continued on to Steenvoorde. He had two further days of rest then crossed into Belgium and marched to a camp at La Clytte. Wilfred was sent into the front line for practical training attached to the 6th Battalion Sherwood Foresters.

At the end of July Wilfred began a tour of duty when the Battalion took over a section of line in its own right near the Verbrandenmolen. Wilfred had only been in the line for a few hours when he came under a heavy artillery barrage that was followed by the enemy blowing a mine. Considerable damage was caused to the trenches that were repaired over the ensuing days. He was relieved late on Friday 13th August and marched back to his billets in La Clytte for twelve days of rest and training.

Wilfred returned to the front line on Thursday 26th and remained on tours of duty in the sector until moving to Hooge in late October. It was a difficult sector to serve in: *"The trenches taken over were in a very bad condition. They had all suffered heavily from both our own and the enemy's shell fire during the fighting between the end of July and the 25th September. Several trenches had been entirely destroyed and in the support and reserve lines it had not been possible to reconstruct them. North of the Menin Road the trenches varied from 80 - 20 yards distant from the enemy's front trenches. The large crater blown up on June 10th when the 3rd Division attacked, is 80 feet*

across and 40 deep. The inside has been constantly shelled and some hundreds of men are buried in it. On the line south of the Menin Road there is a gap of 200 feet between C.1 and C.3 trenches. It has never been possible to reconstruct the intervening trench C.2 as it is constantly destroyed by enemy shell fire. Zouave Wood is a mass of débris and broken trees. The enemy opposite are Wurtemburgers and regiments from Alsace. They appear to have little enterprise, but the whole line is subjected to enfilade fire and north of the Menin Road to reserve hostile gun fire."

Following his first tour of duty in the sector Wilfred was relieved on Monday 1st November and marched to a camp for rest and training. He undertook tours of duty in the front line, was in reserve in *'York Huts'*, or in a rest camp from where he left on Sunday 26th December to return to the trenches for the last time. Early on Monday 27th the enemy raided the Battalion's line and in the defence of his position Wilfred was killed.

He is commemorated on the War Memorial in St Mark's Church, Newport.

1684 PRIVATE HARRY BARR
1st/4th Battalion East Yorkshire Regiment
Died on Sunday 2nd May 1915, aged 16
Commemorated on Panel 21.

Harry was born in Cottingham, Yorkshire, second son of William Barr, of 8 Londesbrough Street, Hull, and the late Sarah Barr. He had an elder brother and sister, William and Doris, with younger siblings Fred, Alice and Hanna. Harry was educated locally.

Harry enlisted in Hull and was sent for training. He left from Folkestone, Kent, on Saturday 17th April 1915, sailing on *HMS Invicta* for Boulogne arriving at

SS Invicta

10.15pm. He marched to camp at St Martin arriving shortly before midnight. The next morning he entrained for Cassel where he was billeted overnight. The next day Harry marched close to Steenvoorde before being sent to Poperinghe by motor omnibus on Friday 23rd. Harry marched to Vlamertinghe passing many refugees struggling to make headway in the opposite direction. The Battalion rested in the village for a short while until 1.40am when they moved to the Yser Canal. Captain Sharp wrote: *"The march to our line* was a queer one. We knew not where we were going, nor what to, and the men's anticipations were not brightened by seeing a dressing station in a very busy state. We crossed over a pontoon over a small canal — a piece of the Yser Canal but not actually it. The banks were very high and we were on the further one which commanded the other side. It was provided with trenches and dug-outs and, after much scrambling in the dark and moving further down and so forth, we got into our position, holding partly some dug-outs and partly a trench. This was about 2 or 3 in the morning of the 24th. When day broke we found that there was an old, small factory with a chimney on our right and several cottages and farms still occupied along our front. Ypres on our right hand and the French line to our left front. There were some Canadian Scottish in the factory who kindly gave the men some beef and tea."* They were not to remain long as they were soon ordered to move towards Wieltje. They approached Fortuin under heavy shell fire and as they closed on *'Bridge House'* intense rifle fire swept across the sector, coupled with shrapnel shells bursting overhead. Captain Sharp continued his story: *"Then came heavy howitzer shells right amongst us which burst and made neat round holes about 30 feet by 10 feet and threw up tons of muck when they hit a field. ... the men never falter but went on and on — a splendid sight — they did magnificently, hungry and tired and weary tho' they were."* Harry and his comrades engaged the enemy but it was reported that it had little effect. They moved to Potijze then onto *'Hell Fire Corner'* to take the line before being promised to be relieved to comparative safety and provided with some overdue rest. The promise had to be broken as the Battalion was ordered to move east of Fortuin to take over the trenches along the St Jan to Passchendaele road, close to the crossroads at Gravenstafel. Harry was on the move again on Thursday 29th April, this time to the line along the Zonnebeke to St Julien road where he was killed in action.

... Hell Fire Corner

451181 PRIVATE
HECTOR BLAKE BEATON
58th Battalion Canadian Infantry
(Central Ontario Regiment)
Died on Wednesday 14th June 1916, aged 17
Commemorated on Panel 30.

Hector Beaton and his signature

Hector was the son of Charles K and Annie Beaton, of 88 Rhodes Avenue, Toronto, Ontario.

He volunteered in Niagara, Ontario, on Wednesday 30th June 1915 when he claimed to have been born in Toronto on Friday 14th August 1896, working as a steel worker, and had served in the Militia. Hector was 5ft 4½in tall, with a 33in chest, a dark complexion, hazel eyes and dark coloured hair.

After training in Canada, Hector sailed to England and sent for further training at Bramshott, Hampshire. He left camp with the Battalion at 8.30am on Sunday 20th February 1916 bound for Southampton. Hector sailed to Le Havre and was greeted by a blizzard at 1.00am the next morning. Following a short rest at *'Sanvic Camp'* on Monday 21st he entrained at 5.00pm, arriving twenty-four hours later in Godeswaersvelde. A short march took him to billets at St Sylvestre Cappel where a series of drills and route marches were undertaken, and General Malcolm Mercer joined them for divine service on Sunday 27th. Hector was trained in the use of gas masks and bombing as well as undertaking fatigues at night.

Malcolm Mercer

Hector marched from Loker to Vierstraat on Thursday 16th March and went into the trenches for the first time. The five-day tour was without incident but still an unpleasant experience for everyone, especially one of such young age. He returned to billets in Loker on Wednesday 22nd where he rested overnight before marching the next day to *'Camp F'* where Hector was provided with a bath. A further move, the next day, took the Battalion to *'Camp D'* and in the evening Hector went to a concert held in the camp cinema. Hector was sent to *'Railway Dugouts'* on Tuesday 28th where he was engaged in fatigues. He experienced his first heavy barrage on Friday 31st where five of his comrades were wounded by shell splinters. Hector moved into the front line on Saturday 1st April when the Battalion relieved the 43rd Battalion and served in the trenches until Wednesday 5th. The Battalion was sent into reserve at 'Camp E': Hector undertook drill, musketry drill, physical exercises and a route march. A further tour of duty began on Sunday 9th until Friday 14th and then marched to 'Camp B'. Everyone was given rest on Tuesday 18th and Wednesday 19th as it was deemed too wet, cold and windy.

Hector was in the line on Monday 1st May when the Germans mounted an attack that he assisted in repulsing. He took alternate tours in the front line and as a member of a working party until Monday 8th under constant observation from German aeroplanes flying above his line. Hector marched to 'Camp D' where on Wednesday 10th he was taken with the rest of the Battalion for a bath. The weather did not improve and everyone was disappointed that the Brigade sports day was cancelled on Saturday 13th.

Hector was sent to the 'Railway Dugouts', arriving at 1.00am on Tuesday 23rd, within two hours there was a gas alert and the Germans began to shell the sector. Throughout the tour of duty Hector was under constant shell fire and so it was with some delight when he reached 'Camp C' at 6.00am on Thursday 1st June. It was to be Hector's last time out of the line. The next day he was sent to Poperinghe where he had a bath and upon return was told to prepare to move off. Hector first went to 'Camp F' before marching on to 'Belgian Château' and then into Ypres itself where he waited in the ramparts. Hector moved into support at 'Zillebeke Switch' that came under shell fire throughout the night. He then went into the front line north of the ruins of the village. Hector was either in the firing line or in support on fatigues until being sent to 'Maple Copse' on Monday 12th. He took part in a bombing attack up 'Gourock Road', 'Hill Street', 'Vigo Street', 'Bydand Avenue' and 'Durham Lane'. It was a complete success but in the action Hector was killed, his body lost during subsequent actions.

2378 PRIVATE
ROBERT WILLIAM BEATTIE
1st/6th Battalion Northumberland Fusiliers
Died on Monday 26th April 1915, aged 16
Commemorated on Panel 12.

Robert was born at home, only son of Hannah Mary Beattie, of 4 Bristol Terrace, Newcastle-on-Tyne, and the late Robert Beattie.

He enlisted in Newcastle and went into training. Robert left with the Battalion and landed in France on Monday 19th April 1915. He entrained to northern France to prepare for the front line. The Germans launched the first gas attack at 5.00pm on Thursday 22nd April. The Battalion was sent to the Ypres Salient and was in action near St Julien under very heavy fire during a series of attacks and counter-attacks. Major Moulton-Barrett was in command of the Battalion who was badly wounded during the day and Captain Auld took command: casualties were particularly heavy amongst the mixed bag of troops fighting together. Despite their losses they put up a good fight convincing the Germans that they faced a much large and stronger force. Sadly Robert was one of those killed in action after only a week since he arrived on the Salient.

445482 PRIVATE MAGLOIRE BERUBÉ
60th Battalion Canadian Infantry
Died on Saturday 3rd June 1916, aged 17
Commemorated on Panel 30.

Magloire's signature

Magloire was the son of Magloire and Rebecca Morin Berubé, of Ste Francoise, County Temiscouata, Quebec.

He volunteered in Sussex, New Brunswick, on Friday 20th August 1915 when he claimed to have been born in Ste Francoise on Monday 15th November 1897 and was working on a farm. Magloire was a Roman Catholic, 5ft 6in tall, with a 33½in chest, a dark complexion, brown eyes and black hair.

He left for England on Friday 5th November 1915 and was sent to 'Bramshott Camp', Hampshire. Magloire embarked in Southampton on Sunday 20th February 1916 bound for Le Havre. From the docks Magloire marched with his platoon to a camp for some rest before entraining to Godeswaersvelde, however, due to a mistake the train continued to beyond Poperinghe so the Battalion had to march over twelve miles back to their billets! Early on Thursday 2nd March they moved to billets in Loker from where Magloire was sent into the front line for practical experience before undertaking tours of duty.

At the end of March he moved into the Salient at 'Maple Copse' where he came under the heaviest shellfire he had yet experienced. Whilst at 'Camp D' in Brandhoek steel helmets were issued to all ranks by Wednesday 19th April; the next day Magloire had his kit inspected prior to returning to the trenches.

The Battalion entrained for the Asylum and moved carefully around Ypres to 'Halfway House' where they relieved the PPCLI. Captain Collingwood Andrews of the Queen Victoria Rifles described the sector: *"Half Way House figures on all the maps as a house of considerable size, but not a vestige of a house was to be seen. It was a large dug-out with several entrances, a veritable warren of galleries and chambers. In it were brigaded 3 Brigade H.Q., a battalion and 2 machine-gun corps, to say nothing of oddments such as sappers and gunners, etc., who sought temporary refuge in what was the only spot with any pretensions to safety on the ridge. Below, the atmosphere was appalling, and conditions were not improved by the constant drip of moisture and the presence of 2 inches of slimy mud on the floor. An engine used to pump day and night to keep the water down; it also lit some of the chambers with electric light. The dug-out was so crammed that men were sleeping in the passages and communication was difficult. It was a perfect maze, but I had a rough plan made and always carried it with me."*

The trenches were in very poor condition with many men up to their knees in thick, slimy mud. Work had to be undertaken to rejoin many parts of the trench together, creating a continuous line, and dig out the stinking unsanitary filth, then create better latrines. The enemy were shelling the sector remorselessly throughout the tour. When relieved Magloire returned to *'Camp D'* in Vlamertinghe where on Friday 5th May six high explosive shells landed in the camp that killed five and wounded fourteen. Magloire remained in camp training and on fatigues until entraining once again to Ypres and marching out to *'Maple Copse'*. It was noticeable that the enemy bombardment of the sector was heavy and constant until he was relieved late on Wednesday 31st. He marched to *'St Lawrence Camp'* where he got some much needed rest, however at 10.00am on Friday 2nd June he was ordered to be ready to move within an hour. Just before midnight Magloire paraded with his platoon and marched via *'Shrapnel Corner'* to *'Halfway House'*. The Battalion had been ordered to follow the 52nd Battalion into the front line to take part in a counter-attack. As Magloire approached *'Regent Street'* he was killed when a number of shells burst amongst his platoon. There would have been very little to recover and less to identify.

2019 CORPORAL JAMES BINNING
1st/6th Battalion Northumberland Fusiliers
Died on Monday 26th April 1915, aged 17
Commemorated on Panel 12.

James was born at home, eldest son of James Wilson and Sarah Binning, of 66 Westminster Street, Gateshead. He trained with his comrades until entraining for Folkestone, Kent, where he sailed to Boulogne on Monday 19th April 1915. James entrained to northern France to begin training around Steenvoorde. Unfortunately for James and the Battalion the Second Battle of Ypres began on Thursday 22nd just after they had settled down in their billets. The Battalion was ordered to rush up to the Ypres Salient to take part in its defence and undertake counter-attacks. James had not been in the front line very long when he was killed in a fierce, close fought action.

L/10392 LANCE CORPORAL SYDNEY HERBERT BIRCH
1st Battalion Queen's Own
(Royal West Kent Regiment)
Died on Monday 22nd February 1915, aged 17
Commemorated on Panel 45.

Sydney's signature Sydney was born at home, son of Mr and Mrs George Sydney Birch, of 33 Holly Road, Chiswick, London.

In the peaceful summer of 1914 Sydney volunteered in Hounslow, Middlesex, on Wednesday 1st July. He was 5ft 9in tall, weighed 129lbs and had been working as a painters labourer.

Sydney was training when the Battalion left with the BEF in August. He remained in England and was appointed Lance Corporal on Saturday 31st October.

The young NCO went out to France on Monday 7th December to join the Battalion in the field whilst they were serving in the Wytschaete to Messines sector. The winter rain had turned the low-lying trenches below the Messines Ridge into a ghastly muddy bog. Sydney had only been with the Battalion for two weeks on tours of duty when he was relieved then spent the end of December resting or training, returning to front line duties in early January 1915. Sydney was resting in Bailleul in mid-February when the Battalion was inspected by General Wanless O'Gowan. A couple of days later, Friday 19th, the Battalion was ordered to march to the trenches southeast of Ypres, via Vlamertinghe. He went into the poorly maintained trenches near Zwarteleen where a considerable amount of time was spent reconstructing them. The enemy became particularly active on Monday 22nd launching a large number of trench mortars against the Battalion's line. German machine gunners played on Sydney's position; he was one of forty casualties the Battalion lost in the action.

S/13019 RIFLEMAN WILLIAM BIRD
9th Battalion Rifle Brigade
Died on Tuesday 18th January 1916, aged 16
Commemorated on Panel 46.

William was born in St Albans, Hertfordshire, on Wednesday 15th February 1899, fourth son of Thomas and Louisa Bird, of High Cross, Aldenham, Watford, Hertfordshire. He went to the local elementary school and was employed as a gardener.

William enlisted on Friday 11th June 1915 and went to France on 17th September joining the Battalion in the field ready to participate in the attack on Bellewaarde. At 4.30am on Saturday 25th September he was sent forward where the Battalion came under heavy fire from 'Oskar Farm' and from the Bellewaarde Spur. From 6.00am the Germans counter-attacked from 'Dead Man's Bottom' that started to push the Battalion back. They were able to hold out on the lip of the mine crater until 4.00pm when they were withdrawn to their original line.

William remained in the Ypres Salient on tours of duty throughout the winter, mainly in the St Jan sector, until he was mortally wounded in the front line as described by his Captain: "We were digging a new trench connecting two other trenches and Bird was hit in the neck by a stray bullet; we managed to get him down on a stretcher to the dressing station, but he died almost as soon as he got there and within an hour of being hit. We buried him just behind our second line. I am very sorry to lose Bird; he had been in my company some time."

William is commemorated on Aldenham War Memorial.

... digging in whilst taking precautions again gas

12325 PRIVATE SAM BLACKWELL
1st Battalion King's Own Yorkshire Light Infantry
Died on Saturday 8th May 1915, aged 17
Commemorated on Panel 47.

Sam was born at home, son of Mrs Emily Blackwell, of 77 Carlisle Street East, Sheffield.

He volunteered in Sheffield and completed his training in Winchester where on Tuesday 12th January 1915 Sam paraded for HM King George who inspected the Battalion prior to their departure to the Western Front. The next day the Colonel of the Regiment, General Sir Arthur Wynne, inspected the Battalion and wished them well for the forthcoming overseas adventure. Sam marched to Southampton where he embarked on the *SS City of Benares* bound for Le Havre on Friday 15th January. Upon arrival he was sent to the station to entrain for Hazebrouck then marched to billets in Outtersteene. Training began the next morning that included visits to the front line where Sam served with battle-experienced men for practical training. Field Marshal Sir John French and HRH The Prince of Wales inspected the Battalion on Thursday 28th.

Sam was taken by motor omnibus to Vlamertinghe from where he marched into the trenches for the first time at Verbrandenmolen on Monday 1st February. It was a grim area where the trenches were flooded with the corpses of French soldiers floating about in them. The walls of the trenches were filled with decomposing bodies and in No Man's Land the bodies of soldiers from both sides and dead animals lay rotting. The tour of duty ended early on Friday 5th, Sam marched to billets in Ouderdom where he got some much needed rest and get the smell of death out of his nostrils. Tours of duty continued with casualties mounting but even larger numbers were invalided with trench foot.

Sam remained on tours of duty in the sector apart from two weeks service in the Wulverghem sector in March. For the story from Thursday 1st April 1915 see Lieutenant James Ferguson below.

10225 PRIVATE LEONARD BLAY
5th Battalion Oxford and Bucks Light Infantry
Died on Saturday 25th September 1915, aged 17
Commemorated on Panel 39.

Leonard was born in Oxford on Sunday 28th November 1897, and was second son and youngest child of eleven children of David and Kate Louisa Blay, of 18 Albert Street, St Ebbes, Oxford.

He volunteered in Oxford and trained with the Battalion until they were ready for overseas service. Leonard went out to France with the Battalion on Thursday 20th May 1915.

The Second Battle of Ypres was drawing to a close as Leonard arrived in Belgium. The sector was, however, never quiet. He began tours of duty in the Hooge sector where he remained surviving the German flame thrower attack at the end of July. The next major action, part of the diversionary attack for The Battle of Loos at Bellewaarde, on Saturday 25th September would be his last. Leonard was mortally wounded in action and died on the battlefield but his body was lost in later battles. He is commemorated on the Holy Trinity War Memorial, St Ebbes, Oxford.

3/2871 PRIVATE SAM BLAYMIRE
1st Battalion York and Lancaster Regiment
Died on Tuesday 30th March 1915, aged 17
Commemorated on Panel 55.

Sam was born at home, eldest son of George and Emma Blaymire, of 1 Stanley Main Street, Eastmoor Road, Wakefield, West Yorkshire.

He volunteered in Pontefract, Yorkshire, and was sent for training. Sam joined the Battalion when they returned from India at the end of December 1914. He trained with them in 'Hursley Park Camp', Winchester, Hampshire, whilst they rekitted and prepared for the move to the Western Front. Sam entrained with the Battalion in Winchester for Southampton and sailed to Le Havre on Tuesday 19th January 1915. He entrained to the Hazebrouck sector then marched to billets west of Bailleul to complete his training.

Sam moved across the border into Belgium and began serving in the ghastly sector around St Eloi where the full horrors of the war were all too apparent. After a month of tours of duty Sam moved for a week of rest and training in Vlamertinghe. When he returned to the trenches it would be further south on the lower slopes of the Messines Ridge, on the Wytschaete to Wulverghem road. Sam remained serving in the front line on tours of duty, or was working on fatigues, for a further seven weeks until he was killed.

7411 PRIVATE
HAROLD FRANCIS BLISSETT
1st Battalion East Surrey Regiment
Died on Tuesday 20th April 1915, aged 17
Commemorated on Panel 34.

Harold was born at home, second son of Edward James and Ellen Blissett, of 60 Balvernie Grove, Merton Road, Southfields, Wandsworth, London. He had two brothers, Ernest Charles and Ivor Stanley.

He volunteered in Kingston-on-Thames, Surrey, and was sent for training until leaving for France on Tuesday 23rd February 1915 to join the Battalion. He was with a draft of fifty men arriving in Neuve Eglise the next day where the Battalion was resting in billets. For a history of the Battalion see Private Albert Burton, see below.

3058 PRIVATE TOM BOLTON
1st/5th Battalion King's Own
(Royal Lancaster Regiment)
Died on Tuesday 27th April 1915, aged 17
Commemorated on Panel 12.

Tom was born at home on Tuesday 16th November 1897, the youngest son of Thomas and Elizabeth Bolton, of Brook House, Caton, Lancaster. He had older siblings, John, Edith and Mary and younger sister, Margaret.

He volunteered in December 1914 in Lancaster and was sent for training in Sevenoaks,

Tom Bolton

Kent. He left with the Battalion for Le Havre on Sunday 14th February 1915. For Tom's involvement on the Western Front see Private James Cathcart, below.

Tom was killed when a shell burst close to him. The 'Lancaster Guardian' published his obituary: "Letters received conveyed the sad tidings that Pte. Tom Bolton, of Caton, had met a soldiers death on the 28th. His death was instantaneous caused by a high explosive shell which also took toll of four or five others. Tom Bolton was the youngest of the Caton recruits. He was born on the 16th November 1897 and enlisted before he was seventeen. Was in France on St Valentines Day this year and perished on the battlefield five months after his enlistment. His bright cheerful exuberant spirit will ever be remembered by those who now deplore his death. His former school mates hoisted the school flag half mast. In a letter, Pte. Harry Shuttleworth (brother-in-law of Bolton) says: 'I am sorry to write this bad news but thought it would be best to let you know. Poor Tom was killed yesterday by a shell, also a few other poor chaps. I have his jack knife and there were some photos in his pay book. I don't know if I can get them if I can I will let your people have them. He died as an English soldier. I did not see him, the stretcher bearer gave me the news today."

12880 RIFLEMAN
REGINALD ERNEST BOWEN
11th Battalion King's Royal Rifle Corps
Died on Tuesday 14th August 1917, aged 17
Commemorated on Panel 53.

Reginald Ernest Bowen
Reginald's signature

Reginald was born in Wrotham, Kent, second son of Thomas and Alice Bowen, of 5 Whatcote Cottages, Platt, Sevenoaks, Kent. He had three brothers and fours sisters.

He volunteered in Dartford, Kent, on Tuesday 19th October 1915 when he claimed to be 18 years and one month old and worked as a gardener. Reginald was 5ft 3½in tall, with a 33½in chest, weighed 112lbs, had a fresh complexion, grey eyes and light brown hair. The next day he was sent to Winchester to begin training. Reginald was posted to the 6th Battalion on Friday 29th October in Sheerness, Kent, where his training continued whilst he also served as part of the Thames & Medway Garrison.

Reginald sailed from Southampton for Le Havre on Tuesday 12th June 1917 to join the Battalion with a draft whilst they were serving on the Somme. The Battalion transferred to Belgium in mid-July 1917 and went for training near Proven. Reginald also went out with working parties carrying ammunition to the front until moving to the line near Elverdinghe on Monday 30th July. At 3.50am on Tuesday 31st the offensive began and he attacked towards the Pilkem Ridge.

Reginald took part in an attack on the Steenbeek on Saturday 11th August that ended in failure as they encountered a German patrol immediately who were able to disorganise the advancing companies. The Battalion was forced to retire and on Tuesday 14th made a further attempt with the support of additional companies from the Rifle Brigade. Reginald was in position at 3.00am and rose from his position as the whistles blew at 4.00am. He waded across the stream under cover of a well laid creeping barrage. The German strong point, a pill-box called 'Au Bon Gite', poured machine gun fire onto the advancing troops. Reginald was killed but his body not recovered.

His father was sent his possessions that included a cigarette case, a book, eight photographs and a metal mirror.

Reginald is commemorated on the Platt War Memorial.

11202 PRIVATE
WILLIAM GEORGE BOYDER
1st Regiment (Infantry) South African Infantry
Died on Wednesday 10th April 1918, aged 17
Commemorated on Panel 15.

William was the son of Henry William and Mary Boyder, of 4 Sydney Road, Bertrams, Johannesburg.

He volunteered in Johannesburg and was sent for training. William sailed with a large number of eager new recruits to England where training continued in November 1917. Due to the success of the German Spring Offensive in March 1918 that decimated the ranks of many Battalions, including all four of the South African Brigade, every able man and boy was rushed across the English Channel. William joined the Battalion about Wednesday 3rd April 1918 whilst they were in 'Ridge Wood Camp', south of Ypres. He was allocated to his platoon and was getting to know them, learning as much as he could of the recent battles when he marched to a hut billet between the Scherpenberg and La Clytte.

General Sixt von Armin launched a major attack at 5.30am on Wednesday 10th and began to move forward with a speed rarely known during the First World War. At 8.00am William was ordered to parade and prepare to move off to take part in the defence of the line or take part in a counter-attack. At 5.15pm William was led forward in an attack against Messines at the point of the bayonet. It initially went well and the enemy was forced to retire. William was killed by machine gun fire from the German strong point at 'Bethleem Farm'.

16980 PRIVATE JOHN BOYLE
7th Battalion Canadian Infantry
(British Columbia Regiment)
Died on Saturday 24th April 1915, aged 17
Commemorated on Panel 24.

John's signature

John was the second son of John and Annie F Boyle, of Revelstoke, British Columbia, he had an elder brother, Allan.

He volunteered in Valcartier, Province of Quebec, on Sunday 13th September 1914 when he claimed to have been born in Manchester, on Tuesday 21st January 1896, and was working as an electrician. John was 5ft 6½in tall, with a 35in chest, a fair complexion, brown eyes and hair, and a burn mark under his right elbow. He was sent over to England for training to join the Battalion who were in 'Lark Hill Camp', Salisbury Plain. They left from Amesbury Station on Wednesday 10th February 1915 and entrained to Avonmouth. The next day they sailed to St Nazaire that was reached on Monday 15th. A long train journey took the Battalion to Strazeele where training began on Thursday 18th. Field Marshal Sir John French, accompanied by General Sir Horace Smith-Dorrien and HRH Prince Arthur of Connaught, inspected the Canadian Contingent on Saturday 20th and wished them well. The next day John marched to Ploegsteert where he was given practical training in front line duties whilst attached to experienced troops.

The Battalion marched south to Armentières, then onward to billets in Sailly on Monday 1st March. During the evening of Tuesday 2nd John began his first tour of duty at La Boutillerie that lasted three days. He moved to billets in Fleurbaix and then undertook three further uneventful tours of duty during the month. John marched to Steenvoorde on Monday 5th April for training and General Sir Edwin Alderson inspected the Battalion on Thursday 8th. General Sir Horace Smith-Dorrien inspected them on Sunday 11th and three days later John embussed to Vlamertinghe from where he marched out to the trenches at Gravenstafel. The sector was far more active than he had been experienced previously and within a few hours four men had been killed and ten wounded.

John was in reserve at Fortuin on Tuesday 20th as the German artillery were pounding Ypres. He was able to get some rest, despite the bombardment, however that changed dramatically on Thursday 22nd following the gas attack. At 7.00pm James was ordered to stand to and two hours later marched to the front, east of St Julien. Throughout Friday 23rd he remained at the front under a heavy bombardment, and at 4.00am on Saturday 24th his line came under a heavy gas attack that was followed at 5.00am by a further artillery bombardment. The enemy rushed James' position at 6.00am dressed in British uniforms, the ruse did not work and the Germans were repulsed. The whole line was subjected to heavy rifle and machine gun fire, James was hit and killed. During the ensuing battle his body was lost on the battlefield.

892010 PRIVATE
CHARLES EDMUND BRADLEY
'B' Company, 8th Battalion Canadian Infantry
(Manitoba Regiment)
Died on Saturday 10th November 1917, aged 17
Commemorated on Panel 24.

Chas' signature

Chas was the son of Mr and Mrs Edmund Bradley, of 80 Harvard Avenue West, Transcona, Manitoba. He worked for the Canadian National Railways in Transcona as a machinist.

He volunteered in Winnipeg, Manitoba, on Wednesday 23rd February 1916, where he claimed to have been born in Superior, Wisconsin, USA, on Sunday 6th March 1898. Chas was a Presbyterian, 5ft 9in tall, with a 35in chest, with a dark complexion, brown eyes and black hair. He was passed medically fit for a Special Service Battalion but for sedentary work only and he should avoid double parades!

Chas trained in Canada and England until joining the Battalion in field. They served on the Salient until August 1916 and after a period of training transferred to the Somme and began serving in the trenches from early September. At the end of the month the Battalion were sent for training before returning to the trenches once again on Monday 9th October at Pozières. Following a another tour of duty they were sent for further training. Chas went into the trenches late on Thursday 2nd November for a three-day tour and he remained on tours in the Berthonval sector. General Sir Arthur Currie visited the Battalion on Monday 27th. Chas marched with his platoon at 9.00am on Monday 18th December and arrived in his billet in Bruay at 2.30pm. Christmas Eve was a holiday and to help the party spirit an enemy aeroplane bombed the village at 10.00pm. Although some damage was done, no-one was injured. Midnight Mass was held in the local theatre and in the morning a further Mass was held in Hospital Chapelat. Chas and his chums enjoyed a good Christmas dinner. He attended a concert given by the band during the morning of Friday 29th and in the evening went to a theatrical concert in The Grand Theatre. Chas remained in Bruay until Thursday 18th January 1917 when he marched to the trenches at Fosse 10 near Bully Grenay. When he was relieved on Friday 26th he marched to Bully Grenay when he had a hot bath the next morning before being sent on fatigues. Chas served in the sector until moving to Ecoivres on Sunday 4th March and went into the trenches the next day. When the Battle of Arras began on Monday 9th April the Battalion was in support. At 6.15am they moved forward as the attacking battalions successfully achieved their objectives. Chas did not move into the front line until early on Friday 13th and into Willerval, that was abandoned, in the evening. The Battalion was relieved by the early hours of Monday 16th to 'Douai Tunnel' for five days. When he went back into the line it was to take part in a successful attack. May was spent training in Hallicourt. Chas moved to Neuville St Vaast on Saturday 2nd June to undertake fatigues for a month. He marched to 'Fraser Camp' on Monday 2nd July for ten days. A series of moves took him to Fosse 7, Hersin, Les Brébis, Hallicourt and Mingoval. Chas took part in the capture of Hill 70, Lens, on Wednesday 15th August. After a period of rest and training he returned to serve in the front line on tours of duty until being sent to 'Aix Noulette Huts' on Thursday 27th September for a week of rest and training. Chas undertook a further tour of duty before beginning training in Bruay and Zuytpeene. Chas arrived in Brandhoek on Monday 5th November and the next day entrained to Ypres Asylum. He marched out to Passchendaele where at 6.05am on Saturday 10th Chas was led forward under a creeping barrage. Chas did not advance far until he was cut down by machine gun fire. Chas is commemorated on the Canadian National Railways Roll of Honour.

2412 PRIVATE JOHN BRADLEY
1st Battalion The Loyal North Lancashire Regiment
Died on Saturday 31st October 1914, aged 17
Commemorated on Panel 43.

John was born at home, eldest son of James and Mary Ann Bradley, of 13 Haydock Street, Bolton, Lancashire. He had an older sister, Annie and younger sisters Hannah and Edith. Following his education John was employed as an iron moulder.

... entraining for the front

He volunteered in Bolton and went out to France on Tuesday 22nd September 1914 to join the Battalion with a draft whilst they were serving on the Aisne. John undertook tours of duty in the Troyon sector until 2.30am on Thursday 15th October but was not involved in any particular action. The situation on the Chemin des Dames was described by one of the officers: *"It was one continual round of trench warfare. The trenches of the West Yorkshire Regiment were still full of their dead, and it was almost impossible to dig in some places without coming upon dead bodies. We were subjected to several attacks, and in no case did the enemy set foot in our trench. One day Major Burrows, Allason, Allen, Calrow and Reid — who had only joined that day — and I were all sitting in the mess talking when a shell burst just at the door. Allason and Calrow were killed, Reid was injured and also Major Burrows, but Allen and I were not touched. One of the mess carts was completely blown up. On another occasion a minenwerfer came into a trench and burst, where five officers and a few men were standing, and only wounded three of them slightly."* (Captain Lionel Allason and 2nd Lieutenant William Calrow are commemorated on La Ferté-sous-Jouarre Memorial.)

John marched via Vendresse, Bourg and Longueville to Vauxcere. He entrained in Fismes late on Friday 16th and finally arrived in Cassel late on Sunday 18th. The Battalion was billeted in and around the town and were given the Monday 19th to rest and relax. John left the town early on Tuesday 20th, crossed the border into Belgium and went via Poperinghe to Boesinghe where he arrived late on Wednesday 21st. At 5.00pm the next evening he was deployed to St Jan where he waited until moving onto the Pilkem Ridge where he arrived at 5.30am on Friday 23rd. The Battalion advanced, as described by Lord Ernest Hamilton: *"In this order they advanced to within 300 yards of the trenches where they began to come under a very heavy shell fire. Major Carter decided to charge at once with the bayonet, and he sent a message to this effect to the K.R.R. on his left, asking them to advance with him. This, however, they were unable to do, and Major Carter accordingly decided to attack alone. Captain Henderson, with the Machine Gun Section, pushed forward to a very advanced position on the left, from which he was able to get a clear field of fire for his guns, and the Battalion formed up for the attack. Captain Crane's and Captain Prince's companies were in the first line; the other two were in support. The order to fix bayonets was given; a bugle sounded the charge, and with loud cheers the Battalion dashed forward, and in less than ten minutes had carried the trenches and cleared them of the enemy. Six hundred prisoners were taken, a number which might have been increased but that the further pursuit was checked by our own artillery."* Later in the day the enemy mounted a concerted attack but it soon subsided and at 9.30pm on Saturday 24th John was relieved then marched into Ypres where he arrived in the early hours of the morning.

John moved out of Ypres into reserve on Monday 26th where he remained until 7.00am the next morning. He packed up his bivouac and marched through Hooge to west of Reutel. The enemy was pushing toward Gheluvelt so the Battalion was deployed: *"As a result of the hasty reinforcing of the line during the day, units were now much mixed up, and sorting and reorganization went on for long after dark. And there was other work to be done. A new line of trenches, roughly north and south through the 8th kilometre-stone, opposite the cross-roads captured by the enemy, and half a mile from them, had to be dug during the night, and the line re-allotted; entrenching tools were scarce and time was lost in trying to find more."*

John spent the night of Friday 30th laying out in a field with little cover under a heavy enemy bombardment. In the early hours of Saturday 31st John was withdrawn to Hooge where he formed up, fixed his bayonet and took part in an attack. In the fierce action John was killed.

Field Marshal Sir John French wrote: *"October 31st and November 1st will remain for ever memorable in the history of our County, for, during those two days, no more than one thin and straggling line of tired-out British soldiers stood between the Empire and its practical ruin as an independent first-class Power."*

20271 PRIVATE JOHN BRAND
1st Battalion Royal Scots Fusiliers
Died on Monday 27th March 1916, aged 17
Commemorated on Panel 19.

John was born in Clydebank, Glasgow, son of Mr and Mrs Alexander Brand, of 4 Station Road, Port Glasgow. He was educated locally.

John volunteered in Greenock, Renfrewshire, and was sent for training and left in early 1916 to join the Battalion in the field with a draft whilst they were serving on the Ypres Salient. He was allocated to a platoon and went into the line for his first tour of duty. John had only been serving for a very short period when he was killed, his grave was subsequently lost in later battles.

12942 PRIVATE WILLIAM BRIDGES
2nd Battalion Suffolk Regiment
Died on Saturday 25th September 1915, aged 17
Commemorated on Panel 21.

William was born at home, the only son of William and Eliza Bridges, of Elmswell, Suffolk. He was educated locally.

He volunteered in Elmswell, following training William went out to France on Tuesday 27th July 1915 with a draft to help bring the Battalion up to strength. He arrived on the Salient as the German launched the first liquid fire attack at Hooge on Friday 30th. Neither he, nor the Battalion, was involved in the action but were soon deployed to the sector assisting in the defence of the line then took part in the main counter-attack on Monday 9th August.

At the end of August William was sent to a camp at Ouderdom, then moved to Vlamertinghe on Thursday 2nd September. From Friday 3rd he began fatigues between 'Moat Farm' and Hooge. The three weeks employed in the front line working as a pioneer Battalion was as dangerous as serving in the front line. William returned to front line duty when he arrived in 'Maple Copse' on Thursday 23rd September. He prepared to take part in an attack on Bellewaarde that was a diversionary attack in support of the main offensive some miles to the south, the Battle of Loos. William went forward on Saturday 25th near 'Sanctuary Wood' and whilst in action was killed.

He is commemorated on the Elmswell War Memorial.

17457 PRIVATE WALTER JOHN BRIGGS
'D' Company, 1st Battalion Suffolk Regiment
Died on Tuesday 25th May 1915, aged 17
Commemorated on Panel 21.

John was born at home, eldest son of Walter and Happy Sarah Sophia Briggs, of King's Lane, Chelmondiston, Ipswich, Suffolk. Following his elementary education John worked on a farm.

He volunteered in Ipswich then went out to France on Wednesday 12th May 1915 with a draft to join the Battalion who were billeted in farms outside Poperinghe. The Battalion had suffered badly during the Second Battle of Ypres and the various drafts that arrived brought the Battalion to a strength of eleven officers and two hundred and sixty-eight men.

John marched with his new comrades to Herzeele on Friday 14th under the command of Major Frederick William Orby Maycock, DSO, who had been appointed the day before (he was killed in the same action as John and is buried in Tyne Cot Cemetery). Major Maycock set about reorganising the Battalion whilst they undertook training. Field Marshal Sir John French visited the Battalion and inspected them in the village square on Thursday 20th.

The Ypres Salient remained a hotly contested battleground without respite. A further German gas attack was launched and on Monday 24th John was moving towards the front line for the first time. It must have been a daunting sight to march through the smoking ruins of Ypres and into the carnage of the battlefield beyond. He went round Zillebeke Lake and arrived at 'Witte Poort Farm' in the early evening. John took cover in his allotted trench where he was ordered to "fix bayonet". Captain Rushbrooke led the men over the top and they charged the enemy who poured deadly fire on the attackers. No progress could be made so they were forced to retire. General Louis Bols ordered that 'Bellewaarde Farm' had to be taken at any cost so shortly before midnight Major Maycock took his men to 'Witte Poort Farm' from where he led his men against the enemy. The attack was a dismal failure for a second time. The Battalion was reduced to only three officers and one hundred and eighty-one men from the action, one of those killed being John.

He is commemorated on the Chelmondiston War Memorial in St Andrew's Church. John's cousin, Private Harry Briggs, died on Friday 17th September 1915 and is buried in the churchyard.

1345 LANCE CORPORAL PETER PAUL BROPHY
2nd Battalion Leinster Regiment
Died on Friday 16th June 1917, aged 17
Commemorated on Panel 44.

Peter was born in Shinrone, King's County, son of the late Kyran and Margaret Brophy, of Shamboe, Borris-In-Ossory, Ballybrophy, Queen's County.

He volunteered in Shinrone and was sent for training. Peter went out to France on Friday 17th December 1915 and joined the Battalion with a draft whilst they were billeted in Gandspette ten miles from St Omer.

Peter crossed into Belgium on Saturday 8th January 1916 and marched to a camp near Poperinghe. His first experience of the battlefield came a week later when he began a tour of duty at Hooge. Peter soon settled down to the routine of front line life, serving in the firing trench, being in reserve, undertaking fatigues, training and some rest.

St Patrick's Day was celebrated with a cinema show in the Divisional Cinema Hall then on Sunday 19th March Peter left the Salient and went to Bailleul. He was sent to serve in the trenches at Wulverghem from Thursday 30th, then the Battalion was to serve slightly north in the Messines sector. It was a busy time as a number of raids were carried out by each side and in May a significant attack was mounted supported by a new form of gas. Later in the month Lieutenant Colonel Winston Churchill, wearing his distinctive French helmet, visited the front line whilst his Battalion was based south of Ploegsteert.

Peter remained in the sector until mid-July; whilst in 'Bulford Camp' orders were received by Colonel Orpen-Palmer that the Battalion should be ready to move at short notice. They moved off by motor omnibus to Flêtre where training began. After a week Peter entrained to Amiens where he arrived shortly before midnight on Tuesday 25th July. A five-hour march took him to billets in Moliens Vidame where four days intensive training began. Some fun was had each evening as Peter was able to watch an inter-brigade boxing match. He arrived close to the front on Monday 31st at Vaux where training continued. The next move was to Bray and all ranks were able to visit the front line between Fricourt and Mametz. Late on Tuesday 8th August he marched to 'The Citadel' where the Battalion went into reserve. The front was finally reached at Carnoy where Peter assisted in the digging of a communication trench from Bernafay Wood to the eastern edge of Trônes Wood. It was not safe from the attention of the enemy as it was often shelled and bullets spattered about.

The first serious engagement on the Somme for the Battalion, and the first for Peter, was at Guillemont. At 8.00pm on Thursday 17th August he marched off and arrived in the assembly trenches at 2.00am. Peter was not to get any rest as he was needed to help carry supplies of ammunition and stores for a few hours. At 3.00pm the preliminary barrage opened with Peter in the support trenches. The attack was not going well and the German defenders were putting up a good show inflicting severe casualties on the attackers — Colonel Orpen-Palmer was wounded whilst organising the Battalion's attack. The Battalion was taking heavy casualties but it was not until the next morning were they relieved. After three days of rest and fatigues Peter returned to the front line. Sadly the relief had been spotted by the enemy and they shelled the position causing a number of casualties. An officer from the 73rd Hanoverian Fusiliers in the line opposite the Battalion recorded: *"The sunken road appeared only as a series of huge shells, filled with uniforms, equipment, arms and dead bodies; the surrounding ground, as far as one could see, had been completely churned up by heavy shells. Not a single blade of grass could be found. A dreadful place — the dead defenders lay amongst the living. Whilst digging funk holes we discovered that they had been buried in strata. One company after another had crowded in and been destroyed by drumfire. The bodies had been covered by the masses of earth thrown up and the next company had taken the place of the fallen.*

The sunken road and the ground in rear of it were full of Germans; the ground in front was strewn with British dead. Everywhere arms, legs and heads were sticking up, torn limbs and bodies were lying in front of our funk holes, partly covered by groundsheets in order to avoid the dreadful sight. Despite the heat, nobody thought of covering the bodies with earth.

Guillemont was only distinguishable by the lighter colour of the craters, due to the white stone of the houses, now pulverised. Before us lay Guillemont Station crumpled up like a nursery toy, and, beyond that, Delville Wood, reduced to chips and splinters."

Following the tour of duty Peter was sent for rest at Dernancourt in a tented encampment. It was particularly unfortunate for Peter and his comrades as the hot summer heat turned to torrential rain that flooded the camp and was too much for many of the tents that collapsed. After a little rest training began once more until returning to the Longueval area on Wednesday 30th. Peter eventually arrived in the support lines, part of the old German line. It had excellent dug outs so everyone was out of the rain and comfortable. Sadly this did not last as long as had been expected as the Battalion was required to take part in a counter-attack that lasted for two days.

Peter was relieved from the line and after some rest

marched to Amiens where he entrained to Longpré then marched to a billet in Beauchamps. A good rest was had before training began. He entrained north to Béthune on Wednesday 20th September and was provided with a billet in Bruay, that was only found after a tiring march.

The next sector where the Battalion would serve was Vimy that, at that time, was quiet and a total contrast to either the Salient or the Somme. Peter was able to relax even when in the front line as for the most part neither side appeared to be too keen to disturb the monotony. However, in October two raiding parties were organised that gained useful information, killed a number of the enemy and destroyed part of their line. At the end of October they moved towards the old Loos battlefield and took the line from Wednesday 8th November.

Towards the end of the year the number of fatigues increased when not in the front line: *"Finding fatigue parties every night for the front line. Bad area. Men never seem to get a rest. Company getting weak, always casualties in the working parties."*

They were in the trenches for Christmas and to ensure that an informal truce would not be declared the following order was issued: *"With the intention of showing the enemy that we have no intention of fraternizing with him, and also with a view to taking advantage of any slackness on his part during Christmas, a special programme will be carried out by the artillery, T.M.s and machine guns during the following hours:—*

24th December —

    4 p.m. to 4.15 p.m.

    7 p.m. to 7.15 p.m.

    10.15 p.m. to 10.45 p.m.

25th December (Christmas Day) —

    1 a.m. to 1.15 a.m.

    9.10 a.m., artillery only, Code B

    12.30 p.m., artillery only, Code B

    4.10 p.m., artillery only, Code B

    7.30 p.m. to 7.40 p.m.

    8 p.m., artillery and T.M.s.

    9 p.m. to 11.15 p.m.

26th December —

    1 a.m. to 1.30 a.m.

    10.15 a.m., artillery only

    11.45 a.m., artillery only

    2.10 p.m., general stafe by artillery

1 In order not to interfere with our patrols which may be out during the intervals of firing, firing will not be carried out (except in case of emergency) except in the hours laid down in the above programme.

2 Rifle grenades will be active during the day.

3 Any attempt on the part of the enemy to show himself is to be met immediately by fire of every possible description.

4 The above programme will not affect any fire called for by observers who see good targets especially as regards para 3. Watches will be synchronized at 2.15 p.m. to-day over the wire.

Code, Apple."

The Battalion's next major action was the attack on Vimy Ridge on Thursday 12th April 1917. Following a number of delays *en route* to the front they finally arrived in their assembly trenches at 4.31am. At 5.00am the artillery bombardment began that was the signal for the infantry to advance under its cover then into a blizzard that obscured the German line. The enemy lines were soon reached and fierce hand-to-hand fighting ensued during which Corporal John Cunningham was awarded the Victoria Cross. The citation for the Victoria Cross reads: *"For most conspicuous bravery and devotion to duty when in command of a Lewis Gun section on the most exposed flank of the attack. His section came under heavy enfilade fire and suffered severely. Although wounded he succeeded almost alone in reaching his objective with his gun, which he got into action in spite of much opposition. When counter-attacked by a party of twenty of the enemy he exhausted his ammunition against them, then, standing in full view, he commenced throwing bombs. He was wounded again, and fell, but picked himself up and continued to fight single-handed with the enemy until his bombs were exhausted. He then made his way back to our lines with a fractured arm and other wounds. There is little doubt that the superb courage of this N.C.O. cleared up a most critical situation on the left flank of the attack. Corporal Cunningham died in hospital from the effects of his wounds."* (He died on Monday 16th April and is buried in Barlin Communal Cemetery Extension)

By noon the Battalion objectives had been taken but at a heavy cost:

	Killed	Wounded	Missing
Officers	4	4	-
Other ranks	48	155	3

By the end of May Peter had arrived in Busseboom, south of Poperinghe, where he undertook fatigues supporting the line during the Battle of Messines. Peter left 'Ottawa Camp' on Wednesday 13th June for 'Micmac Camp' from where on Saturday 16th the Battalion relieved the 8th Battalion The Buffs at Hill 60 for a tour of duty. They came under the constant attention of enemy aeroplanes patrolling above their line that fired on them until being driven off by the Royal Flying Corps and anti-aircraft fire. Shortly after arriving in the front line Peter was killed after serving in the front line for a year and half but still only 17 years old.

2144 PRIVATE JOHN BRODIE BRYANT
53rd Battalion Australian Infantry, AIF
Died on Wednesday 26th September 1917, aged 17
Commemorated on Panel 29.

John's signature

John was born in Saltburn, Yorkshire, son of the Reverend Harry and Edith Bryant, of St Paul's Rectory, Burwood, New South Wales.

He volunteered in Bathurst, New South Wales, on Wednesday 23rd February 1916 when he claimed to be 18 years and 2 months old and a student. John was 5ft 2in tall, with a 34in chest, weighed 168lbs, a fair complexion, blue eyes and brown hair. His mother wrote on Tuesday 4th April giving her consent for John to become a member of the army.

He embarked on the *SS Vestalia* in Sydney on Tuesday 11th July 1916, arriving in England on Saturday 9th September. Whilst training John was admitted to Fargo Military Hospital with pyrexia (fever). He returned to duty on Friday 3rd November but two days later was sent to Fovant Military Hospital, Wiltshire, for a short time. Whilst in camp on Tuesday 12th December John went absent without leave for twenty-four hours and when he returned was kept in custody for a day. Major Cooke Russell awarded him seven days Field Punishment No 2 and forfeiture of eleven days pay. John continued training but from Saturday 7th April 1917 until Monday 9th he went absent without leave again and was fined £1 10s 0d. On Tuesday 15th May John did not comply with an order from an NCO and was absent from a defaulters parade for which he was awarded twenty-eight days detention.

John left Hurdcott, Wiltshire, for Southampton on Thursday 14th June and sailed to Le Havre. He joined the Battalion whilst they were training in Lynde on Wednesday 1st August. John hardly had time to settle down when he was collected by motor omnibus and driven to Lumbres from where he marched to Affriques where training continued for five days. He returned to Lynde then marched to Blaringhem where the Battalion paraded for General Sir William Birdwood who took the salute then undertook an inspection. Training finally ended on Monday 17th September, the Battalion marched out of camp to Steenvoorde and the next day onto a camp in Reninghelst. Late on Saturday 22nd John marched via 'Château Segard' to 'Halfway House' where he bivouacked. John joined members of his platoon and went out to the front line on fatigues, his first experience of the battlefield. At midnight on Tuesday 25th he marched into his allocated assembly position where he arrived at 3.15am. At 5.30am a creeping

barrage was laid down and John was led forward at the double. He then knelt down in No·Man's Land then began to crawl forward. John came under heavy machine gun fire and was killed.

John had been serving in uniform for nineteen months but only spent a couple of hours at the front in action before he was killed.

His father was sent his British War Medal no 43850, Victory Medal no 43366, Memorial Plaque and Scroll no 332175.

2925 PRIVATE THOMAS BUCHAN
2nd Battalion Royal Scots
Died on Sunday 5th March 1916, aged 17
Commemorated on Panel 11.

Thomas was born at home, son of Andrew and Mary Buchan, of 9 Bridgegate, Peebles.

He volunteered in Peebles and sent for training. Thomas went out to France on Monday 9th August 1915 to join the battalion who were serving in the Hooge sector, a scene of a series of intense battles over the previous ten days. Thomas soon settled into front line duties and his only major action would come on Saturday 25th September. The Battle of Loos opened and to help support the offensive a series of diversionary attacks were planned. The Battalion took part in one at Bellewaarde.

Thomas moved into the trenches at 'Sanctuary Wood' where he waited to attack the German lines. At 3.50am the preliminary bombardment began and just before the whistles were blown four mines went up under the German trenches. Thomas charged forward with fixed bayonet and with his comrades they successfully captured their objectives. As Thomas was consolidating the position the enemy mounted a number of counter-attacks. The Battalion suffered very badly, mainly during the counter-attacks, taking losses of ten officers and two hundred and forty-four men, killed, wounded or missing. Thomas was relieved on Monday 27th to Ouderdom for some rest and the next day he had to clean up for an inspection by General Sir Edmund Allenby. Whilst out of the line the Germans had blown a mine and the line was in a terrible state when Thomas returned to the trenches on Wednesday 29th.

Thomas remained in the sector on tours of duty without taking part in any further action until the end of October. He was sent for training and rest in northern France throughout November, returning to the line at St Eloi on Monday 29th. It was an unpleasant sector but was relatively quiet whilst Thomas served there on tours of duty throughout the winter. At the beginning of March 1916 he was on a tour of duty at *'The Bluff'*, whilst he was assisting in burying the dead Thomas was shot and killed.

8525 PRIVATE
GEORGE ECCLES BULLEID
2nd Battalion Canadian Infantry
(Eastern Ontario Regiment)
Died on Thursday 22nd April 1915, aged 15
Commemorated on Panel 18.

George Bulleid
George's signature

George was the youngest son of John and Lena Bulleid, of 3 Sutherland Road, Belvedere, Kent. He had four older siblings.

George volunteered at Valcartier, Province of Quebec, on Tuesday 22nd September 1914, when he claimed to have been born in Plumstead on Sunday 6th October 1895 and therefore aged 18 years and 11 months. He gave his mother as his next of kin, living in Greenock, Scotland. George was 5ft 7in tall, with a 34in chest, a dark complexion, brown hair and eyes, and a mole on his left arm.

George was sent for training prior to departing from Gasepé Bay on Saturday 3rd October 1914 on board *SS Cassandra*, arriving in Devonport on Thursday 15th. His training continued at *'Bustard Camp'*, Salisbury Plain until Sunday 7th February 1915. George marched to Amesbury and entrained to Avonmouth where he embarked on *SS Blackwell* for St Nazaire. He arrived on Thursday 11th then entrained for Strazeele marching to billets in Merris. George went with his platoon for practical front line training near Armentières, attached to the North Staffordshire Regiment prior to undertaking his first tour of duty. He served around Bois Grenier and Fleurbaix until the end of March when he was sent for training at Neuf Berquin. George marched to Winnezeele on Tuesday 6th April for further training from where he left at 9.26am on Sunday 18th April then marched to billets close to Poperinghe for two days followed by a camp in Vlamertinghe.

Shortly after 5.00pm on Thursday 22nd April the Battalion was ordered to stand to following the first gas attack. Later in the evening he marched towards Ypres with the sound of battle raging around St Julien. Preparations for a counter-attack were hurriedly put together. George's position came under particularly heavy fire and he was killed. The battle raged on and George's body was lost in the subsequent battles.

33823 PRIVATE
FREDERICK GEORGE BUNCE
13th Battalion Cheshire Regiment
Died on Sunday 10th June 1917, aged 17
Commemorated on Panel 22.

Frednick George Bunce.
Frederick's signature

Frederick was born at home in February 1900, second son of Frederick and Martha Bunce, of Braughing, Hertfordshire. Following his education Frederick was employed as a farm labourer.

He volunteered in Bedford and first served with the Bedfordshire Regiment with service number 30630. He was sent for training then transferred to the Cheshire Regiment on Thursday 19th October 1916. Frederick was 5ft 4in tall, with a 32in chest and weighed 104lbs. He left to join the Battalion in the field on New Year's Eve 1916 who were serving in the Ploegsteert sector. Frederick was soon assimilated into his platoon and began tours of duty, but was not involved in any particular action. Frederick was wounded on Saturday 14th April 1917 and taken to the 2nd Australian Casualty Clearing Station. Four days later he was taken by a hospital train to No 14 General Hospital in Wimereux followed by a hospital in Rouen from Saturday 28th. Once he had recovered Frederick was able to rejoin the Battalion on Wednesday 23rd May.

Frederick trained for the forthcoming offensive on the Messines Ridge that began at 3.00am on Thursday 7th June when a series of nineteen mines shook the ground like an earthquake. The roar of the mines and artillery could be heard and felt for miles. Frederick followed his Colonel, Lionel Finch, across two thousand yards of No Man's Land towards the German lines. During the advance Frederick was hit by multiple gunshots and died on the battlefield.

He is commemorated on Braughing War Memorial.

205441 PRIVATE
CHARLES BERTRAM BURDEN
10th Battalion Queen's Own
(Royal West Kent Regiment)
Died on Tuesday 31st July 1917, aged 17
Commemorated on Panel 45.

Charles was born in Hampshire, son of Mr and Mrs Burden. As a young boy he moved with his parents to Hemel Hempstead, Hertfordshire.

He volunteered in Watford, Hertfordshire, and was posted to the Northumberland Fusiliers with service number 19564. Charles continued to train with them until transferring to the Queen's and left to join the Battalion in the field.

The Battalion participated in The Battle of Messines in June 1917 and then prepared for the next offensive, The Third Battle of Ypres.

Charles went into the front line on Wednesday 25th July where he came under heavy enemy shelling every day until he was killed on the opening day of the offensive. The objective for the Battalion was to capture Hollebeke and to clear the area east of 'Battle Wood'. The whistles blew and the officers led their men over the top and across No Man's Land. The Bavarian troops in the trenches opposite put up a determined resistance and their machine guns held up the attack. It took until 8.00am before the second objective was achieved. Charles moved forward to attack a series of well placed pill boxes on the ridge ahead of him that poured their fire down on the Battalion as they struggled forward. The attack failed and a large number of casualties were taken, one being Charles.

He is commemorated on the Hemel Hempstead (Boxmoor) War Memorial.

3832 PRIVATE
HERBERT FRANCIS BURDEN,
SHOT AT DAWN – DESERTION
1st Battalion Northumberland Fusiliers
Executed on Wednesday 21st July 1915, aged 17
Commemorated on Addenda Panel 60.

Herbert was born on Tuesday 22nd March 1898 at 47 Silvermere Road, Lewisham, London, the fourth son of Arthur and Charlotte Burden.

Herbert volunteered and was sent for training before being sent out to the front with a draft.

In late April 1915 Herbert was in the trenches at St Eloi when at 5.00pm on Thursday 22nd the Germans launched the first gas attack. Despite being five miles to the south of the attack the gas drifted in the wind and many of the men complained of sore eyes and dry throats. Herbert remained in the sector until Wednesday 26th May when the Battalion was relieved and sent to camp at Ouderdom. After two days rest he was sent to the support trenches close to Potijze Château. During his four days in the line the Château was set on fire during a bombardment but Herbert was not involved in any particular action, he was then sent into reserve south of Hooge. After being relieved at Hooge the Battalion was sent for rest. He paraded at 4.45pm on Tuesday 15th June at his bivouac and marched eight miles to the assembly trenches. He went along the cobbled tree-lined road via Vlamertinghe and rested for two hours shortly before arriving in

Ypres. The town had taken a heavy battering over the previous two months and was no longer a bustling medieval town but a charred ruin. Herbert marched through the town and out via the Menin Gate and along the Menin Road to 'Hell Fire Corner' and took shelter in the shallow assembly trenches. At 2.50am on Wednesday 16th the preliminary bombardment commenced, the third bombardment ended at 4.00am and the Germans then believed the attack would commence. They took to the parapets and started to fire at the British front line. At 4.10am a further barrage fell on the German lines killing many of the defenders and cutting up their line. The whistles were blown, the Battalion went over the top and by 6.30am the second objective was taken. The Germans made a determined counter-attack at 2.30pm, the line came under extreme pressure and they were pushed back to their first objective. Herbert was lucky to survive, with four hundred and one casualties taken by the Battalion, killed, wounded or missing. Later that night he marched back to bivouac at Ouderdom for some well-deserved rest.

Herbert went absent without leave on Saturday 26th June 1915 from near the front line where he had been detailed to dig trenches. He was arrested on the following Monday at 'Dickebusch Huts' where he claimed that he gone to see a friend who was serving in that area.

He was sent for Court Martial that was presided by Major Duncan Harcourt Grant of 1st Battalion Lincolnshire Regiment, together with one of his colleagues Captain Robert H Johnston and Lieutenant Eric Edward Dorman-Smith, of the 1st Battalion Northumberland Fusiliers. Herbert did not have a good Army record that was presented to the Court which included seven other cases of being AWOL whilst in England, one case in France, other minor offences together with a history of claiming to be sick. Four witnesses were called for the prosecution:
8628 Lance Serjeant Charles Dawson of the 1/5th Northumberland Fusiliers stated: "At Vlamertinghe Camp on 26 June in the afternoon I warned the accused for trench working party to parade at 7 p.m. the same date. I called the roll at 7 p.m. The accused was absent. I did not see him again till 9:40 p.m. on the 28th when he was brought in by an escort of the R. W. Kent regiment." (Serjeant Dawson was later awarded the DCM and was killed on Tuesday 8th August 1916 and is buried in Dantzig Alley British Cemetery, Mametz.)
10353 Private John O'Callaghan, 1st Battalion Royal West Kent stated: "On the 26th June 1915 I saw the accused in the transport lines of my Regiment near Dickebush between 12 noon and 1 p.m. he told me he was on a pass. I saw him again on the morning of the 27th at about

9.00 a.m. He was then leaving the transport lines. I saw him again on the 28th at about 18.30 p.m. near Dickebush Huts where my battalion was coming on relief from the trenches. The huts are about 2 miles nearer Dickebush than the transport lines. It was nearer 12 noon than 1 p.m. when I saw the accused." (Private John O'Callaghan was accidentally drowned on Tuesday 7th September 1915 and is buried in Carnoy Military Cemetery.)

472 Lance Corporal Amos H Chapman, 1st Battalion Royal West Kent stated: *"On 26th June 1915 at about 12 noon I saw the accused in the transport lines of my Regiment. I saw him again at about 9 a.m. on the 17th June in the same place. I again saw him on the 28th inst. near the huts which my battalion were coming on relief from the trenches that night."*

Lieutenant and Quartermaster Harry George Rogers, 1st Battalion Royal West Kent stated: *"At about 8.30 p.m. on the 28th June 1915 in the huts of the battalion near Dickebusch I saw the accused & asked him for his reason for being there. He told me that he had permission from the Transport Officer to visit 1 R.W. Kent Regt. to see a friend."* (Lieutenant Harry George Rogers was later promoted to Captain, awarded the Military Cross, was Mentioned in Despatches twice and created an MBE.)

Lieutenant Colonel Clement Yatman, 1st Battalion Northumberland Fusiliers stated: *"This man was punished for being absent on 11th inst. and reported sick the following day. He had only just returned when, on being warned for the trenches, he absented himself. No officer of the company left who knows the man but his platoon sergeant states he is a man you cannot trust. Defaulter sheet shows he is much addicted to absence. In the absence of any officers who know this man I do not feel justified in expressing an opinion. I know very little of the man and it seems to me wrong to express an opinion with so little to back it up. I trust the G.O.C. will realise how hard it is to answer this question fairly in the present circumstances and will not press for a reply."* (Clement Yatman was later promoted to Brigadier General and awarded the DSO.)

Herbert was sentenced to death by the Court and it was passed to the chain of command to confirm: Brigadier General Douglas-Smith agreed, General Aylmer Haldane wrote: *"No remarks to offer in mitigation of the order of the court."* General Sir Edmund Allenby and General Sir Herbert Plumer both agreed with the sentence. Field Marshal Sir John French queried if Herbert knew he was going into the firing line and not for training. Colonel Yatman wrote the following reply to the Field Marshal: *"Burden was warned for duty with a working party which was ordered to proceed to the trenches occupied by the 9th Brigade at Hooge. The party was to remain there for 2 days and took their rations for that period with them. Their duty was to dig at night in the vicinity of the firing line etc. The duty was liable to the usual dangers to be met with in the vicinity of the trenches."* The final signature of Sir John French was added on Sunday 18th July and at 4.00am on Wednesday 21st Herbert was taken out, tied to the execution post and shot. The firing squad was commanded by Captain Charles Rich.

Herbert was one of the youngest soldiers Shot At Dawn, however, Private Joseph Byers was also 17 years old and is buried in Loker Churchyard, see accompanying publication *Boy Soldiers Killed in Belgium 1*.

The National Memorial Arboretum was created at Alrewas, near Lichfield in Staffordshire that was designed by Andy de Comyn and unveiled by HRH The Duchess of Kent. In the centre is a memorial with a statue of Herbert Burden. It shows him standing, blindfolded and strapped to a wooden execution post, eternally awaiting the order to fire. Behind his statue are three hundred and forty other posts each labelled with an executed soldier's name. The site is by the river at a point where the dawn light first reaches the arboretum.

Herbert is commemorated on the War Memorial at St Laurence, Catford, London.

3551 PRIVATE PATRICK BURLACE
2nd Battalion Leinster Regiment
Died on Thursday 12th August 1915, aged 16
Commemorated on Panel 44.

Patrick was born in Athlone, County Westmeath, son of Private Thomas Burlace and Mrs Mary Burlace.

He enlisted in Athlone and after training was sent to France, joining the Battalion in the field with a draft, arriving on Boxing Day 1914. The Battalion had been in the front during Christmas and participated in the Christmas Truce being relieved as Patrick was arriving in Chapelle d'Armentières. His first task was to join in the belated Christmas celebrations and learn all about the events of the previous couple of days.

Patrick's first experience of the front line began on New Year's Eve at Rue de Bois where, for the time being, all was quiet. The High Command of both sides were particularly unhappy with the unofficial truce and orders soon arrived for the resumption of fire on the enemy. Patrick was relieved on Sunday 10th January 1915 to the bustling town of Armentières and comfortable billets. He was provided with a hot bath and clean clothes before exploring the town with its many and varied attractions. After four days Patrick was sent to the trenches at l'Épinette that were flooded up to three feet deep, with many sections being totally unusable. When not on guard duty in the front line he was sent on fatigues digging a communication trench. Until Thursday 11th March Patrick remained on tours of duty with rest in Armentières and could therefore consider himself luckier than many when out of the line. He took part in a successful minor attack that pushed the front line forward to the Portegal to l'Épinette road. Patrick remained at the front to consolidate the newly acquired position. One of his officer's, 2nd Lieutenant Frederick Andrews, was approaching the front line on Monday 15th when challenged by a sentry that was not heard and he was shot dead. Lieutenant Andrews is buried in Ferme Buterne Military Cemetery, Houplines.

One diversion that Patrick thoroughly enjoyed was the 6th Division Horse Show at Erquinghem in early April and was thrilled when many of the prizes were awarded to Battalion horses. General Sir John Keir inspected the Battalion on Thursday 29th April whilst they were billeted in Armentières. The Second Battle of Ypres began a week earlier on Thursday 22nd April when the first gas attack was launched. With the advent of the new terror weapon simple nose and mouth pads were issued to all ranks that may have initially given them some confidence but were to prove to be woefully inadequate.

Patrick marched across the border into Belgium on Wednesday 2nd June and to bivouac near Poperinghe. Three days later he was issued with a new, but equally useless, veil respirator before taking the line near La Brique. When Patrick arrived the scene in front of him was pleasant, almost picturesque. The meadowland was high with plant life, wild flowers growing in abundance. Patrick was sent out to cut down the grass and flowers as its height obscured the line of fire. As he worked the beauty of the field soon changed into a field of death as many bodies lay decomposing and Patrick helped bury many of them. During the afternoon on Tuesday 8th Ypres was being bombarded and Patrick was able to see two of the pinnacles on the Cloth Hall hit and knocked down. After nearly three weeks in the front line Patrick was finally relieved to billets northeast of Poperinghe. After a week of rest Patrick marched overnight and returned to the line on Saturday 3rd July for two days. When he was relieved Patrick marched for a mile through an area that had been attacked by gas that caused him, and his comrades, to suffer with stinging eyes and throats. Patrick continued on tours of duty until he was killed in the line at Hooge. He had been in reserve from Monday 9th August until Wednesday 11th Patrick was sent to take over a series of captured trenches that were under heavy fire. Shortly after he arrived Patrick was shot, dying instantaneously.

His father died on Wednesday 9th December 1914 and is buried in Beuvry Communal Cemetery Extension.

10645 PRIVATE
ALBERT EDWARD BURTON
1st Battalion East Surrey Regiment
Died on Tuesday 20th April 1915, aged 17
Commemorated on Panel 34.

Albert was born in Brixton, only son of Frederick and Louisa Burton, of 121 Fountain Road, Tooting, London. He volunteered and enlisted in Kingston-on-Thames, Surrey and was sent for training. The Battalion went out to France with the BEF in mid-August whilst Albert continued training. He went out to France on Saturday 19th September 1914 to join the Battalion with a draft. Under the command of two officers, Albert was one of two hundred and one men that arrived in St Marguerite on Thursday 24th. The next day the Battalion crossed the Aisne and marched to billets in Jury. At 3.00am on Sunday 27th Albert was stood to as reports arrived that the enemy were advancing on the bridge at Condé, The Battalion marched off to assist with the defence of the position but when they arrived in Serches a report arrived to say the previous information was incorrect so they turned round and returned to Jury.

Albert was not to serve in the front line on the Aisne as at 6.30pm on Thursday 1st October he was told to pack his kit and be ready to move off an hour later. He marched for six hours to billets in Nampteuil that was followed each night by further route marches that took him to Longueil on Tuesday 6th where he entrained to Crécy. Albert detrained to Noyelles-sur-Mer and marched to billets at Château Bois de l'Abbaye near Abbeville. A seventeen mile march took Albert to Vaulx where he waited to be collected by motor omnibus. Due to communication difficulties and general confusion the omnibuses arrived nearly ten hours late.

... boarding omnibuses

Finally, late in the evening of Saturday 10th Albert arrived in Béthune from where he was deployed to the La Bassée Canal where he entrenched. The move towards the enemy continued via Locon towards

Richebourg l'Avoué where Albert had his first experience of engaging the enemy. As the German infantry advanced Albert was ordered to rapid fire that, coupled with the Battalion's machine guns, brought down large numbers of the enemy. Not only did Albert see his first action he witnessed at first hand the reality of war as a number of his comrades were killed and wounded. The Battalion pushed on towards Richebourg l'Avoué where again he took part in another engagement. Albert had a day of rest on Thursday 15th and was able to catch up on sleep then cleaned himself up. The Battalion marched towards Lorgies on Saturday 17th where there was a short skirmish and were then held in brigade reserve at La Tourelle. Albert returned to the trenches on Wednesday 21st near Lorgies as large numbers of fresh German troops were being concentrated in the sector. Early on Thursday 22nd the enemy captured Violaines and the Battalion was sent to assist in a counter-attack. The line was not sustainable and as a result the Battalion was ordered to retire towards Richebourg l'Avoué. The German artillery had been brought close to the front and began to shell the British lines on Sunday 25th. The bombardment continued over the next days coupled with a number of attacks on the line that were repulsed. Albert was relieved on Friday 30th and was first sent to Les Glatignies, secondly onto La Couture. Shortly after he had settled into the latter village it came under shell fire forcing a move to Lestrem, via Le Touret, the next day.

Albert marched towards the Belgian border on Monday 2nd November and arrived in Bailleul expecting to be sent to Ypres. Orders arrived that the Battalion should return to support the Indian Corps. Albert embussed to Lestrem then went into billets and awaited further orders. He returned to the trenches near Vieille Chapelle for an eight-day tour on Friday 6th. Once relieved Albert began his move to Belgium once again. He marched to Méteren where he rested overnight, the next day he crossed the border and went into the trenches at Lindenhoek in the shadow of Mount Kemmel. The enemy kept the trenches under a constant bombardment until Albert was relieved on Tuesday 24th and marched to billets in Dranouter. Albert was able to enjoy his first hot bath since leaving England when he marched to the asylum outside Bailleul on Friday 27th. The next day he returned to the trenches in front of Wulverghem for a four-day tour. When relieved Albert marched to billets in St Jans Cappel. Following some rest he had to clean up and prepare for an inspection in the afternoon of Wednesday 2nd December by Field Marshal Sir John French who addressed the parade: *"I am very glad to have the opportunity of addressing you to-day and of thanking you for the work you have done.*

On the way here I asked your Corps Commander, Sir Horace, what special occasion I could mention in which you have distinguished yourselfs. 'Whatever you mention, and whatever you say,' he said, 'it will not be too much. They have been splendid throughout.' No regiment could wish for higher praise than this, and I thank you personally for what you have done and the way

Sir John French

you have helped me. The 5th Division have had more than their share of the fighting in this campaign. On the terrible retirement after Mons and Le Cateau you had the brunt of the fighting, and immediately after, at the Battle of the Marne, you had to attack the most difficult section of the line, and the attack was brilliantly carried out. Not a week later you were engaged on the Aisne and held the extremely difficult position of Missy, into which an incessant rifle and shell fire was poured from the commanding position above. Less than a month after this the Regiment was in the thick of the terribly severe fighting round La Bassée, where you were faced by three if not four times your numbers and experienced some of the fiercest fighting of the war. Lately in the trench fighting you have gallantly defended your lines against the most determined attacks and the most vigorous shelling. In fact, you have crowded into the four months of this campaign enough fighting to fill the battle honours of an Army Corps, and by your conduct throughout you have not only upheld, but greatly added to the fame of a grand old Regiment. In conclusion, as Commander-in-Chief, I wish once more to thank you for your endurance and for the splendid work you have performed and to tell you how glad I am to have this opportunity of being able to tell you so."

Albert marched to billets in Neuve Eglise on Saturday 5th December then returned to the trenches at Wulverghem. He took part in an abortive attack on Wytschaete between Monday 14th and Wednesday 16th but it was defeated by a combination of a stout defence by the enemy and the unforgiving mud. Late on Thursday 17th a very tired Albert trudged back to St Jans Cappel where he remained for six days and then went to billets in Dranouter. The Christmas period was spent on fatigues but he did not take part in or witness first-hand the Christmas Truce.

It was a great relief to all ranks when they were relieved from the line and sent to billets in Bailleul early on Tuesday 5th January 1915 for four days.

Albert marched to billets in Neuve Eglise on Sunday 10th

January and returned to the trenches at Wulverghem on Saturday 16th. He remained on tours of duty in the sector up to Messines. In the early afternoon of Wednesday 27th February the enemy began to shell the north of Neuve Eglise and the Battalion had to evacuate their billets. By 4.00pm it had quietened down and it was considered safe enough for each platoon to return to the village and rescue their kit but as the process was under way more shells began to fall.

Albert marched out to the trenches and began a tour of duty in a blizzard below the Messines Ridge early on Thursday 28th. After four days he returned to Neuve Eglise for some rest where again the village was targeted by enemy artillery. After undertaking fatigues Albert returned to the line on Monday 8th March and remained in the sector until Tuesday 23rd when he marched the short distance to serve in front of Kemmel with billets in Loker.

With two weeks of service completed in front of Kemmel Albert was moved to Zevecoten on Monday 5th April for two days then on to the cavalry barracks in Ypres. He was able to visit the damaged but thriving town where the cafés were still doing a good trade. Albert paraded in Ypres town square on Saturday 10th as the 2nd Battalion marched through the town and they were given a rousing cheer. Albert was sent to serve close to Hill 60 until Thursday 15th but returned once more on Sunday 18th. The mines had been blown the day before and there was a large battle taking place. Albert's first task was to help rebuild and repair the damaged trenches and clear the dead from the trenches whilst under heavy shell fire. At 11.00am on Tuesday 20th a heavy bombardment was laid on the Battalion and Albert was killed by shell fire.

... the Battalion's position at Hill 60

8900 PRIVATE JOHN CAIRNS
1st Battalion Argyll and Sutherland Highlanders
Died on Friday 16th April 1915, aged 17
Commemorated on Panel 42.

John was born in Enniskillen, County Fermanagh, son of Mr and Mrs Timothy Cairns, of 11 South Sterling Street, South Side, Glasgow. He enlisted in Paisley and was sent for training. John went out to France on Saturday 6th March 1915 with a draft to join the Battalion in the field. He joined them whilst they were serving in the St Eloi sector. After only six weeks of service on the Western Front John was killed whilst in the front line.

6674 PRIVATE ALEXANDER CAMERON
2nd Battalion King's Own Scottish Borderers
Died on Tuesday 15th December 1914, aged 16
Commemorated on Panel 22.

Alexander was born in Old Monkland, Lanarkshire, son of James and Mary Cameron, of 11 Summerlee Street, Coatbridge, Lanarkshire. He was educated locally. He enlisted at Coatbridge and was sent for training, joining the Battalion in the field on Saturday 5th December 1914. Alexander was sent into the line at Wulverghem where the trenches were waist deep in cold sludgy water. Some of his comrades became so badly stuck in the mud they could only be hauled out by ropes. From Monday 14th December until Wednesday 16th the King's Own took part in an attack in the area of Wulverghem. Alexander was killed, one of five to die over the three-day tour of duty, with twenty-seven wounded.

He is commemorated on Coatbridge War Memorial.

... Coatsbridge War Memorial

22722 PRIVATE
HECTOR MCDONALD CAMERON
14th Battalion Canadian Infantry (Quebec Regiment)
Died on Wednesday 21st April 1915, aged 15
Commemorated on Panel 24.

Hector was the son of Lachlan and Annie Cameron, of Lepreaux, New Brunswick. He was educated locally. Hector volunteered and was sent for training before leaving for Devonport. He was sent to Salisbury Plain where training continued until 9.00pm Wednesday 10th February 1915 when he left camp and entrained at Amesbury Station for Avonmouth. He boarded *HMT Australind* commanded by Captain Sidney Angell. He

SS Australind

was crowded in with his comrades and at 11.00pm sailed into tempestuous seas. The gale raged for two days with one man being killed when he was thrown against an iron stanchion. On Sunday 14th the seas calmed and the convoy arrived in St Nazaire early on Monday 15th. The Battalion marched to the station to entrain for Hazebrouck where they arrived at 6.00am on Thursday 18th. Hector detrained and formed up with his platoon then marched via Caëstre to Flêtre where

Prince Arthur

he was billeted. As he arrived in the village HRH Prince Arthur of Connaught rode passed and wished them well. Field Marshal Sir John French arrived on Friday 19th to inspect the Brigade in a field near Caëstre.

At 8.00am on Tuesday 23rd February Hector marched to Méteren then onto Nieppe where General William Pulteney watched the Battalion train. He was sent to Armentières, arriving in the afternoon where billets were provided in the Asylum and in a large warehouse. Over the next few days he was sent into the trenches with the North Staffordshire Regiment to gain front line experience. The Battalion left their billets at 4.00pm on Tuesday 2nd March and marched to Bac St Maur where they were billeted. His senior officers went to Corps Headquarters for a briefing and were told: *"Gentlemen, you are about to face a cunning, cruel, and unscrupulous enemy. If you make a mistake, you will not get the chance to make a second one."* Shortly before dawn on Wednesday

3rd Hector paraded then went into the line opposite Fromelles at Rue Petillon where the Battalion relieved the Northumberland Fusiliers and the 1st Battalion Grenadier Guards. He started work on strengthening the trenches and came under shell fire at noon plus there was the constant danger of snipers who killed one of his comrades in the early afternoon. Hector remained in the line until Saturday 6th when he was relieved to Rue de Quesne until Tuesday 9th and returned to the line at Rue Petillon. The next day the Battle of Neuve Chapelle began although Hector was not called upon to take part. During the night of Saturday 13th Hector was relieved and returned to Rue du Quesne for a period of rest: a football match was organised on Tuesday 16th. He returned to the line on Wednesday 17th for a three-day tour of duty followed by a period of rest then a further tour. He was sent to Estaires on Saturday 27th being provided with comfortable billets near the cemetery. His daily routine was six hours training per day that included trench digging, instruction on wiring, route marches and bombing practise.

... outside the billets

At 6.00am on Wednesday 7th April he paraded and marched to Cassel via Neuf Berquin, Strazeele, and Caëstre. Hector remained there until 1.30pm on Thursday 15th when he marched to Steenvoorde, arriving at 4.00pm where he spent the night before being taken by motor omnibus to Poperinghe the next morning. He was given a hot meal at lunchtime before marching via Vlamertinghe to Ypres. Hector continued via St Jan to Wieltje where he halted and rested. A group of guides arrived to lead the Battalion to the line to relieve the French Infantry along the St Julien to Poelkapelle road where he remained in the line until he was killed, one of seven who were killed during the tour of duty. Hector was buried in the northwest corner of the churchyard in St Julien.

18300 PRIVATE ERNEST CAPEY
10th Battalion Royal Welsh Fusiliers
Died on Thursday 17th February 1916, aged 17
Commemorated on Panel 22.

Ernest was born at home, eldest son of Joseph and Mary Capey, of 35 William Street, Burslem, Staffordshire. He had two older and two younger siblings. Ernest was educated locally.

He volunteered in Tunstall, Stoke-on-Trent, Staffordshire, and was sent for training. Ernest left with Battalion for Dover, Kent, on Monday 27th September 1915 and embarked on *SS Onward* bound for Boulogne. He entrained for Caëstre where training continued until Tuesday 5th October when he marched to Bailleul. Following thirty-six hours in billets Ernest was sent to the Ploegsteert sector for practical training with experienced troops from the 2nd Battalion Royal Scots. He then began tours of duty in the trenches around Hooge that had seen considerable action only a couple of weeks earlier. His first tour of duty began on Friday 15th October and he remained in the sector until the end of November. The Battalion was then deployed to the St Eloi sector, a much grimmer set of trenches to serve in than those at Hooge. The area constantly flooded, particularly in the heavy winter rain and the ground constantly revealed decomposing bodies from the previous months of action. Whilst on a tour of duty Ernest was killed.

He is commemorated on the Tunstall War Memorial.

111078 PRIVATE JOHN WILLIAM CARR
5th Canadian Mounted Rifles (Quebec Regiment)
Died on Friday 2nd June 1916, aged 16
Commemorated on Panel 32.

John Carr

John's signature

John was born in Aldershot, Hampshire, England, the son of Benjamin and Annie Carr, of 995 Barrington Street, Halifax, Nova Scotia.

John volunteered on Wednesday 2nd June 1915 when he claimed to have been born on Monday 10th August 1896 and was employed as a pipe fitter. John was 5ft 2in tall, with a 32in chest, a fair complexion, blue eyes and red hair.

John was sent for training before leaving for England where training continued. He was sent out to join the Battalion in the field in Flanders. He served at Hill 63 and at Kemmel, spending Christmas 1915 in Méteren with only light duties assigned to the Battalion. John served in the southern sector of Belgium until the

end of March 1916 when he moved into the Salient at *'Sanctuary Wood'*. He was relieved from *'Maple Copse'* on Wednesday 5th April and entrained at the Asylum for *'Camp A'*. Whilst an evening party was being held in the Sergeants Mess on Monday 10th three bombs were dropped by a German aeroplane at 9.15pm but they did not cause any casualties. John was sent to Poperinghe on Wednesday 12th where hot baths were provided for all ranks. At 6.30pm the Drum & Fife Band and the Trumpet Band led John and the Battalion to the station from where they returned to Ypres Asylum then marched in small groups, at three minute intervals, through Ypres out via the Lille Gate to *'Railway Dugouts'* and *'Maple Copse'*. Working parties were sent out to *'Romers Lane'*, and *'Hill Street'* and repairs made to *'Railway Dugouts'*. During the night German machines flew low over their positions and dropped a couple of bombs. John came under high explosive shell fire on Sunday 16th whilst fatigues continued at *'Davidson Street'* as well as repairing the damage caused during the bombardment. John was relieved on Saturday 29th and returned to *'Camp A'*.

... in camp washing up

Training continued coupled with rest and sports, on Friday 5th May the Officers played the Sergeants at baseball, losing 26-14 and the next day 'A' Company lost a football match against the 2nd Canadian Mounted Rifles in the Brigade Championship. At 7.15pm on Sunday 7th John was moved to *'Camp F'* from where he was sent on fatigues. John returned to the line on Monday 15th near *'Sanctuary Wood'* for an eight-day tour of duty. When relieved he was sent to *'Camp H'* on Tuesday 23rd, spending Wednesday 24th resting and cleaning his equipment. He marched to Poperinghe on Thursday 25th where a hot bath awaited, as was clean underwear!

John returned to the line for the last time on Wednesday 31st May. He took the usual route of entraining to the Asylum before marching to *'Maple Copse'*, arriving at 1.35am on Thursday 1st June. The morning of Friday 2nd June began bright and clear with a slight northwesterly wind. Early in the morning a German mine was blown and the telephone wires were cut, a terrific bombardment was placed on the line and the German infantry assault began. During the horrific onslaught John was killed and his body never recovered.

36057 PRIVATE LLOYD CHARLES CASSELL
'A' Company, 1st Battalion
Worcestershire Regiment
Died on Wednesday 1st August 1917, aged 17
Commemorated on Panel 34.

Lloyd was born at home, elder son of George Davey Cassell and Mary Jane Cassell, of 30 Court, 4 House, Bishop Street, Birmingham. He had an older sister, Florence, and a younger brother, George.

He volunteered in Worcester and joined the Battalion in the field whilst they were serving in Flanders. Lloyd undertook tours of duty in the newly established front line following the Battle of Messines. The Battalion served in front of Wytschaete both in the trenches and on fatigues. In the build up to the opening of The Third Battle of Ypres on Tuesday 31st July a huge artillery duel was raging with each side pounding the other. Before Lloyd could take part in the offensive he was killed by shell fire.

3430 PRIVATE JAMES CASSELLS
2nd Battalion South Lancashire Regiment
Died on Thursday 17th June 1915, aged 17
Commemorated on Panel 37.

James was born in Bury, second son of Thomas and Margaret Cassells, of 8 Uncle Sam's Place, Rochdale, Lancashire. Following his education James was employed in a cotton factory as a bobbin carrier.

He volunteered in Bury and after training went out to France on Monday 3rd May 1915 to join the Battalion in the field on the Salient during The Second Battle of Ypres. James was deployed as soon as he arrived as fresh troops were required to replace the losses taken over the previous two weeks. He saw a good deal of action before he took part and was killed in the Battle of Bellewaarde as recorded in the Battalion War Diary:

"Tuesday 15th

During this evening the whole of the Units of 3rd. Division moved from their bivouacs, marching in an Easterly direction through Ypres, in preparation for the attack on enemy's line in vicinity of Hooge. Beyond this moment there was very little activity in the sector.

Wednesday 16th

The work on which 'A' and 'B' Companies were occupied was completed soon after midnight, when they withdrew to reserve at Ypres.

Casualties – 4 other ranks wounded, 2 of whom died of wounds during the night.

The whole of the assembly trenches which had been constructed during the past few nights were occupied by various units before 2 a.m. shortly after that hour the whole of our guns east and west of Ypres opened a heavy fire on enemy's line in vicinity of Hooge, and about an hour later the infantry of 7th, 8th and 9th Brigades moved forward. The enemy's trenches were successfully carried and a number of prisoners taken. The Battalion still in reserve at Ypres was detailed to take over and dispose of all prisoners, in accordance with special orders issued on the subject. During the whole day fire from our guns and those of the enemy was heavy – many of the enemy's shells pitched into Ypres and there, together with falling buildings, placed the battalions in very considerable danger. Whole battalions moved forward from Ypres about 9 p.m. to consolidate the ground won and still held by units of 8th Brigade. As companies moved up to the positions they were exposed to enemy's fire of shrapnel; high explosions, and gas shells, sustaining a number of casualties, and the move was really slow. On arrival at the position there was a certain amount of companies amongst the units in occupation and it was found impossible to carry out the work intended."

An officer rides to his men who were resting in billets at the outbreak of the Second Battle of Ypres

2093 PRIVATE GEORGE CATHCART
1st/5th Battalion King's Own
(Royal Lancaster Regiment)
Died on Friday 23rd April 1915, aged 19
Commemorated on Panel 12.

George was born at home, eldest son of John and Mary Cathcart, of 97 Dale Street, Lancaster.
For his story, see his brother James, below.

George and James Cathcart

2091 PRIVATE JAMES CATHCART
1st/5th Battalion King's Own
(Royal Lancaster Regiment)
Died on Tuesday 4th May 1915, aged 17
Commemorated on Panel 12.

James was born at home, second son of John and Mary Cathcart, of 97 Dale Street, Lancaster. George and his brother James were educated locally and both were a member of Bailrigg Cricket Club, Mr Aldous' Choir, the Male Voice Choir and St Peter's Church Choir. They had an older sister Annie.

James, with his brother George, enlisted in Lancaster on Friday 4th September 1914 and were sent for training in Didcot, Oxfordshire, and Sevenoaks, Kent. It is recorded that they were amongst the first dozen men to enlist in the Pals Battalion. They entrained with the Battalion in Sevenoaks, Kent, on Sunday 14th February 1915 for Southampton. They embarked on an old cattle boat and sailed to Le Havre at 7.00am, arriving twenty-four hours later. James and George marched in the rain for some distance to a tented camp where they were able to dry out and get some much needed rest. They marched four miles to the station to entrain at 3.00am on Wednesday 17th bound for Cassel. The train was terribly crowded and little rest or comfort could be found, to make it worse the journey took until 7.00am the next morning before they could stretch their legs on the platform. A seven-mile hard march took them to a grim billet in a barn near Winnezeele that they

shared with one hundred and fifty of their comrades! They were able to have a couple days relaxing with his chums before being sent on a long march to help dig trenches for two days. General Sir Horace Smith-Dorrien visited the Battalion on Monday 22nd to inspect a parade. The next few days were spent on route marches and fatigues, however, at 4.00pm on Sunday 28th the Battalion was sent into a series of trenches constructed at Steenvoorde for training purposes and marched back to billets each night at 9.30pm. A fleet of motor omnibuses collected the Battalion that trundled slowly to Bailleul where they arrived at 10.30am on Tuesday 2nd then marched to billets in a school. The next few days James and George were able to enjoy the pleasures of the bustling town with their comrades. Bailleul was filled with troops going to and from the battlefield so no doubt they took the opportunity of chatting with men who had first-hand experience of the reality of war.

... Bailleul town centre

The brothers left Bailleul at 1.45pm on Sunday 7th March and marched five miles north to a billet in a farm. The sight and sound of battle was all around them: for the first time they experienced live shelling that was not part of a training programme. Some of the shells were shrapnel and coupled with the aeroplanes buzzing overhead directing the German artillery it was quite frightening. They remained in position for two days before moving to Neuve Eglise — the village was already badly damaged by shell fire. The Battalion was subsequently moved to the rear and accommodated in St Jans Cappel.

The brothers first experience of the front began on Sunday 14th March when they marched to 'Pack Horse Farm' and were accommodated in a barn. The loudest and heaviest bombardment anyone in the Battalion had experienced continued throughout the night. With the noise and the barn shaking from the explosions, little sleep was achieved! They moved into the front line for two days, from the support trenches, at Wulverghem on Tuesday 16th for thirty-six hours. It was a shock to experience the sight, and particularly the smells, of the decomposing bodies. Tours of duty and fatigues with long, tiring marches to and from the front line became the norm until the end of March.

Generals Smith-Dorrien and Plumer inspected the Battalion on Wednesday 7th April and the next day James and George marched to billets in a school in Ypres. Following a period of rest they marched out to the front near Hill 60 at 7.30pm on Monday 12th. The German artillery became particularly active the next day that increased in intensity by the hour. Enemy activity at the front continued that resulted in casualties amongst the Battalion mounting by the hour. James and George tramped out of the line late on Friday 16th and went for some rest in a wood to the rear before marching to billets in Ypres. The town was under the constant attention of the German artillery so none of the men from the Battalion were allowed to go into the town itself. The Battalion was moved from the billets to a bivouac outside the town on Wednesday 21st due to the shelling.

... the centre of Ypres in flames due to the bombardment that heralded the German offensive on Thursday 22nd April

The Second Battle of Ypres began at 5.00pm on Thursday 22nd when the enemy launched the first gas attack. At 11.30pm James and George were ordered to stand to and then marched to the front that was under immense pressure from the German attacks. James and George fought hard in the poorly planned counter-attack on Friday 23rd where in the initial wave George was killed. James had to continue to fight on until being relieved on Wednesday 28th.

James returned from the front without his brother, he had not had the opportunity of being able to bury George but now he had the unenviable task of writing home to tell his parents that George had been killed. A concert was held on Friday 30th but it was unlikely it raised James' spirits. He left the rest camp and marched back to the front line on Sunday 2nd May where the Battalion had to defend the line that came under a constant artillery barrage. James survived for forty-eight hours before he was killed by shell fire, now the parents had to cope with the loss of their two boys within ten days of each other. Lance Corporal Ernest Harlowe, wrote home on 22nd May: *"The great battle of Ypres is now over, and the German push checked, I trust for good. The city is in flames and at night presents a scene of unparalleled splendour. The spires of the churches, especially showing up prominently, and rather singular. These seem to stand days after all the surrounding buildings have been burnt out and fallen.*

Doubtless you will have read in the papers all about the terrific bombardment we were subjected to all last week so I need not repeat it here! Therefore I will confine myself to our own share in the awful struggle, we first noticed the great concentration of Germany artillery on the 4th May, after the previous nights retirement and on the 5th it was more violent than ever, all sorts of shells beings hurled at us. I say at us because our battalion was in the centre of the fire line and the enemy were advancing in that direction. Our boys were occupying the fire trench and here we have suffered terribly. Whole trenches being occupied by perhaps only one or two individuals, the rest being killed or wounded. Shrapnel is our greatest enemy. The Germans belching this at us for all they are worth, but I thank God we held out although if they had the pluck of a mouse and advanced towards our trench I question if one of us would have escaped either being killed or captured. However, we were relieved on Wednesday evening by our second battalion but were called back out again on Friday and Saturday when the bombardment was worse than ever. It commenced at daybreak and finished in the dark, for fourteen hours we were dodging shells fired at a rate of 60 to 80 a minute. It was awful that at times we could not hear one another speak and even then they could not shift us from our position. All battalions have suffered severely but even then the enemy would not advance but sheltered behind their trenches like rats in a hole. They are a cowardly lot and sniped at us with their rifles.

Our losses last week were very severe, many of the 200 being killed or wounded. Both the Cathcarts that were billeted with Mrs. Workman are among the fallen and Mr. Peel also got wounded with shrapnel – but whether seriously I cannot say. I do know however, that as a battalion we have now practically ceased to exist.

What I have seen this last month will never efface from my memory. Poor wounded fellows making their way to the dressing station in droves – some with arms blown off, hands off and other injuries. Dead lying by the road side, horses lying in heaps in all stages of decomposition. These are some of the horrors of war let alone the fact that shells are bursting all about us as we enter or leave the trenches."

James and George are commemorated together on the War Memorial in St Joseph's Church, Lancaster.

1026 Private
Cecil Hubert Cray Cattell
Essex Yeomanry
Died on Friday 14th May 1915, aged 16
Commemorated on Panel 5.

Cecil was born in West Ham, London, only child of Henry Richard Trist Cattell and Maude Elise Cray Cattell, of Shencliffe, 19 Leighton Avenue, Leigh-on-Sea, Essex.

He enlisted in Leigh-on-Sea and sent for training. Cecil entrained in Woodbridge on Sunday 29th November 1914 for Southampton. He had a rough crossing to Le Havre where he arrived at noon the next day but did not disembark until early on Tuesday 1st December. After parading on the quay he marched to a cold muddy rest camp. At noon on Thursday 3rd Cecil marched to the station to entrain to St Omer then marched through a blizzard to billets in Wardrecques. He moved to Grand Sec Bois, via Hazebrouck, on Friday 11th.

Field Marshal Sir John French and HRH The Prince of Wales inspected the Yeomanry on Wednesday 27th January 1916 and the next day Cecil was moved to Sec Bois. An omnibus collected Cecil and his comrades on Wednesday 3rd February that drove them to Ypres. The first experience he had of the trenches began on Monday 8th in front of Zillebeke. Whilst in the front line a number of the men constructed a periscope from a drain pipe that had been 'borrowed' from a reformatory in Ypres. The 20ft long pipe was camouflaged to look like a tree and was a great success giving the Yeomanry, and those who followed them into the line, a far better view of the enemy in relative safety. On the first day of the tour one of Cecil's comrades, Private William Roberts, was killed while carrying rations into the front line (he is commemorated on the Menin Gate). After a month Cecil was sent to La Motte for training that continued until the Second Battle of Ypres began on Thursday 22nd April. The next morning Cecil marched via Hazebrouck and Caëstre to Abeele station where he bivouacked.

Cecil returned to the Salient on Monday 3rd May, arriving on the canal bank near Brielen with a backdrop of Ypres engulfed in flames and smoke from a heavy bombardment. After four days Cecil was taken back to Mount Croquet until returning by omnibus on Sunday 9th. Cecil was sent to help construct a long communication trench in the area of Potijze on Wednesday 12th May. Throughout the night Cecil and his comrades were kept pinned down under heavy fire but eventually the work was completed. The German attack began on Thursday 13th following a preliminary barrage that had commenced at 4.00am. Cecil was in

... fighting in a communication trench

the line close to Potijze Château garden; the barrage had taken its effect and a large force of infantry was seen advancing on their line. During the afternoon a counter-attack was organised and Cecil charged the German line at the point of the bayonet. The attack was successful despite taking heavy casualties, including the most senior officers. The Yeomanry consolidated the line and were pleased to find in the captured trench a good supply of sausage and coffee — and considerable quantities of war material. The Germans mounted an artillery bombardment prior to mounting a counter-attack to recapture their lost ground. The rain was falling heavily, the mud played havoc with the men and their rifles that became clogged with mud and were rendered useless. The 10th Hussars, to their left, were forced to retire and at 6.00pm the Yeomanry were ordered to concentrate round the Headquarters on the main road. Later that night Cecil was killed.

21407 Private William Cawtheray
1st/4th Battalion
King's Own Yorkshire Light Infantry
Died on Monday 4th October 1915, aged 16
Commemorated on Panel 47.

William was born at home, youngest son of Mrs E Pontefract, of 9 Kennedy Street, Kirkstall Road, Leeds. He was educated locally.

He enlisted in Leeds and was sent for training in York; he cheered the Battalion when they marched out of barracks bound for France on Saturday 10th April 1915. He left for France on Wednesday 19th May to join the Battalion in the field with a draft whilst they were serving in the Bois Grenier sector.

William was soon working hard with his comrades on fatigues and was introduced to serving in the support and firing trenches. He served in the sector until Saturday 26th June when the Battalion was relieved from the line and were marched to a camp at Watou on the French-Belgian border.

Following a period of rest and training William marched via Poperinghe and Vlamertinghe to serve in the trenches to the north of Ypres around Boesinghe. William was destined to serve on tours of duty in the area without being involved in any particular action until he was killed by a sniper.

25303 PRIVATE
ALBERT NORRIS CHAMBERS
2nd Battalion Cheshire Regiment
Died on Tuesday 25th May 1915, aged 16
Commemorated on Panel 22.

Albert was born at home in 1898, youngest son of Evan and Esther Chambers, of 15 Queen's Place, Lower Tranmere, Birkenhead, Cheshire, he had six siblings. His four brothers served in the war, three in the army and one in the navy. Albert was educated at St Catherine's Church of England School in Tranmere, then worked as an assistant for the British Leather Company.

He volunteered in Birkenhead and was sent for training. Albert joined the Battalion when they returned to England from India in late 1914. He sailed to France on Wednesday 5th May 1915 and was deployed immediately to Ypres where he began tours of duty. Albert was not involved in any particular action until the Second Battle of Ypres.

Albert's first action was at Frezenberg that began on Saturday 8th May when the enemy launched a further gas attack supported by a heavy barrage. The German infantry attack successfully moved forward and pushed the Battalion back. Losses suffered by the Battalion were terrible and included the commander Major Arthur Stone (he is commemorated on the Memorial). The remnants of the Battalion were withdrawn from the field but it was so reduced in numbers it had to form part of a composite Battalion with men from the Northumberland Fusiliers, the Suffolks and the Monmouthshires.

The final action that Albert would participate in began on Monday 24th May. An attack was developing at Bellewaarde and whilst Albert was east

of Vlamertinghe waiting for a hot meal he was ordered to parade. Without his meal he marched towards the ruins of Ypres and out along the Ypres to Roeselare railway. At 5.00pm the attack began but due to poor planning it had little chance of any success. Again the Battalion took very heavy losses, as did the enemy, and no further action took place as both sides were totally exhausted. Albert was mortally wounded, he was first listed as missing, but it was not for over a year until his parents were given the sad news.

The local newspaper printed the following article:

Tranmere Boy Hero Killed a Year Ago

Mr. and Mrs. Chambers, 15, Queen's Place, Lower Tranmere, have just received the sad news that their 16-year-old son, Albert Norris Chambers, fell in action exactly a year ago. Not having heard a word from their son for all that length of time, Mr. and Mrs. Chambers had hoped that he had been taken prisoner, or at worst wounded. The formal information that the lad's death was now presumed reached Birkenhead on the anniversary of the day when he was purported to have been taken prisoner.

Albert is commemorated on Birkenhead War Memorial.

9524 PRIVATE REUBEN CHANDLER
1st Battalion Hampshire Regiment
Died on Monday 26th April 1915, aged 16
Commemorated on Panel 35.

Reuben was born at Vernham Dean, Berkshire, sixth son of Sydney and Martha Chandler. He was educated locally.

He enlisted at Andover, Hampshire, and gave his brother William Chandler, of 20 Abbots Ann, Andover, Hampshire, as his next of kin. He was sent for training before leaving for France. Reuben joined the Battalion with a draft on Friday 29th January 1915 whilst they were serving in the Ploegsteert sector. The trenches were dreadful, constantly flooding with freezing water that caused a large number of the men to be invalided with trench foot. Reuben began tours of duty and fatigues in the sector. Throughout his time in the area soldiers from other Battalions came for practical experience in the trenches. Reuben left Ploegsteert for the last time on Thursday 15th April and went to Noote Boom for rest and training. Whilst there he was able to visit Bailleul, a bustling town full of fun and diversions where the troops could relax.

Reuben entrained at Bailleul for Poperinghe on Saturday 24th April. As he marched to his billet the smell of chlorine gas was in the air and large numbers of gas-wounded troops and refugees struggled passed him. He marched to the Salient and went into the line running from St Julien towards *'Berlin Wood'*. Throughout

Monday 26th Reuben was under heavy artillery fire. As soon as the early mist cleared the German infantry advanced and during the heavy fighting Reuben was killed together with twenty-six others listed as killed or missing, with fifty-nine wounded.

11910 PRIVATE ALEXANDER PAGE CLARKE
1st Regiment (Infantry) South African Infantry
Died on Thursday 20th September 1917, aged 17
Commemorated on Panel 15.

Alexander was born in Canning Town, London, in late 1899, eldest son of Alexander Gloag Clarke and Emma Elizabeth Clarke, of 151 Sutton Court Road, Plaistow, London.

Alexander arrived in Brandhoek on Friday 14th September 1917 and trained for the next three days. He moved into the line in front of the Frezenberg Ridge on Monday 17th. It was a difficult route to the front as everyone had to balance on the slippery duckboards over the deep slimy mud. To fall off them could spell death as with a heavy pack and equipment a man would be swallowed never to be seen again. As Alexander was led forward against the German strong point at 'Potsdam' he was killed.

3103 PRIVATE REUBEN CLIPSTON
2nd Battalion East Surrey Regiment
Died on Sunday 9th May 1915, aged 17
Commemorated on Panel 34.

Reuben was born at home, fourth son of James Payne Clipston and Alice Clipston, of Rushton, Kettering, Northamptonshire. Following his education he was employed as a farm labourer.

He enlisted in Kettering and went out to France on Tuesday 27th April 1915 to join the Battalion whilst they fighting on the Salient during the Second Battle of Ypres where every able man, or boy, was needed. He arrived in Poperinghe on Tuesday 4th May to join the Battalion after they had been relieved from Frezenberg. Reuben paraded for an inspection on Wednesday 5th May for General Edward Bulfin and the next day by General Sir Herbert Plumer. He had a day of rest on Friday 7th but the next morning Reuben marched into the line to help support the front following a German attack that was threatening the line at Frezenberg. He marched through Potijze and took position: at 4.00pm Reuben was led forward to counter-attack. Throughout Sunday 9th he was in the trenches under very heavy shell fire, one burst close to him and Reuben was killed.

He is commemorated on Rushton War Memorial. Reuben's brother, Private Percy Clipston, died on Monday 2nd December 1918 and is buried in Rushton (All Saints) Churchyard.

12805 PRIVATE LEVI COLES
1st Battalion Lincolnshire Regiment
Died on Wednesday 16th June 1915, aged 17
Commemorated on Panel 21.

Levi was born in King's Cliffe, Northamptonshire, only son of Thomas and Sarah Ellen Coles, of 67 Heavy Gate Avenue, Sheffield.

He enlisted in Stamford, Lincolnshire, and was sent for training. Levi went out to France on Friday 16th April 1915 to join the Battalion on the Salient. He arrived just as the Second Battle of Ypres was about to begin. Levi went into the front line for the first time on Thursday 22nd along the Comines to Ypres Canal, to the south of the town. He immediately began to repair and strengthen his trench whilst under the constant attention of the enemy. To the north of his position the gas attack had taken place, Ypres was in flames and a major battle was in progress. It was not until Wednesday 5th May did Levi become involved in a serious action when the Germans launched a gas attack in the sector. It was not followed up by the infantry and thankfully for the Battalion no losses were suffered from the gas.

Levi continued on his tour of duty until being relieved on Tuesday 25th, nearly five weeks of continuous service. He marched to billets in Ouderdom for five days where he was able to clean up and rest. Levi returned to the front on Tuesday 1st June, this time at Hooge that had seen considerable action and the dead from both sides littered No Man's Land. When relieved he went by light railway to a camp at Brandhoek where he rested and trained for the next action. He was issued with a gas and smoke helmet that was a slight improvement on the rudimentary pads that he had been given shortly after he arrived.

Levi returned to the front line for the last time during the evening of Tuesday 15th June. He went round Ypres and along the Menin Road to 'Hellfire Corner', 'Birr Cross Roads' to 'Cambridge Road'. He finally arrived in the assembly trench at 1.15am. The preliminary bombardment began at 2.30am that lasted until 4.15am when the first wave attacked. Levi was held back and then moved forward at the point of the bayonet with the second wave against the German lines, or what was left of them, to help support the Royal Fusiliers. In the fierce hand-to-hand fight Levi was killed.

He is commemorated on King's Cliffe War Memorial.

S/10704 PRIVATE
THOMAS GEORGE COLLINS
2nd Battalion The Buffs (East Kent Regiment)
Died on Monday 3rd May 1915, aged 17
Commemorated on Panel 14.

Thomas was born at home, son of Thomas George
Collins, of 17 Fenham Road, Peckham, London, and
the late Agnes Collins.

He volunteered in Woolwich, London, and was sent
for training then went out to France on Wednesday
21st April 1915. Thomas could not have arrived on the
Salient at a worse time. As he was entraining north
through France to Belgium the Second Battle of Ypres
opened at 5.00pm on Thursday 22nd with the first gas
attack. Thomas did not arrive to join the Battalion until
Saturday 1st May where he, and the other members of
the draft, were immediately put to work together in
a trench. The next day his position came under heavy
shell fire and Thomas was mortally wounded. He had
served at the front line for less than a day.

S/9017 RIFLEMAN
EDWARD ARTHUR COLMAN
'C' Company, 9th Battalion Rifle Brigade
Died on Thursday 6th January 1916, aged 17
Commemorated on Panel 48.

Edward Arthur Colman

Edward's signature

Edward was born in Dalston, London, son of Cecil
Robert and Edith Colman, of 43 Cremer Street,
Shoreditch, London, he had a brother and sister,
William and Kathleen.

He volunteered in Shoreditch on Monday 15th March
1915 when he claimed to be 19 years old, working
as a builder's assistant. Edward was 5ft 2in tall, had
a 35in chest and weighed 120lbs. He was sent for
training during which he was fined ten days pay for
overstaying his leave on Monday 23rd August.

Edward left to join the Battalion in the field on
Wednesday 6th October that helped to bring it back up
to strength following the costly action at Bellewaarde
on Saturday 25th September. He remained on tours of
duty in the St Jan sector until he was slightly wounded
on Wednesday 5th January 1916 and subsequently
killed the next day.

His mother was sent Edward's personal possessions
of four photographs and some letters in 1916 and after
the war his 1914-15 Star, British War Medal, Victory
Medal, and his Memorial Plaque.

NB The CWGC records his surname as Coleman.

1170 PRIVATE JOHN HUGH COMPTON
2nd Battalion East Surrey Regiment
Died on Sunday 25th April 1915, aged 17
Commemorated on Panel 34.

John was born in Walthamstow, London, eldest son
of Hugh and Flora Compton, of Rosedale, Central
Avenue, Southchurch, Southend-on-Sea, Essex. He
had three siblings, Arthur, Thirza and Edmund. John
was educated locally and also worked as a milk boy.
He volunteered in Southend-on-Sea and went out to
France on Wednesday 24th March 1915 with a draft
of ninety men. John joined the Battalion on Sunday
28th at a camp in Dickebusch from where, later that
evening, he began his first tour of duty in the trenches
around St Eloi. The area had suffered badly two
weeks before during a fierce battle that included the
enemy blowing a mine. The trenches were in a terrible
condition with remnants of the dead rotting in the
mud. John remained in the line for two days then
returned to camp for twenty-four hours. He did not
have much time to rest as he had to clean up ready
for an inspection by General James Haldane. John
undertook a further tour in St Eloi, then on Sunday
4th April he was taken through the bustling town of
Ypres to the trenches near Château Rosenthal where
he remained for twenty-four hours. John marched
back through the town and along the pavé to a camp
at Vlamertinghe where he began training.

The Battalion once again marched through Ypres on
Saturday 10th where they were given a great cheer by
their friends and comrades of the 1st Battalion who
were outside the Cloth Hall. The march took John
out to the line between Broodseinde and Gravenstafel
where he arrived at 2.00am the next morning.
Throughout Monday 12th the enemy artillery increased
their shelling and their snipers accounted for three of
John's comrades. The intense work being undertaken
by the Germans indicated
that an attack would soon
be taking place but nothing
developed until the gas
attack began at 5.00pm on
Thursday 22nd. John was
due to be relieved later in
the evening but that was
cancelled and he remained
in the trenches.
Late on Friday
23rd an abortive
attack was
made against
the Battalion's
position and in

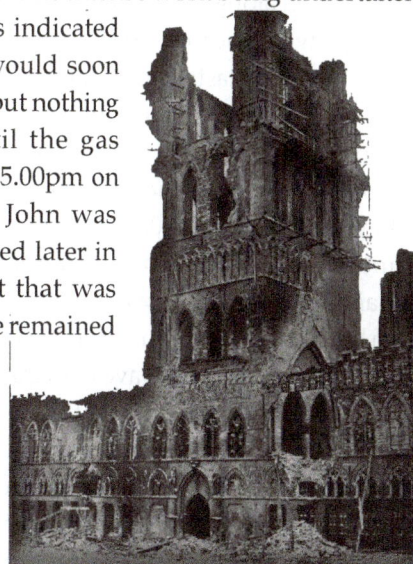

... the partly damaged Cloth Hall

the heavy shelling of the position John was killed early on Sunday 25th.

1665 LANCE CORPORAL
JAMES ALFRED CONNOLLY
2nd Battalion Royal Irish Rifles
Died on Saturday 25th September 1915, aged 17
Commemorated on Panel 40.

James was born in Salford, Lancashire, elder son of James and Amelia Connolly, of 22 Clay Street, Gorton, Manchester.

He volunteered in Manchester and following training went out to France on Thursday 29th April 1915 with a draft. The Salient was ablaze as the Second Battle of Ypres was raging. James' first experience of the front line came on Thursday 6th May following a gas attack on Hill 60. He marched from 'Canada Huts', Dickebusch, via 'Shrapnel Corner', passing large numbers of wounded at Zillebeke Lake that must have brought the realities of war home to young James. The sound of battle had been ringing in his ears since he arrived but now it grew in volume with bullets splattering about and shells exploding close by. Battalion Headquarters were established at 'Dormy House' and James was moved into the front line. The tour of duty ended on Wednesday 12th May when he marched to camp at La Clytte. He spent the rest of the month in the trenches in front of Kemmel, a very quiet area in comparison to the fighting that was taking place only a few miles to the north around Ypres.

James returned to the Salient on Thursday 3rd June when the Battalion was sent to camp southwest of Vlamertinghe. He was sent out on the dangerous duty of fatigues, taking barbed wire to the front line for five days. He marched along the road to the shattered ruins of Ypres then along the Menin Gate to 'Birr Cross Roads' to Hooge where he took position in front of 'Cambridge Road'. The tour lasted until late on Friday 11th then James went into bivouac for three days rest. He arrived in the assembly trenches at 'Witte Poort Farm' late on Tuesday 15th ready to take part in an attack at Bellewaarde. From 2.50am to 4.15am a preliminary bombardment pounded the German trenches. The initial waves moved forward well and at speed but it soon broke down in confusion. James and his comrades were part of the second wave with the responsibility of supporting and consolidating the captured positions. The enemy were able to reorganise themselves; they poured heavy fire on the attacking forces and mounted a series of counter-attacks. At 3.35pm another attack began with James charging across the battlefield. All ranks did very well and they kept fighting until the

early hours of Thursday 17th. Although some gains were made the main objectives were not taken and it was therefore a failure.

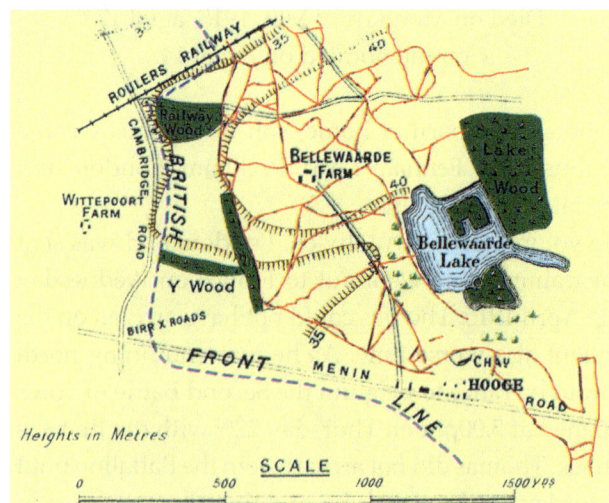

The Battalion was relieved and sent for some rest in the Brandhoek area. When James returned to Hooge at the beginning of July it was almost impossible to recognise the area he had been in only two weeks before. The furious battle had completely changed the landscape. He undertook a four day tour of duty before marching back to a hutted camp west of Vlamertinghe where a large draft of men arrived that brought the Battalion up to strength. James remained on tours of duty in the Hooge sector until Wednesday 11th August when he was moved to Wieltje. At the end of the month, following relief, James marched to a camp near Dickebusch.

James returned to fatigues for the first two weeks of September before returning to the front line at Hooge on Saturday 18th. Here again the Battalion would take part in another attack on Bellewaarde on Saturday 25th to support the Battle of Loos that began the same day. Late on Friday 24th James was in position ready to go over the top following the blowing of four mines at 4.19am. James rose from the trench and he charged across the pitted ground towards the German trenches until was hit by rifle fire and killed.

20410 PRIVATE
CHRISTOPHER CONSTANTINE
8th Battalion King's Own
(Royal Lancaster Regiment)
Died on Thursday 2nd March 1916, aged 16
Commemorated on Panel 12.

Christopher was born in Clapham, Yorkshire, and was the nephew of Alice Constantine, of 7 Grey Street, Barrowford, Nelson, Glamorganshire. He was educated locally.

He enlisted in Nelson and was sent for training but

remained in England when the Battalion left for France on Monday 27th September 1915. Christopher left for France to join the Battalion in the field on Saturday 11th December 1915. He undertook tours of duty, fatigues, training that was interspersed with some rest throughout the winter. Whilst Christopher was in the front line at 'The Bluff', St Eloi, he was killed when a shell blew him to pieces.

18289 PRIVATE
ALFRED LIONEL COOPER
5th Battalion Oxford and Bucks Light Infantry
Died on Thursday 5th August 1915, aged 16
Commemorated on Panel 39.

Alfred was born in Spelsbury, Oxfordshire, eldest son of John Edward and Emily Mary Cooper, of Leafield, Witney, Oxfordshire. He was educated locally.
He enlisted in Oxford and was sent for training. Alfred joined the Battalion on Wednesday 7th July 1915 with a draft. The Salient was a hot and active sector when he went into the line on Thursday 22nd in front of 'Railway Wood'. The enemy blew a mine two days later at Hooge, he then served through the horrors of the German attack where flammenwerfer (flamethrowers or liquid fire) was used for the first time. Alfred continued to serve in the front line in the sector until he was killed during a tour of duty.
Alfred is commemorated on a plaque in Spelsbury Parish Church.

195715 PRIVATE FREDERICK COOPER
5th Canadian Mounted Rifles Battalion
(Quebec Regiment)
Died on Wednesday 31st October 1917, aged 17
Commemorated on Panel 32.

Fred Cooper

Fred's signature

Fred was the son of Frederick Walter and Maud M Cooper, of Morrow, Peterborough, Ontario.
He volunteered in Peterborough on Friday 11th February 1916 when he claimed to have been born in London, England, on Friday 30th September 1898, employed as a clerk, having served for a year in the 57th Regiment, Militia. Fred was a Baptist, 5ft 7in tall, with a 37in chest, a fair complexion, brown eyes, light brown hair and a scar on his right lower jaw.
Following training in Canada and in England Fred joined the Battalion in December 1916 whilst they were in Étrun training. He went into the front line for the first time on Sunday 17th for a six-day tour then had a relatively enjoyable Christmas whilst in Brigade Reserve. He returned to the front line on New Year's Eve then sent for training once more at Étrun.

From Monday 22nd January 1917 a series of marches took Fred to Mont St Eloy, Villers-Brûlin then on to Estrée-Cauchy. He returned to Mont St Eloy and into the front line on Monday 5th February. Fred served in the trenches for a tour of duty, followed by fatigues before moving to Raimbert for rest, training and nightly fatigues. A

Mont St Eloy

route march took him to Cauchy-à-la-Tour at the end of the month for twenty days of fatigues. Fred marched to the training ground at Houdain on Monday 19th March where upon arrival in camp the Medical Officer carried out a foot inspection. After five days he moved to bivouac in 'Woodman Camp' where the sound of the heavy artillery pierced the night. Fred was given a day of rest before returning to fatigues delivering ammunition from Mont St Eloy then worked at Neuville St Vaast to construct a First Aid Post. Fred attended a burial service at Ecoivres Cemetery for eight NCOs and men conducted by Chaplains Captain Duncan and Lowry. At the end of March Fred returned to 'Woodman Camp'. He marched out of camp at 11.00pm on Sunday 8th April and marched via 'Chassery Trench' to the 'Pylones', coming under heavy shell fire at La Targette. At 2.00am Fred began supplying material to the front.
The Battle of Arras began at 5.30am the next morning that was described in the War Diary: *"Intense artillery bombardment — one continuous roar. The ground trembles and is mingled with the roar of the guns, the swishing and screeching of the shell-filled air. 60 guns are covering our own advance, forming a 'rolling barrage'. Smoke and débris thrown up by the bursting shell, give the appearance of a solid wall."* At 5.50am it was the turn of the Battalion to emerge from the tunnels to move forward. As they approached 'Zwischenstellung' a group of forty Germans began to fire on them. Half were killed in the fight and the rest taken prisoner. Fred and his comrades then began to supply the front line with large quantities of ammunition whilst under heavy shell fire. Fred was relieved to 'Woodman Camp', arriving

at 3.55am on Thursday 12th, when the roll was called it revealed that eighty-nine officers and men were casualties. After five days of tiring fatigues he marched to the 'Quarries Line' to take the line from Thursday 19th. Fred went out on a number of dangerous patrols into No Man's Land to the German front to gain useful information. Following a further five days he was relieved and sent to billets in Villers-au-Bois. Fred once again undertook a tour of duty at the 'Quarries' before moving to Vimy Defences until mid-May. He returned to billets in Villers-au-Bois and moved to 'Winnipeg Camp' on Sunday 20th May for a week. Fred was sent to the support trenches on Sunday 27th to begin fatigues at 'Vimy Defences' followed by front line duties there then in the 'Quarries Line'. He remained on tours of duty in the sector or in training at Villers-au-Bois until moving to 'Seaforth Camp' on Monday 2nd July. He went into reserve where the Battalion witnessed a heavy bombing around Lens two weeks later. Fred arrived at 'St Lawrence Camp', Château de la Haie, at 4.30pm on Thursday 19th, spending the next day resting and cleaning up. Six days later Fred marched to a camp at Raimbert. He marched to Gouy Servins on Wednesday 15th August from where he was collected by motor transport and dropped off in Les Brébis to march into the front line. He spent nearly two weeks either in the front line or in close support until returning to Les Brébis then marched onto Bouvigny-Boyeffles. Fred returned to tours of duty and fatigues in the Neuville St Vaast sector until Tuesday 18th September when he was sent for training for the next offensive at Maisnil-Bouché where the Battalion was refitted.

Fred marched to Savy on Monday 15th October and, following a hot meal served at the station, at 2.30pm entrained for Caëstre. A long and tiring journey followed and upon arrival he marched to billets in St Sylvestre Cappel. Fred continued his training until entraining at 7.00am on Monday 22nd to Ypres, arriving at 10.30am. A stiff march in full kit took him to a reserve camp at Wieltje where the first task was to erect a tent and secondly help create a reasonable camp. As Fred was resting a number of German aeroplanes flew low over the camp and no doubt reported its existence to the artillery. After a quiet day throughout Tuesday 23rd at 1.00pm on Wednesday 24th a fleet of bombers flew over the camp and began bombing it as well as the surrounding area. The bombing run was repeated at 8.00pm.

Fred marched out of camp to 'California Trench' in the reserve area, arriving at 1.00pm on Thursday 25th where final preparations were made for the forthcoming attack. At 5.00pm the next evening he moved to 'Capricorn Keep', remaining there until 6.00pm on Sunday 28th when he moved into the front line. The Battalion Headquarters were established at 'Kronprinz Farm' that came under constant shell fire and Battalion casualties began to mount. Fred was in the assembly trench by 5.00am on Tuesday 30th, the night lit by a bright moon: it was fine but cool. As the rain had stopped some days before the ground had dried out somewhat and was not the swampy morass normally associated with the battlefield. The shell holes that had been there for some time were filled with water but those recently created were not. As Fred rested and waited for the order to advance an artillery duel was fought overhead. The supporting barrage began at 5.50am, Zero Hour, and four minutes later the whistles were blown. Fred rose up and charged forward towards 'Vapour Farm', 'Source Farm' and 'Vine Cottages'. The attack was successful, at 7.55am three white flares were put up, the signal to Headquarters that the final objective had been reached. During the fierce battle the Regimental Aid Post had been hit and only two stretcher bearers survived.

A series of counter-attacks had to be repulsed. A report came in from Lieutenant Otty: *"Enemy is digging in on the right. About 300. Am holding Source Farm with about 8 men and am in touch with Lieut. Gifford on the right. Need reinforcements and ammunition."* Another from Captain Pearkes: *"Germans are digging in on top of ridge about 200 yards away. Are in force. … All very much exhausted. Ammunition running short. Do not think we can hold out much longer without being relieved. Both flans still in the air."*

During the action Fred was killed shortly before the Battalion was relieved and marched to Ypres Asylum where they were collected by a fleet of omnibuses to be driven to 'Mills Camp' in Watou.

1911 PRIVATE JOHN COOPER
4th Battalion Gordon Highlanders
Died on Saturday 25th September 1915, aged 17
Commemorated on Panel 38.

John was born in Old Machar, Aberdeenshire, son of George and Catherine Cooper, of 66 Gerrard Street, Aberdeen.

He volunteered in Aberdeen and went for training with the Battalion in Bedford until they went out to France. He entrained to Southampton and sailed to Le Havre on Friday 19th February 1915. John moved through northern France and then crossed the border to a camp at La Clytte. He settled down to tours of duty and served on the Salient until being killed during a fierce action designed as a diversionary attack for The Battle of Loos that was taking place some miles to the south.

20772 PRIVATE ARTHUR COSGROVE
1st Battalion Northumberland Fusiliers
Died on Monday 27th March 1916, aged 17
Commemorated on Panel 12.

Arthur was born at home, fifth son of Patrick and Mary Cosgrove, of 3 High Row, Unsworth, County Durham. He had seven siblings, five older and two younger. He volunteered in Newcastle-on-Tyne and went out to France on Friday 3rd September 1915 to join the Battalion in the field with a draft whilst they were serving on the Salient at Hooge. He undertook a tour of duty in mid-September in Hooge but did not take part in the diversionary attack on Saturday 25th September in support of The Battle of Loos. Arthur was able to see the battle unfold as he was held in reserve near Zillebeke.

... an action at a mine crater

Arthur returned to the line at Hooge on Wednesday 29th September where the enemy blew a mine and attempted an attack that was successfully repulsed. He remained on tours of duty in the sector until Friday 22nd October when he was sent for rest and training in the Steenvoorde area with billets in Godeswaersvelde and later in Winnezeele. With just over four weeks out of the line Arthur marched back into Belgium to a camp at Dickebusch from where he retuned to the trenches around *'Shelley Farm'* in the St Eloi sector. Arthur settled down into the routine of eight days at the front followed by eight in either Poperinghe or Reninghelst. Christmas was spent in the trenches but no truce occurred, however, Arthur was able to celebrate the festive period in Poperinghe after he was relieved. Tours of duty continued until Sunday 6th February 1916 when he was sent for a month's training around St Omer and had billets in Ruminghem. Arthur returned to the line at St Eloi and whilst on a normal tour of duty was killed by a bursting shrapnel shell.

L/10420 PRIVATE JOHN HENRY COSHALL
1st Battalion Queen's Own
(Royal West Kent Regiment)
Died on Sunday 18th April 1915, aged 17
Commemorated on Panel 45.

John was born in Crayford, Kent, fourth son of Eliza Coshall, of 34 Arthur Street, Erith, Kent, and the late James Coshall. He was educated locally and was then employed as a labourer.

He enlisted at Woolwich, London. John was 5ft 5½in tall, had a 34in chest, weighed 110lbs, had a fair complexion, hazel eyes, light brown hair and scars on both knees.

John was awarded twenty-one days detention from Tuesday 6th October 1914 for gambling and helping a soldier under arrest to break out of camp.

He went out to France on Monday 7th December and joined the Battalion in the field whilst they were serving in the Wytschaete to Messines sector. The winter rain had turned the low-lying trenches below the Messines Ridge into a ghastly muddy bog.

John had only been with the Battalion for two weeks on tours of duty when he was relieved then spent the end of December resting or training. He was given seven days Field Punishment No 2 on Friday 6th February 1915. John was resting in Bailleul in mid-February 1915 when the Battalion was inspected by General Wanless O'Gowan. A couple of days later, Thursday 19th, the Battalion was ordered to march to the trenches south of Ypres, a march that took John via Vlamertinghe. He went into the poorly maintained trenches near Zwarteleen where a considerable amount of time was spent reconstructing them. The enemy became particularly active on Sunday 22nd launching a large number of trench mortars against the Battalion's line. He was given eight days Field Punishment No 2 on Thursday 2nd April for a minor offence.

In early April the Battalion relieved the French between Broodseinde and Zonnebeke; throughout the tour of duty he strengthened and repaired the trenches that were in particularly poor condition. He returned to Vlamertinghe where he rehearsed and trained

... Hill 60 shortly before the attack

for the attack on Hill 60. During the late evening of Friday 16th John marched with his platoon into the line; throughout the day he lay *'doggo'* and kept quiet as the element of surprise was imperative; and the skies were constantly patrolled by the Royal Flying Corps to stop any German spotter planes observing the activity. After a long, tiring, and boring day at 7.00pm the mines were blown that took the top off Hill 60 that was coupled with an artillery barrage. With bayonets fixed John and his comrades made their way forward up the slopes of the shattered hill and consolidated the line. Shortly before midnight, when he was due to be relieved, the first German counter-attack commenced. He remained in the line, assisted in repulsing the attack and they successfully repulsed a further two. At 4.30am a very heavy counter-attack was mounted and he was killed by a hand grenade. John was initially listed as missing before his death was confirmed.

8940 PRIVATE REUBEN COWLING
2nd Battalion Suffolk Regiment
Died on Tuesday 2nd March 1915, aged 17
Commemorated on Panel 21.

Reuben was born in Whittlesea, Cambridgeshire, son of Reuben and Elizabeth Cowling, of 3 Council Houses, Coates, Peterborough, Cambridgeshire. He had an older and four younger sisters. Reuben was educated locally and then worked as a farm labourer.

He volunteered in Whittlesea and went out to France with a draft on Thursday 3rd December 1914 to join the Battalion in their billets in Westoutre just after they came out of the line. Reuben's first experience of the trenches and an action began on Monday 14th whilst in front of Kemmel in the trenches that ran along the Kemmel to Ypres road. At 7.00am the British and French artillery laid down a large bombardment that was followed by an infantry attack at *'Petit Bois'*. Part of the Battalion moved forward to relieve the Royal Scots and the other members of the Battalion was employed on fatigues at the front.

Reuben did not witness the Christmas Truce as he was in billets in Westoutre. He returned to tours of duty in the Vierstraat sector where Reuben remained until he was killed.

Reuben is commemorated on Coates War Memorial.

418395 PRIVATE
JOHN RUSSELL CROOK
'B' Company, 42nd Battalion Canadian Infantry
(Quebec Regiment)
Died on Saturday 19th August 1916, aged 17
Commemorated on Panel 28.

John's signature

John was the son of George Russell Crook and Margaret Coakeley Davies Crook, of 126 Victoria Avenue, St Lambert, Chambly County, Province of Quebec.

John first volunteered in 1914 but it was not until Friday 12th March 1915, in Montreal, did he enlist. He claimed to have been born on Wednesday 12th August 1896 and worked as a labourer. John was 5ft 7¼in tall, with a 36in chest, a fair complexion, blue eyes, light brown hair, two vaccination marks on his arm and a birth mark on his left foot.

For John's history and that of the Battalion until Friday 2nd June 1916, see Private Francis Savoie, below.

John was relieved from the battlefield late on Monday 5th after fighting hard for three days and sent for training whilst the Battalion refitted. At the end of the month the Battalion was sent for eleven days into Divisional Reserve in *'Ottawa Camp'*. He returned to front line duties on Tuesday 11th July for eight days on a relatively quiet tour and after being in reserve was sent to billets in Steenvoorde where he arrived on Sunday 23rd.

John left his billet on Monday 31st and marched across the border to *'Camp A'* situated between Brandhoek and Vlamertinghe. He moved to billets in the cavalry barracks in Ypres from where he undertook a day of fatigues when 'C' Company suffered fifty-nine casualties when a high explosive shell burst amongst them. Late on Friday 4th August he moved into the front line between 'Warrington Avenue' to 'Gourock Road'. The sector was particular active during the tour of duty with twenty-three casualties being suffered by the Battalion. In the early hours of Sunday 13th John arrived in 'Zillebeke Bund' for six days of fatigues. Shortly before the Battalion was relieved, and the last day the Battalion would serve on the Salient after five months, John was killed by shell fire.

He is commemorated on the St Lambert Soldiers Memorial that was unveiled by General Sir Arthur Currie on Sunday 9th July 1922.

415769 PRIVATE
KEITH BRUCE CROSBY
24th Battalion Canadian Infantry (Quebec Regiment)
Died on Tuesday 11th April 1916, aged 17
Commemorated on Panel 26.

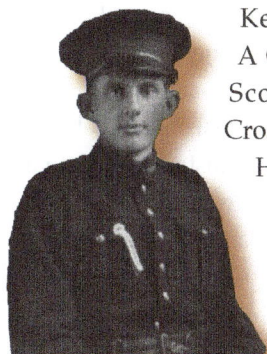

Keith was the son of Howard A Crosby, of Hectanooga, Nova Scotia, and the late Lillian S Crosby.

He volunteered on Friday 6th August 1915 when he claimed to have been born in Carleton, Yarmouth County, New Brunswick, on Friday 23rd April 1897 and worked as a labourer. Keith was a Presbyterian, 5ft 5½in tall, had a fresh complexion, hazel eyes, light brown hair and vaccination marks on his left arm.

Keith sailed with the Battalion to England and was sent to 'Sandling Camp', Shorncliffe, Kent, for training. HM King George V inspected the Battalion on Thursday 2nd September 1915; on Wednesday 15th Keith marched to Folkestone Docks to embark on the SS Queen bound for Boulogne. On arrival he marched to 'Ostrohove Rest Camp' where he remained until the early hours of Friday 17th when he entrained to St Omer. A march via Fort Rouge and Hazebrouck took him to his billet and on Sunday 19th General Sir Edwin Alderson inspected the Battalion. He moved to bivouac at Bailleul on Tuesday 21st and the next day to Loker where on Thursday 23rd billets were provided for everyone. Keith was sent into the line for practical training before going on his first tour of duty on Tuesday 28th in front of Wytschaete, near 'Siege

Farm'. Although it was considered to be a quiet sector, German snipers made their presence felt and machine gun fire splattered across the parapet continuously. Late on Wednesday 29th Keith experienced his first time under shellfire when the enemy sent a variety of shells and mortars over. He was relieved late on Monday 4th October and the next day began fatigues before once again returning to the front line. Keith remained on tours of duty in the sector in the front line or on fatigues without being involved in any particular action. Late on Christmas Eve Major General Richard Ernest William Turner, VC, CB, DSO, visited the Battalion and wished them well for the festive season. Shortly afterwards Keith returned to and celebrated Christmas Day in the front line. When relieved Keith went to camp at 'RE Farm' and sent out on fatigues. He also undertook training and was able to get a hot bath and clean clothes. He returned to front

Richard Turner

line duties on Monday 17th January 1916 when he marched to the Kemmel-La Clytte barrier and out to the front line, with Battalion Headquarters established at the 'Rossignol Estaminet'. From Saturday 5th to Thursday 10th February Keith was sent for training in preparation for an assault on the Spanbroekmolen. Keith remained in the sector on tours of duty, or on fatigues, with a few periods of rest until he was killed by shell fire.

2718 PRIVATE GEORGE CROSSMAN
3rd Battalion Royal Fusiliers
Died on Monday 24th May 1915, aged 17
Commemorated on Panel 8.

George was born in St Pancras, London, fourth son of Mary Ann Crossman, of 2 Compton Villas, Pretoria Road, White Hart Lane, Tottenham, London, and the late Henry Crossman. He had nine siblings, Henry, Frank, John, Mary, Isabella, Charles, Edward, William and Louisa.

He volunteered in Tottenham and went out to France on Saturday 13th May 1915 to join the Battalion with a draft whilst they were in bivouac at Poperinghe. George was coming to the end of his first tour of duty when he was killed.

3901 PRIVATE JAMES S CRUICKSHANK
'C' Company, 4th Battalion Gordon Highlanders
Died on Saturday 25th September 1915, aged 17
Commemorated on Panel 38.

James was the nephew of Mrs Annie Adam, of 18 Marischal Street, Aberdeen.

He enlisted in Aberdeen and went out to France on Monday 4th September 1915. James joined the Battalion in the field on the Salient. He was allocated to a platoon and began to serve at the front.

James took part in a fierce action to support the Battle of Loos and was killed in his first battle, only three weeks after leaving England.

G/2422 PRIVATE FRANCIS CLAUD CRUST
8th Battalion Queen's Own
(Royal West Kent Regiment)
Died on Tuesday 8th February 1916, aged 17
Commemorated on Panel 45.

Francis was born at home in 1898, the eldest child and only son of George and Annie S Crust, of 14 Taunton Road, Northfleet, near Gravesend, Kent.

He volunteered in Gravesend and was sent for training in Shoreham, Sussex, and Blackdown, Wiltshire. Colonel Eden Vansittart led the Battalion from camp to embark for France, landing on Wednesday 30th August 1915. Francis was sent for three weeks training near Montreuil. The long march to the front line began on Thursday 21st September. As the Battalion marched towards the Loos battlefield the roads became busier and increasingly crowded with troops, horses and limbers. Finally the Battalion arrived close to Vermelles where they could hear and see the battle unfolding, however, worse of all they saw the sad sight of the hundreds of wounded being carried to Casualty Clearing Stations. Late in the evening Francis advanced toward Hulluch where he took part in an attack on the village. The initial stages of the attack went well with a steady advance being achieved despite the heavy rifle and machine gun fire. It was the failure of the initial bombardment to cut the German wire that caused the attack to fail. It was impossible to break through and losses began to mount including the Colonel who was badly wounded (subsequently taken prisoner). Orders

Eden Vansittart

were finally given to withdraw and when the roll was called in Mollinghen it made depressing reading. Only Lieutenant Tillie remained of the twenty-four officers, and of eight hundred men that went into action only two hundred and fifty were in fighting order.

Little time was given for rest and recuperation as the Battalion was brought up to strength by drafts from England, coupled with officers and men returning to duty once they had been patched up. Francis was sent north, crossed into Belgium and began nine weeks of tours of duty between St Eloi and the 'Spoilbank'. Francis was sent for rest and training at Bonningues, St Omer, from the end of November to early January 1916. Francis returned to front line duties at Hooge where he remained for a month before he was killed during the course of his work in the trenches and not in any particular action.

373424 RIFLEMAN WILLIAM WILEY CUNNINGHAM
1st/8th Battalion London Regiment
(Post Office Rifles)
Died on Thursday 7th June 1917, aged 17
Commemorated on Panel 54.

William was born in Battersea, eldest son and child of Mrs Alice Kate Cunningham, of 14 Caistor Road, Balham High Road, London. He was educated at the County Council School in Broomwood Road, Battersea, London. William volunteered in Wandsworth, London, and went to train with the East Surrey Regiment with service number 6504 before transferring to the Post Office Rifles.

The Battalion had taken heavy losses during the Battle of the Somme and when they arrived in Ypres in mid-October 1916 they were in much need of reinforcements. William arrived in the Salient with one of the many drafts sent from England.

William began to serve on tours of duty between 'The Bluff' and Hill 60 where he remained until May 1917. He moved with the Battalion to billets in Quercamps where a specially constructed model of the ground they would be fighting over had been constructed for the Battalion to practice on. The area that the Battalion would support the attack included 'Oak Trench', 'Oak Support', 'Oak Reserve', 'Oak Switch' and 'Dammstrasse'. From Monday 4th June an immense bombardment was laid on the German lines that was deafening, even for those some way behind the front. A series of nineteen mines were blown at 3.10am that shook the earth like an immense earthquake and that was the signal for the main attack to begin. A creeping barrage was laid down for the men to move forward under but to the amazement of everyone there were German defenders alive who were able to fire accurately on them. The enemy machine gunners in *'White Château'* were a particular problem so the Battalion assisted the 1st/7th Battalion in capturing it. The fight was intense and closely fought, during the action William was killed.

... advancing on a German machine gun position

2638 PRIVATE THOMAS CUNNISON
'D' Company, 1st Battalion Black Watch
(Royal Highlanders)
Died on Wednesday 11th November 1914, aged 17
Commemorated on Panel 37.

Thomas was born at home, son of the late Thomas and Isabella Cunnison, of Edinburgh.

He enlisted in Edinburgh and went out to France on Sunday 20th September 1914 to join the Battalion who were serving on the Aisne.

Thomas did not become involved in any particular action and on Friday 16th October the move north began. He arrived in Hazebrouck at 6.00am on Monday 19th October where Thomas was billeted for twenty-four hours before marching across the border to Poperinghe, a long and tiring march.

The Battalion was ordered to Pilkem, via Elverdinghe and Boesinghe, where on Thursday 22nd and Friday 23rd they mounted a counter-attack followed by an attack, both were successful — the first action that Thomas had experienced. The French infantry relieved the Battalion on Sunday 25th and they were sent to Verbrandenmolen Wood. After a short period of time Thomas was ordered to the Zandvoorde to Gheluvelt road where on Tuesday 27th the Germans mounted a heavy attack that killed 75% of 'A' Company. As the next few days passed the German attack intensified until Gheluvelt fell on Saturday 31st. From Tuesday 3rd to Wednesday 11th November Thomas was in the line under constant attacks. A very heavy barrage was laid down by the Germans on Sunday 8th and their infantry advanced, penetrating the line but they were finally driven back to *'Inverness Copse'*. At 6.30am on

Wednesday 11th the German artillery commenced the heaviest bombardment of the war — thus far. Their infantry broke through from Polygon Wood and in the fierce defence of his position Thomas was killed.

3/5918 PRIVATE
HORACE HENRY CURREY
'D' Company, 6th Battalion
Duke of Cornwall's Light Infantry
Died on Saturday 31st July 1915, aged 17
Commemorated on Panel 20.

Horace was born at home, third son of Elizabeth Currey, of 5 Norfolk Street, Forest Gate, London, and the late William Currey.

He enlisted in Forest Gate and trained in Aldershot, Hampshire. Horace left with the Battalion by train bound for Folkestone, Kent, and sailed to Boulogne on Friday 21st May 1915 under the command of Lieutenant Colonel Thomas Richard Stokoe. Horace entrained to Cassel, via St Omer, to continue training. At the end of the month he had crossed the border into Belgium and marched to camp at La Clytte. He was sent into the front line at Kemmel to gain practical experience with battle-hardened troops.

Horace was able to enjoy four days in Poperinghe beginning on Sunday 20th June from where he left to undertake his first tour of duty on the Salient. He marched along the cobbled road, via Vlamertinghe, to the ruins of Ypres and into the dugouts in the ramparts. Horace initially went out on fatigues taking supplies each night into the front line, hazardous and dangerous work. From late on Sunday 18th July the Battalion went into the trenches in their own right at Hooge and remained on tours of duty in the sector.

A mine was blown under the German lines at 7.00pm on Monday 19th July that was the signal for Horace and his comrades to open rapid fire on the German lines that supported the capture of the crater. The attack brought an immediate response from the enemy with their artillery laying a heavy bombardment on the Battalion's position. Late on Monday 26th Horace was relieved and marched to a bivouac in Vlamertinghe for four days rest and recuperation. The Germans launched the first liquid fire attack early on Friday 30th July and shortly afterwards Horace was ordered to stand to. At 5.30am he began the march towards the battlefield and rested in the dugouts close to Ypres to await the order to continue marching. Horace arrived in *'Zouave Wood'* in the late afternoon where at 7.00pm the Germans attacked once again using liquid fire and bombed their way forward. In the ghastly mêlée Horace was killed.

17991 PRIVATE RUPERT JOHN CURTIS
5th Battalion Oxford and Bucks Light Infantry
Died on Saturday 25th September 1915, aged 17
Commemorated on Panel 39.

Rupert was born at home, eldest son of John and Daisy Curtis, of Cressex Cottage, Cressex, High Wycombe, Buckinghamshire.
He enlisted in High Wycombe and went out to France on Thursday 10th June 1915 and joined the Battalion in the field whilst they were serving on the Salient.
For his story, see Private Leonard Blay above.

17742 PRIVATE JOHN DALTON
2nd Battalion Royal Irish Fusiliers
Died on Thursday 13th May 1915, aged 17
Commemorated on Panel 42.

John was born at Waterford, Ireland, son of Edward and Mary Dalton, of 110 Queen Street, Govan, Glasgow. He enlisted in Glasgow and after training went out to France on Tuesday 27th April 1915. John arrived to join the Battalion with a draft as The Second Battle of Ypres was under way. There was little time for the niceties of assimilating John into the Battalion or providing practical training in the front line as he had to go immediately to the trenches. The battle was hard fought and after only ten days with the Battalion John was killed in action.

26518 PRIVATE JONATHAN DAVIES
1st Battalion Welsh Regiment
Died on Tuesday 25th May 1915, aged 17
Commemorated on Panel 37.

Jonathan was born in Dale, Pembrokeshire, son of Thomas and Phyllis Davies, of Tree Hill Cottage, Murchin, Marloes, Milford Haven, Pembrokeshire.
He enlisted in Haverfordwest, Pembrokeshire, and went out to France on Wednesday 28th April 1915 with a draft to help bring the battered Battalion up to strength. For Jonathan's story see Private Edmund Jones below. Jonathan is commemorated on the Marloes and St Brides War Memorial.

10141 PRIVATE WILLIAM DAVIES
'B' Company, 1st Battalion
King's Shropshire Light Infantry
Died on Monday 9th August 1915, aged 16
Commemorated on Panel 49.

William was born at home son of John and Margaret Davies, of 3 Southall's Buildings, Willow Street, Oswestry, Salop. He was educated locally.
He enlisted at Shrewsbury and was sent for training. William joined the Battalion in the field with a draft. The Battalion was relieved from the line at Hooge on Saturday 31st July 1915 and sent to a camp near Vlamertinghe before being billeted in Poperinghe. William marched into the line on Thursday 5th August to relieve the 6th Somerset Light Infantry. Due to the

recent fighting the trenches were badly damaged and some work was undertaken to make them usable. A British bombardment began on Friday 6th that brought a massive retaliatory bombardment so the proposed attack was postponed. Throughout Sunday 8th reconnaissance was undertaken over the German lines. At 3.15am on Monday 9th William went over the top and advanced over a thousand yard front. The attack was successful but casualties were heavy, including William, one amongst forty-one other ranks. One hundred and sixty-nine were wounded and eighteen listed as missing.

A/584 RIFLEMAN
WILLIAM GEORGE DAVIS
7th Battalion King's Royal Rifle Corps
Died on Friday 30th July 1915, aged 17
Commemorated on Panel 53.

William was born at St James, Birmingham, son of Mrs Emma Jane Davis, of 4/126 Spring Hill, Birmingham. For William's story and that of the Battalion, see Rifleman Wilfred Huxtable, below.

18764 PRIVATE ISAAC DEWHURST
8th Battalion King's Own
(Royal Lancaster Regiment)
Died on Thursday 2nd March 1916, aged 17
Commemorated on Panel 12.

Isaac was born at home, second son of Isaac and Ann Dewhurst, of 11 High Street, Blackburn, Lancashire. He had three older and three younger siblings. Following his education he was employed in a cotton factory.
He enlisted in Darwen, Lancashire, and was sent for training. Isaac entrained for Folkestone, Kent, under the command of Lieutenant Colonel Antoine Dominique Thorne, on Monday 27th September 1915. Isaac embarked on the SS Duchess of Argyle bound for Boulogne and after he disembarked marched to a rest camp. He entrained to Caëstre and marched to billets in Merris, a further march took him to Lampernisse where he was attached to the Canadians for practical training in the Ploegsteert sector. Isaac's first tour of duty began on Thursday 7th October and five days later he experienced his first serious bombardment when shrapnel shells fell on the line for four hours. He was relieved on Thursday 14th and marched to 'The Piggeries' for a few hours of rest until marching to Bailleul. A further strenuous march on Friday 15th took Isaac to Poperinghe. He went into the front line at 'Sanctuary Wood' and continued to train in the hot

spot with the 1st Battalion Northumberland Fusiliers and 1st Battalion Lincolnshire Regiment. Isaac began tours of duty, training and resting until marching to Eecke on Thursday 21st October for a month of hard training. Unfortunately shortly after he arrived it started raining heavily that continued for the ensuing few days that turned the camp into a swamp. Due to the dreadful weather conditions many from the Battalion were taken ill, including their Colonel who was sent home.
Isaac returned to the trenches at 'The Bluff' where he served on tours of duty in the sector until he was killed. Isaac celebrated Christmas out of the line whilst in camp in Reninghelst where the officers did their best to give their men the best time possible. Isaac began tours of duty in the trenches again on Wednesday 5th January 1916. The enemy blew a mine to the right of Isaac's position on Saturday 22nd and he was stood to but as no enemy infantry attack followed, he was stood down. In mid-February he was relieved and sent to northern France for a special training programme that would prepare him for an attack to recapture 'The Bluff'. Isaac marched to the station at Watou and entrained at 7.00pm bound for Poperinghe where he arrived at 11.30pm. A stiff march took him to a camp on the Ouderdom to Vlamertinghe road where training continued until Wednesday 1st March. He marched to the assembly trenches and throughout the night the German lines were bombarded. At 4.30am on Thursday 2nd Isaac was led over the top and immediately came under heavy gun fire from the enemy. Isaac was killed during the attack.

12793 PRIVATE PHILIP WILLIAM DIX
2nd Regiment (Infantry) South African Infantry
Died on Thursday 20th September 1917, aged 17
Commemorated on Panel 15.

Philip was the son of Mr Robert A and Mrs E M Dix, of 20 Berg Street, Pietermaritzburg, Natal.
He volunteered and following training was sent to join the Regiment whilst they were serving in France. The Regiment had served through The Battle of Arras and after training on the Somme moved to Havrincourt Wood.
Philip arrived in Brandhoek on Friday 14th September 1917. He settled into the camp and began training for the attack he would take part in. Late on Wednesday 19th Philip was led across the duckboards into the allotted assembly position. The next morning he was led forward against heavily defended German positions at 'Waterend Farm' and Hill 37. The enemy machine gunners kept up a heavy curtain of fire and as Philip charged the German positions he was killed.

2560 PRIVATE
OWEN THOMAS DOMENEY
40th Battalion Australian Infantry, AIF
Died on Thursday 7th June 1917, aged 17
Commemorated on Panel 25.

Owen's signature

Owen was born in Zeehan, Tasmania, son of Lemuel Albert Edward and Edith Domeney, of Mostyn Brae, Flowerpot Channel, Tasmania.

He volunteered in Claremont, Tasmania, on Monday 25th September 1916 when he claimed to be 19 years old and worked as an 'orchardist'. Owen was 5ft 10¼in tall, with a 33in chest, weighed 159lbs, had a medium complexion, brown eyes and hair with the top joint on his right middle finger missing.

He sailed from Melbourne on the *SS Ulysses* on Monday 23rd October, arriving in Plymouth on Thursday 28th December. He was sent for training, first at Durrington followed by Lark Hill, Salisbury Plain. Owen left camp and sailed to Boulogne on Friday 20th April 1917 and marched to Base Camp in Etaples, joining the Battalion in the field four days later.

Owen's first tour of duty began on Monday 30th April in the Ploegsteert sector where he remained as the build-up to The Battle of Messines began. From Friday 1st to Wednesday 6th June Owen undertook fatigues supplying the front from 'Regina Camp' on the Ploegsteert road. Late on Wednesday 6th Owen marched into the jumping off trenches near 'La Plus Douve Farm'. As he moved forward the enemy began to lay down a heavy gas barrage so respirators had to be worn. The Battalions were led forward by guides, sadly the one allocated to the 40th took the wrong route that wasted a lot of time and caused considerable confusion amongst the senior officers. Owen finally reached his position by 2.10am and settled down for an hour of rest whilst an immense barrage was pounding the German front line. The whole area shook like an earthquake as the nineteen mines were blown just after 3.10am. He was able to move forward at some speed as the Battalion captured its objectives. Owen was killed later in the day whilst consolidating a newly captured position.

His father was sent his possessions that included two identity disks, a prayer book, photographs, a notebook, cards and two letters. He also received Owen's British War Medal no 51488, Victory Medal no 50807, and his Memorial Plaque and Scroll no 326098.

His younger brother, Corporal Rowland Domeney, died on Wednesday 1st July 1942 and is commemorated on Rabaul Memorial, Papua New Guinea.

11379 PRIVATE
STEPHEN HAROLD DOMLEO
1st Regiment (Infantry) South African Infantry
Died on Wednesday 10th April 1918, aged 17
Commemorated on Panel 15.

Stephen was the son of William Henry and Frances Mary Domleo, of Hilton Road, Natal.
For Stephen's story see Private William Boyder above.

207 PRIVATE WILLIAM DONNACHIE
11th Battalion Highland Light Infantry
Died on Friday 12th November 1915, aged 17
Commemorated on Panel 38.

William was born in Derry, Stirlingshire, son of Manus Donnachie, of 15 Matilda Street, Pollokshaws, Newlands, Glasgow.

He enlisted in Pollokshaws and was sent for training at Bordon and Bramshott, both in Hampshire. William entrained with the Battalion for Folkestone, Kent, and sailed to Boulogne on Thursday 13th May 1915.

HM King George sent a message to the Ninth Division that was read to all ranks: *"You are about to join your comrades at the Front in bringing to a successful end this endless war of more than nine months' duration. Your prompt patriotic answer to the Nation's call to arms will never be forgotten. The keen exertions of all ranks during the period of training have brought you to a state of efficiency not unworthy of my Regular Army. I am confident that in the field you will nobly uphold the traditions of the fine regiments whose names you bear. Ever since your enrolment I have closely watched the growth and steady progress of all units. I shall continue to follow with interest the fortunes of your Division. In bidding you farewell I pray God may bless you in all your undertakings."*

William entrained to St Omer and after two days marched to new billets in Bailleul. He went into the front line for the first time from Saturday 22nd for practical training. Following the tour of duty William had to clean himself and his equipment ready for an inspection by Field Marshal Sir John French on Saturday 29th. During the night of Sunday 6th June William marched to the training area at Busnes. He remained there until marching to the Festubert sector late on Saturday 26th, an area where he would serve until mid-August. He undertook tours of duty, fatigues and training without being involved in any particular action. After two weeks of training William marched to Vermelles on Thursday 2nd September and took the line on what would become the Loos Battlefield.

The whole of the Loos sector was alive with work, akin to an ants nest. Men and equipment were moving to and from the front line, everywhere trenches were being constructed or strengthened. Even though the majority of the men had no idea of the extent of the offensive or when it would begin but it was clear that something major was about to happen. Shortly before the opening of the offensive one thousand, two hundred gas cylinders were lugged into the front line. Each one weighed between 130lbs to 160lbs and were carried by hand over two thousand yards into the trenches. The preliminary bombardment began at 7.00am on Tuesday 21st September. A number of testing raids against *'Little Willie'* and *'Madagascar Trench'* were made by the Brigade but they failed to check the condition of the German wire, this would prove to be a costly and fatal error.

Zero Hour was finally set for 5.50am on Saturday 25th when the gas and smoke was released that floated towards the enemy trenches. At 6.30am the infantry began its attack. William fought in the battle from Saturday 25th to Monday 27th and was lucky to survive. Many of his friends and comrades he had trained with who had come to France with him now lay dead on the battlefield in front of the German wire.

When William was relieved he was sent to Béthune. He was caked in mud, extremely tired and shocked at what he had seen during the battle. He was not given much time to recover as on Wednesday 29th he moved to Belgium, partly by rail but mostly on foot. William was sent to serve in the trenches between Zillebeke and Hooge, the latter sector having seen a fierce action on Saturday 25th to support The Battle of Loos. The detritus of a battle was clear for all to see.

William would not take part in a further serious action but whilst on a tour of duty he was killed.

He is commemorated on Pollokshaws War Memorial.

16476 PRIVATE HERBERT DOWSE
1st Battalion Bedfordshire Regiment
Died on Monday 19th April 1915, aged 17
Commemorated on Panel 33.

Herbert was born in Abbots Langley, Hertfordshire, second son of Henry and Lizzie J Dowse, of Vicarage Lane, King's Langley, Hertfordshire.

He went out to France on Tuesday 2nd February 1915 with a draft of sixty men under the command of Captain Francis Hyde Edwards. They joined the Battalion on Tuesday 9th whilst they were billeted in Bailleul. The next evening Herbert marched to the Wulverghem sector near *'Bus Farm'* and *'Cooker Farm'*. He was instructed in working in the front line from being on guard duty

to helping to repair damage and bailing the trenches out. From Sunday 21st Herbert went into reserve at Dranouter for two days before returning to the front line. At the end of the month Herbert returned to billets in Bailleul, a town much enjoyed by the troops when resting. Being behind the line it was relatively safe, the cafés did a roaring trade and there were a wide range of other distractions available.

Herbert marched from Bailleul to a newly constructed hutted camp at Ouderdom on Wednesday 3rd March. The next day he moved towards the front line and went into the trenches south of the Ypres to Comines canal. There was considerable sniping and bombing that kept both sides alert at all times. The tour of duty ended on Tuesday 16th and he marched into Ypres where he rested over night before moving to a camp in Vlamertinghe to enjoy two days of rest and recuperation. Herbert returned to Ypres from where he again went back to the front line until the end of the month.

The first five days of April were spent in a camp near Vlamertinghe where the Bishop of London arrived to addressed the Battalion. Herbert returned to billets in Ypres where on Tuesday 6th April a few shells hit the town, a number of buildings were damaged with civilians and soldiers being injured. Late on Wednesday 7th he marched through the Lille Gate and onward to Reninghelst where the Battalion was held in reserve.

The last tour of duty that Herbert would undertake began on Monday 12th when he went into the trenches opposite the still intact Hill 60. He was hard at work over the next four days constructing communication trenches, preparing dugouts and enlarging dugouts. The attack on Hill 60 began at 7.00pm on Saturday 17th whilst the Battalion was in the rear ready to give support if required. The enemy launched a series of counter-attacks and on Monday 19th Herbert was sent into the line to assist in consolidating the position. There was considerable shelling, bombing, mortaring, as well as constant rifle fire and in the general mêlée Herbert was killed.

He is commemorated on King's Langley War Memorial.

2076 PRIVATE JAMES DUCHART
1st/7th Battalion Argyll and Sutherland Highlanders
Died on Sunday 25th April 1915, aged 16
Commemorated on Panel 44.

James was born at home, third son of Alexander and Elizabeth Sorley Duchart, of 16 Church Square, Grahamston, Falkirk. He was educated locally.

He enlisted in Falkirk and was sent for training. James left for France on Wednesday 16th December 1914 from where he entrained for northern France. James' training continued that included being attached to troops in the front line for practical experience before his Battalion took the line for the first time.

The Germans launched a gas attack on Thursday 22nd April 1915 against the French colonial troops and Ypres was under threat. James was sent with the Battalion to assist in the defence of the town and in a counter-attack at St Julien. He was in the assembly positions on Saturday 24th awaiting the order to move against 'Kitchener's Wood' (Bois des Cuisinières), the counter-attacks commenced at 3.30am. As James was led forward the Germans in the heavily defended 'Kitchener's Wood' poured their machine-gun and rifle fire into the attacking troops. Despite moving forward at speed the attack failed and during the fierce battle James was killed.

A/1384 RIFLEMAN JAMES DUFFY
8th Battalion King's Royal Rifle Corps
Died on Friday 30th July 1915, aged 17
Commemorated on Panel 53.

James was born in New Town, Birmingham, second son of Edward and Sarah Anne Duffy, of G Court, 8 House, Moland Street, Birmingham. He was educated locally. He went out to France on Wednesday 19th May 1915. For James' story and that of the Battalion see Rifleman Herbert Ashdown, above.

435613 PRIVATE JOHN BURT DUNLOP
49th Battalion Canadian Infantry (Alberta Regiment)
Died on Friday 2nd June 1916, aged 16
Commemorated on Panel 30.

John's signature

John was the son of Daniel and Annie Dunlop, of Frank, Alberta. He was educated locally.

John volunteered on Wednesday 25th August 1915, in Blairmore, Alberta, where he claimed to have been born in Kilmarnock, Scotland, on Wednesday 25th August 1897, so therefore he volunteered on his '18th' birthday. John was a Presbyterian, 5ft 4in tall, with a 33in chest, fair complexion, blue eyes, dark hair and employed as a labourer.

John sailed to England with the Battalion and was sent to train at 'Shorncliffe Camp', Folkestone, Kent. He marched through the town to the docks and embarked on HMT Golden Eagle bound for Boulogne on Saturday 9th October 1915. John marched to 'Ostrohove Camp' where he remained for three days then returned to the

... training in Shorncliffe

town to entrain at La Brique Station bound for Caëstre. The Battalion was sent to billets in and around 'English Farm' in Belgium where their training continued. At the beginning of November the Battalion went into the line close to 'Westhof Farm' where John served on tours of duty until Monday 20th December, with billets in Loker. He marched to Berthen where the Battalion was billeted and remained out of the line for both Christmas and New Year.

John paraded then marched from his billets at 8.30am on Sunday 9th January 1916 to Dranouter and went into reserve for three days. He moved the short distance into the line at Wulverghem and remained on tours of duty until Tuesday 8th February when he moved into reserve at 'Kemmel Shelters'. John was sent with his comrades on working parties during the day until the Battalion relieved the Princess Patricia's Canadian Light Infantry in front of Kemmel. John left the southern sector on Monday 20th March and marched at 8.30am from Loker, via Boeschepe and Wippenhoek, to Poperinghe, arriving at 11.00am. He was able to spend twenty-four hours in the town to enjoy the cafés, shops and relaxing activities that were available. In the early evening of Tuesday 21st John entrained to the Asylum at Ypres and marched with the Battalion to relieve the 1st Battalion Royal Fusiliers close to 'Warrington Avenue', 'Vigo Street' and 'Cumberland Dugouts'. By the end of March John had been sent into the front line between 'Maple Copse' and 'Railway Dugouts'. The line occupied by John came under heavy fire on Monday 1st May and later in the day the Battalion came under attack, Leutnant Wilhelm Binder of the 121st Württembergers was captured together with an NCO, both badly wounded and the NCO died shortly after being captured. The Battalion was relieved by the Princess Patricia's Canadian Light Infantry on Wednesday 31st May for a short period of well earned rest.

At 1.00pm on Friday 2nd orders were received to stand to then marched to 'Belgian Château' an hour later. They came under very heavy shell fire and the Battalion was forced to proceed in small groups to Ypres ramparts. John was mortally wounded by a shell that burst close to him and was buried in the field, his body being lost in subsequent shelling.

8422 Private
Gilbert Andrew Dunn
2nd Battalion Oxford and Bucks Light Infantry
Died on Sunday 1st November 1914, aged 17
Commemorated on Panel 39.

Gilbert was born and brought up in High Wycombe, fourth son of Harry Percival and Mary Ann Dunn, of Clay Lane Farm, Marlow, Buckinghamshire.

He volunteered and enlisted in Oxford and went out to France on Saturday 12th September 1914. Gilbert joined the Battalion with a draft whilst they were serving on the Aisne in the area of La Cour de Soupir. By the time Gilbert began serving in the trenches the Battle of the Aisne was a stalemate. Field Marshal Sir John French stated: *"Futile attempts were made all along our front up to the evening of 28th when they died away and have not since been renewed."*

Private Jim Stallard, a fellow Private in the Battalion, wrote from the Aisne: *"A few words regarding our advance and the state the Germans left the places they came through when we were following them up. They looted everything and everywhere; hardly a house escaped their evil work. They threw things about that were not a bit of use to them, smashed open the doors, and broke everything they could lay their hands on. Tables were carried out of the houses, cloths spread, and plates, etc. were used in the open. Lamps, beds, everything from the houses were scattered in the roads and the street. Never have I seen or even dreamed of such sights. Farms were in an awful state; they absolutely emptied them and destroyed every mortal thing. One place we came through I particularly noticed. All children's and women's clothes were thrown about from the houses; mirrors, lamps, beds, furniture all broken and scattered in the streets, fancy chairs, in fact the entire contents of good houses, so you can perhaps picture the sights.*

But as we got further, instead of household things lying about, it was the Germans themselves lying in all directions. At first it appears rather a ghastly sight – but one has to get used to more than this – things I am not allowed to speak of. We can hear them (shells) screaming as they come but, worse luck, don't know where they are going to settle (settle, what a word!). It is all bobbing up and down (we hear some of the boys shout "Look out!").

Still, it is surprising how the boys keep up their spirits. It is beautiful to see and hear them; there is plenty of life in them. We are all the same; set faces one minute, joking and laughing the next. Still, it is a good game of luck, nothing else. Jack and I are still side by side. We are both all gay. The winter will be awful, I bet, it is terrible at nights now. …" (Jim, and his brother Jack, were killed together on Wednesday 11th November 1914 and are both commemorated on the Menin Gate.)

Gilbert left the Aisne in mid-October and arrived in St Omer on Thursday 15th from where he moved to billets in Godeswaersvelde before marching to Poperinghe on Monday 19th. Gilbert marched along the pavé towards the medieval town of Ypres, still the resplendent medieval jewel of Flanders. He continued his march onto the Pilkem Ridge to take part in the opening battle of The First Battle of Ypres that was recorded by Lieutenant Colonel Henry Rodolph Davies: *"21st October - (Fight near Langemarck.) About 3.00 am I was sent for to go to Brigade Headquarters (in the village of Pilkem) to get orders. The Brigade was ordered to rendezvous, at 6.30 am, at the road junction half a mile north of St Julien. When we arrived at this rendezvous, orders were received that the 1st Division would attack Poelcapelle from Langemarck, while the 2nd Division, on their right, would advance on Passchendaele, the movement to be by the left, ie, the 1st Division directing.*

The 5th Brigade orders were that we on the left and the Worcestershire on the right were to be in front line, the Highland Light Infantry on the left, and the Connaught Rangers on the right in second line. I deployed along the Langemarck-Zonnebeke road, with our left on the Haanixbeck, so as to get in touch with the 1st Division. Front line was 'C' Company (Ponsonby) on the left, 'D' Company (Harden) on the right; second line, 'B' Company (Wood) on the left, and 'A' Company (Kirkpatrick) on the right.

Between 8.00 and 9.00 am we got in touch with a company of the South Wales Borderers - the right regiment of the 1st Division The Captain of the company said that the 1st Division were advancing. So I went back to the Brigade Commander (Lieut-Colonel Westmacott, Worcestershire Regiment), told him, and received orders from him to advance. By this time shrapnel had begun to fall, but it did not do a great amount of harm. The advance began, the men going forward under fire excellently. Bullets came almost at once, and it soon became evident that most of our losses were from fire from the left front, from ground which the 1st Division were to attack.

A good many men were hit, but in spite of losses we advanced quickly and steadily, delay being caused chiefly by the difficulty of getting through the thick fences. We finally got a line with our left about the centre of Haanixbeck, and our right joining up with the Worcestershire on the lower part of the Stroombeek. Here the fire from the left enfiladed us, and the Captain of the South Wales Borderers' Company sent a message to say he was in front of the rest of the 1st Division, who did not seem to be coming on. It was obviously impossible for us to go on unless the 1st Division came on also, so we stayed where we were, hanging on to the ground we had gained.

The Germans had trenches in front, the nearest being about 300 yards away, along the track which leads from near the junction of the Haanixbeck and Stroombeek to the m of Langemarck. Their men could be seen running into these trenches, either to occupy them or to reinforce them, and our front line was able to shoot a good many of them as they did this.

I had been coming along with 'A' Company on the right of the second line, and at this stage got into the upper storey of a farm house, about 200 yards behind our front line, just north of the Kilometre post 7. From here I could see to some extent in three directions. I kept looking northwards, hoping for the appearance of the 1st Division, but nothing more appeared beyond the one company of the South Wales Borderers who, unsupported on their left, were unable to advance any farther. From the front and right front there were movements of Germans towards the front of the Worcestershire on our right, but they were well taken on with shrapnel by our artillery, and they made no real attack in that direction.

The fight was now becoming stationary, and remained so for the rest of the day. There were occasional outbursts of firing, but at other times it died down almost entirely. I had sent messages to say that we wanted the 1st Division up in line with us before we could advance farther, but they did not come on. At dusk we began to entrench. It was a fairly good line that we had got, and a company of the Highland Light Infantry, under Mayne, came up on our left, and filled a gap between us and the company of the South Wales Borderers. During the night we were able to get up rations and ammunition, also the big entrenching tools from the tool wagons; and water-bottles were filled at the farm where I had my headquarters. A great many of the wounded were brought into our farm, but there was some delay in getting up the ambulances, owing, I believe, to a mistaken order having been given to them by someone to turn back when they were on their way up. Having some 50 wounded in the farm, with the probability of its being shelled, was a great anxiety; but to my intense relief some motor-ambulances arrived just in time, and we were able to get all the wounded away before daylight".

The night before Gilbert died he was on the Zwarteleen Hill, Private Jim Stallard wrote home: "Well, I'm sitting down, buried like a rabbit, but not as deep as I should like to be under the conditions, but you can take my word for it I'm deep enough to be safe from the 'Little Snipers'. They do not appear to worry us to a great extent. Of course, we don't put up our heads etc. to feel them; it is bad enough when we are compelled to. It is the 'coalboxes' or 'Jack Johnsons' that worry us. It is bad enough to hear them screaming over us through the air, but it is like being in hell to get them bursting in front or anywhere near us. The terrific noise, shake, smoke and the waiting for them to drop as one hears them coming is a thing I cannot explain. It is awful waiting to hear and feel the explosion so as to be able to breathe once again freely and wait for the scream of the next one. They leave a hole large enough to bury a horse.

Never did I dream that any of the different sort of things to be done by a European race that has been done here. The hundreds of thousands of homes in Belgium and France that have been purposely robbed and ruined is a disgrace to any nation. It is an awful sad sight for us to see as we came through the villages and towns but what in heaven's name must have been in the thoughts of the French 'Tommy'. The Germans were left strewn all up the roads and in the hedges, also the woods. Some were ghastly.

It is really a game of luck and we shall be glad to be out of it. There's no doubt our boys are in wonderful good spirit. Perhaps you may be sitting in the trenches holding a mother's meeting, when all of a sudden one of our big guns may fire from right behind us and not noticing which way it is fired at first it is sport to see us all bob down. It is sport of a good sort, played slow, but only let me scrape through safely and I shall always think of all the boys and their splendid spirit. When we have had the chance to buy a loaf of bread out here, we have had to pay as much as 1/2d. Still I expect we must not grumble."

Gilbert was in the front line when a shell burst close to him and he was killed instantaneously.

He is commemorated on the War Memorial at High Wycombe Hospital.

13021 LANCE CORPORAL WALTER HAROLD DUNN
'D' Company, 2nd Battalion
Duke of Cornwall's Light Infantry
Died on Sunday 14th March 1915, aged 17
Commemorated on Panel 20.

Harold was born in Small Heath, third son of Walter William and Ada Dunn, of 79 Sycamore Road, Handsworth, Birmingham.

He volunteered in Birmingham and went out to France on Tuesday 23rd February 1915. Harold joined the Battalion with a draft whilst they were serving in the St Eloi sector. He settled down to tours of duty without being involved in any particular action until Sunday 14th March when Harold was killed.

Harold marched from camp and went into the trenches late on Saturday 13th March. The German artillery bombarded the lines intermittently from early the next morning. At 5.00pm the enemy blew a series of mines, as recorded in the Battalion Diary: "At 5p.m. a terrific explosion took place under The Mound which collapsed, burying the machine-gun team which was stationed on it. At the same moment Trenches 17 and 18 were blown up by mines." As the mines went up the enemy artillery began to plaster the sector with all calibre of shell and their infantry began their attack. The Germans bombed their way forward and despite the best efforts of Harold and his comrades the enemy could not be held back. Harold was one of the very many casualties suffered by the Battalion in the action.

2175 PRIVATE NELSON VICTOR EDGE
1st Battalion East Surrey Regiment
Died on Monday 19th April 1915, aged 17
Commemorated on Panel 34.

Nelson was born in Fenny Stratford, Buckinghamshire, second son of Charles Edge, of 52 George Road, New Malden, Surrey. He was educated locally and was employed as an errand boy.

He volunteered in New Malden and went out to France on Tuesday 23rd February 1915.

Nelson died of wounds but his grave was lost in later battles. For the history of the Battalion see Private Albert Burton above.

11553 PRIVATE JOSEPH EDWARDS
2nd Battalion King's Own Scottish Borderers
Died on Wednesday 18th November 1914, aged 15
Commemorated on Panel 22.

Joseph was born in Everton, Liverpool, and was the nephew of Elizabeth Hardwick, of 38 Smollett Street, Kensington, Liverpool. He was educated locally.

He enlisted in Bedford and was sent for training before leaving for France on Wednesday 2nd September 1914. Under the command of Lieutenants Dixon and Robertson, Joseph arrived with a draft whilst the Battalion was serving on the Aisne. He immediately went into the front line where he remained until the beginning of October.

Joseph marched, entrained and was driven by omnibus until arriving in Verquin on Sunday 11th October where at last he was provided with a warm and comfortable billet. After a much-needed nights' sleep Joseph went into the line that was under fire. Two days later he took part in a short sharp attack on Cuinchy and the next day a further attack was mounted then the position was consolidated. In two days the Battalion lost sixty killed and wounded. Early on Thursday 15th Joseph was relieved and marched for two miles to Beuvry. After only twenty-four hours rest he marched four miles to Le Touret where he spent the day before moving into reserve late in the evening at Richebourg l'Avoué. Joseph took part in an difficult assault on Beau Puits where enemy machine-gunners, supported by their artillery, caused a further sixty casualties. General Sir Charles Fergusson wrote to Colonel Coke: *"Will you please*

Charles Fergusson

tell your battalion that their work during the last three days has been spoken of in the highest terms by General Hickie, and the Corps Commander directs that you and your men should be informed of his great admiration and appreciation of their pluck and grit.

I can't say how proud I am of them, and the fact that we are all Scotsmen adds to the pleasure. I will take the first opportunity of coming to see you, but shall not bother you till you've had a rest of sleep, of which you must all be in need. With many thanks to you and your battalion."

Joseph was sent to bivouac and rested until being collected by an omnibus in Merville and driven to Wulverghem in the early hours of Saturday 31st October. A battle for Messines was raging with the enemy getting the upper hand. Joseph was sent into battle at 1.00pm and took part in some fierce hand-to-hand fighting. The next morning a retirement was ordered and Joseph was sent for some rest. Early on Friday 6th November he marched via Loker and Dickebusch to Ypres. Joseph was in the line at Nonne Boschen on Tuesday 10th November when the sector came under heavy shell-fire with the position being attacked on Wednesday 11th. After a fierce fight the Germans were repulsed and more than sixty of the enemy were killed or wounded. For nine hours on Friday 13th he was under sustained bombardment. On Tuesday 17th the Germans launched another attack that was again repulsed by rapid fire. The next day *'minenwerfers'* poured down on his line and the King's Own were assisted by the Royal Engineers in digging a section of new trench. During the work Joseph was killed.

6663 PRIVATE DAVID ESPIE
2nd Battalion Royal Scots Fusiliers
Died on Saturday 24th October 1914, aged 17
Commemorated on Panel 19.

David was born in Ayr, eldest child of John and Matilda Espie, of 22 Rochester Street, Whitevale, Glasgow.

He volunteered in Glasgow and went out to Belgium on Sunday 4th October 1914. David marched to Brugge from where he was sent south, a long winding route to Roeselare thence to Ypres. David arrived at Wieltje on Thursday 15th and took the line before moving between Reutel and Poezelhoek. After being relieved from the line, at 5.00am on Wednesday 21st October David marched to billets in St Jan from where the Battalion was sent to help plug a gap in the line that was developing towards Polygon Wood. The Battalion occupied one thousand yards of front between the Passchendaele Ridge and the Keiberg Spur. He was in action desperately defending the position from one attack after another when David was shot and killed.

1440 PRIVATE
MATTHEW FARRELL
1st/5th Battalion King's Own
(Royal Lancaster Regiment)
Died on Wednesday 14th April
1915, aged 16
Commemorated on Panel 12.

Matthew was born in Scotforth, Lancashire, third son of Matthew and Elizabeth Farrell, of 6 Little John Street, Lancaster. Following his education he went to work at Story Brothers of Lancaster.

He enlisted in Lancaster and was sent for training. Matthew sailed for Le Havre with the Battalion, arriving on Monday 15th February 1915.

For Matthew's story and that of the Battalion, see Private James Cathcart, see above.

*Matthew Farrell
at camp*

Matthew was commemorated on the Story Brothers War Memorial, now lost.

26934 PRIVATE
WILLIAM ALFRED FAULKNER
(SERVED AS PRIVATE WILLIAM BOOTH)
1st Battalion Worcestershire Regiment
Died on Sunday 29th July 1917, aged 17
Commemorated on Panel 34.

William was the second son of Alfred Edward and Mary Ann Faulkner, of 2 Camden Street, Derby.

He volunteered in Blandford Forum, Dorset, and sent for training. William joined the Battalion in the field with a draft whilst they were serving in Flanders.

William undertook tours of duty in the newly established front line following the Battle of Messines. He served in front of Wytschaete, both in the trenches and on fatigues. In the build up to the opening of The Third Battle of Ypres on Tuesday 31st July a huge artillery duel was raging with each side pounding the other and William was killed by shell fire.

3582 PRIVATE WALTER FELTON
50th Company Machine Gun Corps (Infantry)
Died on Friday 14th February 1916, aged 17
Commemorated on Panel 56.

Walter was born at home, only son and eldest child

of Walter and Kate Felton, of 7 Punderson Gardens, Bethnal Green, London. He had five younger sisters. Walter was educated locally.

He enlisted in Hackney, London, as 20681 Private Walter Felton with the Leicestershire Regiment. Walter served in France and Belgium before joining the newly formed 50th Company, Machine Gun Corps. He had been serving in Belgium for some time and whilst in action at St Eloi he was killed.

2543 PRIVATE
ARTHUR PETRIE FERENS
1st/6th Battalion Durham Light Infantry
Died on Monday 26th April 1915, aged 17
Commemorated on Panel 36.

Arthur was born at home, son of Frances Ferens, of Ormesby House, Bishop Auckland, County Durham, and the late Arthur Ferens. He was educated locally and was an active member of the Church.

He enlisted in Bishop Auckland and was sent for training. Arthur was billeted in Gateshead from where he left with the Battalion and entrained in Newcastle, on Monday 19th April 1915 bound for Folkestone, Kent. The Battalion sailed to Boulogne and after a night in camp at Ostrohove he marched to the station for a long and tiring journey to Cassel. A short march took Arthur to billets in Hardifort where he arrived at 5.00pm on Wednesday 21st. Two days later Arthur marched to Steenvoorde where the Battalion was collected in the early evening by a fleet of omnibuses and driven, via Poperinghe, to a camp in Vlamertinghe.

The Germans launched the first gas attack on Thursday 22nd April that heralded the opening of the Second Battle of Ypres. The British line was hard-pressed and all available troops were called upon to help save the day. Arthur marched through the smoking medieval town of Ypres that was under shellfire and out to Potijze. He experienced the front line for the first time on Sunday 25th at Potijze where he spent the day under shellfire until being relieved and marching to Velorenhoek. The Battalion received the following order: *"The Germans have broken through our line and are advancing southwest. The Durham Light Infantry (6th Battalion) will advance and take up positions between Zonnebeke level crossing and Hill 37."* When the Battalion arrived in their allotted position enemy artillery fired all types of projectiles, including gas, on their position. In the evening they advanced on the Gravenstafel Ridge where Arthur was killed during a German attack.

He is commemorated on the Four Clocks Centre War Memorial, Bishops Auckland.

LIEUTENANT
JAMES ARTHUR ROSS FERGUSON
3rd Battalion Royal Sussex Regiment attached
1st Battalion King's Own Yorkshire Light Infantry
Died on Sunday 9th May 1915, aged 17
Commemorated on Panel 20.

Ross Ferguson

Ross was born in Thornton Heath, Surrey, on Wednesday 12th May 1897, only son and eldest child of Dr Robert Ross Ferguson, MD, and Mrs Gertrude K Ferguson, of 10 St George's Place, Canterbury, Kent. He was educated at the Abbey Preparatory School in Beckenham, London, and Durston House Preparatory School in Ealing, London, before attending The King's School Canterbury, Kent, from January 1911 to July 1914. In December 1912 he was awarded a Junior Scholarship. Ross was a good sportsman being a member of the XV and the rowing IV, and was appointed captain of both in 1914. He was an active member of the OTC, rising to Serjeant, and Ross was appointed a School Monitor.

When the war broke out Ross was with the OTC on annual camp in Tidworth. He immediately volunteered and was commissioned to the Royal Sussex Regiment. Following training he was sent out to France. Ross was confirmed in his rank from probation on Tuesday 16th March 1915 and was attached to the King's Own Yorkshire Light Infantry on Wednesday 31st March. Ross joined his new Battalion in Belgium. He marched with his platoon through Ypres on Thursday 1st April and out to the front, via the Menin Gate, to relieve the 2nd Battalion East Yorkshire Regiment in the woods near Zonnebeke. The war was yet to reduce every tree to matchsticks or stumps and the Battalion found the trenches in poor condition with German snipers making life more difficult. The British attack at Hill 60 began on Saturday 17th April and on Thursday 22nd the German launched their gas attack to the left of Ross line that opened the Second Battle of Ypres. One of the NCOs, later Lieutenant F K Lambert, serving with Ross and the Battalion, wrote of the gas attack: *"In the early afternoon a greenish-yellow cloud was seen to be approaching the French Colonial Div. line from the Boche trenches. Men looked at it in wonderment, such a phenomenon had never before been seen, and nobody realised what it was until the French Colonials were seen leaving their trenches.*

The enemy with his terrible ingenuity had selected a junction of two armies composed on the one hand of native troops of simple mind, and a worn-out British division on the other. There was no doubt that he meant the full force of his new

and horrible weapon to fall on the simple-minded Africans, to whom witchcraft and magic were dreadful and fearsome things to be avoided. These poor fellows had suffered terrible bombardments and attacks, but in this new weapon there was something uncanny. Men gripped their throats as the terrible gas went to their lungs, and writhed in agony as they slowly succumbed to its effects. The rain of shells and machine-gun bullets poured unceasingly and pitilessly amongst them, but these did not account for the effects of the yellow-green cloud about them. It was some unseen hand, some new and terrible 'white man's magic' brought against them, it was too much for their simple minds to grasp, and they fled terrified from it. The whole of the French Colonial Div. streamed off in panic back across the fields to Vlamertinghe and Poperinghe, leaving a tremendous gap in the line. The 84th Bde., which was holding the extreme left of the British line, was also caught by the gas cloud. They hung on to their trenches. Men dipped handkerchiefs or socks in filthy water and put them over their mouths and nostrils, and stuck to their rifles until the deadly gas overpowered them.

It was not until about six days after the first gas cloud that any preventive measures were received. Then small respirators made of a strip of muslin enclosing a wad of tow soaked in chemicals began to arrive. Two came at first to the battalion with instructions that they were to be issued to the front line sentries, then half-a-dozen, each day bringing a larger number, until every man in the battalion had one. As the supply increased a second one per man was issued. These respirators were worn with the wad of tow over the mouth and packed round the nostrils and tied behind the head with the muslin strip. The taste and smell were horrible and at first many men were averse to using them. They soon learnt their value and took great care to protect them. These respirators were superseded by the flannel helmet with mica eyepieces about a month later, and these in their turn gave way to an improved pattern, which was eventually replaced by the small box respirator of the present day."

Ross wrote of his experiences in the trenches: *"I am writing this just outside my dugout on a table pinched from a farm on our right. After having had quite a good time at Rouen, we marched from our billets which are about seven miles behind the trenches at —. The Company is in support in a wood, a hundred behind them. The Germans shell the wood every now and then, just to keep our heads down, and yesterday we had thirty shells in three quarters of an hour; they make a priceless scream. —, another Sub, who shares my dugout, and I pushed forward to the edge of the wood and were watching the Germans shelling a village with high explosives, which throw an enormous column of earth into the air, when shrapnel began to burst about a hundred yards in front, we scooted back to our dugout and soon shells were bursting overhead. About a hundred yards behind, in the wood, was a farmhouse, which was the scene of fierce fighting between 3rd Coldstreams and the Germans about three months ago. Yesterday a spent shrapnel shell, fired by one of our own anti aircraft guns at a Taube, came down within ten paces of me and exploded. I got some earth in the back and one casualty, one button off my breeches!*

On our way to inspect a line of trenches, six miles from out huts, we passed through a village, nearly ruined, close to the trenches, and I went in to the little chapel, — all the images etc. were smashed, and there was half a six inch shell unexploded, sticking in the floor.

We've been in these trenches now for three times as long as usual. That's our share of this 'do' for Calais. We're peppered with bullets, hand grenades, rifle ditto, trench mortars, shrapnel any old thing in fact. These trench mortars are beastly things; you see them coming about the size of a whisky bottle, full of the highest explosive turning over and over in the air, and when they come down there is some explosion! The other day about twenty fell, all within twenty yards of me — most cheery! Here's another one now — Bust! One came down as I was partaking of some eggs and bacon it put out the candle, sent the bacon flying, covered me with earth and made me bite my tongue. Another burst just above an officer's dugout; one piece went through and sent a roast chicken which they'd been looking forward to for days, flying through the doorway.

At night we and the Germans send up flares — sort of very bright rockets — and these set the wood on fire every now and then. Blooming weird sight!

We've just had the Brigade band playing outside the huts; all the old things, dear old waltzes etc. which bring back all the peace and fragrance of England makes one realise that it is jolly well worth fighting."

Due to the collapse of the line to his left, Ross' sector was becoming dangerously exposed and the line was ultimately untenable. A plan was devised for the reorganisation of the line: on Tuesday 4th May Ross led his men back towards Ypres to their new front line at Frezenberg. Late that night the Battalion was relieved but it was short-lived as the Germans mounted an attack on the position they had occupied and the Battalion was needed to support the line. The German attacks became heavier by the day, Saturday 8th brought a storm of high explosive shells on Ross' trench and he rallied his men to counter three separate infantry attacks. Ross was shot and wounded in the head late on Saturday evening and he died the following day.

Colonel Bond wrote: *"Your son was shot through the head in the same trench that I was in. before he was shot we were being heavily shelled, and he behaved in a most gallant way keeping his platoon cheerful, under the most trying circumstances. By his death we have lost a most gallant and dashing officer. I have forwarded his name to Headquarters for his gallant conduct on that day. His cheerful disposition and his keenness will remain with me for many years"*

James is recorded on Canterbury War Memorial.

36108 PRIVATE
FREDERICK LEWIS FIDO
1st Battalion Welsh Regiment
Died on Tuesday 25th May 1915, aged 17
Commemorated on Panel 37.

Fred was born at home, only child of Alfred and Emily Fido, of 33 Sandbed Road, Mina Road, Bristol.
He volunteered in Newport, Monmouthshire. For Fred's story see Private Edmund Jones below.

10496 PRIVATE
JOHN JEFFREY FILLINGHAM
2nd Battalion York and Lancaster Regiment
Died on Monday 9th August 1915, aged 17
Commemorated on Panel 55.

John was the second son and youngest child of Harriett Fillingham, of 50 Thompson Street, Shipley, Yorkshire, and the late John Fillingham (he died on Tuesday 30th September 1913). He was educated locally and worked as a carter.
He enlisted in the army in Pontefract on Thursday 12th March 1914 when his work ran out. He was given a good reference from his employer. John was 5ft 9in tall, with a 35in chest, weighed 128lbs, had a fresh complexion, grey eyes and brown hair. He did not leave with the Battalion when it went out to France in September 1914. He remained in England until leaving with a draft for France on Tuesday 9th February 1915. John saw considerable action on and around the Salient until he was in action at Hooge when a counter-attack was made against the German lines. They had used flammenwerfer on Friday 30th July that captured a significant area and inflicted heavy casualties: the High Command were determined to reverse the loss. In the action to recapture the lost ground John was killed, he was listed as missing believed killed until his death was confirmed on Tuesday 2nd May 1916.

3626 PRIVATE JOSEPH FLETCHER
2nd Battalion King's Own
(Royal Lancaster Regiment)
Died on Friday 5th February 1915, aged 17
Commemorated on Panel 12.

Joseph was born in Holborn, London, son of Joseph and Rachel S Fletcher, of 118 Britannia Street, City Road, London N1.
He volunteered in Finsbury, London, and was sent for training in Winchester, Hampshire. The Battalion was given a Royal Review by HM King George V, a

signal that their move to the Western Front would take place shortly afterwards. As Joseph was about to leave he was given a printed message from the King that read. *"I was very glad to have been able to inspect the 28th Division, and I wish to express my entire satisfaction with the general appearance of the Troops.*

In spite of the bad weather and of the difficulties attending concentration and training, it is evident to me that no time has been lost in establishing between the various units of this recently formed Division that esprit de corps which counts for so much on the field of battle.

I have been unable to inspect you in the field, but from all I saw to-day I have carried away the impression that a resolute spirit pervades all ranks to join their comrades at the front in maintaining the glorious traditions of my Army.

Farewell my Soldiers. May God bless you and protect you. 12th January, 1915."

Joseph left with the Battalion and embarked in Southampton bound for Le Havre where he arrived on Saturday 16th January 1915. He entrained to northern France for final training and was billeted between Bailleul and Hazebrouck. Joseph was sent into the trenches for practical experience. During his first tour of duty in the Salient he was killed by a shrapnel shell. Joseph was buried in the field but the grave was lost in subsequent battles.

... controlling the traffic

126680 PRIVATE FRANK SYDNEY FLIN
13th Battalion Canadian Infantry (Quebec Regiment)
Died on Tuesday 13th June 1916, aged 17
Commemorated on Panel 17.

Frank was born at home, son of George Warrior Flin, of 129 Brunswick Street, Stratford, Ontario.

He volunteered in Stratford on Wednesday 22nd September 1915 when he claimed to have been born on Saturday 23rd January 1897, was working as a boiler maker, and had served for two years with the 28th Perth Regiment, Militia. Frank was a Methodist, 5ft 4¼in tall, with a 34½in chest, a fair complexion, brown eyes, and light brown hair.

For Frank's story, see Private Percy Wright, below.

18111 PRIVATE JONATHAN FLOYD
'C' Company, 1st Battalion
East Lancashire Regiment
Died on Tuesday 29th June 1915, aged 17
Commemorated on Panel 34.

Jonathan Floyd

Jonathan was born in Huncoat, Lancashire, in November 1898, son of Jonathan and Elizabeth Floyd, of 5 Lane Ends, Hapton, Burnley. Following his elementary education he worked as a cloth looker at Walton's Mill, Hapton, Lancashire. He enlisted on Monday 28th December 1914 in Accrington, Lancashire, and after training went out to France on Thursday 13th May 1915. Jonathan joined the Battalion with a draft when it was in desperate need for reinforcements after two hard weeks of action in The Second Battle of Ypres. The fighting continued and the Salient was never a quiet place to be, Jonathan completed five weeks of service on tours of duty before he was killed by shell fire.

10931 PRIVATE WILLIAM HENRY FORD
'A' Company, 6th Battalion
Duke of Cornwall's Light Infantry
Died on Saturday 31st July 1915, aged 17
Commemorated on Panel 20.

William was born in Whitechapel, London, son of William Henry and Ellen Sarah Ford, of Ivinghoe, Cippenham, Slough, Buckinghamshire.

He went out to France on Friday 21st May 1915, for William's story and that of the Battalion, see Private Horace Currey, above.

41781 GUNNER HENRY SCOTT FOREST
2nd Brigade Canadian Field Artillery
Died on Sunday 25th April 1915, aged 17
Commemorated on Panel 10.

Henry's signature

Henry was the son of John and Mary Forest, of Coaticook, Province of Quebec.

He volunteered on Friday 8th January 1915 claiming to be born on Saturday 8th August 1896, working as a farmer. He was a Presbyterian, 5ft 7in tall, with a 34½in chest, a fair complexion, blue eyes, brown hair, with a triangular scar below his left buttock and three grey spots.

Henry's comrades had left for England with the First Canadian Contingent and were training in Market Lavington on Salisbury Plain when he volunteered. He spent some time training in Canada before he sailed to England from where he was sent out to France to join his comrades in the field in April whilst they were training in Watou. Henry moved towards the front, via Abeele and Poperinghe, arriving in position by Monday 19th April. He had arrived at the most 'inconvenient' time as the German armies were preparing their offensive on the Salient that would be launched on Thursday 22nd when poison gas was used for the first time. The first duty of the gunners was to register them on the German lines. At 5.30pm on Thursday 22nd the German artillery began to target the Canadian lines with an intense barrage. The German infantry made their attack to the Canadian left against the French Colonial troops. Henry moved with the guns to Wieltje early on Friday 23rd and he was ready to open fire from 3.30am. An hour later he began to assist in a barrage but at 5.10am it was halted. Enemy infantry were spotted massing at 9.30am and a request was received that the artillery begin shelling their position. The Germans laid a further gas attack at 4.05am on Saturday 24th that fell not only on the front line but around the batteries too. Henry's guns continued to fire on the enemy to support the infantry and eventually the Germans were halted, however, ammunition ran very short by 9.30am. The artillery continued to fire but with the desperate fighting it was impossible for the Forward Observation Officers to report accurately. The enemy was advancing in large numbers on St Julien from dawn on Sunday 25th. Gas, high explosive, and shrapnel rained down across the sector, it is not know if Henry was killed by shell fire or in a more ghastly manner if he was gassed.

S/13206 PRIVATE GEORGE FORSYTH
2nd Battalion Cameron Highlanders
Died on Wednesday 12th May 1915, aged 17
Commemorated on Panel 38.

George was born at home, son of Robert and Mary D Forsyth, of 44 High Street, Renfrew.

He volunteered in Clydebank, Lanarkshire, and went out to France on Monday 25th January 1915 to join the Battalion with a draft whilst they were based in the southern section of the Ypres Salient. George's first action was at St Eloi in March following the blowing of mines at 'The Bluff'. He then took part in the Second Battle of Ypres that began on Thursday 22nd April. George spent just over two weeks fighting to defend the line until he was killed.

He is commemorated on Renfrew War Memorial.

17362 PRIVATE JOHN LEONARD FORSYTH-INGRAM
2nd Regiment (Infantry) South African Infantry
Died on Thursday 11th April 1918, aged 15
Commemorated on Panel 16.

Leo was the son of John Forsyth-Ingram, of 381 Loop Street, Pietermaritzburg, Natal. He was educated locally.

Leo volunteered and was sent for training. He joined the Regiment with a draft in the field following the Ludendorff Offensive was launched on Thursday 21st March 1918. He arrived in camp in the 'Ridge Wood' area, south of Ypres, in early April and the whole Brigade was reorganised under General William Tanner. The German offensive was slowing and grinding to a halt at Amiens and their attention was turning towards Flanders.

Leo marched to hutments on the Loker to La Clytte road on Monday 8th April and the next morning Ludendorff's offensive was launched against the La Bassée sector and around Ploegsteert. The latter village was lost, as was Messines. The line was breaking around 'Pick House' so the South African troops were sent to counter-attack and stem the tide. By the evening of Wednesday 10th the Germans had succeeded in establishing a new line from Hollebeke, along the Messines Ridge, to west of Ploegsteert. Throughout the night Leo and his comrades held on in front of Messines. During the afternoon on Thursday 11th a further offensive was launched by General Sixt von Arnim that took Hill 63 and drove the 2nd Regiment back more than six hundred yards towards 'Hell Farm'. During the counter-attacks Leo lost his life.

14622 PRIVATE NORMAN FOX
2nd Battalion Duke of Wellington's (West Riding Regiment)
Died on Wednesday 5th May 1915, aged 17
Commemorated on Panel 20.

Norman was born in Honley, Yorkshire, second son of Robert and Sarah Fox, of 75 Lower Houses, Almondbury, Huddersfield. Following his education he was employed as an office boy.

He enlisted in Huddersfield and following training went out with a draft of two hundred and fifty officers and men to France on Thursday 29th April 1915. Norman arrived on Sunday 2nd May whilst the Battalion was in reserve near Kruisstraat following the fierce battle at Hill 60. Norman only had two days to be organised into his fighting unit before he was deployed to the front line. The Battalion was ordered to relieve the Devons on Hill 60 and Norman arrived in the trenches by 3.30am for his first and only tour of duty. Sadly Norman only survived a matter of hours and he died a ghastly death by affixation in the gas attack. The day was recorded by Captain C W G Ince, MC: *"Alas, what would have happened under natural circumstance was impossible under supernatural ones. At 8 a.m. the Germans, aided by a favourable wind, sent over asphyxiating gas with disastrous effects, a proceeding rightly described by the Commander-in-Chief in his despatch of June 15th as 'a cynical and barbarous disregard of the well-known usages of civilized war, and a flagrant defiance of the Hague Convention'. Gas had been first employed by the enemy on April 22nd at the commencement of the Second Battle of Ypres and fully effective counter-measures had not yet been established. We had not received gas masks yet, only a piece of gauze soaked in a preparation prepared by the medical authorities. This solution after a few minutes required renewing, a procedure absolutely impossible, of course, in action. On came this terrible stream of death, and before anything could be done, all those occupying the front line over which it swept were completely overcome, the majority dying at their posts — true heroes. By this foul means the Germans quickly got possession of trenches 40, 43, 45, there being practically no one left to hold them. Capt. G. W. Robins, East Yorkshire Regiment, attached to the Battalion was the last man to leave of the few who managed to crawl away, and he, poor fellow, died in agony that night from the effects of the gas.*

Our support trenches 38, 39, some 100 yards in rear, were held secure, also a small portion of the front line trench 40 on the lower slopes of the crest line was reoccupied. The few holders of these, assisted by strong reinforcements from the Dorset Regiment, counter-attacked and regained some of the lost trenches, but the actual crest of the hill remained in the enemy's hands.

The Battalion suffered over 300 casualties that morning, large numbers dying as a result of this barbarous gas. The writer will never forget the sight of men writhing in agony and slowly dying from the asphyxiating effects of the chlorine, nor the feeling of helplessness at being unable to do anything for them."

Norman is commemorated on Almondbury War Memorial.

SR/7027 Private
Walter Michael Francis
4th Battalion Middlesex Regiment
Died on Wednesday 29th September 1915, aged 17
Commemorated on Panel 51.

Walter was born in North Kensington, London, second son of John and Elizabeth Francis, of 2 Heathfield Street, Holland Park, Notting Hill, London.
He volunteered in Willesden, London, and went out to France with a draft on Tuesday 15th June 1915. Walter joined the Battalion after they had completed a difficult sixteen-day tour of duty at Hooge. The Battalion was resting or undertaking fatigues from a camp near Vlamertinghe where Walter remained until 7.45pm on Monday 12th July. He paraded then marched to Ypres and out to Hooge where the Battalion prepared to take part in an attack. A mine was blown on Monday 19th at 7.00pm that was described: *"… the ground trembled, and there was a terrific roar, as earth, débris and bodies of men shot up into the air amidst, a cloud of smoke and dust. Three distinct shocks were felt, the ground heaving and rocking in a sickening manner; then clods of earth bricks, wood and the mangled remains of Germans began to fall."* The whistles blew and Walter was led forward through a heavy cloud of mud and detritus as the German artillery began to pound the area. The German bombers did their best to hold the attackers back that was followed by a number of counter-attacks that continued until dawn the next morning. Walter remained on the battlefield fighting hard until late on Wednesday 21st when he was relieved and sent to Brandhoek for rest. It had been a costly affair for the Battalion as they lost approximately three hundred officers and men, killed, wounded or listed as missing. Walter was able to rest before starting training and did not return to the front until Monday 9th August, again at Hooge for a two-week tour where he came under constant shell fire and the attention of German snipers. He was relieved to Dickebusch for some rest until Sunday 12th September when he was sent to the dugouts in the ramparts at Ypres. Walter spent a week on fatigues before being moved into the trenches at *'Sanctuary Wood'*. Late on Thursday 23rd Walter was moved forward ready to take part in a diversionary attack for the Battle of Loos, at Bellewaarde on Saturday 25th. Four mines were blown, two at 4.19am and two more at 4.21am, but it was not until later in the morning that Walter was called upon to take part in the action. In the

… dug outs in Hooge crater

evening he moved into the trenches to relieve the Royal Scots and Walter spent the night strengthening the badly damaged trench. The work continued over the next two days and at 4.30pm on Wednesday 29th the Germans blew a mine then rushed the Battalion's position. They bombed their way forward and Walter opened rapid fire. The enemy were supported by their artillery and during a bombardment Walter was killed.

18591 PRIVATE BARON PERCY GALE
5th Battalion Oxford and Bucks Light Infantry
Died on Saturday 25th September 1915, aged 16
Commemorated on Panel 39.

Percy was born in Cheddington, Buckinghamshire, in November 1898, son of the late Arthur Gale and of Agnes Elizabeth Fitzroy (formerly Gale), of 9 Nelson Terrace, Aylesbury, Buckinghamshire. He had an older and a younger brother, Arthur and George.

He enlisted in Watford and sent for training. Percy joined the Battalion with a draft, going to France on Friday 3rd September 1915. Percy entrained to Belgium where he met his comrades in camp and allocated to a platoon. The Battle of Loos began on Saturday 25th September and a series of diversionary attacks were mounted to confuse the enemy. One such attack was made against Bellewaarde Farm and in his first action, and one of his first tours of duty, Percy was killed.

He is commemorated on Aylesbury War Memorial and on the War Memorial in Cheddington Church.

... an attack under the cover of a smoke screen

3245 PRIVATE FRANCIS GAYNOR
1st/5th Battalion Durham Light Infantry
Died on Tuesday 29th February 1916, aged 17
Commemorated on Panel 36.

Francis was the only child of Francis Joseph and Bridget Gaynor, of 6 Garden Place, Thornaby-on-Tees, Yorkshire.

He enlisted in Stockton-on-Tees and went out to France on Sunday 31st October 1915. Francis joined the Battalion with a draft whilst they were serving in the Armentières sector. He had only been with them for a couple days when the Battalion was sent to the area around Merris for training. Francis moved to the Ypres Salient in the latter half of December and began tours of duty between 'Sanctuary Wood' and Hill 60 sector. The area was described: *"Mud! mud! mud! Ankle-deep, knee-deep and sometimes waist-deep, in which men carried on an agonising existence during the whole tour in the front line, then emerging like half-drowned rats, smothered in mud from head to foot, aching and shivering!"*

Francis was in the line between Hill 60 and 'The Bluff' when he was killed on a tour of duty.

Z/1436 RIFLEMAN PERCIVAL ANGUS GIBBONS
1st Battalion Rifle Brigade
Died on Monday 10th May 1915, aged 17
Commemorated on Panel 48.

Percy's signature

Percy was born in Witham, Essex, youngest son of Lucy Gibbons, of 216 Uphall Road, Ilford, Essex. Percy's father had not lived with his mother since his birth. He was educated locally and worked as a engineer.

He volunteered in Stratford, Essex, on Tuesday 1st September 1914. Percy was 5ft 6½in tall, with a 34½in chest, a fresh complexion, blue eyes, brown hair and a large scar on the front of his right soldier.

He went out to France on Saturday 1st May 1915 with a draft that joined the Battalion two days later in Elverdinghe. Percy was soon allocated to a platoon and the next day the Battalion was sent into reserve. He went into the front line for the first time on Saturday 8th near 'Mousetrap Farm'. The German artillery began shelling the sector and was targeting the remnants of the farm buildings, however, a shell burst close to Percy and he was mortally wounded. He died shortly afterwards and was buried behind the lines but the grave was subsequently lost in the ensuing battle on Thursday 13th.

18934 PRIVATE JOHN GILLARD
8th Battalion King's Own
(Royal Lancaster Regiment)
Died on Thursday 2nd March 1916, aged 17
Commemorated on Panel 12.

John was born at home, only son of Mary Ann Spencer, of 19 Wellington Street, Dalton-in-Furness, Lancashire, and the late John Gillard.

He volunteered in Dalton and was sent for training. John left with a draft on Saturday 11th December 1915. For his history, see Private Christopher Constantine above. John is commemorated on Dalton-in-Furness War Memorial.

18103 Private Walter Godbehere
1st Battalion York and Lancaster Regiment
Died on Saturday 8th May 1915, aged 17
Commemorated on Panel 55.

Walter was born in Heeley, Sheffield, eldest son of Mrs Mary Beard (formerly Godbehere) and the late Walter Godbehere, of 1 Court, 3 House, Milton Street, Sheffield.

He enlisted in Sheffield and was sent for training. Walter remained at the Depôt when the Battalion went out to France on Sunday 17th January 1915. Walter joined them with a draft on Saturday 1st May whilst they were serving on the Salient and the Battalion had suffered badly in the opening stages of The First Battle of Ypres. Walter was on his first tour of duty when he was killed defending the line during a German attack. His brother, Private William Godbehere, died on Monday 9th August 1915 and is commemorated on Helles Memorial.

11588 Private Joseph Gough
2nd Battalion Royal Scots
Died on Tuesday 29th December 1914, aged 17
Commemorated on Panel 11.

Joseph was born at home, son of Eliza Gough, of 104 Wolverhampton Road, Heath Town, Wolverhampton. He volunteered in Wolverhampton and went out to France on Friday 23rd October 1914. Joseph joined the Battalion with a draft whilst they were serving in northern France. He moved across the border into Belgium to serve in the trenches between Messines and Wulverghem. General James Haldane inspected the Battalion on Monday 30th and afterwards marched to billets in Loker. HM King George V and HRH The Prince of Wales walked through the village on Thursday 3rd December as Joseph and his comrades lined the road to cheer them.

Joseph's first tour of duty was in front of Kemmel from where he took part in an attack on Monday 14th December against the German line at 'Petit Bois'. With bayonets fixed the Battalion charged across No Man's Land and captured two of the enemy's lines. Joseph remained in the line under heavy shellfire until he was relieved later that night and marched back to Kemmel. Joseph remained on tours of duty in front of Kemmel until he was killed during a relatively quiet period at the front.

19692 Private Frank Goulden
1st Battalion Wiltshire Regiment
Died on Wednesday 16th June 1915, aged 17
Commemorated on Panel 53.

Frank was the fourth son of James and Maria Goulden, of 7 Lansdowne Street, Coventry.

He volunteered and went for training. Frank was sent with a draft out to France on Tuesday 4th May 1915. For Frank's history see Private Charles Williams below.

3/6177 Private Daniel L Graham
1st Battalion Gordon Highlanders
Died on Wednesday 13th January 1915, aged 17
Commemorated on Panel 38.

Daniel was born at home, son of Mrs Charlotte Graham, of 3 Millar Place, Morningside, Edinburgh. He volunteered in Edinburgh and went out to France on Wednesday 7th October 1914. Daniel joined the Battalion in northern France following their service on the Aisne. His first action was in Flanders in the trenches in front of La Bassée and after some desperate fighting in the sector Daniel was sent across the border to assist with The First Battle of Ypres.

Daniel was sent for training in early December and the various drafts that arrived helped to bring the Battalion up to strength following its losses at La Bassée and Ypres. Daniel took part in another operation on Monday 14th December at Messines. It was a particularly fierce fight and the Battalion took heavy losses. Daniel survived yet again and continued to serve in the southern sector. When out of the line he was billeted in Loker and Westouter. Daniel celebrated the New Year in billets then returned to front line duty at Vierstraat then moved billet to La Clytte. Whilst on a tour of duty Daniel was killed.

S/3339 Private Hugh Graham
'E' Company, 1st Battalion Gordon Highlanders
Died on Monday 14th December 1914, aged 17
Commemorated on Panel 38.

Hugh was born at Neilston, Renfrewshire, son of James and Agnes Graham, of 55 Kelburn Street, Barrhead, Renfrewshire. He was educated locally.

He enlisted in Barrhead and went out to France on Friday 4th December 1914. He joined the Battalion in Loker. Hugh only undertook one tour of duty when he participated in an attack on Messines where he was killed, just a week after he had arrived in Belgium. There is a headstone in Irish House Cemetery to commemorate thirty NCOs and men of the Battalion killed in the action at Messines. One of those buried in the grave could be Hugh.

He is commemorated on Barrhead War Memorial.

S/15589 PRIVATE JAMES GRANT
2nd Battalion Cameron Highlanders
Died on Monday 10th May 1915, aged 17
Commemorated on Panel 38.

James was born at home, son of William and Janet Grant, of 27 Buchanan Street, Leith, Edinburgh.

He enlisted in Edinburgh, and following training went out to France on Sunday 3rd January 1915 with the Battalion.

James was sent to northern France to complete his training before beginning tours of duty in the southern section of the Ypres Salient.

James' first action was at St Eloi in March following the blowing of mines at 'The Bluff'. He then took part in the Second Battle of Ypres that began on Thursday 22nd April. James spent two weeks fighting to defend the line until he was killed.

1675 PRIVATE HARRY GRICE
1st/5th Battalion King's Own
(Royal Lancaster Regiment)
Died on Tuesday 27th April 1915, aged 16
Commemorated on Panel 12.

Harry was born at Scotforth, Lancashire, third son of Alfred and Jane Grice, of 7 Ripley Street, Lancaster. He was educated locally.

He enlisted in Lancaster and was sent for training. The Battalion embarked for Le Havre, arriving on Monday 15th February 1915.

For Harry's story and that of the Battalion, see Private James Cathcart, see above.

10111 PRIVATE
WILLIAM JAMES GRINHAM
2nd Battalion Yorkshire Regiment
Died on Friday 30th October 1914, aged 17
Commemorated on Panel 33.

William was born in Elvetham, Hampshire, son of Thomas and Louisa Jane Grinham. Following his education he worked as a painter on the local estate before enlisting in the army. He gave his brother, Mr C Grinham, of 102 Cornwall Road, Lambeth, London as his next of kin.

The Battalion was serving on the Channel Islands when the war broke out. They returned to Southampton on Friday 28th August 1914 and went to a camp outside the city before moving onto Lyndhurst, Hampshire, where mobilisation was completed. They prepared for six weeks for the move to serve on the Western Front and were sent with General Sir Henry Rawlinson's force to Belgium. "At 3.15 p.m. on Sunday, October 4th, we received our long-expected orders. At 3.50 p.m. 'A' and 'B' Companies marched out and were followed an hour later by 'C' and 'D' Companies. The two half-battalions did not meet again for three days. The right-half battalion embarked at about 10 p.m. in the Leyland SS California and set sail early next morning under sealed orders. At 4 p.m. we found ourselves off Dover, where we got more orders, and soon we were all trying to find if Zeebrugge was marked on our war maps. We arrived at Zeebrugge early on the 6th and entrained for Bruges. We were the first British troops to arrive in Bruges and our reception was a very hearty one. We were conducted to billets which had been selected for us. The officers were accommodated in private houses and the office of the Tramway Company, while the companies were put up in the tram sheds. ... We spent the 7th October at Bruges and were joined by the left-half battalion".

With the military situation confused, as the city of Antwerp was being evacuated, orders were received to march to Ostend on Thursday 8th. The Battalion bivouacked in a field at Klemskerke for twenty-four hours before returning to their billets in Brugge. A march of seven miles took them to Beernem on Saturday 10th, in the direction of Ghent, where orders were received to proceed to Ypres and join the BEF that was arriving from the Aisne. They marched via Koolscamp and Roeselare arriving in Ypres at noon on Wednesday 14th. Major Pickard recorded: "The Battalion marched with Brigade up the Menin Road and after a time I received orders to proceed to Kruisstraat and billet the Battalion there. The village was about half a mile from the Ypres railway station on the road to Dickebusch. On arrival there I rode through the village in order to get an idea of the size of it and the type of houses it contained. I then came back to the Ypres side of the village and commence to mark up the houses for the Battalion. Suddenly, a small boy appeared out of a by-road, shouting 'Uhlan! Uhlan!' I had my regimental quartermaster-sergeant with me, and Sergeant Bell was actually at the door of the house. I seized Sergeant Bell's rifle and some information off him and dashed off to the corner of the road. There about twenty yards away were two Uhlans. My Q.M.S. and I dropped on our knees and blazed off. The Uhlans, who, in my opinion, should have charged us, turned round, crashed into each other, and dashed away, but not before we had got them both in the back. A naval party, who had an aeroplane on the Dickebusch Road, was in Ypres when we started firing, and thought their aeroplane was in trouble, so dashed out in a light lorry. I told them what had happened and asked them to get down the Dickebusch Road as fast as they could and try and capture those two Uhlans. Off they went as fast as possible and returned about ten minutes later with the two. One was an officer who was very badly wounded and died shortly after in Ypres, the second was a non-commissioned officer who was also seriously wounded in the back. … My Q.M.S. and I were the first to open fire in the 7th Division."

Later in the day the Battalion marched to Ypres that was recorded thus: "On arriving near Ypres we met two armoured cars who told us they had fired on and brought down a German aeroplane … but when the cars came up with it they found the machine intact but the pilot and observer gone. This was the firing we heard. … Whilst we were on the road we saw a car coming down the road at a great pace. We then discovered it contained the two German officers who had escaped from the aeroplane, they having been captured further up the road and were being brought back to Ypres. They were sitting on the back seat with a large Gendarme between them, who was holding them firmly by the scruff of the neck and shaking them hard the whole time; a French dragoon was standing on the step beside them, and another Belgian Gendarme was leaning over the front seat waving a large revolver under their noses. I never saw two men look so annoyed in my life or two such awful looking blackguards; both had lost their hats and, like all Germans, had their heads entirely shaved; the result was not flattering. One of them, we discovered, had got the Iron Cross for being the first man to throw a bomb on Antwerp."

The Battalion was held in reserve on Thursday 15th and the next day marched down the Menin Road, through Gheluvelt to Klein Kruiseik where they entrenched, as recorded by one of the officers: "We were told to entrench a line which, as far as our Brigade was concerned, ran from the ninth kilometre stone through Poezelhoek and then back in the direction of Poezelhoek. The 22nd Brigade carried this line on facing almost due north, and on our right the 20th Brigade continued the line facing south and south-east through Zillebeke. So, as will be seen, the Division faced roughly three ways — north, east, and south. The Battalion had to hold about a mile of ground which included the village at the cross-roads by the ninth kilometre stone, and continued from that to the left towards Poezelhoek. 'A' Company had the village and the cross-roads, 'B' Company was on their left, then 'C', and then 'D'. Headquarters, to begin with, was in the village.

The men had tea and breakfast and while this was going on a small patrol which had gone out from 'A' Company under Phayre came back very full of themselves, having captured a German patrol. They had gone down the road a bit and been fired on from a farmhouse, so they moved up against the place and saw about eight Germans run across the road from the house into a barn. They shot one as he was running.

The remaining Germans were summoned to surrender, and as they flatly refused to do so, Phayre set the barn on fire. Eventually they came out, but not until their boots were nearly burnt off their feet; and when asked why they had not surrendered before, they said they had been told that the English always shot their prisoners! They were agreeably surprised when they found that, instead of being killed, they were given some food; and said if they had known that they would have surrendered long ago. They were reservists of the 19th Hussars, and we told them it was only fitting they should be captured by the 19th Regiment!" (Lieutenant Richard Phayre died on Monday 26th October and is commemorated on the Menin Gate.)

Throughout Saturday 17th William and his comrades dug in and strengthened the line. Orders were received to take part in an attack on Menin on Monday 19th, however, as they went beyond Dadizeele they had to return as columns of German troops were advancing towards Ypres. During the morning of Tuesday 20th the sector was bombarded by high explosives, the first time that William had experienced such a barrage, *The Green Howards' Gazette* printed: "That day was our first experience of shell fire and though we had only shrapnel against us it was not very pleasant. The enemy's snipers came into action too, and wonderfully good they are in utilizing ground for cover. … There was a certain amount of shooting on the left during the afternoon, and when dusk fell we were able to get out of our trenches and found out what had happened generally." Two days later, during the afternoon of Thursday 22nd, the enemy advanced in close formation on their position: the Battalion's rapid fire brought them to a halt. The Germans recorded: "… the well-aimed fire from the enemy's prepared positions reaped a great harvest."

It was recorded on Friday 23rd: "… we could see quite clearly columns of Germans massing on our left flank; our artillery made excellent practice, but how we prayed for more and heavier guns. On the evening of this day we heard that the enemy had broken through the line on the left. They were attacking in mass for all they were worth and fully determined to break through, but were stopped in a most gallant manner by ' A' Company and the machine guns under Lieutenant Ledgard and by a party of our men who volunteered to attack and clear a wood under Captain Jeffery." (Lieutenant Frank Ledgard who died in the attack is buried in Harlebeke New British Cemetery.)

William remained at the front fighting hard, he came under constant shell fire from Friday 23rd to the end of

Monday 26th. Whilst the enemy were expending vast amounts of ammunition on their attack, so were the British getting through all forms of 'materiel'. Each night, for example, the Battalion was supplied with ninety-six thousand rounds of ammunition.

'The Green Howards' Gazette' recorded the events that led to William's death: *"At daybreak on the 29th October, 'A' and 'C' Companies went up to support the Royal Scots Fusiliers; at about 11 a.m. the Germans in great strength broke through a regiment on our left and threatened our left rear, which forced those on the right to retire about 1000 yards. Colonel King reorganized the Regiment and, collecting anyone he could find from other units, led an attack which was successful in retaking our former position and gaining another 200 yards. This advance was terrible, as the enemy simply poured shrapnel into us and our casualties were heavy. Major Walker was killed whilst in charge of his Company, 'C', by a shrapnel bullet; his death was very much felt as we lost a very fine soldier and a good friend. … When dawn broke the Battalion took up a position which formed a salient, with 'D' Company on the left and the other companies in the order 'A', 'C' and 'B'. We little knew what a terrible day it was going to be for us. We were fired at fairly heavily during the morning, but this caused no casualties; it was through the deadly accuracy of a few snipers who never seemed to miss, that the Battalion had a loss which those who get through this war will never forget — I refer to Colonel King; every officer and man felt his loss more than I can describe, Brown and Hatton were both killed by snipers."* (Colonel King, Brown, Captain Ernest Broun (correct spelling), and 2nd Lieutenant Frederick Hatton are commemorated on the Menin Gate.)

Frederick Hatton

11052 PRIVATE
ALBERT EDWARD GUNNELL
1st Battalion South Wales Borderers
Died on Saturday 14th November 1914, aged 17
Commemorated on Panel 22.

Albert was born in Bromsgrove, the eldest son of Walter Albert and Nellie F Gunnell, of 53 Worcester Street, Bromsgrove, Worcestershire.

He volunteered in Brecon and at the outbreak of war he was stationed in Bordon, Hampshire. Albert left with the Battalion from Southampton for Le Havre on Thursday 13th August 1914. The Battalion entrained to northern France and took part in the Battle of Mons on Sunday 23rd August. Orders were received for the Battalion to withdraw from the battlefield and they retired south that soon became 'The Retreat'. The Marne was crossed and on Saturday 5th September orders were received for the Battalion to turn and engage the enemy. Albert marched with an additional spring in his step as they chased the German armies back across the Marne and onto the Aisne. He took part in an attack on the Chemin des Dames against the enemy on Wednesday 23rd September and three days later the Battalion held off a significant counter-attack. The two actions cost the Battalion dear as they lost over three hundred and fifty officers and men, killed, wounded or listed as missing. General Sir Douglas Haig wrote: *"The conduct of the South Wales Borderers in driving back the strong attack made on them is particularly deserving of praise"* and visited the Battalion to thank them in person.

In early October Albert was sent north to serve in Flanders. He crossed into Belgium and was deployed to Ypres to participate in the First Battle of Ypres. Albert was in front of Gheluvelt Château on Saturday 31st where the Germans were pressing hard on the line. He followed his officers forward and attacked the enemy position that initially went well. A large number of Germans were killed and over sixty surrendered. The enemy brought more troops to counter-attack and in overwhelming numbers successfully pushed the Battalion back. Colonel Leach collected his men, and a number from the Scots Guards, and led a bayonet charge that put the enemy to flight.

Albert survived another two weeks serving on the battlefield until he was killed as the First Battle of Ypres was running out of steam.

… the bayonet charge at Gheluvelt

G/5849 LANCE CORPORAL
ALFRED JOHN GUTTERIDGE
4th Battalion Royal Fusiliers
Died on Tuesday 2nd March 1915, aged 17
Commemorated on Panel 6.

Alfred was born at home, second son of James and Susan Gutteridge, of 36 Clarence Street, Southall, Middlesex.

He volunteered in Hounslow and went out to France on Wednesday 10th February 1915. He joined the Battalion in the field and began tours of duty in the St Eloi sector. Alfred was on his second tour of duty when he was killed.

L/15284 PRIVATE EDGAR WALTER HERBERT HALL
3rd Battalion Middlesex Regiment
Died on Saturday 8th May 1915, aged 17
Commemorated on Panel 51.

Herbert was born in Kensington, London, eldest son of Herbert Charles and Ada Florence Hall, of 25 L Block, Dufferin Street, White Cross Street, St Lukes, London EC1.

He volunteered in Hounslow and was sent for training. Herbert left with a draft and went out to France on Wednesday 21st April 1915. It was hardly good timing to arrive on the Salient as the Second Battle of Ypres began the next day! There was not time to go through the usual pleasantries as he was rushed into the line to help support the Battalion who were fighting with the Canadians at St Jan. Following his 'blooding' Herbert was relieved late on Saturday 24th and sent to rest on the Ypres Canal whilst being held in reserve. The German artillery pounded the area that resulted in the Battalion being withdrawn to a field slightly to the rear. Late on Monday 26th Herbert moved into the Salient and held in reserve to support the Lahore Division. After two days he marched to Verlorenhoek and dug in whilst under constant shell fire. There was a constant battle raging with each side shelling the other. Herbert remained on the tour of duty until late on Monday 3rd May when he was relieved to Poperinghe.

Herbert had some welcome rest and was able to clean up for a couple of days before he marched back to the trenches to take part in an attack at the Frezenberg Ridge. The Battalion moved forward under a heavy enemy bombardment coupled with a hail of machine gun bullets. It was not surprising, therefore, that the Battalion lost heavily, one of those killed being Herbert.

B/3366 RIFLEMAN WILLIAM HALL
9th Battalion Rifle Brigade
Died on Sunday 1st August 1915, aged 17
Commemorated on Panel 48.

William was born at home, son of Malcolm Campbell Hall and Annie Hall, of 67 Chester Road, Hulme, Manchester.

He volunteered in Manchester and was sent for training. He went out to France on Friday 21st May 1915 with a draft. For William's story and that of the Battalion, see Rifleman David Ross below who had accompanied William in the draft.

352544 PRIVATE FREDERICK HANSON
1st/7th Battalion London Regiment
Died on Monday 9th July 1917, aged 17
Commemorated on Panels 54.

Frederick was the only son of William and Matilda Hanson, of 72 Huntsmoor Road, Wandsworth, London. He was educated locally.

He enlisted in Sun Street, London, and after training went out to join the Battalion in the field.

The Battalion was sent for training in Zudausques from Tuesday 15th May 1917 where they practiced over a model of the ground that would be attacked at Messines. Plenty of time was given to all ranks to enjoy sporting events and to visit the bustling town of St Omer. Frederick entrained in St Omer on Wednesday 30th May bound for Poperinghe then marched to 'Patricia Camp'. He was sent into the town for a bath and again was able to enjoy the estaminets et al when not required on fatigues.

Late on Tuesday 5th June Frederick paraded with his comrades then marched to the front at 'Spoilbank'. It took much longer than normal as the roads were very congested with troops moving into the line ready for the attack that would begin on Thursday 7th. He went into the maze of tunnels that afforded good protection from the enemy and ensured that the troops could not be spotted from the air. At 11.00pm on Wednesday 6th Frederick emerged and moved into the front line. He took part in a successful attack on 'White Château' where some eighty of the enemy surrendered or were taken prisoner. Private Frank Dunham recorded the events: *"Toby and I were just wishing each other good luck when we heard a mighty rumble and a roar; to our left and right we could see flames and smoke from the mines.*

The attack was in full swing; prisoners taken looked scared and fatigued. We came across a few of our chaps slightly wounded and all had attended to their wounds with their field dressings.

Hostile shelling was now severe and casualties began to increase. We bandaged several; one poor chap had a smashed leg, so we used a piece of wood from a trench as a splint and made him comfortable.

I then came across Capt. Wallis with a shrapnel wound in the thigh. He had roughly dressed it but I made a proper job of it and left him to await the arrival of a carrying party. We came next to Cpl. Short, unfortunately he was beyond our aid. (He is commemorated on the Menin Gate.)

Using a door from the Château as a stretcher, and with the aid of two officers' servants, we collected several casualties and put them under cover of the Château. This was very tiring work owing to the rough ground and the door being awkward to carry. The poor chaps had a job to keep on it when it tilted; no doubt it was an uncomfortable journey for them, but they did not complain."

Frederick remained on the battlefield until late on Monday 11th when he was relieved to reserve and the next day marched to 'Alberta Camp' in Reninghelst for three days much needed rest. A strenuous march to Lynde began on Friday 15th that was reached two days later with a rest in Caëstre. Frederick was able to enjoy the warm summer weather whilst taking part in a number of sporting events, swimming in the canal and generally relaxing. He attended a swimming gala and carnival on Monday 25th in Blaringhem followed by a divisional tattoo in the evening. The Battalion began its march back towards the front on Thursday 28th, resting in Méteren overnight where everyone attempted to dry out from the march in the pouring rain. The next day they crossed the border into Belgium and went to a camp at 'Ridge Wood'. HM King George visited the area on Wednesday 4th July so the Battalion lined the road and gave him a great cheer as he drove by. Later in the evening Frederick left camp for 'Alberta Camp' from where he visited 'Chippewa Camp' for a bath and he was given a gift parcel from HM Queen Alexandra. Frederick went back into the trenches for the last time on Sunday 8th around 'Optic Avenue'. Frederick had not been in the line very long before he was killed by shell fire.

16644 PRIVATE
HENRY THOMAS HARFORD
1st Battalion Norfolk Regiment
Died on Wednesday 26th May 1915, aged 17
Commemorated on Panel 4.

Henry was born in Wandsworth, London, eldest son of Thomas Fred and Rosina Martha Harford, of 37 Goldyke, Wrydecroft, Peterborough, Cambridgeshire. Henry was brought up and educated in Wandsworth. He volunteered in Norwich, Norfolk, and went out to France on Wednesday 12th May 1915. Henry joined the Battalion whilst they were in a camp at Ouderdom following a twenty-six day tour of duty, the latter part being constant fighting in the Second Battle of Ypres. On Henry's first tour of duty, and within hours of serving at the front, he was killed.

6249 PRIVATE JOSEPH HENRY HARRIS
'C' Company, 2nd Battalion Royal Irish Regiment
Died on Thursday 6th May 1915, aged 17
Commemorated on Panel 33.

Joseph was born in Smallheath, Birmingham, son of Joseph Henry and Henrietta Harris, of 21 Colville Road, Bayswater, London.

He volunteered in Fermoy, County Cork, and went out to France on Sunday 3rd January 1915. Joseph joined the Battalion in the field and undertook a month of tours of duty before being sent for training. The Battalion completed its training on Sunday 14th March and took the line at Le Bizet, remaining in the sector until the end of April with their billets in the village or in Ploegsteert. The Germans used gas for the first time on Thursday 22nd April against the French colonial troops and followed that with an attack on the Canadians that opened the Second Battle of Ypres. The pressure in the northern section of the Salient was increasing. Joseph was ordered to La Brique via Ouderdom, on Friday 30th when the Battalion relieved the 1st Battalion The Queen's Own. As he went forward for the relief Joseph came under heavy shellfire. Over the next few days he was not involved in any particular action but losses continued to be taken by the Battalion. The Battalion experienced its first gas attack on Monday 3rd May and despite the German assault were able to hold the line. Joseph was killed by shell fire whilst in the front line.

110227 PRIVATE
CHARLES JOSEPH HARRISON
5th Canadian Mounted Rifles Battalion
(Quebec Regiment)
Died on Friday 2nd June 1916, aged 17
Commemorated on Panel 32.

Charles' signature

Charles was the son of Thomas Joseph Harrison, of Sherbrooke.

He volunteered on Thursday 11th February 1915 in Sherbrooke, Province of Quebec where he claimed to have been born on Sunday 13th September 1896, in Windsor Mills, Province of Quebec, working as a printer and had served with the 53rd Regiment, Militia, in Sherbrooke. Charles was a Methodist, 5ft 4in tall, with a 33½in chest, a dark complexion, brown eyes, dark coloured hair and a scar on his right thigh.

For Charles' story, and that of the Battalion, see Private John Carr above.

Charles is commemorated on the Sherbrooke War Memorial.

2380 PRIVATE GEORGE HART
'C' Company, 1st/4th Battalion
South Lancashire Regiment
Died on Sunday 27th June 1915, aged 16
Commemorated on Panel 37.

George was born at home, the son of Mr and Mrs George W Hart, of 4 Eustace Street, Warrington, Cheshire.

He enlisted in Warrington and was sent for training. George embarked in Southampton for Le Havre on Friday 12th February 1915. The Battalion sailed on *SS Queen Alexandra* and *SS Trafford Hall* and after disembarkation marched to *'No 2 Rest Camp'* for two days. He returned to the town and entrained for Bailleul. George marched the short distance to the *'Grapperies'* where he was billeted for five days and undertook training. He moved the short distance to the Belgian border on Sunday 21st and onward to a camp in La Clytte, via Loker. After a further five days of training and preparation for the front line George was sent to Kemmel on Friday 26th for his first tour of duty.

... the dead lying uncollected on the battlefield

On Thursday 25th March he marched further north to billets in Dickebusch where after a night's rest he was sent into the line at St Eloi. The view from the trenches was nothing short of a charnel house, bodies of soldiers and civilians who had been killed over the past months lay rotting in front of him. After six days he was relieved by the 2nd Battalion — George returned on tours of duty over the next three weeks. The Battalion relieved the 2nd Battalion in the line near Elzenwalle Château on Saturday 1st May. A gas attack began on Sunday 2nd at Hill 60, the wind blew the gas in their direction, George and his comrades suffered irritation of their eyes as a result. Throughout the rest of the month he undertook tours of duty without participating in any significant action. The Battalion relieved the 2nd Life Guards and 8th Hussars at *'Sanctuary Wood'* on Saturday 5th June. George charged forward in the attack on Bellewaarde

... entrance to dugouts at Ypres and a plan showing a section below

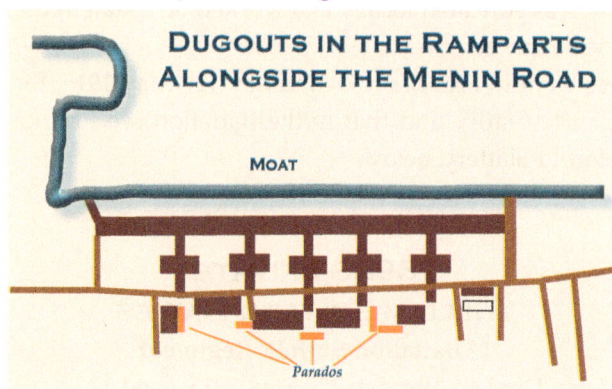

Ridge on Wednesday 16th where he lost many friends who were killed as they advanced into the path of the British barrage. It was a furious fight, where they were pushed back and counter-attacked throughout the day. After a hard and long tour of duty George was relieved from the line and sent to the relative safety of Ypres, being billeted in the dug-outs in the thick walls of the ramparts. After three days rest he went back into the line for the last time, returning to Hooge. George's short life ended in the front line three days later.

L/16919 PRIVATE
GEORGE BADEN POWELL HARVEY
2nd Battalion Royal Fusiliers
Died on Tuesday 7th August 1917, aged 17
Commemorated on Panel 8.

George was the eldest son of Alfred and Ada Harvey, of 31 Holly Road, Twickenham, Middlesex.

He enlisted in St Paul's, London, and after training was sent out to France to join the Battalion with a draft. The Battalion had taken losses during The Battle of Arras, a battlefield they left from Thursday 21st June 1917 and were sent to the area between Arras and St Pol. A series of moves took them to Flanders and across the border to train near Proven. Between leaving Arras and arriving in Proven a number of drafts reinforced the Battalion.

George did not participate in a significant attack during

The Third Battle of Ypres but was in the line on the Pilkem Ridge when he was killed by shell fire.

G/5757 PRIVATE
CHARLES WILLIAM HARWOOD
2nd Battalion The Buffs (East Kent Regiment)
Died on Tuesday 25th May 1915, aged 17
Commemorated on Panel 14.

Charles was born at home, second son of George Grint Harwood, of 18 King John Street, Stepney, London. He was educated locally and worked on a stall in the local markets.

He went to France on Wednesday 12th May 1915, for Charles' story and that of the Battalion see Private Harold Slattery, below.

16933 PRIVATE
WILLIAM EDWARD HAWES
1st Battalion Suffolk Regiment
Died on Tuesday 25th May 1915, aged 17
Commemorated on Panel 21.

William Hawes

William was born at home in 1898, eldest son of Edward and Mary Hawes, of New Cottages, Redlingfield, Eye, Suffolk. He volunteered in Eye and went out to France on Monday 3rd May 1915 and joined the Battalion in the field. For William's story, and that of the Battalion, see Private Walter Briggs, above.

He is commemorated on Redlingfield War Memorial.

A/1643 RIFLEMAN JOSEPH HAWTIN
8th Battalion King's Royal Rifle Corps
Died on Tuesday 6th July 1915, aged 17
Commemorated on Panel 53.

Joseph was born at home, only son of Joseph and Annie Elizabeth Hawtin, of Evesham Street, Alcester, Warwickshire. He was educated locally and was then employed as a hook maker.

He volunteered in Birmingham and went out to France on Wednesday 19th May 1915. For Joseph's story and that of the Battalion see Rifleman Herbert Ashdown, above. Joseph is commemorated on Alcester War Memorial.

6601 PRIVATE JAMES SCOTT HAY
2nd Battalion King's Own Scottish Borderers
Died on Tuesday 15th December 1914, aged 17
Commemorated on Panel 22.

James' signature

James was born in Galashiels, son of George and Janet Hay, of 20 Gullan's Close, Holyrood Road, Edinburgh. James was educated locally and then worked in a local mill.

He volunteered in Galashiels on Monday 25th August 1913 and joined the King's Own Scottish Borderers, Special Reserve. James was a Presbyterian, 5ft 3½in tall, with a 32½in chest, weighed 105lbs, with grey eyes, auburn hair and dots tattooed on the back of his right forearm.

He went out to France on Saturday 5th December 1914, for James' story, and that of the Battalion, see Private Alexander Cameron, above.

He is commemorated on Galashiels War Memorial.

21131 PRIVATE HERBERT HAYHURST
6th Battalion Royal Berkshire Regiment
Died on Tuesday 31st July 1917, aged 17
Commemorated on Panel 45.

Herbert was born at home, fourth son of Christopher Hayhurst, of 51 Raglan Street, Barrow-in-Furness, and the late Frances Hayhurst. He was educated locally.

He volunteered in Reading, Berkshire, and joined the Battalion in June 1917 whilst they were in the rear areas either in reserve or in training.

The Battalion entrained to Cassel from their training grounds on the Somme on Tuesday 3rd July and were provided with billets in Steenvoorde. Whilst there they undertook specialist training for the part they would play at the opening of the Third Battle of Ypres.

The Battalion marched to Reninghelst on Saturday 28th July and the next day to 'Canal Reserve Camp' in Ouderdom, where the men were fully equipped for the attack. The offensive began in the early hours of Tuesday 31st July, the Battalion attacked from the Menin Road towards Polygon Wood, having to first pass through 'Shrewsbury Forest', 'Inverness Copse' and 'Glencorse Wood'. During the advance, Herbert was killed.

15469 PRIVATE
CHARLES HENRY HAYNES
15th Battalion Canadian Infantry
(Central Ontario Regiment)
Died on Saturday 3rd June 1916, aged 17
Commemorated on Panel 24.

Charles' signature

Charles was born in Liverpool, second son of Agnes Ford (formerly Haynes), of Sea Grange, Marine Parade, Tankerton, Whitstable, Kent, and the late Charles Henry Haynes.

He volunteered in Valcartier, Province of Quebec, on Thursday 24th September 1914, where he claimed to have been born on Thursday 16th January 1896 and was working as a jeweller. Charles was 5ft 7½in tall, with a 37in chest, a fair complexion, light blue eyes, fair coloured hair and five vaccination marks his left arm. He trained with the Battalion until they sailed to England in October 1914 and sent for training on Salisbury Plain. During the early hours of Thursday 11th February 1915 Charles marched to Amesbury Station and entrained for Avonmouth. He embarked on *SS Mount Temple* before lunchtime and sailed through rough seas to St Nazaire where he arrived on Monday 15th. At 7.30pm he entrained for Hazebrouck, a long and tiring journey. He marched from the station at 9.30pm on Wednesday 17th to bivouac in the hospital. Following a good nights' rest the march continued at 10.30am along the pavé to Caëstre where he arrived at 3.30pm. Charles remained in the village until moving to billets in Armentières on Tuesday 23rd from where he was sent into the trenches attached to experienced troops for practical training.

Charles packed his kit during the morning of Tuesday 2nd March and in the afternoon marched towards the battlefield. He rested overnight in Bac St Maur where, the next morning, General Sir Edwin Alderson inspected the Battalion. In the afternoon Charles moved onto Pointe de Justice where he remained until 9.30pm on Saturday 6th when the Battalion went into the trenches at Rue Petillon for his first tour of duty. Throughout the next day they experienced an artillery duel with the British scoring a direct hit on a German observation tower at Fromelles, much to the delight of everyone. The Colonel decided that the glengarries worn by all ranks attracted too much attention from the German snipers and gave them clear targets so ordered that 'Tam O'Shanters' should be worn in the future. He also ordered that all the officers must ensure their men removed their boots, putties and socks once a day and dry them off to help prevent trench foot. Shelling

continued every day and at 3.30pm on Monday 8th the Headquarters was hit by a 4in shell that cracked the roof but did little damage, and upon inspection it was noted that the area was strewn with duds. The tour of duty ended on Tuesday 9th and they marched to Rue du Quesne for some rest, however at midnight the Battalion was stood to so they could support the Battle of Neuve Chapelle. At 5.30am Charles blew his bugle to signal the Battalion moving off to its allotted position near Rue de Tilloy. Throughout the day Charles waited, chatting with his mates as the battle raged close by but the Battalion was not required and at 5.30pm they returned to their billets. At 5.00am Charles paraded and was to have returned to the support trenches but the order was cancelled so during the day was taken with his platoon to the baths on the Sailly to Bac St Maur road where he was able to clean up. The Battalion returned to front line duty on Saturday 13th for a four-day tour.

Training began during the last week of March that continued until moving to Cassel on Wednesday 7th April, with Headquarters established at Ryveld, and training continued. Although Cassel was not a large town it had a sufficiency of bars, estaminets and other distractions that were enjoyed by Charles and his chums — so much that the Colonel ordered that no-one was allowed to visit the town after 8.00pm!

Charles marched to Watou on Thursday 15th and the next day on to Abeele where he was collected by a motorised omnibus and driven to Poperinghe. A tiresome march over the pavé to Ypres followed and Charles was billeted in the town. The Colonel was concerned by the constant aerial activity over the town so ordered that the men should not congregate in the streets if an enemy aeroplane was spotted. During the second evening Charles was in the town the most tremendous explosion shook his billet and nearly deafened him. Towards Hill 60 it looked like Dante's 'Inferno' as the mines blew all manner of detritus high in the air, the artillery duel was in full swing coupled with the firing of thousands of rounds every minute. Ypres began to come under heavier shellfire from Monday 19th and one of Charles' officers, Lieutenant Gibson, was hit by a shell splinter in the leg and Captain Turnbull Warren was killed in the market square by the Cloth Hall on Tuesday 20th (he is buried in Ypres Reservoir Cemetery). At 8.00pm that evening the Battalion marched to relieve the 16th Battalion in the trenches in front of St Julien not knowing what was about to befall them.

At 5.00pm on Thursday 22nd the Germans launched their gas attack against the Trench Colonial troops to the left of the Battalion's position. It was not long before Headquarters was swarming with badly wounded and terrified Turcos. The Second Battle of Ypres had begun. Charles marched to a camp halfway between Ypres and Vlamertinghe at 2.00am on Monday 26th for a short rest and 8.00am marched to reserve at La Brique. Orders were received for the Battalion to move forward to the front line at Wieltje at 2.30pm where they came under heavy shellfire during the twenty-four hours they remained there. After a day of rest on the Ypres to Poperinghe road Charles was sent to serve at St Jan, close to No 4 Pontoon Bridge.

Charles was relieved from the Salient on Tuesday 4th May and marched at 6.30pm to billets near Bailleul. Over the next eleven days he undertook training and went out on route marches. The town was bustling with life that provided many enjoyable distractions for Charles and his friends. He moved to Rubecq on Saturday 15th for four days then marched to the trenches near Richebourg in the Festubert sector. The Battalion attacked the enemy on Thursday 20th and Charles was out rescuing the many wounded and helping to take them to the Field Dressing Station. The tour of duty ended late on Saturday 22nd and the Battalion marched to billets in Essars where all ranks got some much-needed rest for four days before returning to the trenches of Festubert.

The Battalion was sent to Oblighem on Tuesday 1st June where the Colonel began to reorganise and the men were able to have a hot bath. They moved to Le Preole, followed by Le Croix de Fer, for training. The Battalion was sent into the reserve trenches at Givenchy for two days on Wednesday 23rd June. Charles began a series of marches that took him back to Bailleul before crossing the border to the Ploegsteert sector where he once again began training, this time at 'Lampernisse Farm'.

Charles was sent out on fatigues digging trenches from Monday 5th July and after four days moved into reserve whilst billeted at La Grande Munque Farm. He had expected to have some rest but the next day he was stood to as a German attack was expected but it did not develop and late in the day was able to relax. The Battalion returned to the front line on Thursday 15th where they constructed new dugouts, strengthened a number of sniper posts and widened the communication trenches. The Battalion was relieved on Monday 19th and sent to 'The Piggeries' to be held in reserve. The Right Honourable Sir Robert Borden inspected the Battalion on Wednesday 21st and at 5.00pm marched to 'Aldershot Camp', Neuve Eglise, where the next day a draft of one hundred and ninety men arrived. The new men were given a hearty welcome and throughout the evening news from Canada and England was given and stories of fighting in the trenches were swapped. Charles went out on fatigues or was undertook training. The

Battalion returned to the front line once again on Thursday 29th in Ploegsteert Wood for a four-day tour and when relieved went into reserve at La Grande Munque Farm. Charles was given some rest before joining a working party.

The Battalion moved to a new position at Hill 63 on Friday 6th August for five days fatigues then marched to 'Aldershot Camp'. The Battalion went into the trenches near 'Ration Farm' from Thursday 19th from where they watched Messines Church being shelled on Saturday 21st that was used as an observation post by the Germans. This pattern of front line duty and fatigues whilst in reserve continued in the Ploegsteert to Messines sector, with considerable amount of time billets being provided in 'Red Lodge' or in Neuve Eglise. Charles moved to Loker on Tuesday 21st September to undertake fatigues on the railway system in front of Kemmel before returning to front line duties at Ploegsteert. Christmas Day was spent in Brigade Reserve in 'Red Lodge' returning to the front line on Wednesday 29th December.

A break from working at the front came on Tuesday 1st February 1916 when Charles marched from 'Red Lodge' to billets in Méteren. The next day he was able to settle down with his chums, relax and enjoy some much needed rest. Early on Thursday 3rd Charles paraded for a kit inspection and in the afternoon the officers toured the billets to ensure they were in good order then on Friday 4th training began. Charles attended Divine Service at 11.30am on Sunday 6th but in the afternoon he was free to spend it with his friends before going into Bailleul to enjoy a concert in the evening. After three weeks Charles returned to billets in 'Kortepyp Huts' and late on Monday 21st marched to the trenches. Tours of duty continued until Saturday 25th March when Charles marched back for rest and training in Méteren for three days then moved to 'Scottish Lines'. The Battalion marched to 'Dickebusch Huts' on Saturday 1st April from where he went into the front line that was significantly livelier that at Ploegsteert. Whilst in the line five German snipers were bagged and a number of their periscopes destroyed. Following a busy tour of duty Charles spent a few days training, followed by reserve before moving to 'Bedford House' on Monday 17th. Two weeks in Brigade Support followed then Charles marched to 'Connaught Lines' on Wednesday 3rd May from where he went into Poperinghe the next day for a hot bath. General Currie visited the Battalion on Friday 5th and carried out an inspection. Various sporting events were organised on Sunday 7th and Monday 8th and after a day of rest on 9th Charles marched to 'Dickebusch Huts' to undertake fatigues. Late on Thursday 18th he returned to the trenches in front of Hill 60 where the aircraft from both sides were constantly patrolling in significant numbers and engaging in constant dog-fights. A significant artillery duel began at 9.20am on Wednesday 24th. As on the previous tour of duty the Battalion snipers did good work destroying, on average, six enemy periscopes a day. The tour ended late on Friday 26th and Charles marched to 'Scottish Lines' where the next evening a band concert was organised. A Memorial Service was held on Sunday 28th for the Battalion's Colonel, William Renwick Marshall, DSO, who was shot by a sniper and died on Friday 19th, he is buried in Lijssenthoek Military Cemetery. Charles enjoyed a sports afternoon on Monday 29th, a concert given by the 3rd Battalion band the next evening and a baseball match against the 14th Battalion on Wednesday 31st. After another baseball game on Friday 2nd June Charles returned to 'Scottish Lines' then moved into the trenches in front of 'Observatory Ridge Road' where he arrived at 2.00am on Saturday 3rd. He prepared to take part in an attack on 'Mount Sorrel'. Following a heavy barrage of the enemy lines six green rockets were sent up that was the signal for Charles and his comrades to charge forward. The action was described by the Battalion Diary: "Formation was completed and advance to position of attack at 2.15a.m. It was broad daylight and as soon as the line started the enemy opened with artillery. Their barrage and curtain fire was simply wonderful. The lines of men advanced as steadily as if on parade and in spite of heavy artillery and machine gun fire the Battalion arrived at the point a little east of Valley Cottages with only a few casualties. For about 100 yards until we reached our position the fire was most severe and the number of casualties increased and by this time reached 6 Officers and 100 Other Ranks. ... The artillery fire increased and at times our own shells were dropping in our new positions where the men were digging in. The number of casualties increased._

Our artillery opened with such a light bombardment we could not believe it was the main one until the rockets were shot up from Brigade. These did not show green and were not observed, only showing like a streak of smoke.

The real attack at 8.35a.m.

Upon the signal being given the Officers and men behaved most courageously immediately getting out, forming line and rushed forward in the face of a perfect HELL of artillery and machine gun fire. It did not seem possible that anything could live through it the right of the line was temporarily held up by a thick hedge and before away was made through it the first line were all shot down. 2nd and 3rd line came up and kept right on. On the left the men took advantage of a little dead ground and rushed right on getting as far as I.24.o.6.1. During the whole of this time the enemy maintained an intense artillery and M.G. fire on our men and on the communication trenches and ground in rear. M.G. were enfilading us heavily from the Snout and

it soon became apparent the objective could not be reached. Accordingly our men fell back to the starting point and dug themselves in along the line."

It will not be know exactly how or when in the action Charles was killed.

1330 PRIVATE MICHAEL JAMES HEALY
6th Battalion Connaught Rangers
Died on Monday 4th June 1917, aged 17
Commemorated on Panel 42.

Michael was born in Cork, Ireland, son of Peter and Margaret M Healy, of New York City, USA.
He enlisted in Cork and trained with the Battalion in 'Kilworth Camp', County Cork, until moving to 'Blackdown Camp', Aldershot, Hampshire, in August 1915. Michael left with the Battalion for Farnborough Station on Friday 17th December and entrained to Southampton. He embarked for Le Havre where he arrived the next day. Michael marched to the station where he entrained for the long and tiring journey through northern France to Hesdigneul near Béthune. From Christmas Eve the Battalion began to send group of men into the front line attached to battle-hardened troops for practical experience, and the rest of the Battalion was sent out on fatigues.
The Battalion went into the line for the first time in its own right on Wednesday 26th January 1916 on the old Loos battlefield in the 'Puits No 14' sector. The enemy artillery began a heavy bombardment of the sector and next day they mounted an attack that was successfully repulsed. Michael took cover throughout Friday 28th as the German artillery continued to concentrate their fire on the line but on Saturday 29th and Sunday 30th the sector quietened down. His first tour of duty ended in the early hours of Monday 31st and he was sent into reserve at Philosophe. The majority of February was spent training and resting behind the lines. General Sir Hubert Gough inspected the Brigade on Monday 21st February and General Sir Charles Monro undertook an inspection on Friday 25th in a blizzard!
Michael moved to Annequin on Tuesday 29th from where he was sent on fatigues before returning to the line at Hulluch. He remained on tours of duty for two weeks, followed by two weeks training in Allouagne before returning to the trenches. The Battalion remained on the Loos battlefield in the line, on fatigues or training until Monday 28th August when they were relieved and marched to Marles-les-Mines, arriving at 8.00pm the next day. After spending time at Bas Rieux, Chocques, they arrived in Méaulte on Thursday 31st August.
From Méaulte they went into the trenches at Guillemont

where they came under heavy shell fire. The Battalion received orders on Saturday 2nd September that they would participate in an attack on Guillemont. Plans were prepared and at 5.00am the next morning they were in position to await the order to attack. An artillery duel began at 8.00am with much damage being caused by the British artillery on 'Rim Trench' held by 'C' Company, and nearly two hundred casualties had been taken by noon. The platoons designated to be in the first wave were so badly cut up that the second wave platoons took their place and they went forward in a series of waves. The Colonel, John Lenox-Conyngham, led from the front and was the first over the top, he was killed almost immediately (he is buried in Carnoy Military Cemetery).

One of the NCO's had an account printed in 'The Freeman's Journal' of Monday 18th September 1916 recorded: "The position we had to carry was bristling with machine-guns. They sent bullets at us in shovelfuls, it seemed. Our commander stepped out and pointed to the position with his cane. 'That, Connaught Rangers, is what you have got to take,' was all he said. We said nothing for reply, but we looked enough to satisfy him we would do all that was expected of us."

A further attack was planned for Saturday 9th September that was recorded by Lieutenant Colonel Rowland Charles Feilding: "From my observation of the terrific fire which the leading companies encountered on leaving their trench, directed not only from the German trench in front, but from numerous shell-holes, I do not believe it would have been possible to do more than they accomplished. Officers and Non-commissioned Officers who actually saw the German trench report that it had escaped our preliminary bombardment almost entirely and that it was thickly manned." Following the failure of the attack some relief was had late on Sunday 10th at 'Carnoy Craters', and two days later Michael marched to Vaux-sur-Somme. After a week he moved to Huppy for a week of training then marched to Abbeville. He entrained to Bailleul and marched to billets at Fonatine Houck, via Méteren.

Michael marched across the border to Belgium into a hutted camp at Loker on Sunday 24th September. He began serving in the line at Vierstraat for a tour of duty from Wednesday 27th. He was then sent out with a working party to dig shelters at 'Siege Farm'. From Thursday 5th to Thursday 12th October Michael rested in billets with his comrades then went on his first tour of duty between 'Turner's Town' and 'Fort Halifax' with his newly perfected respirator. His next tour of duty was at 'Siege Farm' and then was sent to a tented camp at 'Butterfly Farm' where he undertook fatigues. From Sunday 5th to Tuesday 14th November Michael was sent for training whilst based in the hutted 'Curragh Camp'

in Loker. Tours of duty continued for a further month, Michael spent a week in billets at 'Canada Corner' near Loker until Wednesday 20th December when he went back to the trenches. He spent Christmas in the front line but although activity from both sides was limited there was no truce. Michael was relieved on Thursday 28th and two days later enjoyed a delayed Christmas in 'Derry Huts'.

Late on Friday 5th January 1917 Michael once again was in the trenches and on Sunday 7th the Germans began an intense bombardment. At 4.30am enemy infantry were spotted leaving their trenches; Michael and his comrades opened rapid fire that repulsed the attack. Throughout the tour the artillery from each side bombarded the front lines which caused considerable damage.

Michael went into the front line on Monday 29th January where the artillery remained active. At 5.15am on Thursday 1st February the Germans began to shell the front line with high explosives and trench mortars, then launched an attack. The enemy were camouflaged in white clothing but could be easily spotted as Michael fired at them. The British artillery began shelling the enemy at 5.25am but shortly afterwards the whole sector quietened down. Another exchange of artillery fire began from 9.30am until 10.15am. Michael was relieved on Friday 2nd and sent to rest in Kemmel Château. Lieutenant Colonel Feilding wrote of the weather conditions in early February: "It was and had been like the arctic, with a biting east wind. The breastworks in the trenches were in a very bad state, frozen hard as stone with the ground white with snow. The troops had to spend four days and nights at a time in the trenches in the paralysing cold, without exercise or heat."

Michael went into Divisional Reserve at 'Kemmel Shelters' on Tuesday 6th. At 10.30am German 5.9 howitzers began to shell the position whilst Michael was resting in his hut. He remained serving in the sector until the end of March when he moved to serve in the Vierstraat sector.

The Battalion prepared to take part in an action on the Wytschaete and was sent to St Omer on Thursday 17th May for special training on a model of the area that would be attacked. Michael took part in a full dress rehearsal in front of senior officers on Saturday 26th.

Michael was destined not to take part in the major assault. He had returned to the front line at Vierstraat on Saturday 2nd June where he took part in a raid on Monday 4th at 'Petit Bois' where he was one of the six men killed.

412475 PRIVATE
HAROLD ALBERT HENRY
26th Battalion Canadian Infantry
(New Brunswick Regiment)
Died on Sunday 18th June 1916, aged 16
Commemorated on Panel 26.

Harold Henry

Henry's signature

Harold was born at home, son of William and Margaret Elizabeth Henry, of 143 London Street, Peterborough, Ontario. He was educated locally.

Harold volunteered at Peterborough on Tuesday 23rd February 1915 and claimed to have been born on Saturday 7th November 1896. He was a Presbyterian, 5ft 3in tall, a 35in chest, a fair complexion, brown eyes, with dark brown hair.

Harold was sent for training prior to sailing to England on *HMT Caledonia*, arriving in Devonport

HMT Caledonia

on Thursday 24th June 1915. Harold entrained for a camp in East Sandling, Kent. He continued to train until Wednesday 15th September when he marched to Folkestone Docks and sailed to Boulogne. After a night in camp at Ostrohove Harold entrained to Wizernes where they bivouacked overnight before being sent to billets near Hazebrouck. Generals Alderson, Currie and Turner, accompanied by HRH Prince Arthur of Connaught, inspected the Battalion on Sunday 19th. The move into Belgium began on Tuesday 21st when they initially moved to Bailleul before moving to *'Hyde Park Corner'* and finally to billets on the Scherpenberg. Harold's first tour of duty took place on Tuesday 28th near Kemmel. He continued on tours of duty and served in the front during Christmas. The Germans attempted to fraternize but all efforts were rejected, in Harold's line there was no repetition of the *'Christmas Truce'* of 1914, but it was a very quiet day in the trenches. *'Normal service'* returned on Boxing Day with shelling from both sides of the line.

He was relieved on New Year's Eve and on New Year's Day was taken to the baths at Westoutre — during the afternoon the officers enjoyed a lecture by Colonel Fotheringham on trench foot. Harold took part in a practice attack on Monday 3rd January 1917 using the taped trenches along the Westoutre to Berthen road. He undertook gas helmet drill before being sent to relieve the 22nd Battalion on Wednesday 5th. He continued to serve in the sector for the next month and from February was based in the *'RE Farm'* sector where he undertook

fatigues, trained and tours of duty in the line. Harold spent a week training in Reninghelst in April until taking the line at St Eloi from Wednesday 12th. For the next two months he continued the usual routine of front line duties and training until he was sent to the Salient on Thursday 8th June when the Battalion moved to *'Railway Dugouts'*, *'Blauwepoort Farm'* and *'Woodcote Farm'*. From there they relieved the 1st Canadian Battalion in support at Hill 60 and *'Square Wood'*. Harold's last period of rest commenced on Sunday 11th when he was sent to *'Dickebusch Huts'* for three days. He returned to the line around Hill 62 taking the line from *'Hedge Street'* to *'Vigo'*. From Thursday 15th the weather improved with the German artillery increasing daily the intensity of its bombardment. Harold was killed by shellfire on Sunday 18th.

16423 PRIVATE HARRY HILL
No 3 Company, 3rd Battalion Royal Fusiliers
Died on Monday 3rd May 1915, aged 17
Commemorated on Panel 8.

Harry was born in Acton, second son of Peter and Mary Ann Hill, of 5 Mills Cottages, Acton Green, Chiswick, London.

He enlisted in Shepherd's Bush, London, and went out to France on Wednesday 24th February 1915. Harry undertook tours of duty in the trenches without being involved in any particular action until he was in the front line when the Germans launched the first gas attack on Thursday 22nd April 1915 and saw its horrific consequences. Terrible for anyone but one can only imagine what such a young, and relatively innocent, mind could conceive and comprehend. Another gas attack was launched on Saturday 24th whilst he was in the line at Gravenstafel that was followed by a significant attack. The German shelling was fierce and they were able to advance around to the left rear of the Battalion and enfilade them. Harry remained fighting on the battlefield until he was killed during a retirement and shortly before the Battalion was relieved.

949 SAPPER
RICHARD BENJAMIN HILLS
12th Field Company Australian Engineers
Died on Thursday 7th February 1918, aged 17
Commemorated on Panel 7.

R. B. Hills.

Richard's signature

Richard was born in Newcastle, New South Wales, son of William and Harriett Hills of 193 Edgecliff Road, Woollahra, New

South Wales, his father died in 1918.

He volunteered in Victoria Barracks, New South Wales, on Thursday 8th March 1917 when he claimed to be 18 years and 4½ months old, worked as a cadet journalist and had been a member of Waverley Cadets. Richard was a Methodist, 5ft 7in tall, with a 31½in chest, weighed 136lbs, had a dark complexion, brown eyes, black hair, with moles on his abdomen and left buttock, and a scar on the back of his left knee. His mother had signed a letter of consent on Friday 2nd March for Richard to give to the authorities when he enlisted.

He embarked in Sydney on the *HMAT Hororata* on Thursday 14th June 1917 and sailed to Liverpool where he disembarked on Sunday 26th August. Richard was sent to train at Parkhouse as a member of the First Corps Cyclist Battalion where he transferred to the Engineers on Thursday 27th September in Brightlingsea, Essex. He sailed from Southampton on Tuesday 8th January 1918 for France and joined the 12th Company in the field on Sunday 13th. Richard was mortally wounded on Thursday 7th February and died shortly afterward. His grave was subsequently lost, his brother CSM F Hills of the 9th Battalion found his grave at the end of the war at Hollebeke. He wrote on Wednesday 19th November 1918 to the Records Department asking if the grave was that of his brother, a record of the reply is not available but it clearly was Richard's grave. Sadly it would appear that due to some administrative error, or similar, that allowed Richard's not to be properly recorded.

His mother, Mrs Harriett Hills, received his personal possessions that included two razors, scissors, wallet, cards, fountain pen in case, letters, two notebooks, YMCA wallet, metal wrist watch, metal cigarette case, French book, photographs, Bible and a leather writing pad. She also received his British War Medal no 59137, Victory Medal no 58057 and his Memorial Plaque and Scroll no 301761.

Y/1109 RIFLEMAN
ARTHUR ROBERT HILSON
(SERVED AS DANIEL CLARKE)
4th Battalion King's Royal Rifle Corps
Died on Monday 10th May 1915, aged 16
Commemorated on Panel 53.

Arthur was born in St Barnabas, Birmingham, son of Arthur Hilson, of 184 Runcorn Road, Sparkbrook, Birmingham. He was educated locally.

He enlisted under the name of Daniel Clarke in Birmingham. After training Arthur was sent out to France on Wednesday 17th February 1915 then entrained to Belgium.

He joined the Battalion in the southern sector of the Salient where conditions in the front line were dreadful: the trenches were totally water-logged; they could only be reached at night as no communication trenches existed. Many of Arthur's comrades suffered very badly from trench foot.

Arthur served at Polygon Wood in mid-April 1915 from where he was sent to Hill 60 where he was engaged in a furious attack and counter-attack. On Saturday 8th May the German artillery intensified. The next day it grew stronger and their infantry attack was repulsed. The Battalion's front line trenches were totally obliterated. However they were able to hang on and repulsed each attack. A further attack was made during which Arthur was killed on Monday 10th.

16049 PRIVATE HERBERT HINDLEY
5th Battalion King's Shropshire Light Infantry
Died on Saturday 25th September 1915, aged 17
Commemorated on Panel 49.

Herbert was born in Ditton, Lancashire, second son of Agur Abner Hindley and Jane Alice Hindley, of 45 Mount Croft, Holcroft Lane, Culcheth, Warrington, Lancashire.

He volunteered in Middleton and went out to France on Saturday 22nd May 1915. For Herbert's story and that of the Battalion until Tuesday 3rd August, see Private Leonard Preece below.

Herbert continued to serve at Hooge after Leonard was killed and took part in a successful attack on Monday 9th August that recaptured the crater and a number of enemy trenches. Late on Tuesday 10th Herbert was relieved and sent to a bivouac north of Brandhoek where he had two weeks rest. He undertook a further four-day tour of duty before returning to the bivouac for a week. Whilst in bivouac a number of drafts arrived that brought the Battalion up to strength.

General Sir Hubert Plumer inspected the Battalion on Friday 17th September whilst the Battalion was rehearsing for the forthcoming attack. Herbert left by train for Ypres late on Thursday 23rd and then marched to 'Railway Wood' where he arrived in the early hours of the next morning. It was not long before the German artillery began to bombard the area heavily from 3.50am to 4.20am but an intermittent artillery duel continued throughout the day whilst he waited in the trenches. The next morning another bombardment began for fifteen minutes at 3.50am and at 4.20am the whistles were blown. Herbert rose from his trench and clambered into No Man's Land. It went well and the Battalion's objectives were achieved but the supporting battalions on each flank were not so successful. The enemy mounted a counter-attack with fresh troops and in the fierce battle Herbert was killed.

20452 PRIVATE HARRY HIRST
1st Battalion King's Own Yorkshire Light Infantry
Died on Saturday 8th May 1915, aged 17
Commemorated on Panel 47.

Harry was born in Woolley, Yorkshire, eldest son of Mary Hirst, of 14 Smithies Moor Lane, Birstall, Leeds, and the late Bennett Hirst.
He went out to France on Wednesday 7th April 1915. For Harry's story and that of the Battalion see Lieutenant James Ferguson above.

13711 PRIVATE ALBERT HIVES
3rd Battalion Royal Fusiliers
Died on Monday 26th April 1915, aged 16
Commemorated on Panel 6.

Albert was born in Dalston, son of Mrs M A Southam, of 14 Alexandra Road, Heeley, Sheffield.
Albert enlisted in Stratford and was sent for training before leaving for the front, joining the Battalion with a draft. For his story see Private Harry Hill, above.

10081 PRIVATE
WILLIAM ERNEST HOLBOROW
2nd Battalion Gloucestershire Regiment
Died on Monday 10th May 1915, aged 17
Commemorated on Panel 22.

William was born at home, son of George and Ellen Holborow, of Rowden Hazel Wood, Nailsworth, Gloucestershire.
He volunteered in Stroud, Gloucestershire, and went out to France on Thursday 25th March 1915. He joined the Battalion whilst they were in camp in Dickebusch. In early April William was moved to the Salient along the Menin Road. He was at the front on Thursday 22nd when the Germans launched their gas attack, as recorded in the Battalion Diary: *"At 12 midnight received wire from Brigade saying French line about Square C5 was broken*

and fell back about 1,000 yards. Canadian left brigade fell back on account of this. French counter-attack ordered from the direction of Boesinghe." At 4.00am on Saturday 24th William came under heavy rifle fire when the German artillery started to bombard from 'Stirling Castle' to 'Sanctuary Wood' however his position was only under fire for an hour. At 2.00pm William was ordered to leave his line and parade ready to march to Potijze. It was a difficult march as during daylight the Battalion made an ideal target for the German artillery. They passed the British artillery who had their guns pointing both north and south such was their position and the field of fire they had to reach. William remained in reserve but was not sent into the line but later in the evening returned to 'Sanctuary Wood'. After a day resting the same orders were received and they were sent to Potijze, again under heavy artillery fire, only to be returned without seeing action. The Battalion relieved the Argyll and Sutherland Highlanders and the Royal Scots during the night of Wednesday 28th where they remained until being ordered to retire to the old line on Monday 3rd May. The next day the Germans advanced on their line in 'Stirling Castle Wood' and after accounting for a large number of the attackers they captured the area that had been previously evacuated. For the next four days a vicious battle continued.

At 7.00am on Saturday 8th May an intense artillery bombardment commenced along the whole sector but the German infantry did not follow-up with an attack. At 6.30am the next morning the bombardment recommenced on their line and the situation became precarious, William and 'C' Company had taken the brunt of the artillery. At 7.15am the German infantry attacked from 'Stirling Castle'. A series of counter-attacks were mounted most of which ended in failure and casualties in the Battalion were particularly heavy. William was relieved to the GHQ line where he set about improving the line and was sent out to restore the barbed wire. William was killed by a sniper whilst in No Man's Land.

His brother, Stoker 1st Class Charles Holborow, died on HMS Black Prince on Wednesday 31st May 1916 and is commemorated on Portsmouth Naval Memorial. William and Charles are commemorated on the Nailsworth and the Woodchester War Memorials.

... an attack on the German front line

12008 RIFLEMAN HARRY HOLLOWS
3rd Battalion King's Royal Rifle Corps
Died on Monday 10th May 1915, aged 16
Commemorated on Panel 53.

Harry's signature

Harry was born at Hollins Grove, Darwen, second son of Edwin and Helen Hollows, of 486 Blackburn Road, Darwen, Lancashire. He was educated locally and was then employed as a weaver.

He enlisted in Blackburn, Lancashire, on Wednesday 9th September 1914 and was sent to Winchester, Hampshire, on Wednesday 30th. Harry was 5ft 6¼in tall, had a 34in chest and weighed 135lbs.

Harry trained with the 6th Battalion from Friday 16th October. He went out to France with a draft then onward to the Salient joining them on Tuesday 26th January 1915. He was allocated to his platoon and after a little training began tours of duty.

At the end of March 1915 the Battalion was in reserve in billets at Poperinghe. Harry was sent to Polygon Wood in mid-April and undertook a series of tours of duty with billets provided in shell-damaged Ypres. In early May he was sent to Hill 60 where the Battalion came under heavy fire and considerable time was spent in reconstructing the trenches and consolidating their position. The Germans commenced a significant counter-attack on Sunday 9th May and after laying down a barrage they mounted an unsuccessful attack. The Germans attacked again the next day and whilst defending the line, Harry was killed.

... in billets with a local family

11775 PRIVATE ALFRED HOLOHAN
'B' Company, 2nd Battalion Royal Dublin Fusiliers
Died on Sunday 9th May 1915, aged 17
Commemorated on Panel 46.

Alfred was born at home, son of James and Jessie Holohan, of 40 Marlborough Street, Dublin.

He volunteered in Dublin and went out to France on Monday 3rd May 1915. He entrained to the Ypres Salient where the Battalion was engaged in fierce fighting during the Second Battle of Ypres. On his first tour of duty and after only thirty-six hours in the trenches Alfred was killed.

A/3464 RIFLEMAN JOHN EDWIN HOLTOM
8th Battalion King's Royal Rifle Corps
Died on Friday 30th July 1915, aged 17
Commemorated on Panel 53.

John was born at home, fourth son of Maria Holtom, of 53, Essington Street, Ladywood, Birmingham, and the late William Richard Holtom.

He volunteered in Birmingham and went out to France on Wednesday 19th May 1915. For John's story and that of the Battalion see Rifleman Herbert Ashdown, above.

17280 PRIVATE GEORGE HOOD
2nd Battalion Duke of Cornwall's Light Infantry
Died on Wednesday 28th April 1915, aged 17
Commemorated on Panel 20.

George was born at home, eldest son of Margaret Louisa Aldridge (formerly Hood), of 127 Fairbridge Road, Upper Holloway, London, and the late Daniel Hood.

He volunteered in Poplar, London, went out to France on Thursday 1st April 1915 to join the Battalion in Ypres the next day. The Battalion was resting amongst the badly damaged buildings until the evening when they marched through the Menin Gate into 'Sanctuary Wood' via Potijze and Hooge. George undertook a series of tours of duty and during the attack on Hill 60 the Battalion was badly shelled losing a dozen men during Saturday 17th and Sunday 18th April. Late on Monday 19th George was relieved and sent to billets in Ypres. The next morning a shell landed on a billet that killed six and injured thirteen; as a result everyone was moved into safer dugouts in the ramparts before being sent to bivouac in the fields adjacent to the town. George was taken into the town on Thursday 22nd for a bath before being sent to bivouac on the Ypres to Brielen road. At 5.00pm the German artillery onslaught began and chlorine gas shells rained down on the French colonial troops: *"What followed almost defies description. The effect of these poisonous gases was so virulent as to render the whole of the line held by the French division ... practically incapable of any action at all. It was at first impossible for anyone to realize what had happened at all. The smoke and fumes hid everything from sight and hundreds of men were thrown into a comatose or dying condition, and within an hour the whole position had to be abandoned together with about fifty guns."*

The Battalion witnessed the consequences: *"French stragglers from the north started coming in, saying the Zouaves had been attacked with asphyxiating gas and that there had been a general French retirement in consequence on a wide front in the direction of Pilkem and Langemarck."* At 2.30am on Friday 23rd George was ordered to Potijze, arriving two hours later where he was ordered to dig in west of Wieltje. Throughout the night ten Battalions moved into the line to plug the gap. Fortunately the Germans had not pressed their attack home because Ypres had been, for many hours, completely exposed and could have been taken. At the request of General Ferdinand Foch an attack on the area between *'Kitchener's Wood'* (Bois des Cuisinières) and the Yser Canal was mounted. The Battalion managed to reach *'Turco Farm'* where a German observer remained at his post directing the artillery until he was killed, telephone in hand. At 9.00pm the Battalion was forced to retire to *'Foch Farm'* where they remained until 3.00am on Monday 26th when they were relieved and returned to Potijze Château. Throughout Wednesday 28th the Battalion remained in the support trenches that came under shellfire and George was killed.

12835 PRIVATE
FREDERICK ARCHIBALD HORNSEY
2nd Regiment (Infantry) South African Infantry
Died on Friday 12th April 1918, aged 17
Commemorated on Panel 15.

Frederick was the son of Mrs M C Mcfarlane Hornsey, of 9 Thrush Road, Stamford Hill, Durban, Natal, and the late Serjeant Archibald C Hornsey ('C' Company 2nd Regiment South African Infantry).
For his story, see Private John Forsyth-Ingram, below. Frederick survived only a few hours longer than John.

16817 PRIVATE FRANK HOWARD
2nd Battalion Northumberland Fusiliers
Died on Monday 24th May 1915, aged 17
Commemorated on Panel 12.

Frank was born in Redford, Nottinghamshire, son of John and Ada Howard, of Dogdyke Bank, Dogdyke, Lincoln.
He volunteered in Sheffield and went out to France on Wednesday 10th March 1915 to join the Battalion in billets in Bailleul. The Battalion had sustained heavy casualties during an attack on Friday 12th at Wulverghem. Frank undertook fatigues each night carrying supplies to the front line from his billets in either, Bailleul, Loker or St Jans Capel. General

Sir Horace Smith-Dorrien inspected the Battalion on Wednesday 7th April and on Tuesday 13th he marched to a camp at Vlamertinghe. After two days rest Frank began his first tour of duty in the trenches at Broodseinde. A large bombardment began in the sector on Saturday 17th and an attack was anticipated. A short, sharp, engagement followed with each side bombing the other. After two days in the front line Frank returned to reserve.
He was in a hutted camp on Thursday 22nd when the Second Battle of Ypres began and he could clearly see Ypres being bombarded and in flames. Late in the evening the Battalion was ordered back into the line at Broodseinde but the main fighting was taking place to his left. The Battalion was ordered to help support the Canadians at St Julien so a detachment was sent to the sound of the guns and the smell of gas. Due to the pressure on the line during Monday 26th a retirement was ordered to straighten the line. Frank witnessed the ghastly sight of the effects of the gas attacks, as twisted bodies of men and animals littered the area. Early on Monday 3rd May he arrived for some rest in camp near Vlamertinghe. At 9.00pm on Tuesday 4th May Frank was ordered up into the line at Wieltje at *'Mouse Trap Farm'*. He endured for three days a heavy German barrage in very exposed positions. At 8.30am on Saturday 8th the grey masses of the German infantry were seen moving forward with attacks following throughout the morning.
Frank was in camp in Vlamertinghe when at dawn on Monday 24th (Whit Monday) the enemy launched a gas attack that was followed by an infantry attack. Frank marched with his platoon at noon towards the battlefield to take part in a counter-attack. They went around to the south of Ypres and via *'Hell Fire Corner'* into the trenches. The Company Commanders moved their men into the assault trenches where they led the Battalion over the top at 2.45pm. They did not get far until Frank fell dead on the battlefield.

10373 RIFLEMAN EDWARD HUDSON
2nd Battalion Royal Irish Rifles
Died on Wednesday 16th June 1915, aged 17
Commemorated on Panel 40.

Edward was born at home, son of Mrs Margaret McGee, of 9 Lower Clanbrassil Street, Dublin.
He volunteered in Dublin and went out to France on Saturday 5th December 1914 to join the Battalion in the Wytschaete sector with a draft. Edward was soon detailed to front line duty and spent Christmas in the trenches but the informal Christmas Truce did not take place in his sector. When out of the trenches

he marched to billets behind the line in either Loker, Dranouter or Westoutre. The front line, below the Messines Ridge, continually flooded during the winter, the tenches were in constant need of strengthening and repairing.

At the end of March 1915 Edward went into the line at Voormezeele with billets in La Clytte. His commanding officer, Lieutenant Colonel James Alston, was killed in the firing line on Thursday 15th April whilst looking through a trench periscope. A large number of the Battalion attended his funeral at Dickebusch on Saturday 17th, he now lies in Dickebusch New Military Cemetery.

The attack on Hill 60, a short distance to the left of where Edward served in the trenches, began late on Saturday 17th with the blowing of mines followed by an infantry attack. Fighting increased in intensity in the sector from that moment. Following a gas attack on Hill 60 on Thursday 6th May he marched from 'Canada Huts', Dickebusch, via 'Shrapnel Corner', passing large numbers of wounded at Zillebeke Lake. Battalion Headquarters were established at 'Dormy House' and James was moved into the front line. The tour of duty ended on Wednesday 12th when he marched to camp at La Clytte. He spent the rest of the month in the trenches in front of Kemmel, a very quiet area in comparison to the fighting that was taking place only a few miles to the north around Ypres.

Edward returned to the Salient on Thursday 3rd June when the Battalion was sent to camp southwest of Vlamertinghe. He was sent out on the dangerous duty of fatigues, taking barbed wire to the front line for five days. Edward marched along the road to the shattered ruins of Ypres then down the Menin Gate to 'Birr Cross Roads' to Hooge where he took position in front of 'Cambridge Road'. The tour lasted until late on Friday 11th when Edward went into bivouac for three days rest then arrived in the assembly trenches at 'Witte Poort Farm' late on Tuesday 15th ready to take part in an attack on the Bellewaarde Ridge. From 2.50am to 4.15am a preliminary bombardment pounded the German trenches. The initial waves moved forward well and at speed but it soon broke down in confusion. Edward and his comrades were part of the second wave with the responsibility of supporting and consolidating the captured positions. The enemy was able to reorganise itself; they poured heavy fire on the attacking forces and mounted a series of counter-attacks. At 3.35pm an attack began with Edward charging across the battlefield. All ranks did very well and they kept fighting until the early hours of Thursday 17th. Although some gains were made the main objectives were not taken and it was therefore a failure. During the attack Edward was killed, his body was lost in the subsequent battle.

3011 PRIVATE ABRAHAM HUNTER
1st/8th Battalion Durham Light Infantry
Died on Monday 26th April 1915, aged 17
Commemorated on Panel 36.

Abraham was the son of Mrs Margaret Hunter, of 35 Fleming Street, Teams, Gateshead.
He enlisted in Houghton, County Durham, went out to France on Tuesday 20th April 1915. For Abraham's story, see Private John Winn below.

2337 PRIVATE THOMAS HURLEY
3rd Battalion Monmouthshire Regiment
Died on Friday 7th May 1915, aged 17
Commemorated on Panel 50.

Thomas was the eldest son of Joseph and Alice Hurley, of 5 Western Terrace, Ebbw Vale, Monmouthshire.
He went out to France on Saturday 13th February 1915, for Thomas' story see Private Joe Norton below.

R/11830 RIFLEMAN
ALFRED HENRY EDGAR HUXTABLE
7th Battalion King's Royal Rifle Corps
Died on Friday 6th August 1915, aged 15
Commemorated on Panel 53.

Alfred Henry Edgar Huxtable
Alfred's signature

Alfred was born in Plumstead, second son of Eliza Jane Huxtable, of 17 Alexandra Road, Erith, Kent, and the late Arthur Ernest Huxtable. He was educated locally.

Alfred volunteered in Holborn on Monday 12th April 1915 and was sent for training. He claimed to be 19 years old, working as a reporter. Harry was 5ft 2in tall, with a 33½in chest, weighed 109lbs, had a fresh complexion, fair coloured hair, brown eyes and a vaccination mark on his left arm.

He arrived in Boulogne on Wednesday 19th May 1915 from where he entrained to northern France. Alfred's training continued in preparation for front line duties. In early June he crossed the border to a camp where he was trained for two weeks in trench digging and trench maintenance, before taking the line for the first time. Alfred marched through Ypres, no longer the beautiful medieval town of only a few weeks before, but a skeletal ruin; gone were the street cafés and shops, destroyed by shelling. It was not a place any more to wander around and relax. The cellars provided shelter but the town was a dangerous place, well pin-pointed by the German artillery. Alfred was given three days confined to barracks for using obscene language to an NCO on Sunday 6th June.

He undertook a series of duties without incident until a German attack at Hooge on Friday 30th June. On Saturday 17th July the British exploded a mine under the German lines at Hooge but were unable to exploit the action and push on further. Various attempts to attack and advance were made over the ensuing days but without success. A German counter-attack was anticipated from late July; the lip of the mine was held, but only just. No communication trenches ran to the rear and it was under constant sniper, shell and trench mortar fire. During the afternoon of Thursday 29th Alfred marched to Ypres and during the night relieved the Rifle Brigade and their comrades in the 8th Battalion, King's Royal Rifle Corps. The relief went well and apparently unnoticed by the Germans who were, however, well aware that the relatively untried and inexperienced 7th Battalion was taking the line. The Germans had been tapping the British telephone wires and listened carefully to communications reporting all movements and reliefs to Headquarters. When Alfred arrived in the line he found himself very close to the German lines; in places they were only fifteen feet apart. Shortly before dawn Alfred was ordered to stand to, and not long afterwards an immense roar was heard as the Germans blew up the ruins of the stables of Hooge Château. At the same time they advanced on the British lines using 'flammenwerfer' (flame throwers or 'liquid fire'). Thick black smoke billowed everywhere and the sky turned crimson from the jets of flame, at the same time a heavy bombardment commenced, trench mortars rained down and the German front line opened rapid fire. Alfred's line was thus heavily attacked and he was ordered to rapid fire at the short distance that brought the 'flammenwerfer' to a halt in front of his line. At 11.30am reinforcements arrived and at 2.45pm he participated in the counter-attack that ended in failure. Alfred survived the horrific attack and was relieved from the line later that evening.

After a period of rest Alfred returned to the line and during a 'normal' tour of duty was killed — a young life lost that had experienced more than most of us today would wish to imagine.

2960 PRIVATE ROBERT INGLIS
2nd Battalion Royal Scots
Died on Thursday 27th May 1915, aged 17
Commemorated on Panel 11.

Robert was born at home, son of Robert Inglis, of 8 Solicitors Buildings, Cowgate, Edinburgh.
He volunteered in Edinburgh and went out to join the Battalion on Tuesday 12th January 1915. Robert entrained to northern France, then crossed into Belgium to join the Battalion whilst they were serving between Kemmel and St Eloi. He settled down to normal trench routine whilst on tours of duty in the front line or in reserve, undertook fatigues, training or had some rest, remaining in the sector until Wednesday 12th May.

Robert moved into the Ypres Salient to the north of Hill 60 where he served until Tuesday 25th May without being involved in any particular action. He was sent into the line in front of 'Railway Wood' where, as usual, the enemy looked down onto and into the trenches. Robert had only been in the line for just over twenty-four hours when he was killed by a sniper.

G/8741 PRIVATE AARON JACOB
4th Battalion Middlesex Regiment
Died on Wednesday 29th September 1915, aged 17
Commemorated on Panel 51.

Aaron was born at home, son of Mr and Mrs H Jacob, of 161 Stepney Green Buildings, Stepney, London.
He went out to France on Wednesday 16th June 1915. For Aaron's story see Private Walter Francis, above.

2576 PRIVATE GEORGE JAMES
3rd Battalion Monmouthshire Regiment
Died on Sunday 2nd May 1915, aged 17
Commemorated on Panel 50.

George was the son of Benjamin and Hannah James, of Upper Levels, Abertillery, Monmouthshire.
He went out to France on Saturday 13th February 1915, for James' story see Private Joe Norton, below.

72837 PRIVATE WILLIAM JOHN JAMES
13th Battalion Royal Welsh Fusiliers
Died on Tuesday 31st July 1917, aged 17
Commemorated on Panel 22.

William was born in Nantymoel, Glamorganshire, second son of Margaret Ann James, of 90 John Street, Nantymoel, Bridgend, Glamorganshire, and the late David James. He was educated locally.
He volunteered in Bridgend and first served in the Army Service Corps as T3/029331 Private William James before joining the Royal Welsh Fusiliers.
He went out to France on Wednesday 15th September 1915 and served in both France and Belgium until he transferred to the Fusiliers whilst they were training near St Hilaire in June 1917.

William was sent to Belgium after nearly a month of training and went into the line from Friday 20th July. After servicing the front for nearly two years William was well aware that a major offensive was about to begin as everywhere there were troops marching, ammunition being supplied and the heavy artillery were also in position. Robert was sent into the line ready to take part in the opening of The Third Battle of Ypres. At 5.00pm on Tuesday 31st July he was led forward towards 'Cactus Junction'. At first the advance went well with little gun fire to slow the troops down. The Germans had been holding back until William's company was close to the strong point and they opened a murderous fire. William was cut down and killed, together with many of his comrades.

He is commemorated on Llanelli War Memorial.

G/7125 PRIVATE GEORGE JARROLD
4th Battalion Middlesex Regiment
Died on Wednesday 29th September 1915, aged 16
Commemorated on Panel 51.

George was born in Lambeth, son of Mrs Jarrold, of 27 Tower Street, Westminster, London.

George enlisted in London and was sent for training before being sent out to France and joined the Battalion on Wednesday 7th April 1915. He had only been with them two weeks when the Second Battle of Ypres began on Thursday 22nd and he was soon in the thick of the action. George was out of the line resting in 'Rosenhill Huts' when ordered to parade after lunch on Thursday 6th May then marched to the front line at Hill 60. The enemy had captured the Hill the night before and a counter-attack was mounted: George remained in reserve but was not deployed. He continued on tours of duty in the Hooge sector and when relieved spent time in camps near Vlamertinghe. George marched from camp at 7.45pm on Wednesday 26th May through Ypres and out via the Lille Gate to take the line once again in front of Hooge for a thirteen-day tour of duty. When relieved George returned to Vlamertinghe and had two weeks of rest, training or on fatigues. He returned to the trenches on Monday 12th July and a week later took part in an attack following the blowing of a mine. The whole ground shook as the ground in front of him roared high into the air and moments later mud and débris was falling on top of him. The Battalion was so close to the explosion they lost ten men killed by falling objects. George was immediately led forward to the lip of the crater and was soon involved in a fierce hand-to-hand fight. He had to repulse a number of counter-attacks until he was relieved late on Friday 20th to Ypres then onto a camp in Brandhoek for an extended period of rest. From Monday 9th August to Monday 23rd George was in the line between 'Trenches 34' and '31', the Battalion had a rough time of it. They were relieved and sent to Dickebusch for rest.

An attack on Hooge commenced on Saturday 25th September 1915 as a diversionary attack for the Battle at Loos taking place some miles to the south. The Brigade Diary records the difficulties that the British forces were under at the time: *"It was thought that the number of guns and the ammunition allotted to them was inadequate for the attack. … Three trench mortar batteries are also to take part in the bombardment, but the ammunition for these is also very limited. … The Brigade was ordered to hand over 90 pairs of wire cutters to 7th and 9th Brigades, as none were available in Ordnance Stores for them, it being thus seen that after 14 months of war even a sufficiency of wire cutters cannot be obtained before an action."* Not an auspicious start to the last battle George would see.

Following the usual preliminary barrage, four

mines were blown, two at 4.19am, and within thirty seconds the second pair were blown. At 4.20am the whistles blew and George went 'over the top' and charged towards the German lines. At 6.30am the Battalion recorded that German prisoners and their wounded were being sent back. The Germans defended their positions well and mounted a tremendous counter barrage. Further gains, and consolidating those taken in the morning, were becoming increasingly difficult, partly due to lack of bombs. George and his comrades held on gallantly but by 2.20pm the supply of bombs was all but exhausted which meant counter-attacks could not be made. Much of the captured ground was lost.

Throughout the night George worked on rebuilding the damaged or destroyed trenches. Late on Sunday 26th the opposing artillery commenced what became a mutual bombardment duel that lasted for nearly an hour. The next two days were, in relative terms, quiet and this allowed the men to rebuild the trenches. At 4.30am on Wednesday 29th the Germans blew a mine to the left of the Middlesex lines that was followed by an immediate attack by the German infantry, including some dressed in the uniforms of the 2nd Royal Scots. Every man was wiped out on the left flank — they had stood their ground until the last, including George.

6378 PRIVATE
WILLIAM ARTHUR JEFFS
1st Battalion Gordon Highlanders
Died on Monday 14th December 1914, aged 16
Commemorated on Panel 38.

William was born in Highgate, Warwickshire, only son of James William and Annie Florence Jeffs, of 100 Avon Street, Upper Stoke, Coventry. He was educated locally and was then employed as a barber's lather boy. He enlisted in Aberdeen and after a short period of training he was sent out to France and joined the Battalion with a draft on Thursday 3rd December 1914. When William undertook his first tour of duty near Kemmel he found the trenches half-filled with thick, cold, liquid mud. On Monday 14th December he took part in the attack on Messines, William was in front of Maedelstede Farm on the Kemmel to Wytschaete road. At 7.45am the whistles were blown and he advanced but came up against stiff resistance. In the fierce fighting William was killed.

10310 PRIVATE
CHARLES THOMAS JOHNSON
'C' Company, 2nd Battalion Essex Regiment
Died on Thursday 13th May 1915, aged 17
Commemorated on Panel 39.

Charles was born in 1897, eldest of six sons of James and Florence Mary Johnson, of 4 Spainscroft, Widford, Chelmsford, Essex. He was educated locally and then was employed at the Clarkson's Works.

He volunteered in Warley, Essex, following the outbreak of war and sent for training. Charles went out to France on Saturday 1st May 1915 with a draft. He arrived on the Salient to join the Battalion and during his first tour of duty in the front line was killed.

'The Widford Parish Magazine' wrote: "Our sympathy goes to Mr and Mrs Johnson in their anxiety as to the fate of their son Charles who is reported 'missing'. No further news comes to hand, and suspense in such a case is very painful to the parents. Let us pray to the Father that this soldier may still be restored to his parents."

'The Essex Weekly News' wrote on Friday 13th August carried the following appeal for information: "Mr. and Mrs. Johnson of 4 Spainscroft, Widford, would be glad to receive any news concerning their son, Pte. Charles Johnson 10310, 2nd Essex, who was reported missing by the War Office on May 13 after the battle of Ypres."

A further article was published on Friday 14th April 1916: "The War Office have intimated in reference to Pte. Charles T. Johnson, 10310, Essex Regiment, who has been missing since May 13, 1915, that they are reluctantly constrained to conclude that he is dead. A communication expressing the sympathy of H.M. The King has been received from Lord Kitchener. Deceased, who was formerly employed at Messrs. Clarkson's Works, was the son of Mr. and Mrs. James Johnson, of Spains Croft, Widford. Another son, Pte. Frederick E. Johnson, 10940, Essex Regiment. Was admitted to hospital on Feb., 29 suffering from diphtheria (suspected), severely. He was formerly employed by Mr. Green, butcher, Moulsham Street, Chelmsford. Mr, Johnson has two other sons serving with the Forces — Ernest, in the Engineers, and James, in the East Anglian Cyclists."

16960 PRIVATE ROBERT JOHNSON
2nd Battalion King's Own
(Royal Lancaster Regiment)
Died on Saturday 8th May 1915, aged 17
Commemorated on Panel 12.

Robert was born at home, third son of William and Isabella Johnson, of 16 Aireworth Street, Wingates, Westhoughton, Bolton, Lancashire.

He volunteered in Horwich, Lancashire, and went out to France on Wednesday 7th April 1915. For Robert's story, see Private Charles Phelps below.

Robert died of wounds but his grave was subsequently lost.

113323 PRIVATE
WILLIAM HODSON JOHNSON
4th Canadian Mounted Rifles
(Central Ontario Regiment)
Died on Friday 2nd June 1916, aged 16
Commemorated on Panel 32.

W. H. Johnson.
William's signature

William was the son of William and Elizabeth Johnson, of Ottawa, Ontario. William was educated locally.

He volunteered in Ottawa on Tuesday 29th June 1915, where he claimed to have been born in Peterborough, Cambridgeshire, on Thursday 30th June 1898. William was 5ft 5½in tall, with a 34½in chest, a fair complexion, grey eyes, light brown hair and a 4in scar on the left of his chest.

William joined the Battalion whilst they were in training in Belgium on Saturday 29th January 1916. Two days later he was sent into the line near Messines and six weeks later they moved to Zillebeke in which sector they remained until mid-May. He went back into the line on Wednesday 31st May after being out of line for some considerable time at rest and training with some periods in reserve.

William paraded in the early evening of Wednesday 31st May 1916 in full kit with his gas mask and iron rations ready to go into the line. The Battalion was sent to Ypres by train then marched via 'Shrapnel Corner', 'Railway Dugouts' to 'Transport Farm' at Zillebeke. They moved slowly into the front line on Mount Sorrel where they found the trenches in good condition. Early on Friday 2nd the men were being made ready for a visit by Major General Malcolm Mercer (who died the next day and is buried in Lijssenthoek Military Cemetery) and at 6.00am Lieutenant Colonel Ussher made a preliminary inspection. The 'peaceful' sunny morning was shattered by an immense barrage that lasted for four and half hours. The well constructed trenches and dug-outs were destroyed or severely damaged. Ahead of them 'Sanctuary Wood', 'Armagh Wood' and 'Maple Copse' disappeared and when the smoke cleared only tree stumps were left. Shortly after 1.00pm, when the bombardment had finished, a huge mine was blown and the grey uniforms of the German infantry were seen moving swiftly towards them. Casualties were high, and during the barrage William was killed.

6900 PRIVATE
ALBERT GEORGE JONES
2nd **Battalion King's Shropshire Light Infantry**
Died on Wednesday 26th May 1915, aged 17
Commemorated on Panel 49.

Albert was born at York Hill, Hereford, son of Mr H A and Mrs J Jones, of Trumpet Cottage, Pixley, Ledbury, Herefordshire.

He enlisted in Ledbury, and joined the Cheshire Regiment with service number 43989 before transferring to the King's Shropshire Light Infantry.

Albert left with a draft to join the Battalion whilst they were resting in Busseboom, just outside Poperinghe, following the Battle of Frezenberg. The Battalion was reorganised and the drafts assimilated.

The enemy launched another gas attack on Monday 24th May, with their artillery pounding the front line between Langemarck and Bellewaarde. By 5.10am Albert was ordered to stand to then at 6.30am he marched around the south side of Ypres and on towards Hooge. At 4.30pm a counter-attack was made that successfully took the German front line. The position could not be held so the Battalion was ordered to withdraw to between 'Witte Poort Farm' and the Menin Road. Shortly before the Battalion was relieved Albert was killed by shell fire.

22152 PRIVATE
EDMUND CLAUD VICTOR JONES
1st **Battalion Welsh Regiment**
Died on Tuesday 25th May 1915, aged 17
Commemorated on Panel 37.

Edmund was born in Buckingham Gate, London, son of Captain F P Jones, DCM, and Haddie Jones, of Bridgecroft Villa, Widdington, Newport, Essex. He was brought up by his grandparents, then by his uncle and aunt in Wales where he was educated.

He volunteered in Cardiff and was sent for training. The Battalion sailed from Southampton to Le Havre on Monday 18th January 1915. The next day they entrained to Hazebrouck then marched to Merris where billets were provided, and final training began. They paraded for an inspection by General Sir Horace Smith-Dorrien on Tuesday 26th who wished them well for their forthcoming work in the trenches.

The Battalion was transported by motor omnibus to Vlamertinghe on Tuesday 2nd February from where

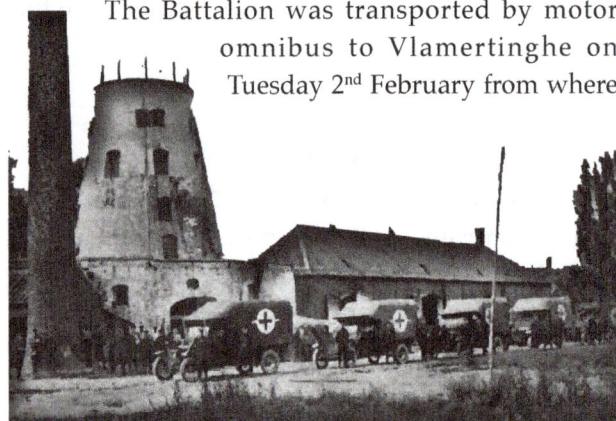

... a convoy of ambulances in Vlamertinghe

they marched along the cobbled road towards Ypres. During the march rations were issued and at Ypres they were met by guides that took them to the lines at Hill 60 and relieved the French infantry: *"They were small men, and seemed very agitated at our being a little behind time. We knew it was only about an hour's march from Ypres to our support positions, and as there were still several hours of darkness, we were rather inclined to think that they had got the wind up. They were of course anxious to get well clear by daylight, to say nothing of wanting to get out to rest, but as we had not yet been in the trenches, we were a bit unsympathetic. To our surprise they were dressed in the old blue overcoat and baggy red trousers of the French infantryman of peace time, and must have made very conspicuous targets. During the next three months we were to see hundreds of dead Frenchmen lying out in No Man's Land, between our front and support trenches and to realise what gallant hearts those theatrical garments had covered. Eventually Battalion H.Q. and two Companies arrived at some brick fields (Tuileries) where the men got into shelters of sorts, and Battalion H.Q. were uncomfortably installed in a kiln, at least so we thought at the time. We little knew* what a palace it was! When day dawned we looked out on our new world, which appeared to be uninhabited. The French had warned us to keep under cover by day, but with true British scorn we did not do so, and got some fairly heavy shelling during the next few days which set 'B' Company's farm, the Moated Grange, close to the Tuileries alight, and killed one man, and wounded seven, besides destroying most of the men's equipment." The area was strewn with the French dead who had not been removed from the field, with a large number of the corpses having been built into the trench walls — and sanitary arrangements did not exist!

The Battalion was relieved on Thursday 11th February and sent to huts in Vlamertinghe where Lieutenant Hilary Evan-Jones wrote home: "We have just finished our first eight days — divided between the supports and the firing line. I had the worst bit of trench to look after with my platoon and did all right, but had a good few casualties, considering the 96 hours I was actually up — two killed and nine wounded. I made two night expeditions by myself with some bombs, which I successfully dropped into the German trenches. During my first I met a German gentleman apparently at the same job as myself. My revolver accounted for him all right, as we were only two feet apart. The trenches are from 30 to 75 feet apart in most places and sometimes closer. We are now off on a four days' rest, which is absolutely ripping. It is splendid to get out of the noise and to get some proper food and sleep. I think, if anything I am rather enjoying myself. Cold feet are the worst part of the show, but my men are such rippers, it makes up for lots. I hate having them hit, though otherwise it is quite cheery. I had a sing-song in my trench the other evening, which did not please the Germans. I sat in a chair, which collapsed, and I went straight to sleep where I lay. The strain is fairly big up there."

The Battalion returned to the line at 'The Bluff' on Sunday 14th February, however, they were not required but took the line the next day.

...mine craters at The Bluff

'Recollections of a Field Officer' records: "It was a miserable, rainy, cold day, and we arrived at Lankhof Château at dusk to find it crowded with officers from all sorts of units, including Belgian artillerists, who kindly gave us some tea, as of course we had nothing but iron rations on us. Guides appeared for the Company Commanders, but none for Lieutenant-Colonel Marden and Captain Westby (Adjutant), who set out to get to Battalion H.Q. in pitch darkness and driving rain, and soon lost their way. They were fortunately rescued by a N.C.O. of the 3rd R.F., returning to the trenches, who walked along running a telephone wire through his hand, or he too would have lost the path. Eventually we arrived at a broken down farm, where we descended into a cellar, the H.Q. Of the 3rd R.F., whom we were to relieve. Here we found the C.O., Lieutenant-Colonel Du Maurier, the author of that well-known play, 'An Englishman's Home,' which had depicted the realities of a German invasion of England, and had had a great run shortly before the war. His forecast of what would happen was more than fulfilled by the Germans, when they took possession of B and put civilians up against the wall and shot them on the slightest pretext. Du Maurier, who was killed a few days later by a shell just outside this farm, was picturesquely attired in semi-civilian kit, which appeared to be much more suited to the climate than our military garments, and he wore a very handsome beard. The cellar was so low that one could just sit upright, and could not stand at all, but at any rate it was dry and warm, though airless. Having been informed of the horrors of the situation we struggled back to the Château to hear that C.S.M. McCarthy, who had won the D.C.M. in the South African War, and was one of our stoutest fighters, had been very badly wounded as he was leaving 'Y' trench. He died the next day. 'Annie' Lloyd (Lieutenant G. Lloyd), his Company Commander, said that he knew he would suffer the same fate when he took over' Y 'trench, and sad to say, his premonition was right. We rode back to Mile Kapellen Farm, where the Battalion was billeted, and had not been in an hour or so when we were ordered out again, and at 3.30 a.m. the Battalion was on the move to Ypres and the Lankhof Château. Half-way we met the N.C.O.s who had been reconnoitring, marching back—we were dead tired, and they must have been even more so. However, we got some hours sleep on some corn sacks in an outhouse at Lankhof during the 15th inst., all except the C.O., who had to go to a Brigade Conference, and then do another reconnaissance."

The Battalion Diary recorded: "The track to the trenches was over a mile long, and deep in holding mud. 'T' trench (Major Hoggan), was on a sort of hillock (The Bluff), but there was a good deal of dead ground in front and to the north of it. It was regularly and accurately shelled twice a day by the enemy. 'X' trench was only a series of small dugouts under a bank with a 40 yards view. It protected 'T' from small parties creeping in under the hillock. 'Y' trench (Lieutenant C. Lloyd) was merely a ditch with a very weak parapet, and under close fire (40 yards) of the very strong German line. There were also ruined houses in advance of both flanks which gave trouble. The trench was knee deep in water, and casualties always occurred when entering and leaving the trench, It was not *properly supported by fire from either 'T' or 'Z', and was untenable, 'Z' trench (Major Toke) had been strong once, but was now only partially held. It was subject to enfilade fire from one of the cottages. The parapets were not bullet proof, and sand bags were shot down as soon as placed. 'B' Company (Captain Montgomery) and the Grenadier platoons had better trenches on the south of the Canal."*

The whole sector was little more than a pool of mud where men and horses were sucked down and drowned. Due to the cold weather many of the Battalion suffered with frostbite and trench foot. They finally left the sector on Tuesday 23rd February and marched to Bailleul having lost sixteen officers and five hundred and forty-one men, killed, wounded or listed as missing. Some much needed rest was provided in good billets and everyone was able to clean up. They returned to the trenches north of Wulverghem where they served on tours of duty until Monday 5th April, except for a three-day tour in Ploegsteert. The Battalion was sent to camp at Poperinghe where General Sir Horace Smith-Dorrien inspected the Battalion on Wednesday 7th and General Sir Herbert Plumer on Sunday 11th. Five days later the Battalion marched to a camp a mile from Ypres where they could witness the shelling of the town with civilians passing them as they fled in terror.

The Battalion began to serve on the Salient at Broodseinde early on Saturday 17th where they felt the ground shake at 7.00pm when the mines were blown at Hill 60. The enemy occupied part of the line who were driven out at the point of the bayonet and the skilful use of the bomb. The success was short-lived as the Germans counter-attacked and forced the Battalion to retire. The next morning, supported by an artillery barrage, another attack was made but it again failed. There was an intensive fight on Thursday 22nd where it was noted that the German infantry were massing for an attack. At 5.00pm the expected attack came to their northwest: *"This was the day of the first German cloud gas attack but all we heard was that the French had bolted as a result of a gas attack, connected in our minds only with gas shells such as had been fired at us, and we little realised the terrible power of the new weapon, or the extent of the catastrophe which had befallen the Allies that day."* Late on Friday 23rd the Battalion was relieved and sent back to the camp west of Ypres. They had to carefully pick their way through the dead horses and the ruins of homes that had been standing when they went into the line.

"No one seemed to know much about the gas attack, except that the French colonial troops had bolted, and some were occasionally seen moving singly across country near the huts. Shelling went on spasmodically, and some 'overs' went near the billets, but no one took any notice of them, and in

... a faithful friend

the afternoon the officers played the sergeants at Rugby football. We were all looking forward to a real night's rest when the order came for the Battalion to move up to the Frezenberg Ridge, in support of the 84th Brigade. We could not start for some time as the circular road was blocked by the 10th Brigade (Hull's) moving up into position to counter-attack at St. Julien. However, we marched off shortly after midnight, and got into some ditches and very indifferent dugouts just behind the crest of the Frezenberg Ridge, from which there was a splendid view over all the northern part of the present front."

Their experience in the trenches were recorded: *"Matters livened up considerably on the 26th. the enemy judged pretty correctly that there were reinforcements in the dip behind our ridge, and started searching for them with field guns. Part of 'C' Company had to clear to another place, and Packe who had just come to Battalion H.Q. for a conference was badly hit be shrapnel and carried away to an 'estaminet' close by to wait till dark for evacuation. Then, sometime in the morning, the 2nd K.S.L.I. and 6th D.L.I. came through us over the top of the ridge in extended order to go to the assistance of someone in difficulties in front. As they advanced the enemy's guns opened on the top of the ridge with shrapnel, but to my surprise hardly anyone was hit, though the shelling was heavy and accurate. Line after line ran the gauntlet and disappeared down the forward slope. It was a great sight. Between 2 o'clock shelling on our ridge stopped and heavy fire broke out to the north. We found out later that it was a combined attack by the French on the west of the Canal, hand in hand with the Lahore Division, just arrived from the First Army.*

We could see the sections advancing by rushes, then falling flat, and rushing on again, just like a typical field day, except that each time some were left lying still, never, alas! to rise again. Then a lot of infantry came through on our left moving towards St. Julien, but didn't seem to know where to go or what to do. No wonder — they were Territorial Infantry of the Northumbrian Division, who had been pushed into the battle without previous reconnaissance, and only given a map reference for direction, and this was their first action. Shortly after we had a message to send a Company to help the 5th Fusilier detachment which was out towards the Canadians, and off 'D' Company went. Our guns were firing furiously over our heads, and the Boche starting 'strafing' them and us, using incendiary shell, which soon set our dressing station in the estaminet on fire, and the wretched wounded had to be carried down the road. What with burning cottages and exploding shells and artillery ammunition wagons coming up to the batteries at the gallop over the open, it was quite a spectacular battle."

The Battalion had its first experience of coming under a gas attack on Sunday 2nd May but quite a lot of the gas cloud floated back onto the Germans! The overall line was untenable and had to be straightened. Over the next couple of days the front line moved back.

"When dawn broke on 5th May, the enemy did not discover for some hours that the trenches lately held by the 10th Brigade were now unoccupied, and we had the pleasure of seeing them shelling empty trenches heavily. The field of fire from our trenches was only good in places, and the enemy could creep up fairly close, unseen, owing to folds in the ground and to hedges. Our positions were soon spotted from the air, of which the Germans seemed to be absolute masters, but we didn't get much shelling till late afternoon, and during the day the men worked hard at improving their front trenches which were only partially dug, owing to R.E. parties failing to put in an appearance. Battalion H.Q. were in some dugouts which the French had made with much ingenuity under three long sugar beet heaps in the corner of a field near the road. These were partly covered from view by a small cottage in which the M.O. placed his aid post. John Westby worked like a Trojan, making a sort of strong point round the three dugouts, and deepening the trenches. His labour was well rewarded during the next two days. At one point we could see the Germans moving about singly and in pairs about 1,000 yards away, and the best shots under Major Toke and the Pioneer Sergeant had turns at a loophole which we had fixed up, and everyone claimed hits. The enemy seemed disinclined to attack, but next morning the usual bombardment commenced, while his infantry began to creep forward. The Boche in his methodical way concentrated his guns in turn on each Battalion for two hours in the morning and the same in the afternoon. The ground rose behind us, and there was no escape. We simply had to grin and bear it. Our artillery had been moved back a good deal, while theirs had come forward, and in any case

were told to reserve their ammunition in case of an attack, as all that could be spared was wanted for the offensive about to start against Aubers Ridge. After we had had our dose we watched with sympathy and interest the other Battalions of the Brigade getting 'strafed'. The H.Q. trenches were soon full of badly wounded men, and not a man could move out of the trenches till dawn. As it was dawn about 3 a.m., and not dark till 9 p.m., the days seemed, and were, hideously long, without anything to relieve the monotony. After dark all the wounded going back, and the ration parties coming up, had to run the gauntlet of the road for several hundred yards, through intermittent shelling and pretty continuous machine gun fire. We felt we were simply cannon fodder. About midday on 6th May the enemy had set fire to the aid post cottage, where we got our water, and when the roof burnt out he spotted our dugouts, and shelled them heavily, smashing in two of the three. The last one, though hit several times, managed to hold out luckily till our relief that night. It was full to the brim with H.Q. officers, orderlies, signallers and wounded, and a shell bursting inside would have made a hideous mess. How we prayed for the enemy to attack, and give us a chance to use our rifles! We were so sure that there would be an attack next day that we envied the 5th Fusiliers who took our places, while we went back to their positions in the G.H.Q. line a few hundred yards in rear. The Boche did attack them a few hours after relief, and got a bad hammering."

The Battalion left the battlefield on Monday 10th May and marched to Ypres where they rested for a day before moving to Herzeele, via Poperinghe, for ten days rest. A number of drafts arrived and were allocated to their platoons that brought the Battalion back up to strength. They returned to the trenches at Hooge on Saturday 22nd for a two-day tour and then marched to Vlamertinghe. Unfortunately their rest was cut short due to a heavy attack on the Bellewaarde Ridge. The enemy had been successful in capturing a large section of trenches so the Battalion was ordered to return to the front. A difficult march took them around Ypres, as they moved up the Menin Road shell fire pounded them and Colonel Thomas Owen Marden, was badly wounded (he later became Major General Sir Thomas Marden, KBE, CB, CMG). They took the line and came under a gas attack. A counter-attack was launched, led by Major Toke and Captain Edmund Westby. As they charged 'Railway Wood' many of the men were killed. They lay dead in a sunken road, the area was subsequently captured by the Germans who did bury the dead, however, the graves were lost in subsequent battles.

Edmund was first listed as missing until his death was confirmed some time later.

His brother, 2nd Lieutenant F L C Jones, MC, MM, died on Sunday 1st September 1918 and is buried in Sailly-Saillisel British Cemetery.

2862 RIFLEMAN
ERNEST HENRY JONES
1st/12th Battalion London Regiment (The Rangers)
Died on Wednesday 10th February 1915, aged 17
Commemorated on Panel 54.

Ernest was the second son of Ernest Morgan and Annie Jones, of 24 Tower Hamlets Road, Hoe Street, Walthamstow, London. He was educated locally.

He volunteered in London and was sent for training, joining the Battalion whilst they were guarding the London and South Western Railway. Ernest returned to Roehampton, Surrey, on Wednesday 16th December 1914 when the Battalion began to train hard in Richmond Park, Surrey. He left with the Battalion for Barnes Station on Wednesday 23rd and entrained to Southampton ready to embark for France. No boat was available so Ernest and his comrades were billeted in a local school over night. On Christmas Eve 1914 he set sail, arriving in Le Havre on Christmas Day. He remained in camp for four days where the rain fell and following a storm on Monday 28th it turned whole camp into a quagmire. The next morning Ernest paraded in the continuing storm then marched to the Station to entrain to St Omer. The Battalion was billeted in Blendecques and for the next month undertook training to

... on the road near Le Havre

prepare for the trenches on the Western Front.

At 9.30am on Saturday 29th January 1915 Ernest left for Hazebrouck and went into billets in a partially built hospital that had just been vacated by horses and was filthy! Thankfully for everyone the next day they marched from their salubrious billets to Outtersteene where they remained until 2nd February when the Battalion crossed the border into Belgium and marched to a camp at Ouderdom.

The final move to the front began on Monday 8th when the Battalion marched to billets in the Cavalry Barracks at Ypres. The town was a strange mixture of the living and the dead, although the majority of the inhabitants had left here and there shops remained open, as were the cafés. Ypres remained relatively intact as the shelling was yet to complete its destruction. Immediately parties were sent to the front taking up vital equipment and stores. They went into the line where they remained for two weeks. Ernest was holding a front line trench under heavy shell fire when he was killed and was buried close to where he fell.

1401 PRIVATE
WILLIAM EDWARDS JONES
Essex Yeomanry
Died on Friday 14th May 1915, aged 17
Commemorated on Panel 5.

William was the son of Ernest Edwards Jones and Clara Jones, of Western Moor, Neath, Glamorganshire. He enlisted in Colchester and went out to France on Thursday 18th February 1915. For the history of the Battalion and William's involvement, see Private Oxley Gordon Askew, above.

7336 PRIVATE ALBERT JUDD
1st Battalion East Surrey Regiment
Died on Wednesday 16th December 1914, aged 17
Commemorated on Panel 34.

Albert was born at home, second and younger son of Mrs Maria Judd, of 33 Duffield Street, Battersea, London.

He volunteered in Kingston-on-Thames, Surrey, went out to France on Monday 26th October 1914 with a draft. For a history of the Battalion see Private Albert Burton above.

SECOND LIEUTENANT
EDWARD ROWLEY KELLY
3rd Battalion Border Regiment
Died on Wednesday 7th July 1915, aged 17
Commemorated on Panel 35.

Edward was the son of the late Lieutenant Edward Kelly, RN, and Mrs Ethel Kelly. He was educated at Hitchin Grammar School and was to have gone up to Merton College, Oxford, but the war intervened.

Edward volunteered on Wednesday 27th January 1915, his next of kin was an aunt, Mrs Bowden, of 64 Carshalton Park Road, Carshalton, Surrey. He was sent for officer training. After receiving his commission Edward left for France joining the Battalion in the field on Tuesday 8th June, attached to the Lancashire Fusiliers. He arrived as the successful Battle of Messines was gaining ground, news that spread around the Ypres Salient to give everyone much cheer. Edward spent only a month on tours of duty until he was killed in action on the Pilkem Ridge.

113335 PRIVATE
JOHN ROCHE KENNEDY
4th Canadian Mounted Rifles Battalion
(Central Ontario Regiment)
Died on Friday 2nd June 1916, aged 17
Commemorated on Panel 32.

John's signature

John was the son of Richard and Ellen Kennedy, of 502 St Clarens Avenue, Toronto, Ontario.

He volunteered at Barriefield, Ontario, on Friday 20th August 1915, where he claimed to have been born in Toronto on Friday 17th December 1897 and worked for a local company as an inspector. John was a Baptist, 5ft 7in tall, with a 34in chest, a dark complexion, grey eyes and black hair.

John was sent for training in Canada and England before joining the Battalion in 'Camp B', Vlamertinghe, on Wednesday 7th April 1915. He quickly settled down with his new comrades and began training with them, listening to the stories of the front line. John paraded at 8.15pm on Tuesday 13th then marched to the station to entrain at 9.00pm for Ypres Asylum. He marched out to 'Maple Copse' to undertake his first tour of duty. He was given practical instruction on how to behave in the front line and also undertook fatigues, repairing the trenches. John watched with some wonderment at the Luftstreitkräfte actively patrolling across the Salient, often chased by the Royal Flying Corps. Throughout the tour of duty the enemy was shelling from 'Sanctuary Wood' to 'Maple Copse' in differing degrees of intensity. He moved to 'Railway Dugouts' on Saturday 24th that came under heavy shell fire being directed from above as the enemy aeroplanes buzzed across the sector. The enemy blew a mine at 6.30pm on Tuesday 27th to the right of John's position and then pressed home an attack. The Battalion was ordered to stand to at 7.00pm and an hour later moved forward but they were not called upon. Late on Thursday 29th John was relieved and returned to 'Camp B' for a week. General Sir Douglas Haig inspected the Battalion on Tuesday 4th May and congratulated the men on their turnout. Two days later John returned to the front via 'Château Belge' and into the trenches at 'Sanctuary Wood' where he served until Saturday 15th. He was then sent to 'Camp F' followed by 'Camp B' to undertake fatigues.

John returned to the trenches for the last time on Monday 31st May. Whilst in 'Sanctuary Wood' on Friday 2nd June John's officers prepared the men to receive a visit from Major General Malcolm Mercer. Colonel Ussher checked all was well first thing in the morning and then left to meet the General and his party. Shortly after 8.00am as they were working their way back to the line a huge German barrage opened, quite unexpectedly. Lieutenant Harvey Douglas wrote of his experience: *"At 6 o'clock I went off duty, entered the dug-out, slipped off my equipment, put my steel helmet on the table and settled down for an hour or two of sleep. At 6.30 I was up again to see Col. Ussher and Capt. Jack Symons who had come to make a preparatory inspection of the trenches. As they went away I bade good-bye, for the last time, to Jack, who was my brother-in-law.*

A few minutes to 8 o'clock breakfast was announced and our 'batman' came in from the little cookhouse in the dug-out across the trench, bearing a large tin plate of beautiful fried eggs and bacon and some prunes. This, with the addition of a little coffee, was the excellent meal we were just about to taste when —crash! Hell was let loose. Shells of all sizes came hurtling through the air, raining in on us from all sides. We slipped on our steel helmets, left that lovely breakfast and rushed outside to see how serious the show might be. We had suffered heavy bombardments before but we at once saw that this was the biggest we had ever been in. Harvey Cockshutt, always thinking of the men, issued the order to take everyone to the front line, where he decided the bombardment was not quite so heavy. In a few seconds every man was lining the firing trench. The shells continued to rain in on us from every direction. The Bosches, as we found out later, had turned every gun around the Ypres salient on the frontage occupied by the 3rd Canadian Division. We received almost as many shells from the rear flanks, as we did from the front. These, of course, we could not always see coming, but wherever we looked towards the German lines we could see 'Minnies' rolling over and over in the air on their way to greet us. These were quite easy to dodge when they came one at a time. All you had to do was to watch where they were going to light and dodge around the traverse into the next bay. You might be knocked down or even buried, but the effect of the explosion of a 'Minnie' is very local although it makes an awful mess of your trench. We had the men distributed evenly along the front line. In addition to the sentry on duty at the periscope in almost every bay, we posted further sentries gazing up to the front and right and left watching for 'Minnies'. They gave no alarm unless there was going to be a direct hit in their own bay, when everyone was warned and dashed around the traverse. Unfortunately, owing to the fact that they were coming so thick, many a man dashed around the traverse to escape the explosion on one Minnenwefer and ran directly into that of another.

By 10 o'clock the bombardment had been so effective that our front line was practically destroyed and a large portion of our men were wiped out. Harvey Cockshutt sent for me and told me to take about half other men who were left — amounting to some twenty — to the support trench on our left. We could not move along the front line so we jumped on the parados and made a dash for it overland. We gained the trench, without a casualty, but found that it, too, was in a sad state. We were moving along to the left when suddenly a large shell or 'Minnie', I don't know which, landed right in the middle of my little party and wiped them all out with the exception of four others and myself in the front, and perhaps one or two in the rear whom I never saw again.

We five moved along a short distance till we found a short angle in the trench which had somehow or other escaped the attention of the German artillery. Here I collected a few men from 'C' Company which was on our left, until eventually we numbered about ten. Had we been spared until the attack came off, the ten of us would probably have succeeded in pumping a considerable amount of lead into the advancing Huns.

By this time we had begun to realise that this was no casual 'strafe' but the preparation for an attack. A German aeroplane, flying very low, noticed this little bit of undestroyed trench. We feigned death. Any man who made a move was properly cursed, as our only hope of being unmolested was that this air-man should think we were already dead. However, he decided to take no chances, and directed fire of what seemed to us like about forty batteries, as well as several Minnenwerfers, on our one little bit of trench. At one moment I looked up and saw three 'Minnies' coming down directly on top of us. We all kissed ourselves good-bye, and hoped for the best, but none of them made a direct hit. One of the three landed in the interior angle, and the other two on the exterior faces of the angle made by the bend in the trench, and all exploded simultaneously. Everyone who had not already been wounded, with the exception of a stretcher-bearer named Barclay and myself, got it then. We were all half buried, but we managed to crawl out.

Barclay and I put field dressings on the wounded men and I gave morphia tablets — which all officers carried — to those in great pain. There were only three besides myself who could move, and I decided to act as Mr. Cockshutt would have wished under the circumstances, and take these men to a shell-proof trench in Mount Sorrel which was commonly known as the Tunnel. We had been given orders that in case of a heavy bombardment, this was where we were to take our men. In order to get there we had to go down a short communication trench known as Canada Street, but we had not gone more than a few yards before we discovered that Canada Street existed no longer. We crawled overland, following the line of the trench by the bits of 'A' frame and revetting material which were protruding from the earth. We soon came to the German barrage, which extended all the way along our frontage just in the rear of the trenches, and prevented any possibility of reinforcements reaching us. We saw that it was hopeless to get through this at the time, and decided to lie there until the barrage might lessen sufficiently to enable us to make a dash for it.

I particularly wanted to reach the Tunnel, as it was there that battalion headquarters were located, and it was necessary to report that our trenches were destroyed and that there were no men left to defend the position when the attack should come. As we lay there we were soon located by a German machine-gunner who ripped off two or three belts at us. We were in full view with practically no cover; the bullets cracked all around us and the dirt flew in our faces. We had been under fire many a time before and had often felt afraid. According to the old saying, any man who says he is not afraid is either a fool or a liar. But none of us had ever experienced anything so terrific as this. We knew we were going to be killed, and we had got to the stage where it did not seem to matter whether we got it then or a few minutes later. I believe it was this feeling that had rendered all the men so cool and collected and I was surprised to see, during the morning, that some of the new men who were under fire for the first time were just as cool as those who were old hands at the game. Of course, they had the advantage of not knowing how dangerous a shell might be, whereas the others had seen so many of their friends 'Go West' that they could appreciate the danger more fully."

At 1.00am the bombardment lifted and those who had survived were both lucky and relieved — it was to be short-lived, the Germans then blew a mine. Not surprisingly very few survived to answer the roll call on Monday 4th June — only seventy-three out of six hundred and eighty.

1828 PRIVATE TOM KIDD
'C' Company, 1st/4th Battalion
East Yorkshire Regiment
Died on Monday 3rd May 1915, aged 17
Commemorated on Panel 31.

Tom was born at home, son of the late William Blakeston Kidd and Mary Ann Kidd, of Hull.

He volunteered in Hull and went out to France with the Battalion on Saturday 17th April 1915. For Tom's story see Private Harry Barr above. Tom survived Harry by a matter of hours.

R/11059 RIFLEMAN JOHN KIERNAN
9th Battalion King's Royal Rifle Corps
Died on Friday 28th January 1916, aged 17
Commemorated on Panel 53.

John was born at home, son of Mrs Ellen Kiernan, of 4 Edgar Street, Oldham, Lancashire.

He volunteered in Shaw, Lancashire, and after training went out to France on Friday 6th August 1915. John joined the Battalion after they had received a mauling at Hooge the week before. He began tours of duty in the sector that clearly had been hard fought over with many of the dead and body parts lying in No Man's Land. John's first and only major action was in the same area, at Bellewaarde. John went into the line on Friday 24th September ready to support the attack the next day which was a diversionary attack for the Battle of Loos. At 4.19am a mine was blown under the German lines and a fierce battle took place. Attack was followed by counter-attack. It was the fiercest battle so far witnessed by the Battalion.

Activity on the Salient quietened down and John returned to the normal round of tours of duty in the front line, fatigues, training and period of rest. Whilst at the front line John was mortally wounded by rifle and machine gun fire and died shortly afterwards.

11374 RIFLEMAN
ARTHUR GEORGE KITCHERSIDE
2nd Battalion King's Royal Rifle Corps
Died on Saturday 31st October 1914, aged 17
Commemorated on Panel 53.

Arthur Kitcherside
Arthur's signature

Arthur was born at home, third son of Thomas Albert and Minnie Kitcherside, of 14 Tennyson Road, South Wimbledon, London.

He volunteered in Kingston-on-Thames, Surrey, on Saturday 17th January 1914 when he claimed to be 18 years and 6 days old, working as a milkman. Arthur was 5ft 6½in tall, with a 34½in chest, weighed 116lbs, a fresh complexion, brown eyes and hair, a burn scar behind his left ear and a scar on his right shin.

At the outbreak of war the Battalion was at '*Blackdown Camp*', Camberley, Surrey. They mobilized and embarked for Le Havre on Thursday 13th August then marched into a rest camp. Arthur entrained for Le Nouvion at 10.00pm on Saturday 15th. He marched towards Mons on Friday 21st and during the battle remained in reserve but was not involved in any action. Arthur was ordered to retire on Monday 24th and continued to march south until Sunday 6th September

with his comrades when at last he halted then turned to engage the enemy. Arthur moved back across the Marne and moved onto the Aisne.

He marched from Vendresse to Troyon in heavy rain and *en route* encountered a German picquet defending a bridge. The Battalion attacked but were unable to get through — it would take a further three days before it was taken. At Moussy-Verneuil the German artillery launched a barrage and the Battalion's successful advance began, capturing more than three hundred prisoners. The Germans commenced a counter-attack and with the 1st Battalion they were able to repulse the oncoming German infantry. Losses were heavy with the Battalion losing three hundred killed or wounded. Arthur remained on the Aisne until early October.

Arthur arrived at Cassel on Sunday 18th October before being sent to Ypres, arriving three days later where they were billeted in Boesinghe. At 6.00am on Friday 23rd he was ordered forward and took part in a counter-attack to regain some lost ground and trenches. The attack was successful partly due to the Germans shelling their own front line!

Arthur was in front of Gheluvelt on Thursday 29th to undertake another counter-attack during which the Battalion took heavy losses. The Germans mounted a heavy attack on Saturday 31st that drove the Battalion towards Ypres and the village was lost. Whilst defending his position Arthur was killed.

He is commemorated on the War Memorial at All Saints' Church, Wimbledon.

2595 RIFLEMAN
WILLIAM RICHARD KLAGGE
1st/12th Battalion London Regiment (The Rangers)
Died on Saturday 8th May 1915, aged 17
Commemorated on Panel 54.

William was the youngest son of Mrs Albetina Klagge, of 79 Chesterton Road, North Kensington, London, and the late Mr Klagge, his parents were born in Germany and subsequently emigrated to England.

William volunteered and was training whilst the Battalion left for France. He embarked on the *SS Balmoral* in Southampton on Tuesday 9th March 1915 and sailed to Le Havre. William joined the Battalion whilst they were in the Cavalry Barracks in Ypres on Wednesday 17th. General Edward Bulfin inspected the Battalion on Monday 22nd then addressed the parade. Shortly afterwards William marched to Bailleul where he was billeted for two days. He returned along the cobbled road to Dranouter and began fatigues in the front line at Lindenhoek crossroads for six days. The first experience William had of serving in the front line began on Sunday 28th for a five-day tour. He marched to Ravelsburg on Saturday 3rd April, passing Dranouter where a service was conducted by the Bishop of London. The Bishop arrived over an hour late, so William and his comrades were left standing around in the freezing cold. His opening remarks included: *"As you could not come to the Church I have brought the Church to you…"* Many of the men replied under their breath: *"Pity you did not bring it a little nearer!"*. A Battalion sports day was organised on Monday 6th together with other events and activities. The next day the Battalion was inspected by General Sir Horace Smith-Dorrien after which they marched to billets in Bailleul through a heavy downpour. They were inspected again, this time by General Sir Herbert Plumer, on Sunday 11th. The next day William was sent to billets in Vlamertinghe where four days later they were bombed by a passing Zeppelin *en route* to attack Bailleul. Many of the men opened fire and hit the Zeppelin but did no damage. The next day a football match was organised between The Rangers and the 9th Battalion London Regiment that was won by The Rangers 2-0.

William returned to the trenches at Zonnebeke on Saturday 17th for a six-day tour. When relieved from the line he went into poor straw-covered bivouacs at Verlorenhoek. He watched helplessly as the wretched remnants of men flooded back from the front line as a result of the first gas attack. Orders were received to advance to St Julien and help support the Suffolks then remained in front of the village until the night of Monday 26th when he was relieved, returning to Verlorenhoek. Whilst in camp an enemy machine flew low over them: it was brought down just outside the camp that was particularly beneficial as it had been helping to direct shell fire on the camp! Late on Sunday 2nd May William went out to dig trenches on the Frezenberg Ridge in preparation for the line to be straightened and the general withdrawal from Monday 3rd to Tuesday 4th. For five days William worked hard under heavy and constant shell fire. He was relieved late on Friday 7th to the GHQ Line that took until 4.00am the next morning. A large number of the Battalion were killed whilst taking shelter in the dugouts. At 11.15am William was led forward to support the front line. Withering machine gun fire greeted them that cut down so many of the Battalion.

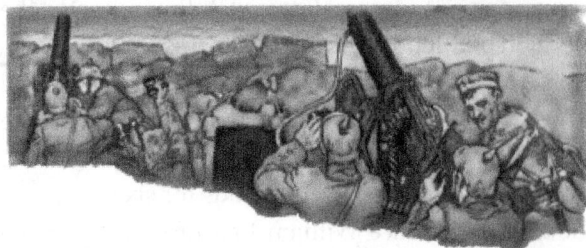

5697 RIFLEMAN ERNEST LAKE
4th Battalion Rifle Brigade
Died on Monday 10th May 1915, aged 17
Commemorated on Panel 48.

Ernest was born in Membury, Devon, second son of William and Martha Lake, of 1 Hope Street, York Road, Battersea, London. Following his elementary education he was employed as a carter.

He volunteered in Wandsworth, London, and went out to France on Wednesday 17th March 1915. Ernest joined the Battalion whilst they were billeted in Poperinghe recovering from the mauling they had received at St Eloi. His first tour of duty began at the end of the month he was then sent to Poperinghe for rest before relieving the French 268th Reserve Regiment in Polygon Wood, facing Polderhoek. He remained on tours of duty over the next three weeks and when out of the line was sent to camp in Vlamertinghe. Following the gas attack on Thursday 22nd April, the Battalion was ordered march from Vlamertinghe to Potijze Wood, from where they were sent to take the line between *'Canadian Farm'* and *'Kansas Cross'*. Their first task was to improve the trenches that were in a very poor state; the second task was to bury the dead as more than a thousand corpses lay ahead of them.

Gas was released on their line on Saturday 24th and as it rolled towards them Ernest was order to rapid fire to forestall an attack. The gas had dispersed by the time it reached their lines although many suffered with minor effects. That night the men went out into No Man's Land to bury large numbers of the dead. The Battalion was were ordered to retire towards St Julien on Monday 26th. Two days later German aeroplane flew low over their lines, Ernest and his comrades opened rapid fire with some success as it crashed behind the lines. The Battalion was to be relieved on Saturday 1st May, but orders were received to proceed to *'Sanctuary Wood'*: *"… a blessed calm prevailed, the only sound was the singing of the nightingale"*. They spent two days digging trenches before being moved to Hooge into a new trench line in front of the Bellewaarde Spur. It was described by one of the officers: *"The position of the companies for the next two days was not pleasant."* The German artillery were able to blast the Battalion's position from almost point blank range and as a result the losses were terrible. In two days one hundred and fifty were killed and two hundred wounded. Ernest spent Saturday 8th in a dugout behind Bellewaarde Lake where the next day he came under heavy shell fire that heralded another German attack and the opening of the Battle of Frezenberg Ridge. The Princess Patricia's Canadian Light Infantry were in the firing line and were under great pressure. The Battalion was deployed to support them that was described by the

Canadians: *"We have seen the angels today, they had R.B. on their shoulders."* The good work provided by Ernest and his comrades stemmed the tide and were able to halt the German advance. One attack after another was mounted and each time it was repulsed. Early on Monday 10th another bombardment was laid down by the German artillery and a further attack was made that pushed the Battalion back. In the fierce fight Ernest was killed.

10792 PRIVATE FRANK LALLY
2nd Battalion Duke of Wellington's
(West Riding Regiment)
Died on Sunday 8th November 1914, aged 17
Commemorated on Addenda Panel 59.

Frank, or Francis as he was christened, was born in Bradford, Yorkshire, eldest son and child of Alice Lally and the late John Lally, of 13 Pine Street, Bradford.
He volunteered in Halifax and went out to France on Sunday 20th September 1914. The Battalion had been serving on the Aisne and as Frank arrived they were preparing to leave the sector. The Battalion arrived in Béthune on Friday 9th October where he joined them. Frank's first experience of the front was at La Bassée. The Germans broke through on Thursday 22nd, Frank remained under heavy artillery fire and constant attack, with the Germans coming within four hundred yards of their trenches. The Black Watch relieved the Battalion on Thursday 29th but it did not last long as they were required to support the Sikhs who were coming under pressure at Festubert. Frank left the line on Monday 2nd November and marched to Estaires where he was taken by bus to Bailleul. From there he marched into Belgium, arriving in Ypres on Thursday 5th November at 5.00pm and took billets in *'Hermitage Château'*. Colonel Harrison recorded: *"Marched 6.45 a.m. were delayed three-quarts of an hour at Dranouter, where a French Cavalry Division passed us. About noon heavy artillery fire was going on in front of us, so the whole Brigade turned left-handed and we spread ourselves out over a largish area behind some woods and hedges, where we stayed for two hours, when the shelling ceased. Roads very bad and knee-deep in mud except on the pavee. Arrived Ypres 5 p.m. As we passed the fine old Town Hall and Cathedral it looked splendid in the twilight, and though a few shells had been dropped in various buildings in the town there had actually been no damage done to these buildings. Later on, however, I believe the greatest part of this place has been destroyed. Marched on till 7.30 p.m., and took over the trenches from the General Commanding 22nd Brigade, of which only some 900 men remained. An attack about 10 p.m. died out, and the fire trenches were taken over by the Bedfords and Cheshires. We remained in support in edge of wood."* From 9.00am on

Sunday 8th the Battalion came under heavy shell fire and the Germans counter-attacked. Whilst defending the line Frank was killed.

1797 PRIVATE ARTHUR AUSTIN LAMB
1st/4th Battalion East Yorkshire Regiment
Died on Saturday 24th April 1915, aged 17
Commemorated on Panel 31.

Arthur was born in Kirkstall, Yorkshire, only son and eldest child of James Arthur and the late Isabella Lamb, of 42 William Street, Hull.
He went out to France on Friday 17th April 1915, for Arthur's story see Private Harry Barr, above.

64055 PRIVATE
PIERRE HENRI LAMBERT, MM
3rd Battalion Canadian Infantry
(Central Ontario Regiment)
Died on Tuesday 13th June 1916, aged 17
Commemorated on Panel 18.

Pierre's signature

Pierre was the son of Jules Lambert, of 3 Rue Emile Bonnet, Saint Leu La Forêt, near Paris, Seine-et-Oise, France.
He volunteered in *'Dibgate Camp'* on Thursday 9th September 1915 when he claimed to have been born on Saturday 29th August 1896 and was a student. Pierre was a Roman Catholic, 5ft 6in tall, with a 36in chest, a fair complexion, brown eyes and fair coloured hair. Pierre was sent for training in Canada before sailing to England where he continued to train until being sent to France. He was held at base for a short time before joining the Battalion in the field whilst they were in billets in Dranouter. Pierre began training with his new comrades and prepared for his first tour of duty near *'RE Farm'*. It was cold in the front line with snow covering the ground, but it was a relatively quiet sector. He marched via Westoutre and Reninghelst to *'Scottish Lines'* on Saturday 1st April where the Battalion was in reserve. The next day Pierre marched to the support lines and billeted in *'Bedford House'* then began fatigues. From Monday 10th the Battalion went into the front lines trenches covering *'Lovers Lane'*, *'Thorne Street'*, *'Grand Fleet Street'* and *'Petticoat Lane'*. German mine workings discovered near *'The Dump'* were blown at 11.00am on Wednesday 12th that rocked the ground as it went up. Pierre watched as the Battalion snipers fired on a number of German periscopes, scoring a number of direct hits much to the enjoyment of all. The

tour of duty ended on Sunday 16th when Pierre was relieved and marched through Ypres to the Asylum where he boarded the train for Poperinghe. Billets were provided in the Boeschepestraat and he was able to get some much needed rest. The next morning he was able to go with his platoon for a hot bath and was issued with clean underwear. Pierre was sent on a working party burying cable during the night. At 7.30pm on Monday 24th he marched to 'Dickebusch Huts' from where fatigues continued until returning to the trenches near 'Larch Wood' on Tuesday 2nd May for an eight-day tour. Pierre spent a week in 'Scottish Lines' before moving back to 'Bedford House' on Sunday 28th. May ended with a four-day tour in the front line then Pierre marched to 'Dickebusch Huts'.

Pierre had been promised a reasonable rest and a break from the trenches but that was not to be as the Germans launched an attack on Friday 2nd June. The Battalion was ordered to stand to and marched off at 3.00am the next morning to the 'GHQ Lines' at 'Château Segard'. Rumours abounded on the progress made by the enemy and the loss of several senior officers. At 10.00am Pierre was moved forward to 'Railway Dugouts' where a group of fifty men of the Battalion had the grim task of going out to bury the dead in 'Square Wood' whilst others were sent on various other working parties. The Germans continued to shell the whole sector and on Tuesday 6th blew a series of mines at Hooge. After a difficult few days for all ranks Pierre was relieved to 'Scottish Lines' on Thursday 8th. The next day he was able to rest, catching up on sleep, and on Saturday 10th was sent for a hot bath before parading for General Currie who addressed the Battalion. Pierre returned to the front line late on Sunday 11th. Throughout Monday 12th the artillery pounded the German lines. From 12.45am until 1.30am on Tuesday 13th an intense bombardment was laid down and as soon as it lifted Pierre was led forward towards 'Machine Gun Trench'. The attack went well, at the point of the bayonet, and a large number of the enemy were despatched in their trenches. The Battalion pressed on before they came under heavy German shellfire from both high explosive and shrapnel shells. During the bombardment Pierre was hit and killed, his body was lost on the battlefield.

10752 PRIVATE CECIL HENRY LANE
2nd Battalion Welsh Regiment
Died on Friday 6th November 1914, aged 17
Commemorated on Panel 37.

Cecil was the third son of Catherine Lane, of 110 Aubrey Street, Everton, Liverpool, and the late James Lane. Following school he became an apprentice cycle fitter.

Cecil went to France on Wednesday 12th August 1914, landing in Le Havre and the next day marched five miles to 'No 6 Rest Camp' at St Martin's. The Battalion entrained on Saturday 15th in a large collection of open trucks for Etreux from where they marched six miles to Leschelle. They marched through Maubeuge to Grand Reng. Captain Rees (later Brigadier General Hubert Conway Rees, CMG, DSO) recorded in his diary the defences of Maubeuge: "… the masses of barbed wire 100 yards deep and lines of well-concealed trenches with splendid fields of fire looked very serviceable."

Just as the Battalion settled into their billets orders were received for them to move forward a further five miles. In the distance they heard the sound of machine gun and rifle fire as cavalry patrols from both sides came under attack. Whilst in billets the Medical Officer inoculated the men. The Battalion entrenched their position on Sunday 23rd; they were not engaged during the battle but from their slit trenches they could see clearly the fight ahead of them. They were ordered to retire on Monday 24th, Captain Rees recorded: "Melville with one machine gun was posted on the railway line to sweep with his gun the approaches from Merbes St. Marie i.e., E. towards the gap between the B.E.F. and the French. We had a very disturbed night, having at the most three-quarters of an hour's sleep on the track. On three occasions during the night did the German Army open rifle fire. It appeared as if tens of thousands of men were all firing as fast as they could. They could not have been very far away as a few, very much spent, bullets reached us. In addition to the cannonade from Mons a still heavier roar of firing began at dawn about the outskirts of Charleroi, and the French were steadily driven back, as far as we could judge, through Merbes St. Marie on Merbes Le Château. By 9 a.m. we seemed to run the risk of being cut off. About 9.30 a.m. we got orders to retire on Croix and Rouveroy, and at the same moment a German cavalry patrol appeared from the Bois Houdiez (about 1,000 yards distant). When we had quite decided they were really Germans a section opened fire, and brought down the whole patrol, both men and horses." This was only a patrol from a large body of cavalry which had approached unseen owing to a fold in the ground."

As the Battalion marched south they were resting next to a French cavalry regiment that had bivouacked, Captain Rees recorded: "The artillery fire was only a distant matter of sound, and I don't imagine anyone was considering the possibility of being attacked. The pandemonium, which ensued when a sharp rattle of musketry broke out from the Queen's, beggars description. The Frenchmen leapt on their horses bareback, firing their pistols, a bolting two-horsed limber charged down the road, and all the men scrambled over the hedges to get out of its way, whilst a 60-pounder Battery somehow got off the road into action, and opened fire at a range of 800 yards on a herd of frightened cows, which were mistaken in the dusk for a Battery of German artillery coming into action."

The Battalion did not become involved in the Battle of Le Cateau but heard the noise of battle in the distance. They continued to march southeastward until Saturday 5th September, Captain Rees wrote: *"The determination of the men during the Retreat passed all belief. The reservists, as I remarked before, were not in any way fit for such a terrific test of endurance. Between 22nd August and 5th September, we marched about 240 miles, and only on one day did we have any semblance of rest. The men were absolutely tired out before the actual retreat began on 24th. At the end of some of the marches it was impossible to maintain our formation, and the column became merely a crow flowing very slowly along the road, the men looking as if they neither saw nor felt anything. Almost without exception their feet were raw and bleeding, and many marched with puttees wrapped round their feet. Their one desire was to halt and fight the enemy, and not being allowed to do so was the cause of bitter complaint."*

The Battalion finally arrived and halted in Rozoy. From Sunday 6th September the Battalion turned to find the enemy. Lieutenant Melville wrote: *"It was here, that we received our first orders to march forward to the Marne, and it was one of the most wonderful illustrations of moral that one could possibly see. The troops, who had before been thoroughly tired and worn out and disheartened, fell in on parade like fresh recruits, eager to be off. Their attitude had altered. Even when moving forward on the dusty roads, when they had to make way for the Field Artillery, instead of cursing them for covering them with dust, they cheered them wildly and wished them good luck."*

After passing the Marne they continued onto the Aisne. The Battalion was the Advanced Guard for the 1st Division on Saturday 12th September and spent a dreadful night on duty in pouring rain and biting cold wind; none of the men had a greatcoat for protection. Captain Rees wrote: *"We were as hard as iron, but a most disreputable gang. Probably not so appallingly filthy as we were after the First Battle of Ypres, but all the men, and most of the officers wore beards, through the impossibility of finding time to shave, and it would have puzzled most of us to remember the last time we had a bath."* The Battalion took position on the Chemin des Dames close to Troyon where they engaged the Germans as Captain Rees wrote: *"We were holding a steep bank on the near crest of the ridge with the Germans among some corn stooks, only 150 yards away. We rushed the Huns, and the remnants of them fled. The ground was littered with their dead."*

Lieutenant Melville wrote: *"Having wiped out this little counter-attack I, suddenly, to my intense excitement, observed the German trenches on my right filled with troops prepared to repulse the attack of the S.W.B. Ranging very carefully with my Barr and Stroud, I started vertical*

searching from both my guns. As the range was only about 700 to 800 yards, the execution was terrible. Eventually the Germans could stand it no longer, and breaking from their trenches ran back over the crest of the hill like a football mob, both my guns pumping into them, as hard as they could fire. I then saw a most beautiful exhibition of shooting by the 113th Field Battery, which was supporting us in the valley below. As soon as the enemy broke from their trenches, the guns opened on them with shrapnel. The slaughter was terrific. Later on in the day the drama was repeated, the Boche being forced back into their trenches only to break once again and retire over the hill. They never returned after that, and the hillside was thick with their dead and wounded."*

The Battalion remained on the Aisne until early October before being sent north, entraining for Hazebrouck where they arrived on Monday 19th October. They were sent to Poperinghe and provided with billets in a convent. From Wednesday 21st they took the line at Langemarck where the next day the German artillery targeted the village that reduced it to rubble. Captain Rees described the barrage: *"I saw a field gun shell strike the spire of the church just below the cross, and send the cross 20 yards in the air. The church shortly afterwards caught fire and went up in a sheet of flame. A little later, Colonel Morland and Battalion H.Q. came to my Company H.Q. He had had two houses blown down over his head in succession in the village, and, as he remarked, it was safer in the front line."* Cecil was at Koekuit, just beyond Langemarck, on Friday 23rd when he came under a concerted attack, with the Germans advancing in close formation who were mown down in droves by British rapid fire. He moved to Bellewaarde on Monday 26th. At 5.30am on Thursday 29th the expected German attack fell on the defenders and pushed the line back. At 2.00pm a counter-attack was mounted towards Gheluvelt. As Cecil reached the edge of the village he saw a large number of Germans advancing and opened rapid fire on them. By the end of the day the advance had been checked. Throughout Friday 30th the Battalion consolidated its position and dug in whilst under constant artillery fire.

By 8.00am on Saturday 31st the fog lifted and the Germans launched a relentless barrage on their lines which destroyed many of the defences and claimed the lives of many. At 10.00am the German infantry advanced in strength and for over an hour the British rapid fire held the advance at bay. However, the superiority in numbers allowed the Germans to move forward. An officer for the Gloucesters recorded: *"Church, houses, and windmill of Gheluvelt were reduced to ruins, and the Welch were practically wiped out where they stood, and soon after, dazed and broken men of this Regiment commenced to straggle back through Gheluvelt and Veldhoek. Whole companies were annihilated, and the marvel is how anyone remained to help break the infantry attacks which were delivered again and again."* Cecil was forced back to the line of the 54th Battery when a shell burst that mortally wounded Lieutenant Colonel Charles Morland who died shortly afterwards and is buried in Ypres Town Cemetery. In the fierce battle Cecil was killed.

19642 Private Edwin Francis Lane
1st Battalion Wiltshire Regiment
Died on Sunday 6th June 1915, aged 17
Commemorated on Panel 53.

Edwin was born at home, third and youngest son of James and Agnes Lane, of Hethe, Bicester, Oxfordshire. He was educated locally and then was employed as a labourer.
He volunteered in Oxford where he was allocated to the Oxford and Buckinghamshire Light Infantry with the service number 11246 before transferring to the Wiltshire Regiment. Edwin went out to France on Tuesday 4th May 1915. For his history see Private Charles Williams below.
Edwin is commemorated on Hethe War Memorial.

14406 Private
William Preston Lear
1st Battalion Devonshire Regiment
Died on Monday 26th April 1915, aged 16
Commemorated on Panel 21.

William was born at home in 1899, the eldest son of William Preston Lear and Caroline Louise Lear, of 38 Torbay View, Overgang, Brixham, Devon.
He volunteered in Paignton, Devon, and went out to France on Friday 12th March 1915. He joined the Battalion whilst they were serving at Kemmel. William remained on tours of duty in the sector until Sunday 18th April. Two days later he was in Divisional Reserve at Kruisstaat when the Battalion was ordered to march to Zillebeke Pond on Tuesday 20th. The next day William moved to Hill 60, a scene of total devastation from the fierce battle that had been raging since the mines were blown and the attack that had begun on Saturday 17th. William came under heavy shell fire as the German infantry poured rifle and machine gun fire onto his position. The fighting was at close quarters often from one shell crater to another that resulted in heavy losses to all combatants. The fighting died down late on Wednesday 21st and in the early hours of the next morning frantic work was undertaken to reconstruct the trenches, collect the wounded and bury the dead. Throughout the day the Germans poured

shell upon shell on the British positions and in the night an attack was mounted that was successfully repulsed. William got some welcome relief from the fighting for two days from Friday 23rd. When he returned the sector was relatively quiet but it was not to last. The enemy began a heavy bombardment late on Monday 26th and then rushed the line held by the Battalion. In defending his position William was killed.
He is commemorated on the Brixham War Memorial.

5644 Private Frank Ledwidge
2nd Battalion Royal Dublin Fusiliers
Died on Monday 24th May 1915, aged 17
Commemorated on Panel 46.

Frank was born at home, son of Frank and Ellen Ledwidge, of 134 Thomas Street, Dublin.
He volunteered in Dublin and went out to France on Sunday 2nd May 1915. For Frank's story see Private John Smullen, below. Frank was first listed as missing until his death was confirmed.

9129 Private Thomas Lennon
2nd Battalion Royal Dublin Fusiliers
Died on Sunday 23rd May 1915, aged 17
Commemorated on Panel 46.

Thomas was born and raised in Dublin the son of Mr and Mrs Thomas Lennon, of Dublin.
He volunteered in Dublin and went out to France on Monday 3rd May 1915. For Thomas' story see Private John Smullen, below.

3093 Private Thomas Liddell
1st/5th Battalion Durham Light Infantry
Died on Sunday 25th April 1915, aged 17
Commemorated on Panel 36.

Thomas was the son of William and Isabella Liddell, of 1 Farm Cottages, Shotton Colliery, Sunderland.
He volunteered in Stockton-on-Tees, and went out to France on Friday 16th April 1915. For Thomas' story see Private Robert Waller, below.
He is commemorated on the Shotton Colliery War Memorial.

9620 PRIVATE
WILLIAM GEORGE LILLEY
'A' Company, 1st Battalion
Royal Warwickshire Regiment
Died on Monday 24th May 1915, aged 16
Commemorated on Panel 8.

William was born at home, eldest son of William and Lucy Lilley, of 82 Conybere Street, Birmingham. He was educated locally.

He enlisted in Birmingham and was sent for training before embarking for France to join the Battalion in the field on Sunday 2nd May 1915. William was sent into the line at Potijze Château on Saturday 8th May where he remained for five days. He was relieved from the line and marched through the Menin Gate into the shattered town of Ypres. Very heavy shelling over the previous four weeks had taken a heavy toll on the town and William would have seen very little other than the movement of troops amongst the ruins. No longer were there open shops selling their wares or street cafés lining the streets and square. The town was also a dangerous place to be as the German artillery had the whole town pin-pointed. His march continued out along the Ypres to Poperinghe road, stopping in the relative safety of Vlamertinghe where he was able to rest for a few days. William was able to clean up, received clean clothes, had regular meals and was able to sleep. He paraded then marched back along the cobbled road to Ypres on Thursday 17th and out via Menin Gate, arriving at the front line in Wieltje. He had been trained and prepared for the attack on *Shell Trap Farm*' which took placed on Monday 24th. William and the Battalion was in support some way behind the front line when the Germans used gas against the British lines so William was not effected by it. His Company was in readiness to advance but the heavy machine-gun fire prevented their deployment. Despite not being in the heart of the battle William was killed: one of more than a hundred casualties.

11673 PRIVATE ARTHUR LITTLE
1st Battalion The King's (Liverpool Regiment)
Died on Wednesday 18th November 1914, aged 17
Commemorated on Panel 4.

Arthur was born in Warrington, Lancashire, third son of Thomas and Ellen Little, of 27 Smithdown Lane, Paddington, Liverpool.

He volunteered in Liverpool prior to the war. Following mobilisation Arthur embarked on the SS *Irrawaddy* to Le Havre on 13th August 1914 under the command of Lieutenant Colonel William Bannatyne.

Upon arrival in Le Havre he, and all the troops, received a tremendous welcome then marched to a rest camp three miles above the town of St Adresse. Arthur entrained to northern France then marched towards the Mons battlefield. Following the battle he took part in The Retreat, Colonel T W S Graham wrote: *"With regard to the men's packs, I distinctly recall that Colonel Bannatyne sent for us Company Commanders during this night (25th/26th) in Maroilles and said that he had been ordered confidentially, to inform us (and us only, the information to be kept to ourselves), that the position was that the brigade could not be got away and therefrom the best available position was to be occupied before dawn and the brigade would fight the matter out to the end on the position selected. I particularly recollect him saying, that under no circumstances would the brigade be surrendered. Further, he ordered that in order to fight light and unimpeded, the men would not need packs, and we were ordered to stack them — these were stacked in a house and not on wagons at all. As far as I remember, the full number of rounds of ammunition were issued per man."*

Captain Sheppard recorded the following incident during The Retreat: *"I remember a young N.C.O. who got a shrapnel bullet through the calf of his leg near Bavai early on the morning of August 25th. Not only did he march fifteen miles with us, but he went up and down the ranks encouraging unwounded men, who were so tired that they just wanted to fall out and go to sleep. During the halts he was unable to sit down as his wound got stiff, so he walked up and down the road, cheering up, and setting an example to his men. He was offered a ride on a horse, which he refused as he said that it was his duty to keep the men 'at it, and he could not do that unless he was on his feet himself'."*

Arthur was *en route* to Meaux on Wednesday 2nd September when between 3.00 and 4.00am he moved off in the cold and mist. However, it soon warmed up and all ranks became exhausted marching in the heat. The 6th Brigade Diary records: *"The day was very hot and the men were about done. The straggling was the worst we had seen, but there every excuse as there was very little chance of getting water. The 1st King's carried on best of the four battalions."* At 8.00pm they arrived three miles east of Meaux. The never-ending march continued the next day as one of the officers related: *"I came across upon our Mess Sergeant walking along with a hen under his arm. A hen is not the thing I should choose to carry under my arm during a twenty mile march and so I asked him why he did not kill it. He replied, in all seriousness, that he was going to keep it alive for a day or two in case it should lay an egg."* The Battalion turned and recrossed the Marne and marched on to take position on the Aisne. Whilst on the Aisne it is recorded that on Monday 21st September Colonel Bannatyne received orders by telephone from Brigade Headquarters, *"... these being the first to be received by a field instrument"* at least the first by the King's Regiment during the war!

Arthur marched to Fismes on Thursday 15th October where he entrained for St Omer that was reached via Paris and Calais; the next night he was billeted in Hazebrouck.

The Battalion marched to Godeswaersvelde on Monday 19th through the rain with everyone being soaked to the skin. After drying out, and a nights' sleep, Arthur marched via Reninghelst and Elverdinghe to Boesinghe. At 4.55am on Wednesday 21st the Battalion was ordered to support Wieltje, *en route* they stopped in a turnip field for several hours with the noise of battle ringing in their ears. They moved forward again but were not required so were ordered back to St Jan late that night where they were billeted. Arthur remained in his billet until 4.00pm when orders were received to move forward. They arrived at Zillebeke at 6.15pm where 'B' Company went into the line on the ridge between Zandvoorde and Hollebeke. At dawn they were relieved and undertook the familiar march back to St Jan where they spent the rest of the day in reserve. Arthur took his men into action on Saturday 24th. They were sent in front of Westhoek to relieve the 1st South Staffordshires and began an attack against Molenaarelsthoek. They advanced to the outskirts of the village where the Germans put up a reasonable defence. They were able to push on and took the village, bar a couple of cottages. The machine-gun fire from the remaining cottages was fierce, Arthur took part in two charges against the guns. He was lucky to survive Monday 26th, throughout Tuesday 27th Arthur remained in the line where the ammunition was running dangerously low. Major Steavenson wrote: *"In a quarter of an hour we had the pack animals up with fifteen boxes; the men had run the whole way; all of them and Company Quartermaster-Sergt. Walsh in charge 'pumped' to a turn, but they had done real good work."* Now replenished with ammunition Arthur was able to effectively open rapid fire on Wednesday 28th that halted a German attack. Late in the evening Arthur was relieved from the line and was sent for some rest in a bivouac. In the morning he enjoyed a good breakfast before setting about cleaning his rifle, equipment and himself. With little real rest, Arthur was ordered to move off at 1.00pm for Polygon Wood, arriving an hour later. As soon as he was in position Arthur and his comrades began to dig in furiously. It was a relatively quiet night so he not only was able to enjoy a hot meal but some rest too. At 6.00am the Battalion was ordered to their old billets at Westhoek where he was able to get some welcome rest. The German war machine was putting all its efforts into breaking through at Ypres by attacking across the sector continuously. At 11.30am on Saturday 31st the situation

at Polygon Wood was precarious and the Battalion was sent back to help defend the line. The enemy advanced and captured Gheluvelt late in the day then the line quietened down — both sides were quite exhausted. For Arthur, Sunday 1st November was a relatively quiet day but on Monday 2nd the German artillery began to pound Polygon Wood.

Arthur remained at the front countering small raids from time to time but the next major action he was involved in began at 7.00am on Wednesday 11th November. He was ordered to rapid fire on the attacking Germans. Targets could not be easily identified in the dark but Arthur and his comrades kept firing. When dawn broke it was clear their firing had been deadly accurate as the great heaps of German dead littered the ground in front of them. The enemy artillery, who had ample supplies of ammunition, bombarded the sector, Colonel Steavenson recorded: *"Our dug-outs were completely blotted out and long swathes cut through the wood as if a gigantic scythe had gone down and taken off the trees three feet from the ground."* The Prussian Guard pressed home the attack, the German armies put nearly twenty thousand men into the field against less than eight thousand British defenders. Arthur's good work helped stop the German advance at Nonne Boschen and one can only wonder how many of the enemy young Arthur managed to kill — the German dead littered the battlefield by the hundred. The First Battle of Ypres had effectively drawn to a close. The Salient had been formed and trench warfare began, although there was no let up in shelling for either side. Late on Monday 16th Arthur was mortally wounded by shellfire.

10755 Lance Corporal Arthur George Llewellyn
'A' Company, 1st Battalion Coldstream Guards
Died on Thursday 12th November 1914, aged 17
Commemorated on Panel 11.

Arthur was born in Nechells, Warwickshire, third son of Annie Llewellyn, of 12 Cross Keys Yard, Atherstone, Warwickshire, and the late Edward James Llewellyn. He was educated locally and was then employed as a warehouse lad.

He volunteered in Nuneaton and went out to France on Sunday 1st November 1914. Arthur arrived in Ypres on Thursday 5th with a draft of one hundred men.

Arthur was to be in the line for only a couple of days before he was killed. The First Battle of Ypres came to its height on Wednesday 11th with a massive attack across the whole Salient. Arthur was in the line at Polygon Wood and was one of only six killed from the Battalion on Thursday 12th that otherwise was considered to be a quiet day.

His brother, Lance Corporal Albert Edward Llewellyn, died of wounds on Thursday 16th January 1919 and is buried in Manchester Cemetery. Arthur is commemorated on Albert's CWGC gravestone.

36003 PRIVATE HENRY LLOYD
1st Battalion Welsh Regiment
Died on Tuesday 25th May 1915, aged 17
Commemorated on Panel 37.

Henry was born in Abertillery, Monmouthshire, second son of John Lloyd, of 1 Cae Felin Street, Llanhilleth, Newport, Monmouthshire, and the late Eliza Lloyd. He had four older sisters and a brother, and a younger brother.

He went out to France on Wednesday 5th May 1915. For Henry's story see Private Edmund Jones above.

S/9004 PRIVATE
WILLIAM THOMSON MACAUSLAN
1st Battalion Gordon Highlanders
Died on Saturday 25th September 1915, aged 17
Commemorated on Panel 38.

William was born in Shawland, Lanarkshire, son of Peter Macauslan, of Castlepark, Lanark.

He volunteered in Lanark and went out to France on Wednesday 21st April 1915. William arrived at the front just as the Second Battle of Ypres had begun. He joined his comrades whilst they were serving in the St Eloi sector and where he remained until moving the short distance to Hill 60 on Wednesday 12th May. A ghastly sight greeted William and the Battalion — the decomposing bodies of the dead, that had been lying there for a week, littered No Man's Land and packed the trenches. He was detailed to help collect the remains then bury them and on the same duty he retrieved large quantities of salvage. Everyone in the Battalion was pleased to be relieved as they marched to La Clytte late on Thursday 20th. Following the German attack at Hooge on Monday 24th William was ordered to stand to and somewhat later in the day he marched to the reserve trenches east of Zillebeke. He came under a heavy and sustained artillery barrage on Tuesday 1st June that was followed by a gas attack. It was a long and difficult tour of duty that had lasted nineteen days before being relieved.

William remained on tours of duty and the next major action was to be his last. As a diversionary action in support of the Battle of Loos that began a few miles to the south on Saturday 25th September, the

1st and 4th Battalions were to take part in an attack at Bellewaarde. Shortly before William went into the line he was inspected by Field Marshal Lord Kitchener who addressed the parade and told them: *"Scotland expected that their work would be thoroughly well done"*.

Late on Friday 24th William arrived in the trenches astride the Menin Road and at 4.10am the next morning he was led forward towards the German line. Unfortunately the artillery had failed to cut the German wire and as a result the Battalion was badly held up and exposed to enemy fire. The German infantry did their worst and as a result the Battalion took considerable losses, the majority before 11.00am:

	Killed	Wounded	Missing
Officers	6	8	3
Other Ranks	36	232	58

One of those killed was William.

435348 PRIVATE JOHN MACDONALD
10th Battalion Canadian Infantry (Alberta Regiment)
Died on Saturday 3rd June 1916, aged 17
Commemorated on Panel 24.

John MacDonald

John's signature

John was born at home, son of Mr and Mrs Daniel C Macdonald, of 910 5th Street North-West, Calgary, Alberta.

He volunteered in Calgary on Tuesday 15th June 1915, where he claimed to have been born on Tuesday 24th August 1897 and worked as a labourer. John was a Presbyterian, 5ft 7in tall, with a 35in chest, a fair complexion, blue eyes and fair coloured hair.

Following training in Canada and England John joined the Battalion with a draft on Saturday 4th September 1915 whilst they were serving in the Messines to Ploegsteert sector. He remained on tours of duty in the sector, serving in the front line, in reserve around *'Grand Munque Farm'*, on fatigues or out of the line training — mainly in *'Bulford Camp'* — until Wednesday 24th November when the Battalion was sent to a camp between Méteren and St Jan Cappel, just west of Bailleul. Two days later training began lasting until Monday 13th December then John marched back to *'Bulford Camp'*. He was able to get a hot bath on Wednesday 15th after which he was issued with his pay. Late on Thursday 16th John returned to the front line once again, Christmas was not celebrated properly although plum pudding and cigars were given out at lunchtime on Saturday 25th. John remained on tours of duty, in reserve, on fatigues, or out of the line resting and training until the end of March 1916. The Battalion undertook a number of small raids against the German lines but were not involved in any significant

... an idealised view of Christmas in the trenches

operations. When he left the sector John was sent into reserve at Eecke.

A joint Church Parade with the 8th Battalion was held on Sunday 2nd April and General Sir Edwin Alderson addressed the men at its conclusion. Two days later John marched along the pavé, passing the many hospitals *en route* to billets in the hop factory next to Poperinghe station. He entrained in the town for Brielen at 7.30am on Saturday 8th from where he marched into the front line for eight days. John was relieved and sent to *'Dickebusch Huts'* from where he undertook fatigues. An urgent telegram was sent to the Colonel on Monday 24th to *"stand to and await further orders"* but it turned out to be a false alarm, however the Battalion was due to go into reserve at *'Scottish Lines'* which was effected late that night. A similar telegram was again received on Wednesday 26th and the Colonel had his work cut out to bring back the work parties and prepare the rest of the Battalion in case they would be needed. Again, the Battalion was not required to support the line as a German attack had been adequately repulsed. General Sir Douglas Haig toured the front and inspected the Battalion whilst they were at work on Friday 28th. John moved into the front line at *'Petticoat Lane'* during the night of Thursday 4th May for six days, then moved into support. He was sent out on working parties until Tuesday 16th when he moved to billets at *'Bedford House'* when the Battalion switched to support. John was able to get a good soak and cleaned up when he was taken for a hot bath on Saturday 20th. He began a few days of training and fatigues until he returned to the front line on Friday 26th for a relatively quiet five-day tour. John went into reserve at *'Swan Château'* where he was when the German attack on Mount Sorrel began on Friday 2nd June. Shells were flying around the whole sector but thankfully the billets the Battalion occupied avoided any direct hits. At 4.40pm the Colonel received orders to move forward and support the line. When they arrived at what had been the front line they did not find a recognisable trench system, it had been obliterated. The fight was hard with the German firepower being used to its best. In the fierce hand-to-hand fighting John was killed.

He is commemorated on Banff War Memorial, Alberta.

2016 Private Thomas Henry Maddock
Leicestershire Yeomanry
Died on Thursday 13th May 1915, aged 17
Commemorated on Panel 5.

Thomas was born at home, third son of Charles Arthur and Elizabeth Annie Maddock, of 75 Moira Street, Leicester. He had an older sister and two brothers, together with three younger brothers and a sister.

He volunteered in Leicester and went out to France on Tuesday 3rd November 1914. Thomas was sent to serve on the Ypres Salient as the First Battle of Ypres was at its height but shortly to reach its conclusion. He soon settled down to tours of duty at front, or when relieved undertaking training coupled with some rest but was not involved in any particular action until the Second Battle of Ypres in April 1915.

He was in bivouac near Brielen on Tuesday 11th May as the Battle of the Frezenberg Ridge began. Thomas' officers visited the trenches where they would be occupying late the next evening. At 6.30pm Thomas paraded then marched to the front line, however, orders were received that sent them to near *'Cambridge Road'* not where the officers had reconnoitred the day before. Thomas was immediately ordered to improve the communication trenches and from 5.00am enemy artillery began firing across the sector that was followed by an infantry attack. Thomas was in his front line trench when a shell burst that killed him instantaneously.

9697 Rifleman Patrick Maguire
2nd Battalion Royal Irish Rifles
Died on Friday 10th August 1917, aged 17
Commemorated on Panel 40.

Patrick was born at home, son of John and Rose Anne Maguire, of Clonroche, County Wexford.

He volunteered in Wexford and went out to France with a draft. For Patrick's story and that of the Battalion see Rifleman James McClelland, below.

5701 Private Myles Mahoney
'A' Company, 2nd Battalion Royal Dublin Fusiliers
Died on Monday 10th May 1915, aged 16
Commemorated on Panel 46.

Myles was born at home, son of James Mahoney, of 10 Lower Bridge Street, Dublin. He was educated locally. Myles volunteered in Dublin and was sent for training before joining the Battalion in the field on Monday 3rd

May 1915. Myles was stood to early on Saturday 9th, at 1.30pm marched through Ypres, La Brique, St Jan to the woods near Potijze Château, and as he approached the Château the shell-fire became intense. Myles was in the line one hundred and fifty yards southeast of *'Mouse Trap Farm'* when he was killed. During the action some of Myles' pals in the Battalion were in reserve north of Potijze Wood. The shelling experienced the day Myles died was the worst the Battalion had faced since the beginning of the war.

2566 PRIVATE PETER MALCOLM
1st/7th Battalion
Argyll and Sutherland Highlanders
Died on Saturday 8th May 1915, aged 17
Commemorated on Panel 44.

Peter's signature

Peter was born at home, the only son of Robert and Janet Malcolm of 26 King Street, Alloa. He had two younger sisters.

He volunteered in Alloa on Wednesday 9th September 1914 when he claimed to be 19 years old. Peter was 5ft 9in tall with a 34½in chest. He was sent for training with the Battalion until entraining to Southampton and sailed to Le Havre on Tuesday 15th December 1914, arriving the next day. He entrained to northern France for final training and after a period of practical experience in the trenches attached to battle-hardened troops Peter served in the southern part of the Salient. He moved to the Salient itself and the Hooge sector where he served on tours of duty until the outbreak of The Second Battle of Ypres on Thursday 22nd April 1915. Peter was soon deployed to defend the line and to take part in a number of counter-attacks. Despite his hard work the line was forced to retire and whilst in action two weeks later Peter was killed.

G/8641 PRIVATE
THOMAS WILLIAM MANNING
4th Battalion Middlesex Regiment
Died on Tuesday 20th July 1915, aged 17
Commemorated on Panel 51.

Thomas was born in Pimlico, London, son of Thomas and Jemima Manning and the brother of Mrs Adelaide Davey, of 91 Glengarry Road, East Dulwich, London. He volunteered in St Paul's, London, and went out to France on Tuesday 15th June 1915. For Thomas' story see Private Walter Francis, above.

2119 PRIVATE ERNEST MARKS
40th Battalion Australian Infantry, AIF
Died on Thursday 7th June 1917, aged 17
Commemorated on Panel 25.

Ernest's signature

Ernest was born at home, son of Gustave and Alice Maud Marks, of Port Augusta, South Australia.

He volunteered in Adelaide on Tuesday 18th July 1916 when he claimed to be 18 years old and worked as a labourer. Ernest was 5ft 7¼in tall, with a 33in chest, weighed 132lbs, had a fair complexion, blue eyes, and light brown hair.

He sailed with the Battalion from Adelaide on *SS Anchises* on Monday 28th August 1916 and disembarked in Plymouth on Wednesday 11th October. He was sent to Larkhill on Salisbury Plain where training continued. Ernest entrained in Amesbury bound for Southampton Docks on Thursday 23rd November and embarked at 6.00pm. After a reasonable crossing the ship arrived at 2.30am the next morning but Ernest and his comrades did not disembark until 9.00am. The Battalion paraded on the docks then marched off to *'No 1 Rest Camp'* where they arrived at 5.00pm. After some rest overnight William marched to the station the next day to entrain to Armentières. For the next week he undertook training and prepared to go into the front line.

Ernest's first tour of duty began on Sunday 10th December that lasted for six days. He returned to the trenches after some rest and spent Christmas at the front where one of his comrades was killed, Private Carl Christensen who is buried in Cité Bonjean Military Cemetery, Armentières. Ernest was relieved on Thursday 28th and sent to billets where he was able to enjoy a delayed Christmas.

Tours of duty in the trenches continued from 3rd January 1917 and at 5.50pm the enemy raided the line with a party estimated to between fifty and sixty. They attempted to enter the Battalion line but were repulsed. After a further two tours of duty Ernest moved to the Bois Grenier sector on Friday 26th where at the end of the month another German raid was mounted but again they were repulsed after suffering a number killed and the loss of a large collection of material!

Ernest was hospitalised on Friday 2nd February with scabies but was able to return to his comrades on Sunday 18th and returned to front line duties until early March. Ernest undertook a number of marches and moves beginning on Saturday 3rd March. He undertook training in Tatinghem until Thursday 5th April when he marched to St Omer, entrained to Steenwerck then marched to Armentières. Ernest returned to the trenches in the Houplines sector from 8.00pm Sunday 8th where he remained for a week. He undertook training until Thursday 26th then marched across the border into Belgium to serve in the Ploegsteert sector where he remained as the build-up to The Battle of Messines began. From Friday 1st to Wednesday 6th June Ernest undertook fatigues, supplying the front from *'Regina Camp'* on the Ploegsteert road. Late on Wednesday 6th Ernest marched into the jumping off trenches near *'La Plus Douve Farm'*. As he moved forward the enemy began to lay down a heavy gas barrage so respirators had to be worn. The Battalion was led forward by guides, sadly the one allocated to the 40th took the wrong route that wasted a lot of time and caused considerable confusion amongst the senior officers. Ernest finally reached his position by 2.10am and settled down for an hour of 'rest' whilst an immense barrage was pounding the German front line. The whole area shook like an earthquake as the nineteen mines were blown at 3.10am. Once the whistles were blown Ernest was able to move forward at some speed and the Battalion captured its objectives. Ernest was killed later in the day whilst consolidating the newly captured position. Ernest was recorded to have been buried at B1056, Sheet 16.

His mother was sent Ernest's brush and two keys, the only possessions to be found. She also received his British War Medal no 46378, Victory Medal no 45846 and his Memorial Plaque and Scroll no 326082.

9580 PRIVATE CHARLES MARTIN
1st Battalion Cameron Highlanders
Died on Wednesday 11th November 1914, aged 17
Commemorated on Panel 38.

Charles was born in Raasay, Broadford, Inverness-shire, son of John Martin, of New Buildings, Bonawe Quarries, Taynuilt, Argyll.

He volunteered in Fort William, Inverness-shire and went out to Le Havre on Friday 14th August 1914 with the Battalion. He entrained to northern France then marched to the Mons battlefield. Following the Battle of Mons on Sunday 23rd August he took part in The Retreat. A hard march of over two hundred miles took Charles to within sight of Paris. Orders were issued on Saturday 5th September for the British Army to turn and engage the enemy on the Marne. With an extra spring his step Charles recrossed the Marne and marched onto the Aisne where he remained in action until early October. Charles entrained to northern France and was sent into the Ypres Salient to take part in the First Battle of Ypres. Charles marched into the medieval town of Ypres that was basically intact and beautiful, the shops and cafés

were doing a roaring trade. In the market square troops were resting, others were marching to and from the front through the Menin Gate, horses were feeding or clopping over the cobblestones. Charles took part in a number of actions as the Ypres Salient began to form and when the battle was at its height he was killed.

S/8434 PRIVATE
WILLIAM MCAUGHTRIE
1st Battalion Gordon Highlanders
Died on Wednesday 21st July 1915, aged 17
Commemorated on Panel 38.

William was the son of William and Christina Mcaughtrie, of 159 Queen Street, Govan, Glasgow. He volunteered in Glasgow and went out to France on Wednesday 21st April 1915. For William's story, see Private William Macauslan, above.

10528 RIFLEMAN
JAMES MCCLELLAND
2nd Battalion Royal Irish Rifles
Died on Monday 6th August 1917, aged 17
Commemorated on Panel 40.

James was born in Bangor, County Down, eldest son of Annabella McClelland, of 9 Ann Street, Newtownards, County Down.

He volunteered in Newtownards and after training went out to France to join the Battalion with a draft in mid-June 1917. The Battalion had taken severe losses during the Battle of Messines and the one hundred and two men that joined them in Radinghem replaced half of the losses. James undertook some training before marching to *'Pioneer Camp'* near Vlamertinghe to begin fatigues. It would the first time that James had seen the true horror of the Western Front as over the next ten days he helped construct roads. He moved to the area around *'Swan Château'* on Monday 30th July where fatigues continued until going into the dugouts in Ypres Ramparts on Saturday 4th August. After a night of rest he moved into the trenches for the first time in front of Westhoek Ridge. It was a difficult relief as the Battalion came under heavy shell fire and whilst taking cover in a front line trench James was killed when a shell burst close to him.

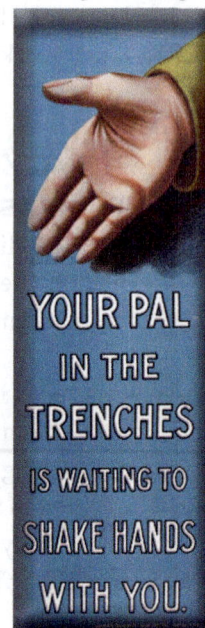

YOUR PAL IN THE TRENCHES IS WAITING TO SHAKE HANDS WITH YOU.

235128 Private
Thomas Henry McGarva
10th Battalion Cameronians (Scottish Rifles)
Died on Saturday 21st July 1917, aged 17
Commemorated on Panel 22.

Thomas was the son of Robert and Catherine Jose McGarva, of The British Consulate, Las Palmas, Grand Canary.

He volunteered and enlisted in Dumfries. Thomas was first allocated to the King's Own Scottish Borderers with service number 2881 before transferring to the Scottish Rifles. Thomas was sent out to join the Battalion with a draft.

The Battalion had served through The Battle of Arras and on Saturday 16th June 1917 entrained from France to Vlamertinghe. Three days later they moved into trenches to the left of 'Warwick Farm' close to the Ypres to Roeselare railway near Potijze. The enemy were well aware of a forthcoming offensive and they did all they could to interrupt the preparations. They introduced to the Salient a new terror weapon, mustard gas, on Thursday 19th July and drenched the artillery positions with nearly four thousand shells. During a bombardment of the area a shell burst close to Thomas that killed him.

5725 Private John McGuinness
2nd Battalion Royal Dublin Fusiliers
Died on Monday 24th May 1915, aged 17
Commemorated on Panel 46.

John was born at home, son of John McGuinness, of Stratford-on-Slaney, County Wicklow.

He enlisted in August 1914 in Naas. Following training he went out to France on Monday 3rd May 1915. For John's story see Private John Smullen, below.

27352 Private Alfred McLellan
2nd Battalion Durham Light Infantry
Died on Friday 21st April 1916, aged 17
Commemorated on Panel 38.

Alfred was born at home, second son of Alice McLellan, of 19, Henry Street, Lytham, Lancashire, and the late John Mclellan.

He was sent for training before joining the Battalion in the field on Saturday 12th February 1916 whilst they were in camp at Poperinghe. Alfred had his first experience of shelling at close quarters when enemy artillery targeted the town and their aeroplanes dropped twelve bombs — not an encouraging introduction to the front.

During the afternoon of Tuesday 15th February Alfred paraded with his platoon then marched to the station and entrained to Ypres Asylum. He marched out to Potijze then into the front line. The German snipers were particularly active and following intermittent shelling a new weapon was deployed by the Germans from 'Oskar Farm', a train mounted gun that became nick-named 'Silent Sue'. Over the ensuing two weeks Alfred only had two days out of the line until he was relieved on Thursday 2nd March to Poperinghe for five days rest, although each day the town was shelled. During the next tour of duty the Battalion mounted an unsuccessful raid on the German lines on Monday 13th but the next night it was mounted again, this time they got into the German lines and killed a good number of the enemy. Alfred returned to Poperinghe in the early hours of Friday 17th, then marched to 'Camp K' the next day. He paraded for an inspection by General Lord Cavan on Wednesday 22nd who addressed the Battalion to congratulate the raiding party, amongst others, for their good work. Four days later the Battalion marched to 'Hopoutre Sidings' and entrained to Calais, then marched to 'Camp C', close to the Dunkerque road, where they arrived at 7.30pm. Alfred began training and went on route marches, however, he was able to visit the town to enjoy the various shops and cafés that were apparently unaffected by the war. To break the monotony of training a series of sporting events were held on the beach and a Divisional Horse Show at Esquelbecq. In addition to the bathing parades some brave souls enjoyed a swim in the sea!

The march back to 'Camp K' was completed on Saturday 15th April and whilst Alfred recovered from his long march his officers went to reconnoitre the trenches to south of the Pilkem Ridge where the Battalion would occupy from Tuesday 18th. At 7.30pm on Monday 17th Alfred took the light railway to the Asylum then went into reserve on the canal bank. He waited for twenty-four hours before going into the front line for the last time and shortly after arriving at 5.00pm was subjected to a heavy enemy barrage. The Germans raided the British line that was repulsed along the Battalion's line. Enemy artillery continued to bombard the line and Alfred was killed.

3/5603 Private Kenneth McLeod
1st Battalion Cameron Highlanders
Died on Thursday 29th October 1914, aged 17
Commemorated on Panel 38.

Kenneth was born in Harris, Tarbert, Inverness-shire, son of Alexander and Mary Mcleod, of 4 Portnaloug, Carbost, Portree, Isle of Skye.

He volunteered in Tarbert. For Kenneth's story, see Private Charles Martin, above.

3/5421 PRIVATE NORMAN MCLEOD
1st Battalion Cameron Highlanders
Died on Wednesday 11th November 1914, aged 17
Commemorated on Panel 38.

Norman was born in Benbecula, Lochmaddy, Invernsess-shire, son of Archibald Mcleod, of Uachdar, Benbecula, Nunton, Lochboisdale, South Uist.
He volunteered in Cairnish, North Uist. For Norman's story, see Private Charles Martin, above.
His brother, Donald, died on Saturday 25th September 1915 and is commemorated on Loos Memorial.

18780 PRIVATE THOMAS MCLOUGHLIN
2nd Battalion East Lancashire Regiment
Died on Tuesday 31st July 1917, aged 17
Commemorated on Panel 34.

Thomas was born at home, son of Margaret Alice Mcloughlin, of 132 Union Buildings, Blackburn, and the late Philip Mcloughlin.
He volunteered in Preston, Lancashire. After a period of training he joined the Battalion whilst they were training in the Merris area in early June 1917. After two weeks he was moved to billets in the ramparts of Ypres from where he went out to the trenches in front of Hooge. It would be the area where Thomas was expected to attack at the opening of The Third Battle of Ypres and therefore experience of the ground was considered to be of great help.
At 3.50am on Tuesday 31st July Thomas was led forward under a covering barrage and charged toward the area between 'Clapham Junction' and 'Glencorse Wood'. He came under heavy rifle and machine gun fire. Thomas was cut down and died instantaneously.

17403 PRIVATE
HARRY JAMES MCMANUS
'D' Company, 6th Battalion Somerset Light Infantry
Died on Thursday 7th October 1915, aged 17
Commemorated on Panel 21.

Harry was born in New Cross, London, son of Harry and Florence Amelia McManus.
He volunteered in Battersea, London, went out to France on Wednesday 14th July 1915. Harry joined the Battalion whilst they were billeted near Vlamertinghe.
At 6.00pm on Sunday 18th July the Battalion formed up in the camp then Harry marched along the cobbled road to Ypres, reaching the Menin Gate at 9.00pm. Harry went into the front line at Hooge where he remained until Thursday 22nd. When relieved the Battalion was sent the short distance to the ramparts of Ypres where they were billeted and from where they supplied the front line with stores and ammunition until Monday 26th. The Battalion was moved to a camp in a hop field between Vlamertinghe and Poperinghe for rest and training for three days.

A telegram was received in Battalion headquarters at 4.30am on Friday 30th July: *"Stand to arms: Germans attacking 41st Brigade."* The British line at Hooge was coming under a severe attack where 'liquid fire' was being used for the first time. By 5.15am the Battalion was ready to move off, but at 7.30am he was ordered to stand down until 6.35pm when he moved off to billets in the ramparts of Ypres. At 3.10am Harry moved forward to the GHQ line, and then into the firing line at *'Zouave Wood'* to support the Durhams. At 8.49pm orders were given to 'C' and 'D' Companies to relieve Harry and his comrades, but this was not an easy task as Lieutenant Foley recorded: *"We moved off but before we had got clear of the town the bombardment recommenced with such violence that it was impossible to go any further. We waited crouching along under a garden wall opposite the ruins of a church, while around us raged a perfect tornado. Branches of trees were strewn about and pieces of brick and masonry hurtled into the roadway, but luckily our hiding-place was not directly subjected to shelling, so that we escaped serious damage."* Harry was finally relieved at 12.50am the next morning. After a short period of rest he returned to *'Zouave Wood'* until being relieved by 'D' Company late on Tuesday 3rd August. Corporal Loxton recorded in his diary: *"Moved up to firing line to-night relieving A Company; worst part of front in the hollow of 'U' facing trench captured by Germans, the space between it and us being open ground covered with long grass, and our position being on the edge of Sanctuary Wood, beautifully marked off by German artillery. The whole hollow of the 'U' was covered with dead bodies of K.R.Rs. and R.B.s., killed in original retreat and subsequent counter-attacks on retreat, and the stench was awful and outlook appalling. The captured trench was on rising ground and also beautifully ranged by our artillery, who were dropping in shells all day. It is doubtful whether the Germans occupy the trench at all. If they do, or did, then their losses must have been frightful, as our fire from 9.2 and other guns were terrible, practically every shell dropping in trench or parapet. We saw several bodies on parapet in German uniform, a sign that their losses had been heavy, otherwise they would have been recovered and buried."*

Harry was relieved from the line and spent four days in *'Camp W'* at Vlamertinghe until Tuesday 10th August when he returned to the line at *'Railway Wood'* for two days. After spending a considerable amount of time on tours of duty the Battalion was relieved for two weeks. Harry left the camp in the early hours on Wednesday 1st

September, marched to Ypres, and was sent to relieve the 6th Battalion Duke of Cornwall Regiment.

Harry was relieved for some rest on Monday 20th September until Thursday 23rd when he wasd ordered back to the trenches. At 3.50am on Saturday 25th the artillery commenced a bombardment and at 4.19am a mine was exploded under the German line at 'O.4'. Three minutes later they advanced. The Battalion Diary recorded:

"4.22 a.m. guns lifted.

4.23 a.m. guns established barrage of fire."

By 9.45am the situation was becoming critical and as the battle intensified many of his comrades were killed in front of *'Railway Wood'*.

He was lucky to survive the ghastly battle and was relieved when sent for some rest. On his next tour of duty Harry was blown to pieces by a shell.

426750 PRIVATE
NELSON CAMPBELL MCMATH
28th Battalion Canadian Infantry
(Saskatchewan Regiment)
Died on Tuesday 6th June 1916, aged 17
Commemorated on Panel 28.

Nelson was the son of Mr and Mrs James A Mcmath, of Humbolt, Saskatchewan.

He volunteered in Regina, Saskatchewan, on Saturday 10th April 1915 when he claimed to have been born in Stratford, Ontario, on Saturday 19th September 1896 and worked as a cattle driver. Nelson was 5ft 9in tall, with a 38in chest, and had a large scar on his left buttock. Nelson was first allocated to the 46th Battalion then transferred to 28th Battalion on Friday 26th November 1915. He joined them whilst they were billeted in Loker undergoing training. Nelson began to undertake tours of duty in the Kemmel sector and spent Christmas Day in the line that was described: *"… front very quiet. Our men greet Fritz at morning Stand To with machine gun & rifle fire, but enemy did not reply, scarcely a shot was fired during the remainder of day, no artillery & no fraternising with the enemy, 2 companies in strong points relieved 2 companies in front line."*

Nelson returned to Loker on Tuesday 28th where a considerable number of his comrades reported sick with influenza and bronchitis. The Christmas and New Year celebrations were rolled into one with a special

dinner on Friday 31st then returned to the line late on Sunday 2nd January 1916. Nelson remained in the sector on tours of duty for a further month then was sent for training. General Malcolm Mercer visited the Battalion on Saturday 12th February and met many of the men. Nelson undertook two tours of duties from Sunday 20th and was then sent to train at Berthen on Wednesday 1st March for a week before moving to Schaexhen then went into the trenches in front of Kemmel. Nelson marched to Méteren on Thursday 30th for three days of training then undertook a route march via Mont Noir and Westoutre to a camp at Reninghelst. After a night of rest Nelson continued onto Dickebusch where the Battalion went into Brigade Reserve. The Battalion began to serve in a new and particularly grim sector — Voormezeele — from Thursday 6th to Sunday 9th April then marched to camp at Zevecoten for ten days. Nelson's next move was a month later to the trenches at *'Spoilbank'* with billets in Reninghelst or Dickebusch when out of the line.

Nelson moved into the ramparts of Ypres late on Friday 2nd June then marched into the line on Monday 5th with Battalion Headquarters established at *'Halfway House'*. The enemy began a heavy bombardment of the sector at 9.00am and at 3.30pm blew four mines. Unfortunately Nelson was blown to smithereens by one of the mines.

11438 PRIVATE JOHN MCSTRAVICK
1st Battalion Royal Irish Fusiliers
Died on Sunday 25th April 1915, aged 17
Commemorated on Panel 42.

John was born in Shankill, County Armagh, son of James McStravick, of 48 Shankill Street, Lurgan.

He volunteered in Lurgan and went out to France on Sunday 27th December 1914 to join the Battalion in the Ploegsteert sector. John soon settled down to trench routine in the sector but was not involved in any particular action. John left the sector for the last time on Monday 12th April and marched to billets in Bailleul. After long weeks of service in the front line John really appreciated the comparative luxury of his billet. He was able to get some much needed sleep and enjoy all that the busy town of Bailleul had to offer each evening. During the mornings he trained and in the afternoons various sporting events were organised. John marched to billets in Merris on Friday 16th where General William Pulteney inspected the Battalion three days later. He wrote to the Colonel, Arnold Burrowes, to thank him: *"The cleanliness of the men show great self-respect on their part, and this reflects much credit on the officers who have looked after them so well. I know full well the arduous time* you have all had in the trenches, and how cheerfully you have met the uncongenial conditions. I also know that the filling of sand-bags is not very interesting work; but you have made your trenches strong, and you who have been behind them know the value of this. It has been a great pleasure to me to hear from time to time whatever duty your Battalion has been called upon to perform, you have at once undertaken that duty and carried it through well and cheerily, and that is the true high spirit which I know so well. The summer is now approaching and you have all got your backs well up, and I know that you will acquit yourselves well."

John was ordered to parade on Friday 23rd April as the Battalion was urgently needed to assist in the defence of Ypres as a result of the German gas attack. At 8.20pm they marched from Merris, through Bailleul to Dranouter where they were billeted at 11.30pm. At 7.30am the next morning they marched the relatively short distance to Loker where they stopped and rested. In the early afternoon they set off for Ouderdom, just a short distance north, where they were issued with additional ammunition. At 7.15pm they reached their allotted position some two miles east of Vlamertinghe where they rested for the night — the men lying by the side of the road, the fellow officers were given the use of a loft in a damaged building. Throughout the night was illuminated by Ypres being consumed by flames from a terrific barrage.

The next night John reached St Jan in the pouring rain, moving into the front line by 5.30am the following morning. The Battalion attacked the area to the south of 'Kitchener Wood' but were driven back, mainly due to British artillery whose shells were falling short. By 8.30am Headquarters were established at Vanheule Farm and the fight was intense. The Battalion brought down a German aeroplane just behind Headquarters, shortly afterwards the Headquarters was shelled, set on fire and destroyed. The area was described: *"… the civil population had fled, leaving everything, and one kind action was to let the wretched cattle free, which had been left tied up in the byres. Years of frightfulness were to convert this smiling landscape into a vast sea of mud and filth which no pen could describe and only sight could convey to the senses."* In the ghastly desperate battle that saved Ypres, John was killed.

3/6575 PRIVATE HAROLD MEAD
1st Battalion Dorsetshire Regiment
Died on Friday 13th November 1914, aged 16
Commemorated on Panel 37.

Harold was born at home, second son of Albert and Letitia Mead, of West Knoyle, Mere, Wiltshire. He was educated locally and became a general labourer.

He enlisted in Gillingham, Dorset, and was sent for training. Harold was sent out to France with a draft joining the Battalion on Tuesday 27th October 1914 at Le Touret from where they moved to Rue de l'Épinette. On Saturday 31st he paraded with the Battalion and marched thirteen miles to Strazeele where a period of rest was anticipated. At 7.00am on Sunday 1st November orders were received for the Battalion to move off and at 10.00am a fleet of buses arrived to take them towards Wulverghem. The Battalion Diary records: *"At 10.15 a.m. the bus column started. The buses still contained the advertisements with which they had been decorated when following their normal routine in London. The journey was pleasant enough. It was a glorious autumn day, and the country was quite untouched by war. While passing Lindenhoek, heavy shelling could be seen at Wytschaete, which had now passed into German hands."* Harold and the Battalion were billeted in Neuve Eglise. At 2.00pm on Monday 2nd Harold was sent into the line for the first and only time at Ploegsteert Wood. The Battalion Diary records: *"As the Germans were maintaining continuous pressure upon the 4th Division line on the front Le Gheer-St. Yves (Ploegsteert Wood), 'A' Company was ordered to move up in support in the wood about half a mile east of the former village, while 'B' and 'D' were sent to entrench a line along one of the rides of the wood, about half a mile further back. During the morning and afternoon of the 3rd, companies remained as stated, but at 6 p.m. they commenced to relieve the 1st Royal Irish Fusiliers in incomplete trenches with 'C' Company astride the Ploegsteert-Messines road, and the front continued by 'A', 'B' and 'D' Companies, the flank of the latter resting on the river Douve. The Battalion thus covered two important tactical features — the Messines road and Hill 63."* Harold came under heavy and sustained artillery fire both day and night. He remained in the line until he was killed.

2163 PRIVATE JAMES MENOCH
1st/9th Battalion
Argyll and Sutherland Highlanders
Died on Monday 10th May 1915, aged 17
Commemorated on Panel 44.

James' signature

James was born in Bridgeton, near Glasgow, the second son of James and Annie Menoch, of 6430 Vanburen, Detroit, Michigan, USA, he had four brothers and three sisters. He was educated locally and then worked on a local estate as apprentice beater.

He volunteered in Clydebank on Thursday 18th May 1914 when he claimed to be 17 years and 1 month old and became a member of the Territorials. James was 5ft 8in tall with a 35in chest.

Following the outbreak of war the Battalion was mobilised at Dumbarton. James then trained with Battalion in Bedford where he was given fourteen days detention on Saturday 30th January 1915 for irregular conduct whilst on sentry duty.

He left with the Battalion for France on Friday 19th February. James was sent to serve in the St Eloi sector from early March. James moved into the Salient and served in the trenches in front of *'Dumbarton Lake'* from Sunday 4th to Thursday 8th April on a tour of duty. He was relieved to a camp in Vlamertinghe for four days then was sent into the line in front of *'Glencorse Wood'*. He remained on tours of duty in the sector and when out of the line was billeted in Ypres. The front line was straightened so when James returned to the trenches he was sent to *'Sanctuary Wood'* on Monday 3rd May. The Germans launched an artillery and gas bombardment of the line on Monday 10th and followed it with an infantry attack. It was a fierce and furious battle that cost the Battalion over three hundred killed, wounded or listed as missing. James was first listed as missing until his death was confirmed.

2178 PRIVATE
ROBERT LIONEL MEREDITH
(SERVED AS
PRIVATE ROBERT FALCONER)
45th Battalion Australian Infantry, AIF
Died on Thursday 7th June 1917, aged 17
Commemorated on Panel 27.

Robert's signature

Robert was born in Bulli, New South Wales, only son of Mr T F and Mrs Lydia Meredith; of St Elmo, Russell Street, Woonona, New South Wales, his father died before 1921. It appears that Robert was estranged from his parents. Robert had first attempted to enlist using the preferred surname of his mother, Lewis, but had failed due to his being under age. On his second attempt he volunteered in Bathurst, New South Wales, on Monday 21st February 1916 when he claimed to be Robert Falconer, born on Tuesday 14th September 1897 thus aged 18 years and 3 months, working as a labourer and giving Mrs Victoria Falconer (aunt) as his next of kin. Robert was 5ft 5½in tall, with a 31in chest, weighed 120lbs, had a fair complexion, blue eyes, black hair, a mole on the right hand side of his cheek and a scar on the inner side of the right knee. He forged his aunt's signature on the consent form although in fact she may not have

been related to him either!

Robert sailed from Sydney on *SS Wiltshire* on Tuesday 22nd August 1916 and disembarked in Plymouth on Friday 13th October. He was initially sent to train in Woolwich, London. Whilst at *'Bovington Wool Camp'*, Dorset, on Saturday 4th November he was fined two days pay for refusing to obey an order. He moved to continue his training at *'Camp 13'*, Codford, Wiltshire, where on Saturday 11th November he was hospitalised until Thursday 4th January 1917.

Robert left from Folkestone, Kent, on *SS Princess Victoria* and sailed to Boulogne on Wednesday 17th January from where he marched to Base Depôt in Etaples. Robert joined the Battalion on Saturday 20th in *'Mametz Camp'* on the Somme. His first tour of duty began in Flers on Thursday 8th February, when the Battalion was deployed to *'Gap Trench'* and *'Switch Trench'*. Robert was introduced to the practicalities of trench life and undertook fatigues. Ten days later he moved forward to Gueudecourt where the Battalion occupied *'Stormy Trench'*, *'Grease Trench'*, *'Pilgrims Way'* and *'Chalk Cliff'*. At 11.30am on Wednesday 21st the enemy laid a heavy barrage on the communication lines and around the trenches occupied by the Battalion. He was relieved on Saturday 24th and returned to Mametz then moved for training in Bresle from Friday 2nd March. Whilst there Robert was hospitalised on Wednesday 21st March with scabies, then developed influenza. He returned to the Battalion on Wednesday 9th May but was again admitted with scabies same day for five days. He rejoined the Battalion two days later.

Robert left Bresle just after he rejoined the Battalion and marched to Aveluy station to entrain for Bailleul where he arrived at 10.00am on Thursday 17th. He paraded outside the station then marched across the border to Neuve Eglise and by the afternoon was out on fatigues. His work at the front line continued until Thursday 31st when he moved to *'Kortepyp Camp'* where he trained for the offensive at Messines.

Following the blowing of the mines early on Thursday 7th June and the initial attack had taken place Robert moved from the camp to *'Stinking Farm'*. At 11.30am the Battalion formed up in No Man's Land and ten minutes later went forward. They advanced to the eastern slope of the Messines Ridge where orders were received to halt. As they waited to continue a heavy shrapnel bombardment fell over them from the German artillery near Warneton. The enemy mounted a counter-attack that as driven off by well-directed artillery and accurate rifle fire. Robert was finally led forward at 3.10pm but came under extremely heavy machine gun fire from a German strong point that had to be silenced. As Robert took part in the attack on the pill box he was killed.

Information came to hand in late September 1917 that Robert was really Robert Lionel Meredith when a number of papers were exchanged with his mother, and his family, that established his true identity.

His mother was particularly distressed that the Memorial Plaque and Scroll had his assumed name and she wrote to the records office: *"Dear Sir, Received safely the scroll and King's message for which I thank you, you state in your communication that the name in which the solder served and died will be the same put on the Memorial Plaque which are to be issued. My son enlisted and died in an assumed name I would just like to say if his own name cannot be put on anything that I am entitled to get I would rather not receive anything at all with another man's name on it. I could not call it mine without my own name on it."*

There is no indication as to the name finally inscribed, however, his mother did receive his British War Medal no 45884, Victory Medal no 45358 and Memorial Plaque and Scroll no 328347.

A somewhat tragic story of a young boy who was eager to enlist whose family circumstances were not good and whilst the Great War may have ended on Tuesday 11th November 1918 but the war within his surviving family did not.

7417 RIFLEMAN ROBERT MILLAR
'C' Company, 2nd Battalion Royal Irish Rifles
Died on Sunday 9th May 1915, aged 17
Commemorated on Panel 40.

Robert was born in Shankill, County Antrim, son of Matilda Freel (formerly Millar), of 14 Harrison Street, Belfast.

He enlisted in Belfast and went out to France on Thursday 8th April 1915 with a draft. For Robert's story, and that of the Battalion, see Lance Corporal James Connolly, above.

10661 PRIVATE HERBERT MILLER
2nd Battalion Connaught Rangers
Died on Saturday 31st October 1914, aged 17
Commemorated on Panel 42.

Herbert was born at home, eldest son of Joseph and Mary Miller, of North Curry, Somerset.

He volunteered in Taunton, Somerset, prior to the war and gave his sister, Mrs Phyllis Shaw, of 26 China Street, Accrington, Lancashire, as his next of kin. At the outbreak of war the Battalion mobilised in Aldershot, Hampshire. During the morning of Thursday 13th August 1914 Herbert marched to the station and entrained for Southampton under the command of Lieutenant Colonel Alexander William Abercrombie (he died on Friday 5th November 1915 as a prisoner of war and is buried in Berlin South-Western Cemetery, Brandenburg). The Battalion embarked on the *SS Herschel* and *SS Seahound* bound for Boulogne that was reached at 5.30pm the next evening. Herbert marched to a camp outside the town where he rested overnight before entraining at 9.00am bound for Busigny. Upon arrival he marched to billets in Mennevret where he remained until Friday 21st. Whilst there the Battalion undertook route marches and training. Over the next couple of days Herbert marched towards Mons, via La Groise and Pont-sur-Sambre, and was cheered all along the route. When he reached Bougnies the sounds of battle could be clearly heard. The Battalion was ordered to dig in, Captain Ernest Graham Hamilton (later Colonel Hamilton, CMG, DSO, MC) wrote: *"Every one was very keen on the idea of meeting the enemy and we were all in the best of spirits. On the evening of the second day we heard the sound of the guns and later on we could see the shells bursting. The Second Corps were engaging the enemy in front and we were moving up to reinforce them. My Battalion was in support on a ridge some mile and a half behind the front line. We had a splendid view of the battle from where we were entrenched. The evening before was a perfect summer evening, and it was a wonderful sight to see the shells bursting. At first we could not make out the heavy German howitzers — one saw columns of black smoke rising as high as a church steeple, and then came the sound of terrific explosions. We thought it must be land mines, but in reality it was a shell that afterwards became known as 'Black Maria' or 'Coal Box', and various other names.*

Of course we could see nothing of what our cavalry was doing, but we saw some of the infantry fighting. On a plateau to our left front we saw long lines of Germans attacking some British infantry who were in trenches. We could also see British supports moving up, and the enemy were either killed or driven back by the heavy rifle fire. At about 9 a.m. the infantry commenced to retire. All the guns, except those detailed for the rearguard, had already withdrawn during the night. We were told that we were to form part of the rearguard, and it was somewhat unnerving to see all the troops moving back. At about 11 o'clock the enemy started shelling our ridge. ... About 12 o'clock we were one of the last regiments on the field. The Germans did not come directly for us, but passed to our left flank. We had to retire and moved in extended order over about one and a half miles of open wheat-fields. We were actually the last battalion to leave the battlefield, and were by then almost surrounded by the enemy. We came now under what was then considered heavy shell fire. The German field artillery was not very good. Most of their shells went high, and we had only about a dozen men hit. Late in the afternoon we passed through the Guards Brigade, who had taken up and entrenched a second position.

This was the beginning of the retirement from Mons. That night we stopped at Bavai. We started off early next morning, having spent the night in a field."

The retirement took Herbert via Bavai to Le Grand Fayt where Captain Hamilton recorded the events of Wednesday 26th: "By 5 a.m. we had reached the point were we were to make a stand, but there was no sign of the enemy following us up so we retired slowly to a series of positions suitable for defence. At 12 noon, I retired my company from one of these positions, where, in my turn, I been holding the rearmost line. Marching my company along the road and through other companies who were taking up positions farther back, I eventually came up with the rear of the transport. At 2 p.m. everything was still quiet, and at 3 o'clock we entered Le Grand Fayt, which was in a hollow. The Colonel, with three companies, was then holding the ridge above the time. … At 3.30 another officer and myself were sitting on a bridge over the stream which runs through the village, when, without the slightest warning a shell burst within fifty yards of us. In five minutes what had appeared to be a peaceful hamlet became a positive inferno."

Following the short, sharp engagement, Herbert was ordered to continue the retirement, leaving many of his comrades on the battlefield, including the wounded Colonel. A series of exhausting marches took Herbert and his comrades south to Marles-en-Brie that was reached on Saturday 5th September where orders were received to halt then turn to engage the enemy. The day he marched in search of the enemy, the War Diary records for Sunday 6th: "At 6 a.m. Battalion moved due east and took up a position about Champlet. Remained in position till 6 p.m. when the enemy retired. The force followed in pursuit and halted for the night."

The Germans were engaged at Orly as recorded by one of the officers: "… the Germans on the far side of the stream commenced to retire almost immediately. …soon rushed on and disposed the platoon in a lump round the end houses of the village. As the Germans retired across the open space in front of the estaminet, O'Brien and our men jumped out and shot them at point blank range. Some of men got into the houses and took a few Germans prisoners.

All the Germans in the village had been slain or had surrendered and Sergeant had several prisoners, including an officer. Sergeant O'Brien then sent out for the wounded and had them brought up to the estaminet in Orly."

The march eastward continued and the Marne was crossed at Charly on Wednesday 9th where the Battalion captured over five hundred German prisoners. They were relatively easy to capture as they had been drinking the wine cellar of a local château dry! Further short engagements continued over the next few days until the Ainse was crossed on Sunday 13th at Pont d'Arcy. Herbert moved onto Soupir and took position where the Germans attacked in force. Lieutenant

Colonel O'Sullivan wrote: "The Battalion arrived at Soupir between 8 and 9 p.m. No enemy were encountered and the village was found practically deserted. The few remaining inhabitants said that the Germans had evacuated the place only a short while before."

The action at La Cour de Soupir was particularly fierce and the Battalion lost heavily. Captain Hamilton wrote: "I think that the first German attack was made with two battalions and machine guns. They also had some guns in action. Unfortunately we had neither guns nor machine guns at first. By 9 o'clock we were in the midst of the hottest fight so far witnessed in the battalion. We had no cover of any description and the ground was perfectly flat for eight hundred or nine hundred yards in front of us and for five hundred or six hundred yards behind us, until one reached the steep ground leading down to the river valley. About three hundred yards to our left flank there was a small tributary valley running down to the main valley. We kept up the fire fight for about an hour. The German fire was not very accurate, but, even so, we suffered fairly severely. They attempted to advance by short rushes of small parties at a time, but did not succeed in getting on very far.

It was the first time that most of us had been under a really heavy infantry fire. There was one constant crackle of the firing, and the hiss of the bullets was like the hiss of steam escaping. At about 10 o'clock the company on our right, which had lost its commander and most of its officers, was forced back to a wood, so that both my flanks were exposed. Shortly after this we found that we were being fired at from the direction of our left flank, so we had to retire to a position further back. I ordered the left half-company to retire, and as soon as they got up the German fire became simply appalling. The right half-company, with which I myself was, kept up as rapid a fire as we could until the other half had got back about a hundred yards. Then they got down and opened fire whilst we retired. In this way we got back about three hundred yards to where there was some cover of sorts, and there we started improving the cover with our entrenching tools. It is surprising that we did not lose more men whilst falling back, but the enemy's fire, although very heavy, was very inaccurate. … The Guards Brigade had now taken on the fight and drove the enemy back to where they had started from. One of our companies which had been in support also took part in the counter-attack. Great numbers of the Germans surrendered and by dark we had take nearly three hundred prisoners, besides two hundred wounded.

As far as could be ascertained, there were about six hundred German dead on the ground within three hundred yards of the farm, and there must have been many more farther away."

Herbert was relieved from the line on Tuesday 15th and marched to Verneuil where he waited all day not knowing if he would be sent back into the line or to billets. Luckily for him, and his comrades, it was for rest in the billets provided for them in the village. He was stood to over the next couple of days but did not return to the line until later on Thursday 17th. The next day Herbert took part in another action as described by Captain Hamilton: *"The position consisted of a series of big caves surrounded by gravel pits. These pits were used as fire-trenches. When we got there in the evening the whole of the area inside the post was covered with shell-holes; this warned us to expect a lively time — and we certainly had it. We manned the trenches all night, and at 4.30 in the morning the enemy commenced to attack. We drove them back easily enough, but they kept up a constant fire on us. At about 7 o'clock they started to shell us, but as they only used shrapnel they did very little damage. At 9 o'clock they bombarded the trenches behind us, which were held by the rest of my regiment and by another regiment. They used some very heavy shell for this and blew in the trenches in several places. At the same time, under cover of this fire, they again attempted to advance. Fortunately, for some reason or another they did not shell the advanced post, so we again drove them back. …*

The bombardment of the trenches behind us was so heavy that they had to be evacuated. … It was a very critical time, as the enemy were constantly massing in front, and I thought a bombardment, followed by an assault, would start any minute. Eventually I got another officer with fifty men as reinforcements, and although the Germans made repeated attempts to advance to some dead ground near our position, we drove them back each time."

At 3.30am on Monday 21st September the Battalion was relieved from the line and sent to bivouac at Dhizal where they remained until Friday 2nd October. They marched to billets in Soupir for four days before going into reserve at Bourg until Tuesday 13th.

At 8.00pm on Wednesday 14th the move to Flanders began. They marched to Fismes and entrained at 3.20pm — a long winding journey took them to Hazebrouck, via Calais and St Omer, finally arriving at 1.30am on Friday 16th. After three days Herbert marched with his platoon across the border into Belgium and billets in Poperinghe where a draft of two hundred and eighty men joined them. Little time was given for the new men to get accustomed to their new situation as the Battalion was sent to bivouac at Boesinghe the next day, Tuesday 20th. They prepared to attack the Germans at St Julien the next day. From 9.00am on Wednesday 21st the German artillery bombarded their line and they came under constant attack. The Battalion headquarters, based in a small estaminet, was hit and partially destroyed but the occupants remained unhurt. Of more concern was the barn that was hit during the bombardment and destroyed all the rations and stores! A further two days of heavy fighting continued before they were relieved to Halte, arriving in their billets at 6.00am, with breakfast provided at 7.00am. A good rest was

anticipated by all, but an hour later Herbert was falling in with his comrades to march along the Menin Road to Veldhoek. Lieutenant Colonel Hamilton wrote: *"After getting no rest the previous night, we were all somewhat tired and not in the best spirits: the prospects of what was ahead of them did not appear very cheerful! In fact, to put it bluntly, we were all somewhat anxious. When we were well within the area of shell fire the Corps Commander — Sir Douglas Haig — with one staff officer and one orderly carrying his Corps Commander flag — overtook us. He rode quietly on ahead of us as though nothing unusual was happening. I remember noticing how immaculately he turned out and how cool and unconcerned he looked. I don't know whether his action was designed in order to create an effect, but it certainly had the effect of bucking us all up and steadying our nerves."*

Herbert moved to Molenaarelsthoek on Wednesday 28th when the Battalion relieved the Berkshires. The next day an attack was made against the German lines along the Becelaere road. As the Germans pressed their attacks home, and partially broke the line, Herbert was killed.

14808 PRIVATE
GEORGE HAROLD MILLS
1st Battalion Dorsetshire Regiment
Died on Monday 5th July 1915, aged 17
Commemorated on Panel 37.

George was born in Finchley, Middlesex, second son of George and Mary Jane Mills, of 32 Courthill Road, Parkstone, Dorset.

He served as 20054 Private George Mills with the Duke of Cornwall's Light Infantry before transferring to the Dorsetshire Regiment. George went out to France on Thursday 6th May 1915 to join the Battalion with a draft whilst they were in Kruisstraat. George began serving at the front between the Ypres to Comines Canal and St Eloi. He remained on tours of duty without becoming involved in any particular action. George was killed during a German bombardment of the line.

3/7176 PRIVATE
CLIFFORD ROBERT MILTON
1st Battalion Somerset Light Infantry
Died on Tuesday 27th April 1915, aged 17
Commemorated on Panel 21.

Cliff was born at home, seventh son of Thomas Milton, of 11 Scotts Lane, Wellington, Somerset, and the late Grace Sophia Milton. He was educated locally.
He volunteered in Taunton, Somerset, and went out to France on Wednesday 24th March 1915. Cliff joined

the Battalion whilst they were serving in the relatively quiet sector at Ploegsteert. Cliff remained on tours of duty, or on fatigues with periods of training and rest in the sector. He left St Yves on Sunday 11th April 1915 and sent to the Nooteboom sector for an extended period, however this ended when the German gas attack was launched on Thursday 22nd.

Cliff was ordered to stand to at 11.30am the next morning. He packed his kit in readiness for the move. Cliff marched to Bailleul and entrained to Poperinghe then marched to bivouac at Busseboom from where the smoke and noise of battle could be seen. He moved to a hutted camp in Vlamertinghe the next day where he waited for orders to take part in the battle. Cliff was sent to Fortuin where he dug in furiously as the Germans shelled the position: *"… kept the supporting trenches under a rain of shrapnel, so that the supports did not dare show their heads above the parapet, and searched the high ground behind with high explosive to stop movements of reserves."*

Cliff was ordered to lay low throughout the day, Monday 26th, as the shelling was so heavy. A half-hearted attack was mounted on the line that fizzled out but a number of casualties were taken by the Battalion. During the night he continued to dig in and improve the defences. During a bombardment of the line the next day Cliff was killed.

2764 PRIVATE JOHN MOGFORD
2nd Battalion Monmouthshire Regiment
Died on Saturday 8th May 1915, aged 17
Commemorated on Panel 50.

John was born in Newport, Monmouthshire, second son of Samuel and Rosannah Mogford, of 5 Holy Oake, Pontnewynydd, Pontypool, Monmouthshire. Following his elementary education he went to work as a collier at Llanerch Colliery, Abersychan.

John Mogford

He volunteered at the outbreak of war although his parents begged him not do so. John was determined so enlisted and was sent for training until leaving with a draft for France on Wednesday 17th February 1915. He joined the Battalion whilst they were serving in the Ploegsteert sector where he remained until mid-April. John was resting in Bailleul when the Second Battle of Ypres began on Thursday 22nd April. Five days later he marched to Hazebrouck where he rested over night before moving back across the Belgian border to a bivouac at Elverdinghe. Late on Friday 30th John marched passed the smoking ruins of Ypres to go into reserve at La Brique. The real ferocity of the battle became all too real when a gas attack, coupled with a tremendous artillery bombardment, fell on the Pilkem Ridge on Sunday 2nd May. Part of the Battalion was sent to support the Essex Regiment who required urgent assistance. John went into the line at Wieltje late on Tuesday 4th and he was in a trench near *'Mouse Trap Farm'* that came under a heavy gas attack, however, it was not followed up by an infantry assault. Throughout Thursday 6th and Friday 7th a series of attacks were mounted but each one was repulsed. In the early hours of Saturday 8th John was killed by shell fire.

John received a commendation for conspicuous bravery in the field: *"Private Mogford, 2nd Monmouthshire Regiment. Your Commanding Officer and Brigade Commander have informed me that you have distinguished yourself by conspicuous bravery in the field. I have read this report with much pleasure."*

6769 PRIVATE
ERIC JOHN SAMUEL MOLLOY
1st Battalion Australian Infantry, AIF
Died on Thursday 4th October 1917, aged 17
Commemorated on Panel 7.

Eric's signature

Eric was born in Newtown, Sydney, son of Walter and Isabella Molloy, of Erricol, View Street, Arncliffe, New South Wales. He was educated locally.

He volunteered on Tuesday 16th May 1916 when he claimed to be 18 years and 8 months old and worked as a machinist. Eric was 5ft 5½in tall, with a 31½in chest, weighed 112lbs, had a fresh complexion, grey eyes and brown hair. Both of his parents signed a note of consent to Eric enlisting.

He embarked on the *SS Port Nicholson* in Sydney on Wednesday 8th November 1916 and disembarked in Devonport on Wednesday 10th January 1917. He was sent to training in Durrington and left from Folkestone, Kent, bound for Boulogne on Wednesday 9th May. He marched to Base Depôt in Etaples from where he was sent to join the Battalion, arriving with them on Monday 14th whilst they were training in Bazentin-le-Petit. The Battalion moved to La Viéville on Tuesday 22nd where training continued until moving to Englebelmer on Friday 29th June. After three days he moved to Mailly Maillet for four days then returned to La Viéville. Whilst in camp Eric paraded for an inspection by HM King George on Sunday 12th August. He moved to Bray on Wednesday 15th for nine days, then moved via Dernancourt to Wallon Cappel on Monday 27th for two weeks. Training was not complete so Eric moved yet again to Sec Bois where he remained until Thursday 13th September.

After five months of continuous training in France Eric began the move towards the battlefield on Thursday 13th September when he marched to Méteren. The next day he crossed the border into Belgium to 'Palace Camp' at Ouderdom. The trenches beckoned on Sunday 16th as he marched to 'Château Segard' then went into the trenches at Hooge on Monday 17th to begin his first tour of duty. It was a relatively quiet sector whilst Eric was there throughout the tour. He returned to 'Château Segard' early on Thursday 20th, then marched to 'Halfway House' were he remained in support for two days undertaking fatigues before returning to 'Palace Camp'. After some rest Eric was collected by an omnibus and driven to Steenvoorde on Monday 24th for training.

Eric's second visit to the battlefield started on Monday 1st October when he left camp in Steenvoorde and marched to 'Château Segard' where he remained overnight. The next day he moved onto the Westhoek Ridge and took part in an attack on Passchendaele Ridge. Eric was killed as he moved forward but his body was lost.

Eric had been in uniform for seventeen months but spent less than a week in the trenches before he was killed.

Eric was listed as Missing In Action before a Court of Enquiry confirmed his death. His parents were sent his British War Medal no 62420, Victory Medal no 51700 and Memorial Plaque and Scroll no 341856.

1958 Private
James Brown Morgan
9th Battalion Royal Scots
Died on Monday 3rd May 1915, aged 16
Commemorated on Panel 11.

James was born in Glasgow, son of Mr and Mrs James Morgan, of 104 Causewayside, Newington, Edinburgh. He was educated locally.

He enlisted in Edinburgh where he remained in training until Tuesday 23rd February 1915, when he marched through the city, being cheered on his way, to entrain for Southampton. He embarked on SS Inventor arriving in Le Havre on Friday 26th. A hearty welcome in the town awaited the Battalion as they marched to their rest camp. The next morning James entrained for northern France from where he marched along the tree-lined cobbled roads into Belgium. He soon heard the sound of battle and after only a few days training for the front was sent on his first tour of duty in front of St Eloi. It was baptism of fire as their line was attacked on Sunday 14th that was repulsed. After a further two tours of duty at St Eloi James was sent in early April to Ypres, where he was billeted. He was in his billet on Wednesday 7th when a salvo of German shells hit the building and more than fifty of his comrades were injured. James returned to the line before being sent to Vlamertinghe for rest and training.

On Thursday 22nd the Germans launched the first gas attack and bombarded Ypres. The black smoke from Ypres billowed into the sky, clearly visible from the camp, coupled with the sound of 'crump, crump, bang', of the shells. Belgian civilians, evacuating what was left of the town and its surroundings, began to stream by with their meagre belongings. The sight of the dog-carts, babies prams filled with a few personnel possessions, frightened and tearful men, women and children was distressing to all. Inter-mingled with them came the French Colonial Troops, the Turcos, in a terrible condition. Many of them by then were totally out of control, dying in absolute agony from gas poisoning. The impression on the men, and particularly on one as young as James, can only be imagined. Despite the fears, the total lack of understanding of the gas attack or whatever his thoughts were, he mustered and marched off at 7.00pm towards the inferno with the sound of the artillery growing ever louder. James marched through Ypres, despite the shell fire, and out through the Menin Gate (the site where his name would later be remembered in perpetuity) to Potijze, arriving at 3.00am the next morning. The sound of battle raged around him as he awaited orders and at noon James was sent to support the Canadians who were coming under pressure. By late afternoon the Battalion was in front of St Jan but it was not until the next day that time was given for them to eat — their first rations in forty-eight hours. James undertook a series of short, sharp counter-attacks designed to keep the Germans at bay. In the early morning of Tuesday 27th he was relieved and returned on the difficult route back to Potijze where he rested for a short time before moving to 'Sanctuary Wood'. His last two days were frustrating for all ranks of the Battalion: on Sunday 2nd May they were marched to Potijze only to be sent back once they arrived and on Monday 3rd they were sent to Frezenberg, again only to be sent straight back. Shortly after his return James was mortally wounded and buried where he died.

SECOND LIEUTENANT HENRY GAGE MORRIS

2nd Battalion Duke of Cornwall's Light Infantry
Died on Sunday 23rd May 1915, aged 17
Commemorated on Addenda Panel 58.

Henry Morris

Henry was born in Bodmin on Saturday 14th August 1897, only surviving child of Colonel Henry Gage Morris. He was educated at Marlborough College from September 1911 as a member of Mitre and passed into RMC Sandhurst on his Headmaster's nomination. He was a popular boy at school, bright and *"a perfect gentleman"*.

Henry was gazetted in January 1915, at the age of 17, and went out to the front joining the Battalion in the field on Friday 23rd April as the Second Battle of Ypres was beginning.

The day before Henry arrived the Battalion had been taken into Poperinghe where baths were provided for all before being sent to bivouac on the Ypres to Brielen road. At 5.00pm the German artillery onslaught began and chlorine gas shells rained down on the French colonial troops: *"What followed almost defies description. The effect of these poisonous gases was so virulent as to render the whole of the line held by the French division … practically incapable of any action at all. It was at first impossible for anyone to realize what had happened at all. The smoke and fumes hid everything from sight and hundreds of men were thrown into a comatose or dying condition, and within an hour the whole position had to be abandoned together with about fifty guns."*

The Battalion witnessed the consequences: *"French stragglers from the north started coming in, saying the Zouaves had been attacked with asphyxiating gas and that there had been a general French retirement in consequence on a wide front in the direction of Pilkem and Langemarck."*

… Zouaves and refugees flee the gas attack

At 2.30am on Friday 23rd the Battalion was ordered to Potijze, arriving two hours later where they received orders to dig in west of Wieltje. Throughout the night ten Battalions moved into the line to plug the gap. Fortunately the Germans had not pressed their attack home because Ypres had been for many hours completely exposed and could have been taken. At the request of General Ferdinand Foch an attack on the area between *'Kitchener's Wood'* (Bois des Cuisinières) and the Yser Canal was mounted. The Battalion managed to reach *'Turco Farm'* where a German observer remained at his post directing the artillery until he was killed, telephone in hand. At 9.00pm they were forced to

Ferdinand Foch

retire to *'Foch Farm'* where they remained until 3.00am on Monday 26th when they were relieved and returned to Potijze Château. Throughout Wednesday 28th and Thursday 29th they remained in the support trenches near *'Hill Farm'* before returning to the château. During Thursday night they moved back to *'Sanctuary Wood'*. They relieved the Leinsters at *'Armagh Wood'* on Thursday 6th May where they came under sustained shell fire for two days. The Battalion was relieved for a short period of time and Henry returned to the front for the last time.

Colonel Tuson wrote of Henry and how he was killed: *"He was such a nice boy and a very brave and gallant lad, and died gallantly. He was killed in a counter-attack we made with the 13th Brigade, the East Yorks., Yorks. and Lancs. and the 4th Canadians on the 23rd. I was commanding the battalion at the time, and the last I saw of him he passed me with a platoon of 'C' Company, which was in reserve. He came past me with a very cheerful face, and laughing, under a very heavy cross-fire from machine-guns, and sang out to me, 'Shall I go on?' and I answered, 'Go on, laddie, as hard as you can'. Poor lad! I did not see him again, but heard he was shot in the head, but he would not let anyone stay with him. He was such a good boy, always cheerful and always ready to do anything that was wanted. He was very popular with everyone — officers and men."*

His Batman wrote: *"Your son was as brave a man as anyone could wish to meet. I was his servant while he was in France, and a better master I never had. The men in the platoon loved him, and would do anything for him. He was always cheerful and had friends everywhere he went. I was not with him when he got hit, but I heard he wanted to go on, and refused to be bandaged, as he said there were men who were hit more badly than himself. He always thought of others before himself."*

2384 PRIVATE WILLIAM MORRISON
1st/6th Battalion Northumberland Fusiliers
Died on Monday 26th April 1915, aged 17
Commemorated on Panel 8.

William was born at home, eldest son of James Potts and Isabella Morrison, of 18 Bulmer Street, Newcastle-on-Tyne.
He went out to France on Tuesday 20th April 1915. For William's story and four days service at the front see Corporal James Binning, above.

19035 PRIVATE AUBREY MORTON
6th Battalion Lincolnshire Regiment
Died on Thursday 7th June 1917, aged 17
Commemorated on Panel 21.

Aubrey was born at home, elder son of Harry Andrew and Rosanna Morton, of 3 Freiston Road, Skirbeck, Boston, Lincolnshire. He had a younger brother, Jack. Aubrey was educated locally.
He volunteered in Boston and following training he left to join the Battalion in the field. The Battalion left the Somme on Thursday 17th May 1917 and entrained for Cassel. They marched to billets in Thieushoek and a week later moved to the training area for the forthcoming offensive at Messines.
Aubrey trained hard on a specially constructed model of the ground over which he would advance and attack. It was complete with trenches, mock pill boxes, barbed wire etc all marked out in great detail. At 11.00am on Wednesday 6th June Aubrey marched to *'Butterfly Farm'*, some two miles behind the front line, where he waited twenty-four hours for the final order to move into the front line. Sadly for the Battalion they were positioned very close to the heavy guns of the artillery and were deafened as the huge shells blasted the German line. The nineteen mines were blown at 3.10am on Thursday 7th that shook the ground like an earthquake. At 11.00am Aubrey moved forward to the *'Vierstraat Switch'* and an hour later he arrived where a hot

... one of the mine craters

meal was provided. At 3.00pm he struggled forward across the battlefield, passing the wounded and other troops moving backward and forward to the front line. A further barrage was laid on the German positions and once that lifted Aubrey charged forward. During the attack Aubrey was killed, one of only three from the Battalion to be die on the battlefield that day.

5673 RIFLEMAN WILLIAM CHARLES MOTT
4th Battalion Rifle Brigade
Died on Monday 15th March 1915, aged 16
Commemorated on Panel 48.

William was born at home, son of William Mott, of 9 Wadding Street, Rodney Road, Walworth, London. William volunteered and went for training being sent to France to join the Battalion in the field whilst they were serving at St Eloi on Wednesday 3rd February 1915. Many of William's comrades, who had only recently returned from India, suffered badly in the awful weather conditions, with more than two hundred being invalided with trench foot. Opposite William were the Bavarian troops — including Adolf Hitler —who mounted constant attacks and raids. It was a difficult line to hold as it was on the lower slopes overlooked by the Germans — sniping was a constant danger as they sapped towards them. William undertook a series of tours of duty without particular incident, and was often sent to a camp at Reninghelst for rest and training. Whilst there on Sunday 14th, at 5.00pm, the Germans blew a mine under *'The Mound'*, coupled with an artillery barrage, then advanced on the village and the British lines. William was ordered to stand to. He marched along the cobbled road to Voormezeele then onward to St Eloi; the condition of the fields meant a cross-country route was impossible. At 4.00am, with bayonet fixed, he charged forward. The fighting was intense and vicious during which William was killed.

2857 PRIVATE GEORGE ALBERT MOUNTCASTLE
4th Battalion Lincolnshire Regiment
Died on Wednesday 30th June 1915, aged 17
Commemorated on Panel 21.

George was born at home, eldest son of George and Fanny Mountcastle, of Spridlington, Lincoln. He had five younger brothers and a sister. George was educated locally and then worked as a farm labourer. He volunteered at Lincoln and went out to France on Friday 25th June 1915. He joined the Battalion whilst they were serving close to the Spanbroekmolen. George was killed within hours of going into the front line for the first time.
He is commemorated on Spridlington War Memorial.

3039 RIFLEMAN
FREDERICK LIONEL NASH
1st/12th Battalion London Regiment (The Rangers)
Died on Sunday 25th April 1915, aged 17
Commemorated on Panel 54.

Frederick's signature

Frederick was the youngest son of Charles Herbert and Florence Nash, of 211 Ontario Street, St Catharine's, Ontario, Canada, previously of Maybank, Palmerston Road, Buckhurst Hill, Essex. After the war his parents, two elder brothers and the youngest of three sisters emigrated to Canada.

He volunteered on Thursday 10th September 1914 aged 17 years and 4 months. Frederick was 5ft 3¾in tall with a 34in chest. He embarked on the *SS Balmoral* in Southampton on Tuesday 9th March 1915 and sailed to Le Havre. He joined the Battalion in the field on Wednesday 17th. For Frederick's story see Rifleman William Klagge, above.

603193 PRIVATE JOHN NICHOLLS
10th Battalion Canadian Infantry (Alberta Regiment)
Died on Wednesday 14th June 1916, aged 17
Commemorated on Panel 24.

John's signature

John was the son of the late John and Lucie Nicholls, of 101 State Street, Galt, Alberta.

He volunteered in Galt on Thursday 7th October 1915 when he claimed to have been born in Staffordshire, England, on Monday 4th January 1897, was working as a labourer, and had served four months in the 39th Battalion, Militia. John was 5ft 6¾in tall, with a 34½in chest, a fair complexion, grey eyes, brown hair, a small mole on his right shoulder and another on his upper right arm.

For the story of the Battalion until Saturday 3rd June 1916, see Private John Macdonald, above.

John remained in the line covering *'Armagh Wood'*, *'Square Wood'*, and *'Leicester Square'* until being relieved at 2.00am on Sunday 4th and sent to *'Dickebusch Huts'*. Over the next twenty-four hours the Battalion reorganised itself and all ranks rested then cleaned themselves up. At 5.00pm on Monday 5th John marched to *'Camp D'* from where he returned to the front line at Hill 60 the next evening. After a five-day tour he was sent into reserve at *'Dominion Lines'* for two days when he marched to *'Camp E'* but after only a few hours was ordered to return to the trenches. The sector was under a very heavy bombardment that was destroying the front line

system. The fire increased in intensity and John was killed when a shell burst close to him.

He is commemorated on Galt War Memorial.

17625 PRIVATE
CHARLES CYRUS NORCOTT
5th Battalion Oxford and Bucks Light Infantry
Died on Friday 11th February 1916, aged 17
Commemorated on Panel 39.

Charles was born at home on Monday 5th December 1898, second of three sons of John and Rose Norcott, of 5 Corner Cottages, Farnham Royal, Slough, Buckinghamshire.

He volunteered in Slough and went out to France on Friday 1st October 1915. Charles was a member of a draft that helped bring the Battalion up to strength following the various actions of the summer on the Ypres Salient, the last one being only a week before at Bellewaarde.

Charles settled down to the routine of a soldier on the Western Front: tours of duty in the front line, in reserve or support, fatigues, coupled with training and some periods of rest. He remained on the Salient that had quietened down following months of intense fighting. Charles did not take part in any particular action but had to constantly face the enemy and put his life at risk until it was lost. Charles was buried close to where he fell but his grave was lost in subsequent battles.

Charles is commemorated on Farnham Royal War Memorial.

2027 PRIVATE JOE ARTHUR NORTON
'A' Company, 1st/3rd Battalion
Monmouthshire Regiment
Died on Saturday 8th May 1915, aged 17
Commemorated on Panel 50.

Joe was born at home, eldest son of Joseph and Laurie Norton, of 5 Brecon Road, Abergavenny, Monmouthshire. He had two younger brothers, Reginald and Bertram. Joe was educated locally.

He volunteered and was sent for training that was completed in Cambridge. He left with the Battalion to entrain for Southampton and embarked on the *SS Chyebassa* late on Sunday 14th February 1915. Once he disembarked Joe entrained to northern France then marched to Steenvoorde for ten days of final training. A fleet of London omnibuses, still with their pre-war advertising on them, collected the Battalion and drove them to Bailleul. Between Wednesday 3rd and Friday 5th March Joe was sent into the trenches attached to seasoned troops for practical training. Joe wrote of his experiences: *"The firing line is not as bad as you would think, at least it is not so bad as we expected it to be. The trenches we have been in are dry ones, and the only thing is the cold nights. We were shelled rather heavily last Tuesday; but our guns gave them something after. The men we were in with didn't seem to mind much. They say 'keep your napper down and you're alright!'"*

Joe's first experience of the front line was at Wulverghem on Friday 12th March where he undertook tours of duty until Friday 2nd April. General Sir Horace Smith-Dorrien inspected the Battalion on Tuesday 6th and two days later they were collected by transport and driven to Ypres. Joe marched out to the trenches in Polygon Wood for a tour of duty then was sent into Ypres for some rest. He returned to the line and was serving when the Second Battle of Ypres began on Thursday 22nd. After fighting for over a week the Battalion was forced out of Polygon Wood and pushed back on Monday 3rd May. The next day a German bombardment fell across the line followed by an infantry attack. Casualties amongst the Battalion began to mount that increased during the various counter-attacks. Joe held on in the line but received some respite on Thursday 6th as the fighting quietened down. The enemy began to shell the sector again with increased intensity on Friday 7th. At 5.30am the next morning a preliminary bombardment was laid on the Battalion's position that was followed by an attack at 8.30am. Joe and his comrades opened rapid fire that drove the attackers back. Shelling and infantry attacks continued throughout the day that virtually wiped out the Battalion. Joe was one of those killed. Private Badham wrote: *"The 8th was the day I shall never forget. They started bombarding the same time in the morning, and about half an hour afterwards we could hear a long blast of a whistle, and the attack started. We were only a handful of men, and they came on in thousands, but we kept them at bay; but I knew we would have to give way before long. The fellows on our left and right were retiring and we had orders to do the same, but we did not go until we put some more shots into them.*

It was in the retirement that we lost a lot of men. They were bayoneting our wounded that we had to leave behind. Well, we got back to our second line of trenches, and reinforcements came up. After that I don't know what happened. I went to the hospital with shrapnel in my back and a big bruise on my shoulders and the gas in my eyes."

Joe is commemorated on the St Mary's Christ Church War Memorial, Abergavenny.

Gilbert Ledward designed the Abergavenny War Memorial that is dedicated to the officers and men of the 3rd Battalion Monmouthshire Regiment.

S/8889 PRIVATE THEODORE ALBERT VICTOR OAKES
1st Battalion Queen's Own (Royal West Kent Regiment)
Died on Sunday 18th April 1915, aged 17
Commemorated on Panel 45.

Theodore was born in Bermondsey, London, second of three sons of Benjamin and Alice Oakes, of 18 Lamerton Street, Deptford, London. He was educated locally and was subsequently employed as a tin box sorter.

He enlisted in New Cross, London, and went out to France on Friday 12th March 1915 to join the Battalion with a draft. For Theodore's story and that of the Battalion see Private John Coshall above. Theodore was initially listed as missing before his death was confirmed some time later.

16715 PRIVATE ROBERT OLIVER
2nd Battalion Northumberland Fusiliers
Died on Saturday 8th May 1915, aged 16
Commemorated on Panel 8.

Robert was born at home, only son of Thomas and Jane Oliver, of 13 Bents, Whitburn, Sunderland. He had two elder sisters, Annie and Selina and a younger sister, Elizabeth.

He enlisted in Sunderland and after training left for France on Wednesday 10th March 1915. For Robert's story and that of the Battalion, see Private Frank Howard, above.

1581 PRIVATE EDWARD CHARLES OVER
3rd Battalion Royal Fusiliers
Died on Saturday 22nd May 1915, aged 17
Commemorated on Panel 6.

Edward was born in Ealing, son of Mrs Florence Mary Over, of 2 Dewsbury Crescent, Chiswick, London. He was educated locally and was then employed as an assistant on a motorised omnibus.

He volunteered in Kingston-on-Thames, Surrey, and after training Edward went out to France with a draft, entrained for northern France and went to Belgium to join his Battalion in the field on Sunday 7th March 1915. After a short period of training he commenced tours of duty in the front line. Edward had the opportunity of seeing Ypres before it was totally destroyed. Many shells and bombs had already landed on the town but it remained relatively intact. It was a vibrant and quite an exciting place for most soldiers, particularly for one so young on his first visit to anywhere outside of London. The shops remained open around the market square selling a wide range of souvenirs that were in particular demand. The cafés continued to ply their trade and expanded their pavement tables into the street that hindered many a marching soldier going into or out of the line.

At the outbreak of the Second Battle of Ypres Edward was back in the line at Gravenstafel. When the Battalion arrived in the trenches it was clear to all the men (and boys) that a German attack was about to commence. Edward had already had the misfortune to witness the first gas attack a couple of days before. At 3.30am on Saturday 24th the Germans launched their second gas attack, Edward and his comrades had little effective defence against gas, the equipment had not yet been invented, nor did they have much conception of the power and affects the gas could have. The attack was followed up by an enormous artillery barrage by the British to counter the German attacks. Attack and counter-attack continued and by the time Edward was relieved on Monday 3rd May he was lucky to be alive, however, totally exhausted. He marched to a bivouac north of the Vlamertinghe to Poperinghe road where he got some much needed rest. Edward was up early in the morning to get his equipment, uniform as well as himself clean and presentable ready for an inspection by General Edward Bulfin. Edward returned to the line on Saturday 8th in support of an attack but took no part. Edward remained on tours of duty without being involved in any distinctive or particular action until he was killed.

446963 PRIVATE
CYRIL ALFRED OWEN
31st Battalion Canadian Infantry (Alberta Regiment)
Died on Tuesday 13th June 1916, aged 17
Commemorated on Panel 28.

Cyril Alfred Owen.
Cyril's signature

Cyril was born in Plumstead, London, the second son of John Henry and Edith Owen, of Trail, British Columbia. He had an elder brother, John.

He volunteered in Calgary, Alberta, on Tuesday 18th May 1915, where he claimed to have been born in Woolwich, London, in 1897 and was working as a clerk. Cyril was 5ft 5in tall, with a 33½in chest, a fair complexion, brown eyes and light coloured hair.

Cyril sailed to England with the Battalion and was sent for training at Lydd and Otterpool in Kent. Whilst training The Right Honourable Sir Robert Borden, Prime Minister of Canada, accompanied by

Major General Sam Hughes inspected them. At 6.15pm on Saturday 18th September Cyril embarked on *SS Duchess of Argyle* that sailed at 7.10pm for Boulogne, arriving at 9.30pm. A short march of two miles took the Battalion to *'Ostrohove Rest Camp'* where they remained overnight before leaving the next morning for the station. At 10.30am the train pulled out of the station and by 3.00pm had arrived in Cassel. The Battalion was billeted at St Sylvestre where General Sir Herbert Plumer inspected them. The Battalion was sent to

Robert Borden and Sam Hughes

'Aldershot Camp' where training continued, including how to deal with a gas attack. At 4.30pm on Friday 24th General Sir Edwin Alderson addressed the Battalion and wished them well for the duties they were to undertake at the front. At 1.15am the next morning the Battalion arrived at *'Kemmel Shelters'* from where they took the line for the first time on Thursday 30th. Cyril continued to serve in front of Kemmel, with his main billets in Loker, until early February when the Battalion billeted in Berthen until the end of March.

On Saturday 1st April Cyril was sent for five days rest in Bailleul, however, the next day the Battalion was ordered to move towards Ypres. They marched via St Jan Cappel, Mount Noir, Westoutre and Reninghelst into *'Camp A'* west of Dickebusch. Cyril went into the trenches at *'Spoilbank'* during the night of Monday 3rd April where the Battalion diary records that *"the sanitary conditions of surroundings bad"*. The German artillery kept up a constant bombardment of their lines and Cyril was wounded in the head by a shell on Wednesday 5th, he was sent to *'Bedford House'* where the Field Ambulance was based. Major Daly, DSO, wrote: *"The continuous bombardment lasted 17½ hours, breaking up all the communication trenches from point 19S right up to the old front line, and made it absolutely impossible to go by daylight there being no cover whatever. The communication trench from the bottom of Convent Line to 19S is flattened out terribly, and troops cannot pass there by daylight in large numbers. The two dugouts at S.19 are intact, all others have been flattened out, the trench filled in at short intervals all along."*

Once Cyril had recovered from his wound he rejoined his comrades and continued to serve in the sector around Voormezeele and *'Scottish Wood'*. The Battalion was relieved to *'Camp E'* on Tuesday 9th May for training and rest until Monday 22nd when they returned to the line until the end of the month.

Cyril was sent to *Quebec Camp* on Thursday 1st June for three days when he moved to *Winnipeg Camp* from where he was taken by motor transport towards the front and as they approached they came under shell-fire. Cyril took the line at Zillebeke and was killed during a terrific artillery bombardment.

3486 PRIVATE HAROLD KEITH PAGE
48th Battalion Australian Infantry, AIF
Died on Friday 12th October 1917, aged 17
Commemorated on Panel 27.

Harold's signature

Harold was born in Adelaide, son of the late Alfred and Sarah Hamilton Page, of 24 Kent Road, Keswick, South Australia.

He volunteered on Monday 4th September 1916 when he claimed to be 18 years and 5 months old, working as a farm hand. Harold was a Methodist, 5ft 7¾in tall, with a 35½in chest, weighed 138lbs, had a medium complexion, blue eyes and brown hair. Both of Harold's parents signed the letter of consent to him enlisting.

Harold embarked on the *SS Seang Bee* in Adelaide on Saturday 10th February 1917 and arrived in Devonport on Wednesday 2nd May. He was sent for training until leaving from Southampton on Monday 16th July. Harold joined his Battalion in the field on Friday 3rd August whilst they were training in Doulieu.

Harold marched via Neuve Eglise and Dranouter to *'Kemmel Huts'* on Monday 6th August. He went into the line at *'Cabin Hill'* on Wednesday 8th where enemy activity varied day by day. He watched a dog-fight involving a large number of aeroplanes over *'Despagne Farm'* at 7.45pm on Monday 13th, cheering as the RFC drove the enemy back from whence they came! The tour of duty ended on Wednesday 15th and Harold spent the next day cleaning his equipment followed by himself. Once he had some rest he returned to working at the front line carrying ammunition. At the end of the month Harold moved via Kemmel to Zuytpeene and on to the training area at Boué where he stayed until Thursday 20th September. A series of moves took Harold via Steenvoorde, to *'Dominion Camp'* in Reninghelst then onto Ypres. Harold's first task was to help collect salvage before taking the support line at Nonne Boschen on Sunday 30th. During the relief a shell burst amongst a platoon that killed three and wounded eight of Harold's comrades. The next day he moved

forward to the Westhoek Ridge for twenty-four hours then was sent for two days rest in *'Halifax Camp'*. He was driven by omnibus to Steenvoorde on Thursday 4th October for rest and training until moving back to the Salient on Wednesday 10th. Harold was mortally wounded on Friday 12th October at Passchendaele and died on the battlefield, the thick mud consumed his young body.

His mother was sent a package with Harold's brush, razor strop, letters and a writing pad. His parents had both died before the issuing of medals so his British War Medal no 56256, Victory Medal no 55333 and his Memorial Plaque and Scroll no 336963 were sent to Harold's siblings.

17691 PRIVATE JOHN PARSONS
6th Battalion Somerset Light Infantry
Died on Sunday 26th September 1915, aged 17
Commemorated on Panel 21.

John was born in Ponders End, Middlesex, fifth son and sixth of nine children of Thomas John and May Parsons, of 77 Northwood Road, Thornton Heath, Surrey.

He went out to France on Tuesday 17th August 1915. For John's story see Private Henry McManus, above.

40365 PRIVATE JOHN PASFIELD
2nd Battalion Northamptonshire Regiment
Died on Tuesday 31st July 1917, aged 17
Commemorated on Panel 45.

John was born at home, second son of William and Mary Pasfield, of 81 George Street, Romford, Essex. He was educated locally.

He volunteered in Romford and was sent for training. John left to join the Battalion with a draft whilst they were serving in France.

The Battalion arrived in Méteren on Wednesday 6th June for a week of rest before moving into the line between the Menin Road and the Ypres to Roeselare railway. Following a tour of duty John was sent for training in *'Dominion Camp'* to train and prepare for the Third Battle of Ypres. Late on Saturday 30th June John went with his comrades into the assembly trenches in *'Kingsway'* and *'Kingsway Support'* with Battalion Headquarters established at *'Birr Crossroads'*. The area was swamped with water that made the mud very difficult to negotiate. The Battalion advanced alongside the Worcesters, then moved to *'Château Wood'*, the area of Bellewaarde Lake was cleared then the advance continued. By 5.30am *'Jacob Trench'*, immediately in front of the Blue Line, was also consolidated. In the fierce battle John lost his life.

His elder brother, Private William Pasfield, died on Tuesday 27th August 1918 and is buried in Ligny-sur-Canche British Cemetery.

14650 PRIVATE ALFRED PATTERSON
1st Battalion Lincolnshire Regiment
Died on Wednesday 16th June 1915, aged 17
Commemorated on Panel 21.

Alfred was born in Plumstead, London, eldest son of Mrs Alice Mary Davison (formerly Patterson), of 22 Abney Street, Sheffield, and the late Vincent Patterson (2nd Battalion Lincolnshire Regiment). He had four younger brothers. Alfred was educated locally.

He went out to France on Friday 30th April 1915 and joined the Battalion with a draft whilst they were serving on the Salient. For Alfred's story, see Private Levi Coles, above.

His father, 9339 Corporal Vincent Patterson, died on Sunday 7th November 1915 and is buried in East Retford Cemetery.

919930 PRIVATE JAMES EDWARD PEACOCK
24th Battalion Canadian Infantry (Quebec Regiment)
Died on Tuesday 6th November 1917, aged 17
Commemorated on Panel 26.

James' signature

James was born at home, son of John Frederick and Margaret Connery Peacock, of 1789 Notre Dame Street East, Montreal, Province of Quebec.

He volunteered in Valcartier, Province of Quebec, on Tuesday 12th September 1916 when he claimed to have been born on Friday 11th March 1898, was working as a machinist and whilst serving in the cadets had qualified as a sharp shooter. James was 5ft 7in tall, with a 35in chest, a dark complexion, brown eyes and dark coloured hair.

James trained in Canada and England before being sent to join the Battalion with a draft. He arrived on Tuesday 5th June 1917 whilst the Battalion was training in Camblain l'Abbé. The next day James followed the programme below:

6th

6.30am	Breakfast
7.30am-8.15am	Physical training
9.00am	Battalion Parade. Inspection and march to training area
10.15am-12.15pm	Section drill, saluting, arm drill
Afternoon	Free

7th and 8th

Morning	Physical training, platoon drill, arm drill, musketry and recruits
Afternoon	Bayonet fighting, recruits

9th

Morning	P.T., box respirator drill, saluting and recruits, musketry
Afternoon	Free

10th

Morning	Church Parade

11th

Morning	P.T., platoons practice in attack, one company at musketry, half an hour at box respirator drill
Afternoon	Each section in its own weapon, the rifle sections being allotted half to the Lewis Gun Section and half to the rifle grenadier section

12th

Morning	P.T., platoons practice in attack, bayonet fighting, throwing bombs, musketry
Afternoon	Each section in its own weapon, the rifle sections being allotted half to the Lewis Gun Section and half to the rifle grenadier section

13th

Morning	Brigade route march
Afternoon	Free

14th and 15th

Morning	P.T., platoons practice in attack, musketry, throwing bombs
Afternoon	Each section in its own weapon

16th

Morning	P.T., one company musketry, remained arm drill, bayonet fighting and saluting
Afternoon	Free

17th

Morning	Church Parade

18th and 19th

Morning	P.T., company in open order drill
Afternoon	Each section in its own weapon

20th

Morning	Brigade route march
Afternoon	Brigade Sports at Château de la Haie

21st

Morning	P.T., company in the attack
Afternoon	Bomb throwing and box respirator drill

22nd

Morning	P.T., company in the attack
Afternoon	Bayonet fighting

23rd

Morning	P.T., arm and company drill, and

Afternoon   Divisional Sports in Hersin

James marched to the Divisional Baths at 7.30am on Sunday 24th and when he returned to camp he attended a Church Parade. He prepared his kit ready for an inspection on Monday 25th the next day HRH The Duke of Connaught watched an arms drill then undertook an inspection on Wednesday 27th.

The move towards the battlefield began on Sunday 1st July when James marched from camp and into Brigade Support at Liévin. As he went into the trenches an artillery duel was being fought with shrapnel, high explosive and gas shells crashing about him. James was given practical training in the trenches but returned to billets at night that also came under shell fire. It was quite an introduction to the reality of war. James moved into the front line at Lens during the early hours of Saturday 7th where he was given further training. At 4.30am on Tuesday 10th he watched the anti-aircraft detachments drive off a flight of enemy aeroplanes as they approached the British lines. James first tour of duty ended late on Tuesday 10th when he marched to billets in Bully Grenay. He was able to get some sleep and rest during Wednesday 11th and marched for a hot bath the next morning. Following three days of training James returned to the trenches at Maroc and upon relief was sent to *'Noulette Wood Huts'* for training. He went back to front line duty at St Pierre from Tuesday 14th August until Wednesday 22nd. When relieved James marched to Bully to embus to billets in Gouy Servins. After a few hours rest he was able to get a hot bath and fresh clothes. He enjoyed a Concert Party given by the 3rd Divisional Party on Thursday 23rd. The next morning he returned to training but to keep spirits up another concert was organised that evening too. The Battalion marched to Maisnil-Bouché at 8.00am on Monday 27th where at 11.20am Field Marshal Sir Douglas Haig inspected the 5th Canadian Brigade. James marched from the camp on Monday 3rd September to Villers-Châtel in full kit and wearing a tin helmet. He settled into billets in Mingoval and the next day began training. He moved back to the front, via Villers au Bois, at *'Goodman Tunnel'* from where he undertook fatigues until Thursday 27th. After rest and training in Villers au Bois he marched to the support line at Méricourt on Friday 5th October. The relatively quiet tour of duty ended on Tuesday 16th and James marched to Zivy where he entrained on the light railway to *'Ottawa Camp'* in Bois des Alleux. After a day of rest he marched to a camp at Bailleul-aux-Cornailles. James marched to Tinques on Wednesday 24th and entrained to Borre where he trained until marching to Caëstre on Saturday 3rd November. He entrained at 6.45am bound for Ypres then marched

through the ruins of the town and out to Potijze. The 'accommodation' provided was not good, it was merely a collection of funk holes covered by tarpaulin. The 'camp' had to be evacuated shortly after he arrived when the enemy began shelling the area. During the afternoon James was prepared to go into the front, and was issued with ammunition, rations and sandbags. He was moved forward to the front line during Sunday 4th with Battalion Headquarters being established at *'Hamburg'* before moving to *'Hillside'* the next day. At 6.00am on Tuesday 6th James was led forward under a heavy barrage. The enemy poured a curtain of lead onto the attackers and their artillery began to shell the sector. During the attack James was killed.

… an HQ

10518 Lance Corporal
Arthur Edwin Pearce
1st Battalion Cheshire Regiment
Died on Thursday 29th April 1915, aged 16
Commemorated on Panel 19.

Arthur was born in St Clement's, Manchester, the only son of George Edwin and Martha Pearce, of 71 Stovell Avenue, Longsight, Manchester. He had two younger sisters, Amy and Beatrice. Arthur was educated locally. He enlisted in Chester, Cheshire, and was sent for training before being sent out to France. Arthur joined the Battalion with a draft in the southern sector of the Salient on Monday 11th January 1915. In March he was in the ghastly trenches between St Eloi and Hill 60, however, as the weather improved, so did the conditions at the front.

Arthur was a popular and good soldier, hence his promotion to Lance Corporal. He served on tours of duty at the front but his severest test came when on Tuesday 20th April 1915 the Germans began a two-day bombardment that ended with the first gas attack at 5.00pm on Saturday 22nd. Arthur was stood to then waited for further orders. He went into the front line in the early evening of Sunday 23rd where the situation was confused and desperate. Arthur took part in a series of attacks and counter-attacks until he lost his young life defending the line.

11205 PRIVATE JOHN JAMES PEFFERS
4th Regiment (Infantry) South African Infantry
Died on Thursday 20th September 1917, aged 17
Commemorated on Panel 16.

John's signature

John was born at home, the youngest and fifth child of William Wilson Peffers of 19 First Street, Bloemfontein, Orange Free State, South Africa and the late Annie Brown Peffers. His parents came from Haddington, East Lothian, Scotland, and emigrated to South Africa where their family was born.

He volunteered in Roberts Heights on Thursday 6th January 1916 where he stated he was 17 years old and was a student. John was sent to join 3rd South African Horse with service number 1833. After training he was taken on strength from Wednesday 23rd February. John took part in the fighting in German East Africa (Tanzania). He was wounded and taken prisoner on Friday 8th September but released soon afterwards. He disembarked on the HMT *Arcadian* on Wednesday 29th November in Durban, John was discharged, temporarily medically unfit, on Wednesday 13th December, due to the bullet wound to his left big toe.

John re-volunteered in Bloemfontein on Wednesday 31st January 1917 where he claimed to be 18 years and 11 months old and was a student. He was 5ft 8in tall, with a 35½in chest, weighed 120lbs, had a fresh complexion, grey eyes, light brown hair and three vaccination marks on his left arm.

He embarked on the SS *Walmer Castle* in Cape Town on Saturday 24th February. After training in England John was sent to Base Depôt in Rouen, arriving on Tuesday 22nd May. He joined the Battalion on Thursday 21st June. For John's story, see Private Forrest Sutherland, below. His brother, Private William Peffers aged 18, died on Thursday 19th October 1916 and is commemorated on Thiepval Memorial.

2587 PRIVATE
ALEXANDER ROBERT PERRY
36th Battalion Australian Infantry, AIF
Died on Monday 1st October 1917, aged 17
Commemorated on Panel 25.

Alexander's signature

Alexander was born in Broken Hill, New South Wales, son of William Charles and Evelyn Perry. He was a Ward of The Victorian Neglected Children's Aid Society from the age of eight.

He volunteered in Melbourne, Victoria, on Tuesday 5th September 1916 when he claimed to be 18 years old and was an ironworker, living at 44 Park Street, Brunswick, Victoria. He gave his aunt, Mrs J Fitzsimmons, of 26 Anderson Street, Alexandria, New South Wales, as his next of kin. Alexander was Presbyterian, 5ft 4½in tall, with a 30in chest, weighed 122lbs, had a medium complexion, brown eyes and hair, a mole on his right cheek and a scar on his left thigh. Ms Nellie Cowlie, the Secretary and Agent for The Victorian Neglected Children's Aid Society, gave her consent for Alexander to enlist as she 'believed' him to be 18 years old.

He embarked on HMAT *Shropshire* in Melbourne on Monday 25th September 1916 and disembarked in Plymouth on Saturday 11th November. He was sent for training in Hurdcott, Wiltshire, then sailed from Southampton on Thursday 23rd August 1917 bound for France. He joined the Battalion in the field on Saturday 1st September whilst they were enjoying a Brigade Sports Day in Le Mesnil-Boutry. The next day he began training with his new comrades in Ledinghem.

Alexander marched fifteen miles from camp to Heuringhem on Wednesday 26th September and the next day a further twenty miles took him to Eecke. After two days of hard marching most of the men were moaning as the roads were in a dreadful condition and had feet to match! A short march of six miles the next morning took him to Winnezeele and during the night of Saturday 29th Alexander was sent into the line for the first and last time in front of Frezenberg. He came under heavy fire from 'Bremen Redoubt' and 'Levi Farm' throughout Sunday 30th. In the early hours the next morning Alexander was blown to smithereens during a heavy bombardment. He had only been in the front line for just over a day and it is doubtful he ever had the chance to fire his rifle in anger.

His British War Medal no 47702, Victory Medal no 47147 and Memorial Plaque and Scroll no 3335321 were sent to his brother, Clement, who lived with his aunt, Mrs Fitzsimmons.

989 PRIVATE ERNEST JOHN PETCHEY
Essex Yeomanry
Died on Thursday 13th May 1915, aged 17
Commemorated on Panel 5.

Ernest was born at home, second son of Laura Agnes and the late William John Petchey, of 8 Princes Street, Maldon, Essex. He had two brothers, William and Clifford. Ernest was educated locally and then worked as a shop assistant in a local grocery shop.
He volunteered in Maldon and went out to France on Monday 30th November 1914 as a member of the Braintree Troop.
For the history of the Battalion and Ernest's involvement in the war, see Private Oxley Gordon Askew, above.

2588 PRIVATE CHARLES PHELPS
2nd Battalion King's Own
(Royal Lancaster Regiment)
Died on Saturday 8th May 1915, aged 17
Commemorated on Panel 12.

Charles was born in Fulham, London, son of John Randle Phelps and Kate Phelps. He was sent to an institution in Manchester for London youngsters.
He volunteered in Manchester and went out to France on Thursday 11th March 1915 to join the Battalion in the field with a draft. Charles soon settled into the routine of serving at the front and was given practical training in the front line then began to undertake tours of duty in the trenches.
Charles marched out of a camp in Vlamertinghe at 8.30pm on Tuesday 4th May and went into the line on the Frezenberg Ridge. Over the next three days the line was shelled intermittently. At 5.30am on Saturday 8th the Germans sent up a bright red rocket that was their signal for the preliminary bombardment to commence. The barrage was ferocious and for four hours shrapnel shells poured down on the front line and high explosive shells played havoc with the trenches. Lieutenant Colonel Aylmer Richard Sancton Martin had his Headquarters in a dug-out some five hundred yards behind the line, with half the Battalion in reserve ready to provide support. The German artillery successfully cut all telephonic communication with the front line and more than one messenger left on a one-way journey from the dug-out never to be seen again. By 7.30am the situation was becoming serious, many of the companies were already almost wiped out. Colonel Martin ordered more of his men to go forward to preserve and support the line and by 8.00am it was relatively secure despite losing most of their machine guns. As the German artillery barrage

lifted their infantry poured forward and attacked, having to cover only two hundred yards of ground. The German attack was checked and the artillery barrage stopped for a short period but at 10.50am their artillery opened up again. One of the high explosive shells hit the command dugout and Colonel Martin was killed instantaneously (he is also commemorated on the Menin Gate). Charles, together with many of his friends, died in the desperate fight and his remains lie in the earth where he fell.

S/8803 RIFLEMAN THOMAS PLATT
9th Battalion Rifle Brigade
Died on Saturday 25th September 1915, aged 17
Commemorated on Panel 48.

Thomas was born in Bethnal Green, London, eldest son of Thomas and Erina E Platt, of 38 Lamprell Street, Old Ford, Bow, London. He had an elder sister, three younger brothers and two younger sisters. Thomas was educated locally.
He enlisted in Shoreditch and was sent for training. Thomas went out to France on Tuesday 31st August 1915 and has not been with the Battalion for two weeks when he took part in his only action.
The Battle of Loos began on Saturday 25th September and diversionary actions were arranged to support the offensive. Late on Friday 24th Thomas marched to 'Railway Wood' ready for the attack on Bellewaarde. At 3.50am the British preliminary barrage commenced which was followed by a mine being blown at 4.18am; two minutes later he was led over the top and charged towards the lip of the crater. German machine-gun fire was intense and Thomas was shot down as he advanced.

19777 PRIVATE
WILLIAM BENJAMIN POWELL
8th Battalion Bedfordshire Regiment
Died on Thursday 4th November 1915, aged 17
Commemorated on Panel 33.

William was born in Birkenhead, Cheshire, eldest child of Edward William Benjamin and Elizabeth Powell, of 42 Manley Street, Regent's Park, London. He had two younger brothers and three sisters.
He volunteered in St Pancras, London, and went out to France on Monday 4th October 1915. William was part of a draft of one hundred and fifteen men that joined the Battalion whilst they were in a camp in Vlamertinghe on Friday 8th. He did not have much time to settle into Battalion life as the next morning he marched along the pavé to the ruins of Ypres and out to the front line for

the first time for a two-day tour of duty. When relieved William marched to a billet in a farm on the Watou to Proven road. He moved to 'Camp B' in the woods on Thursday 14th where two days later he was able to have a bath before the Battalion was inspected by General Sir Herbert Plumer. William returned to front line duty until the beginning of November. He was relieved late on Tuesday 2nd November where he was able to get some rest the next day. During the morning of Thursday 4th he undertook drill and physical training then in the afternoon William was sent to the front with a working party where he was killed.

6779 PRIVATE LEONARD PREECE
5th Battalion King's Shropshire Light Infantry
Died on Tuesday 3rd August 1915, aged 16
Commemorated on Panel 49.

Leonard was born in All Saints, Hereford, second son of Mrs Alice Preece, of 3 Limes Terrace, Maylord Street, Hereford. He was educated locally.

Leonard volunteered in Hereford and was sent for training, He left the training ground at Aldershot, Hampshire, on Wednesday 19th May 1915 to entrain for Folkestone, Kent, and embarked for Boulogne. After a long and winding train journey he arrived in Cassel from where he endured a tiring march to billets in Erkelsbrugge. He undertook training before moving to the line on Monday 31st May at Zillebeke, taking part in the attack on Bellewaarde in June.

Leonard returned to Ypres on Thursday 8th July and was billeted in the ramparts. The Battalion was held in reserve and each night he carried large quantities of rations along the Menin Road to the trenches in front of 'Railway Wood'. During the day Leonard went out into the town to help clear the rubble and detritus of war from the streets. Leonard went into the trenches at 'Railway Wood' from Tuesday 13th and when relieved was sent to bivouac at Busseboom, a short distance south of Poperinghe He again undertook fatigues, both during the day and night, at 'White Château'. At 7.00pm on Monday 19th, from his position only a short distance from Hooge, Leonard watched, heard and felt the blowing of the mine near Hooge Château. Following the German attack on Friday 30th July at Hooge, where flammenwerfer was used for the first time, a number of counter-attacks were mounted against the enemy. The Battalion was ordered into the line late on Saturday 31st, for Leonard and his comrades it was a difficult relief that took many hours to complete. The sight that greeted him as dawn broke was not a happy one. The whole area had been blasted by shellfire and many of the trenches were destroyed. Bodies, and parts of

bodies, lay out in No Man's Land uncollected with large numbers of the wounded lying in agony awaiting rescue. Leonard remained in the trenches and was killed the day before he was due to be relieved.

His elder brother, Private Albert Preece of the 1st Battalion King's Shropshire Light Infantry, died on Monday 15th May 1916 and is buried in Lijssenthoek Military Cemetery, grave reference VI.D.33.

26237 PRIVATE BERT ARTHUR PRESANT
14th Battalion Canadian Infantry (Quebec Regiment)
Died on Monday 26th April 1915, aged 16
Commemorated on Panel 24.

Bert's signature

Bert was the son of Philip H and Emma A Presant, of 27 Eighth Avenue, Toronto, Ontario. He won the Strathcona Gold Medal at Toronto for shooting at the Cadet School Contest.

He volunteered on Tuesday 22nd September 1914 when he claimed to be 19 years and 11 months, supposedly born on Thursday 17th October 1895, employed as a factory hand and a member of the Wesleyan Church. Bert was 5ft 6in tall, with a 38in waist, a fair complexion, blue eyes, brown hair, four vaccination marks on his left arm and a scar on the back of his left hand.

Bert was sent to St Nazaire from Avonmouth on Monday 11th February 1915 from where he entrained for Strazeele. His training continued until taking the line at Neuve Chapelle. After surviving the battle Bert continued to serve in the sector until being sent to Belgium on Friday 16th April.

Bert was in camp at Poperinghe when the Germans launched the first gas attack on Thursday 22nd April and he was ordered to march via Vlamertinghe into the line near St Julien. He marched along the cobbled, tree-lined road toward Ypres to the sound of the artillery; Ypres was under heavy attack and on fire. Bert marched out towards St Julien and took the line. He moved forward at 11.00am on Saturday 24th April under heavy fire and counter-attacked. The Germans launched a gas attack in the afternoon which he survived. The battle raged on and Bert was killed in the front line two days later.

B/1358 RIFLEMAN PERCY PRICE
7th Battalion Rifle Brigade
Died on Friday 30th July 1915, aged 16
Commemorated on Panel 48.

Percy was born at home, second son of Sarah E Price,

of 37 Corser Street, West Smethwick, Staffordshire, and the late John Price. He had one older and three younger brothers and a younger sister. Percy was educated locally.

He enlisted in Smethwick and was sent for training, moving to 'Whitley Camp', Godalming, Surrey, in February 1915 before moving to Salisbury Plain in March. Conditions in the camps were dreadful, thick mud and cold huts; the training was made more difficult due to the shortage of rifles and the lack of uniforms. Percy was sailed to Boulogne on Wednesday 19th May 1915, entraining to Watten where he continued to train before going into the line for his first tour of duty. For two months he did not become involved in any particular action. On Thursday 22nd July the British engineers blew a large mine on the ridge in front of Hooge; his tour of duty was delayed as a result, and he took the line the next day. Once Percy arrived in the line he was ordered to set about rebuilding his section of trench that was undone on Saturday 24th when the Germans blew a mine next to the British one! This was followed by an advance that was successfully repulsed. After a difficult tour of duty, late on Friday 29th Percy and the Battalion was relieved by the 8th Battalion to camp in Vlamertinghe. He arrived tired and exhausted at 3.45am, having been told he would be out of the line for a few days; one hour later he was ordered to stand to. The Germans had launched a major attack against the 8th Battalion and along the line at Hooge. At 7.00am Percy wearily marched back along the cobbled roads to Ypres — he had neither food nor rest. The Battalion was halted at Ypres whilst Colonel Heriot-Maitland visited Headquarters to receive final orders for the counter-attack in which they were to participate. Finally, at 1.30pm Percy was back in the line at 'Zouave Wood' with the battle raging ahead of him. At 2.45pm the counter-attack was launched but his progress was held up on the uncut wire and heavy machine gun fire poured down from the ridge above them. He was ordered to dig in and consolidate and whilst in the line Percy was killed.

2338 RIFLEMAN FREDERICK THOMAS GEORGE PULSFORD
1st/12th Battalion London Regiment (The Rangers)
Died on Wednesday 21st April 1915, aged 17
Commemorated on Panel 54.

Frederick Pulsford

Frederick was the only son of Frederick Luke and Blanche Bertha Pulsford, of 10 Tradescant Road, Lambeth, London. He had a younger sister, May. Frederick was educated at Westminster City School.

He volunteered on Tuesday 8th September 1914 and was sent for training. He embarked on the SS Balmoral in Southampton on Tuesday 9th March 1915 and sailed to Le Havre. He joined the Battalion in the field on Wednesday 17th.

For Frederick's story see Rifleman William Klagge, above.

2nd Lieutenant H H Bentley wrote of Frederick: "On 21 April your son and his friend Elvin were in a dug-out at Zonnebeke tending to the pressing wants of a comrade who was dreadfully wounded. As they busied themselves with him, a German shrapnel fell into the dug-out and burst. The violence of the explosion and the deadly hail of shrapnel bullets annihilated all the occupants of the dug-out, and The Rangers lost two fine soldiers in the painless heroic deaths of your son and his friend Elvin. It gives me great pain to have to break this sad yet heroic news to you, because he was always a great friend of mine and one who always did the utmost of his duty."

Frederick is commemorated on the Stockwell War Memorial.

... repulsing an attack

2051 Lance Corporal
William Thomas 'Tom' Purnell
2nd Battalion Gloucestershire Regiment
Died on Tuesday 20th April 1915, aged 16
Commemorated on Panel 22.

Tom was born at home, second son of Sidney Charles and Marry Ellen Purnell, of 18 Stratton Road, Gloucester. He had an older brother, Sidney James. Tom was educated locally.

He enlisted in Gloucester and was sent for training prior to leaving for France to join the Battalion in the field on Thursday 4th March 1915 whilst billeted in Westouter. Tom's first experience of the front line began in front of St Eloi where on Sunday 14th the Germans blew a mine under 'The Mound'. The terrifying noise pierced the air as the ground shook beneath Tom's feet, none of his training had prepared him for that. The fight that took place raged around him but Tom was not asked to take part. Late on Tuesday 23rd he was relieved and marched to huts at 'Rosenhill Camp' near Reninghelst. The camp was so grim many of the men bivouacked rather than occupy the huts!

Robert moved to the Ypres Salient in early April and on Saturday 17th April Tom was in the line at Hill 60. The next morning, he, together with his comrades, were subjected to a heavy mortar attack. The Germans were counter-attacking, attempting to retake Hill 60, but the Battalion doggedly stuck it out. During one of the bombardments Tom was killed.

He is commemorated on the City of Gloucester War Memorial.

13314 Private
George Frederick Quincey
2nd Battalion Worcestershire Regiment
Died on Friday 13th November 1914, aged 16
Commemorated on Panel 34.

George was born in Aston during early 1898, second son of Christopher and Rose Quincey, of 189 Montgomery Street, Sparkbrook, Birmingham. He was educated locally.

He volunteered in Birmingham in April 1913, aged 15 years old. At the outbreak of war George was mobilised with the Battalion in Aldershot, Hampshire, from where he left by train on Thursday 13th August 1914 for Southampton. The Battalion sailed to Boulogne on board the *HMT Lake Michigan* and the *Herschel*, arriving the following day to a great welcome from the local inhabitants. After a tiring march they arrived at 'Camp de Marlborough' high above the town where Field Marshal Sir John French

The Worcesters from Mons to the Aisne
The route taken by the 2nd and 3rd Battalion

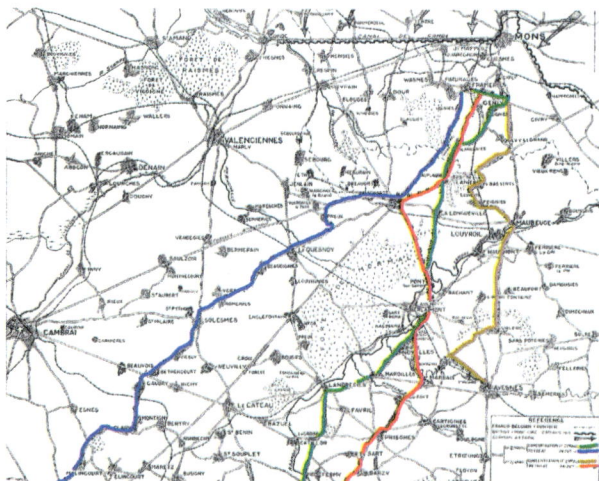

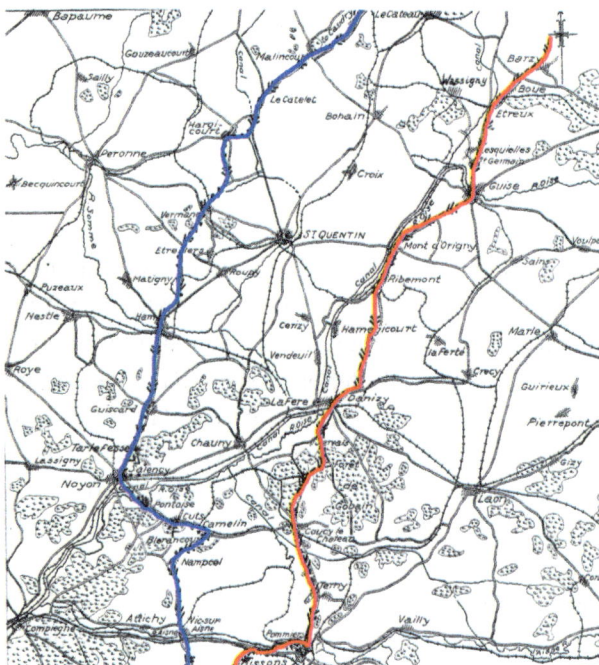

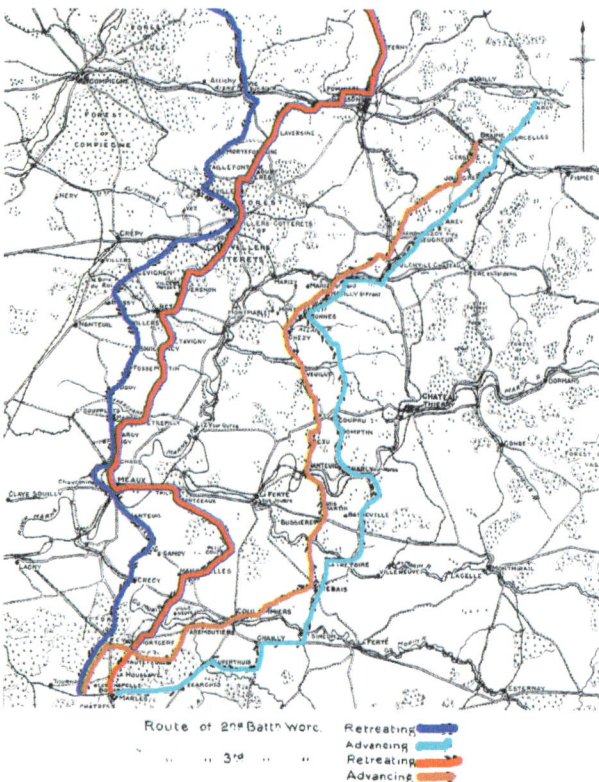

Route of 2nd Battn Worc.   Retreating
.." 3rd "..   Advancing
                             Retreating
                             Advancing

and General Joffre visited them the next day.

George entrained to Wassigny from where he marched and rested until eventually arriving close to the Mons battlefield during the afternoon of Sunday 23rd where they could see the action ahead of them. Before the Battalion could be fully involved in the battle they were ordered to Frameries and ordered to assist with the withdrawal. They came under German shell fire before they were also ordered to retire. After a night bivouacked in Bavai the retreat continued to Maroilles, one of George's officers wrote: *"We were all dog-tired and when we halted at Marbaix for half an hour we were all sound asleep on the road"*. The seemingly endless march south continued, on Thursday 3rd September a German aeroplane flew low over the Battalion and was brought down by rifle fire. Three days later George's Battalion were ordered to turn and find the German armies — they reached the Petit Morin where he was involved in a short, fierce action. The advance to the Aisne continued where the Battalion dug in and took part in continuous action for a month.

During the night of Monday 12th October George and his comrades were relieved by the French; the Battalion was sent to Fismes where they entrained. The train pulled out of the station in the black of night and it wound on its slow mysterious journey that took George to the outskirts of Paris. The train turned north and via Abbeville, Etaples, St Omer it arrived in Hazebrouck during the early evening of Friday 16th, a short march took George to billets in Morbecque. Following a rest in camp George was sent to Poperinghe on Monday 19th and the next day marched along the cobbled roads to Boesinghe, via Elverdinghe. In the distance the medieval spires, towers and high tiled roofs of Ypres were clearly seen by all ranks. George was sent along the Pilkem Ridge where he dug in and prepared for action. At dawn on Wednesday 21st George moved forward towards St Julien where he came under attack from small groups of German infantry, who were spread out in the hedges and fields, who were beaten off. After spending Friday 23rd under a constant bombardment it was of some relief to leave the battlefield in the early hours of Saturday 24th. He marched via St Jan to *'Hell Fire Corner'* that at this time was a fair distance from the front line and was a peaceful spot. George settled down and was looking forward to breakfast then begin three days of promised rest. Within twenty minutes he was ordered to stand to as there was a serious attack on Polygon Wood and support was required. He marched along the Menin Road and to the edge of the still standing wood that would soon be reduced to matchsticks. A fierce hand-to-hand combat ensued with the bayonet being used more often than the bullet that forced the Germans from the wood. Over the next couple of days

George was able to get some rest during the day in a bivouac near Veldhoek. Throughout Wednesday 28th and Thursday 29th the Battalion remained in reserve as a series of attacks took place ahead of them, none of which made any headway.

A fierce battle began at Gheluvelt early on Saturday 31st whilst the Battalion remained in reserve west of Polygon Wood. With the situation becoming increasingly desperate and a counter-attack needed, General Charles FitzClarence, VC, ordered the Battalion to undertake the task. The Battalion's commander, Major Edward Barnard Hankey (later Brigadier General Hankey, CB, DSO), led his men forward at the point of the bayonet at 2.00pm along the shallow valley of the Reutelbeek. They moved to the crest of the Polderhoek Ridge where they came under shell fire. Major Hankey ordered the men to charge towards Gheluvelt Château and into withering fire. The artillery supported the attack and shelled the grounds of the Château. The Battalion charged into the grounds and attacked the enemy — one of the German defenders was Adolf Hitler and his comrades of the List Regiment. The German infantry were forced out and the fighting continued in the houses in the village until the fighting died down. General FitzClarence realised that the position could not be maintained so ordered a retirement to Veldhoek where they began to dig in. George was relieved and marched back into reserve where he, like all ranks, lay in the field totally exhausted. During the afternoon of Sunday 1st November George marched to Zillebeke where he rested overnight before moving forward close to the line and held in reserve. He did not take part in any action and marched to Polygon Wood on Friday 6th and took the line on Sunday 8th. George's last action was the Battle of Nonne Boschen and despite surviving the initial battle on Wednesday 11th was killed in action two days later.

S/8981 RIFLEMAN
BERNARD THOMAS QUINN
9th Battalion Rifle Brigade
Died on Saturday 25th September 1915, aged 16
Commemorated on Panel 48.

Bernard's signature

Bernard was born at home, the only son of Mrs Annie Quinn, of 7 Stone Terrace, Storer Street, Nottingham. He had an older sister, Mary Ann and two younger sisters, Beatrice Ann and Catherine.

He enlisted in Nottingham on Saturday 13th March 1915 when he claimed to be 19 years and 2 months old and was working in a colliery as a pony driver. Bernard was 5ft 6½in tall, with a 34in chest and weighed

120lbs. He was sent for training in Winchester and was hospitalised with tonsillitis from Friday 2nd to Saturday 10th April. He was sent to the dentist on Wednesday 21st where he had four extractions and two fillings.

He joined the Battalion in the field whilst they were serving on the Salient on Thursday 9th September 1915. Bernard was listed as missing but it was not for another year was his death confirmed.

For Bernard's service at the front and the history of the Battalion see Rifleman David Ross, below.

His mother was sent Bernard's identity disc and after the war she received his war medals and Memorial Plaque.

20496 PRIVATE HARRY RADFORD
2nd Battalion King's Own Yorkshire Light Infantry
Died on Friday 7th May 1915, aged 17
Commemorated on Panel 47.

Harry was born at home, eldest son of Herbert and Annie Elizabeth Radford, of 2 Chapel Square, Greenhead, Chapeltown, Sheffield. He had two older and three younger sisters and a younger brother. Harry was educated locally and then worked at the screens in a pit shop in a local colliery.

He volunteered in Sheffield and went out to France on Thursday 21st April 1915. For Harry's story and that of the Battalion, see Lance Corporal Vincent Renshaw, below.

3/8988 PRIVATE ERNEST READ
1st Battalion Suffolk Regiment
Died on Saturday 24th April 1915, aged 17
Commemorated on Panel 21.

Ernest was born in Eaton, Norfolk, eldest son of William and Elizabeth Read, of 12 Nicholas Street, Norwich, Norfolk.

He volunteered in Norwich and went out to France on Tuesday 23rd February 1915. Ernest joined the Battalion whilst they were in billets in Bailleul. His first experience in the trenches began on Saturday 27th when the Battalion marched to 'Bus House' and went into reserve at Wulverghem. His first tour of duty in the front line lasted five days, from Wednesday 3rd to Monday 8th March then he returned for rest in Bailleul. Ernest undertook a two-day tour of duty in Ploegsteert before moving into the trenches in front of Kemmel on Sunday 21st March. He remained in the sector for another two weeks with billets in Dranouter.

Ernest marched from the village on Monday 12th April to comfortable billets in Poperinghe, at this stage well behind the lines. As he marched through Westoutre a great cheer went up from the 2nd Battalion who were billeted in the village. The senior officers of both Battalions decided to allow the men some time to meet with family and old friends before the 1st Battalion continued their march. After three days in the bustling town of Poperinghe Ernest marched along the cobbled road towards the spires of Ypres, halting at Vlamertinghe for two days then onward through Ypres to the trenches in front of Zonnebeke. Whilst in the line the sound of the German bombardment of Ypres grew ever louder and great plumes of black smoke billowed in the wind. From the trenches opposite the enemy kept up a constant fire from rifle, machine gun and trench mortar.

The Second Battle of Ypres began on Thursday 22nd April, late on Friday 23rd Ernest was relieved from the front line and sent into reserve between Frezenberg and Verlorenhoek. He set up a bivouac and got as much rest as was possible. It was not long, however, before he was ordered to prepare himself to go into battle. Captain Balders led the men to assist the Canadian forces and engage the enemy. It was not long before they came up against the German infantry. Ernest was shot and killed.

3/6742 PRIVATE WILLIAM READ
1st Battalion Dorsetshire Regiment
Died on Saturday 14th November 1914, aged 17
Commemorated on Panel 37.

William was born in Hook, Dorset, youngest son of Sarah Burden (formerly Read), of 1 Bridge Street, Overton, Basingstoke, Hampshire.

He volunteered in Dorchester, Dorset, and went out to France on Friday 23rd October 1914. For William's story, see Private Eric Widmer below.

40318 PRIVATE JOSEPH REDMAN
2nd Battalion Royal Scots Fusiliers
Died on Tuesday 31st July 1917, aged 17
Commemorated on Panel 19.

Joseph was born in Moston, Manchester, the eldest son of James and Ellen Redman, of 52 Brampton Street, Newton Heath, Manchester.

He volunteered in Manchester and was sent for training. Joseph joined the Battalion with a draft.

The Battalion had served through The Battle of Arras and following a period of training during which they received a number of drafts to bring them back to strength. Joseph marched from camp and went into the line along the Menin Road. The Battalion, under the command of Lieutenant Colonel W L Campbell, was part of the second wave. The Manchester Regiment attacked the line between *'Stirling Castle'* and *'Clapham Junction'*. They captured *'Stirling Castle'* but the enemy was stoutly defending the area between *'Glencorse Wood'* and *'Inverness Copse'*. Joseph was led against the enemy and whilst consolidating the position on the ridge came under a number of counter-attacks that had to be beaten off. It was a fierce fight during which four officers and sixteen men were killed, six officers and one hundred and fifty one men wounded and thirty-one men listed as missing. One of those lost was Joseph.

16074 PRIVATE
HENRY 'HARRY' REEVES
2nd Battalion Gloucestershire Regiment
Died on Monday 10th May 1915, aged 17
Commemorated on Panel 34.

Harry was born in Leigh, Lancashire, eldest son and child of Peter and Elizabeth Reeves, of 79 Sutton Veny, Warminster, Wiltshire. He had a younger brother and two sisters. Harry was educated locally.
He enlisted in Bristol and went out to France on Friday 2nd April 1915. For Harry's story and that of the Battalion, see Private William Holborow, above.

2047 PRIVATE
LEWIS THEODORE SINCLAIR REID
1st/14th Battalion London Regiment
(London Scottish)
Died on Sunday 1st November 1914, aged 17
Commemorated on Panel 54.

Lewis was born in Balham, Surrey, eldest son of John and Annie Battley Reid, of 42 Sheepcote Road, Harrow, Middlesex. He was educated at Magdalen College School, Brackley, Northamptonshire, as a boarder.
For Lewis' story see Private Archibald Angus, above.

3/1408 LANCE CORPORAL
VINCENT RENSHAW
2nd Battalion King's Own Yorkshire Light Infantry
Died on Friday 7th May 1915, aged 17
Commemorated on Panel 47.

Vincent was born in St Philip's, Sheffield, second son of Mrs Ada Renshaw, of 3/1 Britannia Road, Darnall, Sheffield. He was brought up in his maternal grandparents home.

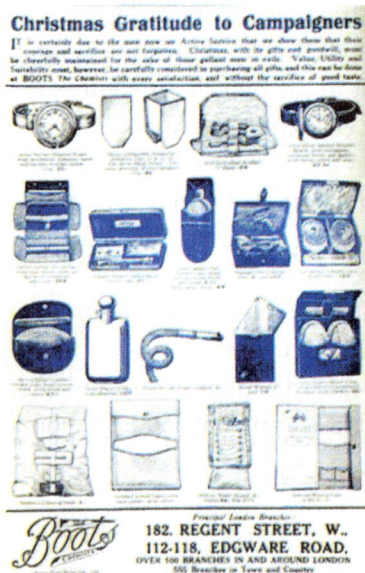

Boots provide a range of handy presents for the troops at the front

He volunteered in Sheffield and went out to France on Friday 4th December 1914. Vincent joined the Battalion at their billets in Loker with a draft of sixty-six men and two officers two days later. He began tours of duty in the southern Kemmel sector where the trenches were never dry and often the tours of duty were completed whilst waist deep in freezing cold water and mud. The Battalion, during this period, lost more men to hospital with trench foot and other such complaints than they did to enemy action. Vincent spent Christmas in billets in St Jans Cappel where he enjoyed a hearty lunch and joined in the six-a-side football matches. He completed a three-day tour of duty before spending New Year's Day billeted in Neuve Eglise.

Vincent marched out of the village on Wednesday 6th January 1915 to return to the trenches where, *en route*, General Sir Charles Ferguson inspected the Battalion then addressed the men. Vincent remained on tours of duty in the sector with billets in Bailleul during January. The First Battalion had arrived in France so on Friday 29th January Vincent marched out from Bailleul towards Outtersteene where the two Battalions met together in a field and enjoyed chatting with family and friends.

Tours of duty, training and rest continued in the sector until Sunday 11th April when the Battalion was relieved and sent to a camp in Reninghelst. Early on Saturday 17th Vincent was ordered to stand to then marched off to Ypres where he later heard the explosions of the mines blown under Hill 60. The enemy mounted a strong and successful counter-attack at dawn on Sunday 18th that pushed the King's Own Scottish Borderers off the crest. A British counter-attack was required: at 7.00am Vincent marched towards the battlefield and at 12.30pm moved into *'Larch Wood'* where he awaited orders. From 5.00pm the Battalion began to go through the communication trenches by company ready for the attack. The crest of the hill was once again in British hands but the position required consolidation, Vincent was detailed to begin entrenching and improving what was left of the trenches. Somehow he managed to survive on the Hill as forty-four batteries of German artillery pounded it and their infantry continuously attacked. At dawn on Monday 19th Vincent was relieved from the field of death where the bodies of the dead and wounded heaped by the hundred on the field. Following twenty-four hours in a bivouac Vincent marched to a hutted camp at Ouderdom where he was able to clean up and rest. Whilst in camp Generals Sir Horace Smith-Dorrien and Sir Charles Ferguson visited to thank the Battalion for their hard work and on Wednesday 21st General Robert Wanless-O'Gowan came to inspect a parade then addressed the men. Field Marshal Sir John French addressed a parade of the 13th Infantry Brigade at 2.30pm on Thursday 22nd where he thanked them profusely for the good work at Hill 60.

The plan was for the Battalion to have the opportunity to refit and reorganise before being deployed to the trenches once more. However, the Germans had different plans, at 5.00pm the first gas attack was launched and thus began the Second Battle of Ypres. At 7.00pm Vincent marched north to the Poperinghe to Ypres road where streams of terrified refugees were packing the road and amongst them were large numbers of French Colonial troops (Turcos) who had taken the brunt of the gas attack. The Turcos were in a terrible state and many collapsed writhing on the ground and died on the spot. Vincent continued on to Brielen from where the next day he went into the front line and dug in. A fierce counter-attack was mounted late on Friday 23rd where the Battalion was badly mauled. Vincent was one of only two hundred and fifty men left able to fight. He was sent to St Jan on Monday 26th where he spent two days digging in whilst under heavy shell fire. Vincent went into the firing line at Wieltje for a few hours before being relieved and sent to rest in Vlamertinghe where messages of thanks were received from General Sir Herbert Plumer and Sir Edwin Alderson.

Yet again Vincent and his comrades were destined not to get any rest as a gas attack had been mounted on Hill 60. He marched to the front where he was in reserve until he took part in an assault at 2.30am on Friday 7th May. As Vincent rushed the German trenches he was shot down by rapid fire.

18102 PRIVATE RICHARD RHODES
1st Battalion York and Lancaster Regiment
Died on Saturday 8th May 1915, aged 17
Commemorated on Panel 55.

Richard was born in Norton, Sheffield, second son of Rufus Gascoyne Rhodes and Hannah Rhodes, of 27 Tannery Street, Woodhouse, Sheffield. He had an older and two younger brothers, and two younger sisters.

Richard was educated locally.

He volunteered in Sheffield and went out to France on Saturday 1st May 1915. For Richard's story see Private Walter Godbehere above.

2782 PRIVATE
HERBERT JAMES RICHMOND
1st/7th Battalion
Argyll and Sutherland Highlanders
Died on Sunday 25th April 1915, aged 17
Commemorated on Panel 44.

Herbert was the eldest son and child of Malcolm F and Annie Richmond, of 71 Dorrator Road, Camelon, Falkirk. Following his elementary education he was employed as an electroplater in the Crown Brass works, Falkirk.

He volunteered in Falkirk and went out to France on Tuesday 15th December 1914. For Herbert's story see Private James Duchart, above.

9757 PRIVATE JOHN ROBERTS
1st Battalion Lincolnshire Regiment
Died on Sunday 1st November 1914, aged 17
Commemorated on Panel 21.

John was born in St Theresa, Southport, Lancashire, son of the late Mary Roberts.

He volunteered in Seaforth, Lancashire, and went out to France on Thursday 22nd October 1914. John joined the Battalion with a draft in Croix Rouge as the Battalion was ending its service in the trenches in the La Bassée sector.

The Battalion left for rest overnight in Estaires on Friday 30th October and at 6.35am the next morning they marched across the border into Belgium. John marched for twelve miles via Lindenhoek to Kemmel. A fierce battle was raging for the possession of Messines and the sight and sound of battle could be clearly heard and seen. The Germans were pressing hard along the Messines Ridge and the Battalion was ordered into the line on Sunday 1st November, the War Diary records: "… at 1.30 a.m. a hurried order was received that the battalion was to march to Wytschaete and retake the trenches from which the cavalry had been driven." At 1.30am John marched toward Wytschaete where the Battalion encountered the enemy pretending to be Indian troops. As the men moved forward they came under fire and the German ruse accounted for many in the Battalion, including John.

3/10512 PRIVATE
GEORGE WILFRED ROBERTSHAW
2nd **Battalion Duke of Wellington's**
(West Riding Regiment)
Died on Wednesday 24th February 1915, aged 16
Commemorated on Panel 20.

George was born at home, second son of John and Alice Robertshaw, of Broad Head End, Hollock Lee, Mytholmroyd, Yorkshire. He had an elder brother and six younger sisters. George was educated locally then was employed whipping blankets in a local factory. He enlisted in Halifax and was sent for training before leaving for France on Saturday 5th December 1914. George joined the Battalion in the field near Wulverghem the next day as Colonel Harrison recorded: *"A new reinforcement of about 200 men and 3 officers, under Capt. C. H. Unwin, arrived at 10 a.m., which makes us up to 850 men and 14 officers."* and the next day: *"Did some parade to-day to smarten and shake the new drafts up. … Most of the new draft are Special Reserves, and it will be difficult to keep the Battalion up to something like Regimental form."*

George was allocated to his platoon and met his new comrades who were able to tell him in graphic detail the reality of the Western Front as he sat chatting with them. He was called to the Medical Officer on Tuesday 8th to check that his inoculations were adequately up to date. George paraded at 1.00pm on Thursday 10th then marched to some rather poor billets in Dranouter where, throughout the night, the enemy shelling kept him and his comrades awake. George went into the trenches for the first time in front of Wytschaete on Monday 14th where he came under heavy shellfire. He was relieved on Tuesday 15th that was difficult, he had to assist in pulling many of his comrades out of the mud with ropes. George spent the winter on tours of duty in the sector.

George was sent with the Battalion to Vlamertinghe on Friday 19th February, arriving at 3.30pm, where they were provided with huts to the south of the village to rest in overnight. The next morning he marched along the cobbled road to Ypres. The area was relatively undamaged: the town, with its medieval towers still standing proud, yet to suffer the terrible damage that would reduce it to rubble in only a few weeks time. The town was buzzing with activity; soldiers were marching to and fro, others resting. The cafés continued to ply their trade and were packed to bursting and the shops were doing a roaring trade selling souvenirs. It must have been a fascinating and exciting time for a young boy whose previous experiences in Yorkshire would have naturally been somewhat narrow. George did not have long to appreciate or enjoy what was

on offer in Ypres as he was sent into the front line at Zillebeke to support the Royal West Kents. On one of his first tours of duty George was killed in action.

793884 PRIVATE
JOSEPH CHARLES VINCENT
ROBICHAUD
42nd **Battalion Canadian Infantry (Quebec Regiment)**
Died on Thursday 15th November 1917, aged 17
Commemorated on Panel 28.

Joseph Charles Vincent Robichaud
Joseph's signature

Joseph was the son of Joseph O Robichaud and Marie Babin, of Upper Pokemouche, Gloucester County, New Brunswick.

He volunteered in Campbellton, New Brunswick, on Monday 21st February 1916 when he claimed to have been born on Thursday 21st January 1897 and was working as a labourer. Joseph was a Roman Catholic, 5ft 7½in tall, with a 35in chest, an olive complexion, grey eyes, brown hair, and numerous scars on his trunk and legs from Pediculosis Corporis (a condition usually caused by lice when they lay their eggs in clothing). Joseph joined the Battalion whilst they were training near Steenvoorde. He entrained at Esquelbecq on Thursday 7th September and after further training he arrived in the Vadencourt Wood on Tuesday 12th. The Battalion took the line in readiness for an attack towards Pozières. He was sent to 'Usna Hill' on Friday 15th before moving forward with their objective of 'Fabeck Graben Trench'. For three days Joseph attacked, consolidated his position and counter-attacked before being relieved to 'Tara Hill'. He continued to serve on the Somme throughout the rest of the year but was able to spend Christmas out of the line. The last days of 1916 were spent in training ready for a raiding party that attacked the German trenches at 1.55am on Monday 1st January 1917. Tours of duty continued throughout January, February and March where Joseph was involved in a series of raids. Training was undertaken in preparation for supporting the Battle of Arras on Monday 9th April. During the night of Saturday 7th April Joseph moved from Villers au Bois and he went into 'Grange Tunnel' before moving the next day to 'Longfellow Trench'. By 5.00am on Monday 9th the advance was going well being described by Major Pease: *"The final objective was reached and consolidation started at about 8 a.m. on April 9th. A short time after this Captn. Hugh Wallis of the Brigade Staff arrived and proceeded to the left where we were in touch with a few of the 54th Battalion who had reached their objective. He soon returned and reported that the Battalion on our left was held up by enemy Machine Gun and requested me to call a few Rifle Grenadiers and see what we could do. This I did and was moving to the left flank, which I had reached, when the sniping became very active from the left and we could see numbers of the enemy on the skyline about 200 yards distant. The rifle grenadiers took over and opened up fire at the enemy and I moved down to the left, warning everyone I could find towards the flank. To our left a Machine Gun and a number of men presumably 54th also engaged this party, and after a brisk exchange of fire the enemy withdrew leaving only a few snipers who took positions in the wood on the brow, and just below the slope."* By lunchtime the wounded remained uncollected but a further supply of ammunition had to be sent to the front:

> 5,000 rounds of SAA
> 3,300 rounds of SAA
>   600 No 23 Mills rifle grenades
>   240 No 5 Mills grenades

By the evening their next objective were being considered as the Germans were reinforcing their line and moving towards Méricourt. Major Nosworthy sent the following message: *"B and D Coys., are dug in the wood. They are in close touch with P.P.C.L.I. on right. Their left flank is in the air and extends a little further north that what was laid down as our Brigade boundary. Total garrison about 150 including 5 Officers, 4 Lewis Guns (42nd Bn) and 2 Colt Guns, 2 Lewis Guns (49th Bn).*

A supply of L.G. Discs, 1½" VERY pistols and SOS flares was sent them to-night.

Their left flank received a considerable measure of protection from the fact that "C" Coy; together with a few men of the 54th Bn., have in addition to garrisoning Strong Point,

pushed well up BLUE Trench and dug a flanking trench on both its East and West side - estimated distance separating companies 100 yards.

Garrison of BLUE Trench and S.P.7 - 2 Officers and 98 O.R. (including 2 or 3 Lewis Guns) and Lieut. Morris and 3 Vickers Guns. Garrison of BEGGAR Trench 2 Officers and 70 men including 2 Lewis Guns. Touch with Left Battalion in BEGGAR Trench was not established until late this afternoon, when it was found that they were manning BEGGAR Trench from S.22.A.8.3 to junction of BEGGAR and BLIGHTY S.22.a.6.4 with 3 Officers and about 130 of 102nd Bn. And 54th Bn. Including 7 or 8 Lewis Guns, their left flank being in the air. In accordance with Brigade advice of pending operation the whole of this garrison was moved south on BEGGAR and temporarily there are 200 men between about S.22.a.8.3 and junction of BEGGAR and BLUE.

Major Pease stated enemy is in considerable force about forty yards distant from outpost line. He snipes actively by day from behind logs of wood. Only one enemy shell has hits on BLUE near S.P.7 this morning caused considerable casualties. On the whole enemy registration of these trenches is not so good as would be expected.

Our men are very tired and would strongly recommend that they be relieved tomorrow night."

Eventually, after a hard tour that saw five officers killed and six wounded, and a total of two hundred and ninety-one other ranks were casualties, Joseph with the Battalion were relieved and set off to Villers-au-Bois. After eight days he returned to the line on tours of duty at Vimy or on fatigues, remaining in the Vimy and Lens sectors until the night of Friday 5th October when he was relieved and sent to dugouts in the 'Thélus Cave' area.

Joseph entrained at Tinques for Godewaersvelde on Tuesday 16th October then marched through Caëstre and was billeted near Hazebrouck where training continued and an inspection took place near Borre by HRH Field Marshal the Duke of Connaught. Following a route march to Caëstre Station the Battalion entrained to Ypres. They rested for a few hours before proceeding to 'California Trench' where they were held in reserve, providing fatigues. They moved to bivouac on the 'Abraham Heights' with the HQ at 'Otto Farm' on Tuesday 30th and considerable casualties were taken

HRH The Duke of Connaught

from shelling in their exposed position. At 7.30pm on Wednesday 31st the Battalion moved forward into the appalling conditions of the front line that were more a collection of shell holes rather than connected trenches. The following evening Joseph was sent to establish an additional post on the south side of the Gravenstafel Road. A successful raid was prepared during the night of Friday 2nd November to capture a pill box with the attack beginning in the early hours the next morning. 'Graf House' was eventually captured and its garrison fled. The Germans mounted a counter-attack under the cover of darkness that was stopped by effective rifle and machine gun fire.

Major Nosworthy recorded the events: *"I then sent word to Hobart that McIntyre's and Macaskill's parties were being withdrawn and that he might use his judgment whether he withdrew or dug in where he was. He replied that he had only got forward about sixty yards, had suffered some casualties from a machine gun on his left, and that he would withdraw.*

At 4.02 Lieut. Shaw, Stokes Gun Officer, reported that the use of the rings necessary to obtain extreme range had so heated his barrels that two guns were out of commission. The other gun remained trained on Graf House but no signal had been received from Lieut. Cohen to open fire. I ordered him to resume fire with the two guns as soon as barrels cooled but to leave one gun trained on Graf. ...

A platoon of C Company, which was in support behind Coy. Headquarters was ordered to report to Lieut. Howard to strengthen his garrison. Meanwhile Party No. 5 had been held up about 50 yards from the German line by a machine gun. A verbal message was received that asked for instructions and I ordered a withdrawal. Party 6 had lost its Officer Lieut. Parkings wounded very soon after zero hour, but had pushed on to its objective i.e. road junction at D.5.d.4.8. Their position was very difficult however owing to machine gun fire from higher ground on their left and Major Willcock whom I had sent out to look over the situation ordered a withdrawal. I had given him authority to take this step if thought advisable. Party No. 7, Lieut. Cohen and 28 O.R. detailed to capture Graf House advanced in three parties, the left party consisting of a Sergeant and 5 men became scattered and appears to have rendered Mr. Cohen very little assistance. The two remaining parties reached Graf House and on their approach its garrison, which consisted of 5 or 6 men, fled. Our party occupied the ruin where they were subjected to considerable M.G. and rifle fire. After about 20 minutes a party of about 15 Germans advanced to the attack but were driven off by rifle and Lewis Gun fire. Later a much larger body advanced but were also halted by fire from our Lewis Gun which expended in all 15 panniers.

The Germans however under cover of darkness were able to creep up to within effective bombing distance and our party suffered a number of casualties from cylindrical stick and egg bombs as well as rifle and M.G. fire. When the ruin had been in our possession about an hour Lieut. Cohen was killed by a bullet through the abdomen. The garrison was now reduced to 5, consisting of Lce. Corl. J. Taylor and 4 others. Their L.G. ammunition had all been expended except half a pannier as well as all their rifle grenades and bombs, and L/Cpl. J. Taylor, who was himself wounded, decided to withdraw.

No message asking for reinforcement was received from Lieut. Cohen, and as only a few of the casualties of his party reported back through their Company Headquarters it was not evident to us that he was being to hard pressed. Our right Company Commander had however sent forward a Lewis Gun and crew with instructions to report to him, but most unfortunately it lost its way and joined Party No. 6.

Next morning the Germans were busy evacuating wounded from the vicinity of Graf House giving proof of the effectiveness of the stand made there by our garrison. The outstanding figures in this desperate resistance were undoubtedly Lieut. Cohen and L.Cpl. J. Taylor, No. 1 of the Lewis Gun. A Company of R.C.R.'s under Lieut. L. E. Longley did excellent work in evacuating wounded." (Lieutenant Myer Tutzer Cohen is buried in Poelcapelle British Cemetery and Lieutenant Robert McIntyre died of his wounds and is buried in Nine Elms British Cemetery.) It was an expensive action, the casualties being:

	Killed	Died of wounds	Wounded	Missing
Officers	2	1	5	-
NCOs	6	3	16	-
Other ranks	32	6	99	4

Late on Saturday 3rd November Joseph was relieved and was sent to rest in 'Pomern Castle' and the next day marched to a camp for twenty-four hours before entraining at Ypres Asylum for Abeele. He marched to billets in and around 'Trappist Farm', Watou. Joseph was able to properly clean up and rest before undertaking training. A fleet of omnibuses arrived on Tuesday 13th to collect the Battalion that deposited them on the Dickebusch road from where they marched to 'California Trench' where they spent the night. The next day Joseph moved into the front line and undertook an operation to establish a post in 'Virtue Farm'. It was unsuccessful and in the attempt Joseph was killed.

16477 PRIVATE
HENRY THOMAS ROBINS
1st Battalion Somerset Light Infantry
Died on Tuesday 27th April 1915, aged 17
Commemorated on Panel 21.

Henry was born at home, eldest son of Thomas and Sarah Robins, of Elberton, Olveston, Bristol, Gloucestershire. He had three younger sisters. Henry was educated locally and then worked with his father who was a local blacksmith learning the craft.

He volunteered in Bristol and went out to France on Wednesday 24th March 1915. For Henry's story see Private Clifford Milton, above, who left for the Western Front with Henry and they died on the same day.

TF/1795 PRIVATE OWEN ROSE
1st/8th Battalion Middlesex Regiment
Died on Friday 30th April 1915, aged 17
Commemorated on Panel 51.

Owen was born at home, son of George T and Mary Ann Rose, of 4 Deburstow Terrace, Bishops Road, Hanwell, London.

He volunteered in Ealing and was sent for training. Owen joined the Battalion when they returned from serving on Gibraltar in February 1915. He left with the Battalion from Hounslow on Monday 8th March 1915 to entrain for Southampton. He sailed to Le Havre where he landed the next day then entrained to Bailleul. Owen undertook training and joined working parties until Friday 26th when he was sent into the front line for practical training attached to battle-hardened troops. Fatigues continued until Sunday 4th April when the Battalion collected at Kruisstraat then moved to Vlamertinghe on Tuesday 6th. Owen's first tour of duty began on Friday 9th at Zonnebeke.

When the Second Battle of Ypres began on Thursday 22nd April, John was serving at the front at Zonnebeke as the War Diary records:

"April 22nd: Shelling continually during the day. Front line trenches mined. Men slept during the day and kept quiet. 'B' Company relieved during the night, and 'A' Company went back into cellars at Zonnebeke. Guns going all night and much rifle fire.

April 23rd: Fairly quiet morning. Shelling commenced afternoon and continued for some hours, intermittent all night. A great man 'non-stops'. Carried for East Surreys, 'B' Company making two journeys. Several men wounded and one killed on railway line. Shelling and rifle fire all night."

The enemy mounted an attack at 7.00am on Saturday 24th and captured St Julien. The Battalion was ordered to move round and support the line, Owen with his comrades began to dig in near St Jan. German artillery shells of all types and calibres began to fall amongst the Battalion on Sunday 25th. The position in front of them was threatened so a counter-attack was planned. The Battalion charged across the field whilst under heavy fire then shot or bayoneted the enemy they encountered. The War Diary records: *"By then, owing to the fact that the parapet had to be lined as the trench was recaptured, there were no more men left, and*

on reinforcements being asked for to enable Lieut. Woods to complete the recapture of the trench, it was found that every available man of the Surrey's and Middlesex were in the fire trench and lining the parapet. It was then about 2.15 p.m., and it was realised that nothing more could be done with the troops present. The troops had become very mixed, and the Middlesex had lost six of their ten officers and well over 100 men out of the 240 taken into the trench. In the early evening a detachment of Cheshires unexpectedly arrived, and their presence was much appreciated. About 7 p.m. the Shropshires arrived and made two assaults on the part of the trench not recaptured." The series of attacks were unsuccessful with a large number of the Battalion lost. Colonel Garner recorded for the events: *"Enemy's sniping and bombing, which now enfiladed us from both flanks, increased daily and became very nerve shaking, making many casualties. Owning to absence of trench mortars and the condition of the parapets as left by the French, hardly any reply was possible on our part."*

From Wednesday 28th the Battalion moved to Verlorenhoek where they dug in under heavy shell, mortar and rifle fire. The work continued, with individual companies going into the firing line for short periods. After serving and surviving through many difficult and dangerous actions, Owen's young life ended in a field on the Frezenberg Ridge.

S/7435 RIFLEMAN
DAVID ARTHUR CECIL ROSS
'B' Company, 9th Battalion Rifle Brigade
Died on Saturday 25th September 1915, aged 17
Commemorated on Panel 48.

David was born at home, second son of James Ross, LRCP, LRCS, and Alice Ross, of Glengariff, Shore Road, South Hackney, London.

He volunteered in Holborn, London, and sent for training in Petworth, West Sussex, followed by Aldershot, Hampshire. He left with the Battalion for France arriving on Friday 21st May 1915.

David was sent for practical training in the front line attached to the 1/5th North and the 1/5th South Staffordshire Battalions. He began tours of duty near *'Railway Wood'* from early June and settled down to front line routine.

The first significant action that David participated in was at Hooge on Friday 30th July. The brunt of the first flammenwerfer (liquid fire) attack by the Germans fell on the 8th Battalion who were serving to the 9th Battalion's right. David saw the huge crimson jets of fire light up the sky and the thick black smoke billowing into the sky. As the attack began a two-hour barrage fell on the line held by David and his comrades. Colonel Villiers-Stewart was informed at 5.30am that the 8th Battalion had been forced to retire and sent Lieutenant John Edward Baroles Gray out to investigate. The Brigade Commander, who was on the field, stated: *"In my opinion situation precludes counter-attack by day. Counter-attack would into a re-entrant and would not succeed in face of enfilade fire."* Sadly the Division disagreed and the counter-attack was ordered for 2.45pm. The 8th Battalion led the way with David and his comrades of the 9th in support. The Battalion made considerable progress as they were fresh, having not been involved in the early action. The 7th and 8th Battalions, who were already totally exhausted, were unable to make any headway despite heroic efforts by both officers and men. The losses between the three battalions were very high, many acts of bravery were rewarded with decorations and those who survived Hooge felt themselves very lucky indeed.

David was relieved from the line and after a short period of rest returned to the same line to continue tours of duty. The area was covered with body parts and the unburied dead from both sides. After six weeks the Battalion would take part in another attack at Hooge. The Battle of Loos began on Saturday 25th September and diversionary actions were arranged to support the offensive. Late on Friday 24th David marched to *'Railway Wood'* ready for the attack on Bellewaarde. At 3.50am the British preliminary barrage commenced which was followed by a mine being blown at 4.18am; two minutes later he was led over the top and charged towards the lip of the crater. German machine-gun fire was intense and David was shot down as he advanced.

6305 PRIVATE
FRANCIS ADRIAN OSCAR HERBERT ROSS
9th Battalion Australian Infantry, AIF
Died on Thursday 20th September 1917, aged 17
Commemorated on Panel 17.

Francis Adrain Oscar Herbert Ross

Francis' signature

Francis was born in Stockinbingal, New South Wales, son of Edward and Alice Ross, of Cannon Vale, Proserpine, Queensland.

He volunteered in Bowen, Queensland, on Monday 10th April 1916 when he claimed to be 18 years and 4 months, working as a labourer that he later changed to be a farmer when undertaking a medical. Francis was 5ft 9in tall, with a 33in chest, weighed 132lbs, had a fair complexion, blue eyes and brown hair.

He embarked on the *SS Clan MacGillivray* in Brisbane, Queensland, on Thursday 7th September 1916 and upon arrival sent to continue his training. Francis sailed on the *SS Golden Eagle* from Folkestone, Kent, to Boulogne on Sunday 17th December. He arrived with a draft of twenty-six men under Lieutenant J S Young to join the Battalion whilst they were serving in front of Flers on the Somme. Francis went into the front line for the first time late on Thursday 21st at *'Smoke Trench'*. He was introduced to trench routine that included helping to strengthen the line. Francis spent his only Christmas on the Western Front in the trenches but was relieved on Saturday 30th and marched to a hutted camp in Bazentin. As Francis had only just arrived and it was deemed that he did not need so much rest Francis was sent out on Sunday 31st with a working party. He remained on fatigues until moving to Dernancourt on Saturday 6th January 1917. After two days of hard work all ranks were given three days complete rest then returned to fatigues. He moved to Bresle for training on Sunday 14th where Francis contracted gastritis on Monday 22nd January 1917 and was sent to 3rd Australian Field Ambulance. He was sent by Hospital Train to the 14th General Hospital, Boulogne where he developed pneumonia and sailed on *HMHS Princess Elizabeth* to England. He was hospitalised in Ward 5 of Norfolk War Hospital, Thorpe, Norwich, from Thursday 8th to

Monday 19th February and again from 5th to 21st March from where he was sent to recover in Dartford, Kent. He remained in England until Friday 20th July when he sailed via Southampton to France and rejoined the Battalion in a camp at Vieux Berquin on Tuesday 7th August where they were training.

Francis began the move to the front on Thursday 13th September when he marched from the camp. He passed through Merris, Strazeele, Caëstre, and Abeele to *'Ottawa Camp'* in Ouderdom where he arrived three days later. At 8.00pm on Tuesday 18th Francis paraded then marched to *'Château Segard'* to spend the night in the dugouts and shelters. After a tense day waiting for the final move into the trenches he finally left at 11.45pm the assembly point at Hooge that came under heavy shell fire. Zero hour was 5.40am the next morning and by 6.25am the first objectives were captured. Francis was taken forward to the Blue Line where he was killed by shell fire.

His mother received his British War Medal no 46670, Victory Medal no 46131 and Memorial Plaque and Scroll no 332921.

16403 PRIVATE JAMES ROSTRON
2nd Battalion King's Shropshire Light Infantry
Died on Tuesday 25th May 1915, aged 17
Commemorated on Panel 49.

James was born in Blackburn, Lancashire, eldest son of Edmund and Margaret Rostron, of 3 Railway Terrace, Rawtenstall, Manchester. He had an older and a younger sister, and two younger brothers. James was educated locally and then employed in a local cotton mill.

He volunteered in Blackburn and went out to France on Wednesday 19th May 1915. For James' story see Private Albert Jones, above.

He is commemorated on the Blackburn Roll of Honour.

S/8927 RIFLEMAN
THOMAS EDGAR RUSHBROOKE
8th Battalion Rifle Brigade
Died on Friday 30th July 1915, aged 17
Commemorated on Panel 48.

Thomas' signature

Thomas was born at home, the youngest son of George and Hannah Rushbrooke, of 100 Bridge Street, Stowmarket, Suffolk. He had three older brothers, three older sisters and a younger sister. Thomas was educated locally.

He volunteered in Stowmarket on Friday 12th March 1915 when he claimed to be 19 years and 3 months old and working as a general farm labourer. Thomas was a Congregationalist, 5ft 5¾in tall with a 34½in chest.

He went out to France on Friday 30th June 1915 to join the Battalion whilst they were serving at Hooge.

The British blew a mine at Hooge on Thursday 22nd July but failed to fully capitalise on it, two days later the Germans blew one of their own. The Germans had lost ground and it was clear that a counter-attack would be launched. The German infantry moved forward with their special backpacks filled with inflammable liquid pouring forth their fire and smoke. It must have been a terrifying sight and it forced the British defenders back. Thomas was killed in the fierce action.

Lieutenant Carey (later Lieutenant Colonel Carey, DSO) wrote a comprehensive account of the action:

"The 8th Battalion left Ypres by the Lille Gate something after 10 p.m. on July 29. 'A' Company was commanded by Lieutenant L. A. McAfee, an old Cambridge Rugger Blue, beloved of both officers and men; he was also in charge of No. 1 Platoon (we lost our original company commander a

week or so earlier at Railway Wood — the first officer of the Battalion killed). I commanded No. 2 Platoon, Lieutenant M. Scrimgeour No. 3 and 2nd Lieutenant S. C. Woodroffe No. 4. 'A' Company was to hold the line on the left of the crater, with my platoon on the right of our sector holding up to the left edge of the crater. No. 4 Platoon was on my left, and Nos. 1 and 3 in a trench running parallel to No. 4's bit, a few yards in rear of it. 'C' Company (Captain E. F. Prior) was to hold the line on the right of the crater; Keith Rae commanded a platoon in this company and I'm pretty sure his platoon's sector was that nearest the right-hand edge of the crater. 'B' Company (Captain A. L. C. Cavendish) and 'D' Company (Captain A. C. Sheepshanks) were in support, in trenches at the near edge of the wood.

I remember having a strong presentiment as I plodded up to the line that night that I should never come back from it alive; in the event I was the only officer in my company to survive the next twenty-four hours.

The relief was complete shortly after midnight. It has been rather a tiring business, for we had had two miles to cover before the line was reached, with the delays inevitable to troops moving over strange ground in the dark; and the difficulty of getting our men into the broken-down trenches while the 7th Battalion were getting out of them was even greater here than we had found elsewhere. I had warned my men of the need for silence, owing to the nearness of the Boche, and I remember when the time came feeling certain that the tramp of feet and the clatter of rifles must have given the show away (I need not have worried — we knew afterwards that the Boche learned from more reliable sources when a relief was to take place). Indeed, the night was ominously quiet. There had been very little shelling on the way up — for which we were duly thankful; but the absence of the sniper's bullet as we filed up the communication trench from Zouave Wood was something more surprising. The continued silence after we got into the line became uncanny. About an hour after we were settled in and the last of the 7th Battalion had disappeared into the darkness, I decided that a bomb or two lobbed over into the Boche trench running close to mine near the crater might disturb him if he were up to mischief there. (It should be mentioned here that in these early days of bombs there was only a limited number of men in each battalion who could use them, and these were organized as a squad under a single officer. Their disposition over the battalion sector and their supply of bombs was under the supervision of the Battalion bombing officer, who on this night had begun his rounds on the 'C' Company sector and had not yet reached mine. I had in the meanwhile posted a few bombers attached to my platoon at what I considered the vital spots, the point where my trench joined the crater, and Point B. Our supply of bombs was small, though more were expected to be up before daylight.) Accordingly I got one of the bombers to throw over a hand grenade; it looked to carry about the right length and it exploded well. We waited; no reply. At short intervals he sent over two more. 'This ought to rouse them,' we said; again no reply. There was something sinister about this.

It was now about half an hour before dawn, and just then the order for the usual morning 'stand-to' came through from the Company Commander. I started on the extreme right of my bit of the line, to ensure that all my men were lining the trench, with their swords fixed. Working down gradually to the Point B, I decided to go on along the stretch of trench which bent back from the German line almost in the form of a communication trench; there were servants and some odd men from my platoon in so-called shelters along here, and I wanted to make sure that these people, who are apt to be forgotten at 'stand-to,' were all on the alert. Just as I was getting to the last of these, there was a sudden hissing sound, and a bright crimson glare over the crater turned the whole scene red. As I looked I saw three or four distinct jets of flame—like a line of powerful fire-hoses spraying fire instead of water—shoot across my fire-trench (see dotted lines in plan). How long this lasted it is impossible to say—probably not more than a minute; but the effect was so stupefying that, for my own part, I was utterly unable for some moments to think — collectedly. I remember catching hold of a rifle with fixed sword of a man standing next to me and making for Point B, when there was a terrific explosion, and almost immediately afterwards one of my men, with blood running down his face, stumbled into me, coming from the direction of the crater. He was followed by one or two others, most of them wounded. The minenwerfer had started, and such men as had survived the liquid fire were, in accordance with orders, giving the crater a wide berth. Then broke out every noise under Heaven! 'Minnie' and bombs in our front trench, machine guns from places unseen, shrapnel over the communication trenches and the open ground between us and the support line in Zouave Wood, and high-explosive on the wood and its vicinity. It was impossible to get up the trench towards the crater while men were coming down in driblets, so I got out of the trench to the right of Point C to try and get a better idea of the situation. I was immediately hit in the right shoulder by a shrapnel bullet, but I didn't have time to think much about it; still less did I realize that it was to prove my salvation. The first thing I saw was men jumping over the edge of the crater into 'C' Company's trench. It was still the grey light of dawn and for some moments I could not distinguish whether they were Boche or British; but, deciding soon that they must be Boche, I told the few survivors of my platoon, who by that time had joined me, to open fire on them, which they promptly did. At this point McAfee came up, followed by Michael Scrimgeour, and we had a hurried consultation. By this time the Boches were in my bit of trench as well, and we saw that my handful couldn't get back into it. It was a death-trap to stay where we were, under a shrapnel barrage; so Mac, after weighing the possibility of going for the Boche

across the open with the bayonet, reluctantly gave the order for me to get the remnant of my platoon back to the support line, and said that he and Michael would follow with the rest of the company. About a dozen men of No. 2 Platoon were all that I could find—those who had faced the flame attack were never seen again—and we started back over the open. I doubt if we could have found the communication trench if we had wanted to, but for the moment there was open fighting to be done (we had no reason to suppose that the Germans were coming no farther than our front line). A retirement is a miserable business, but there can be nothing but praise for the conduct of the men in this one; there was nothing approaching a 'run,' and at every few yards they lay down and fired with the coolness of an Aldershot field day at any Boches who could be seen coming over into our line. There was a matter of four hundred yards of open ground to be covered under a regular hail of machine-gun and shrapnel fire, and I have always marvelled how anyone got over it alive; as it was, most of my fellows were wounded during that half-hour's retirement, if not before, and one was shot dead within a yard of me while in the act of firing. Eventually, I (literally) fell into the main communication trench about twenty yards ahead of the support line; it must have been then about 4.30 a.m. Here I was joined almost at once by Cavendish (O.C. 'B' Coy.), who, on learning that our front line was lost, suggested that we should there and then build a barricade in the communication trench—it was still expected that the Boche would come on. My small party set to, using sandbags from the side of the trench, and a supply of bombs came up while we were working. It was rather ticklish work when it came to the upper part of the barricade, as the Boche was using shrapnel very accurately, and there were a lot of rifle and machine-gun bullets flying about. But the men in the support trenches behind us were having a worse time, for Zouave Wood was being heavily bombarded and 'B' and D' Companies were 'suffering a lot of casualties. During this time, Mac, having got his survivors back to the supports, came up to see how I had fared. He was very cool, but terribly unhappy at our losses of men and ground; and especially at having been unable to get into touch with Woodroffe. I was thankful at finding him safe, and still more so to learn that Michael also was all right. He went off almost at once to reorganize the remainder of the company. We continued to stand by our barricade, and I borrowed a rifle and tried to do a bit of sniping; the Boche could be seen throwing up the earth in our front line, and it now looked as if he were going to stay there. About this time came our first bit of consolation. Our artillery had begun to retaliate, and we could see shells bursting in our old front line; but the effort was feeble as compared with the German bombardment. Some hour and a half later Mac came back with the grievous news that Michael Scrimgeour had been killed while reorganizing his men in the wood. He also began to fuss about my wound, and eventually gave me a direct order to go back to the dressing-station. I had to go, and that was the last I saw of poor McAfee, who was killed that afternoon leading his men in a counter attack."

Thomas' father was sent Thomas' personal possessions of a Gospel and a bundle of letters.

S/12387 PRIVATE JOHN RUSSELL
2nd Battalion Cameron Highlanders
Died on Sunday 9th May 1915, aged 17
Commemorated on Panel 38.

John was born at home, son of James and Margaret Russell, of South Row, Carnwath, Lanarkshire.

He volunteered in Tarbrax, Edinburgh, and went out to France on Sunday 3rd January 1915 with the Battalion. John was sent to northern France to complete his training before beginning tours of duty in the southern sector of the Ypres Salient.

John's first action was at St Eloi in March following the blowing of mines at 'The Bluff'. He then took part in the Second Battle of Ypres that began on Thursday 22nd April. John spent two weeks fighting to defend the line until he was killed.

18292 PRIVATE ARTHUR ALBERT SADLER
5th Battalion Oxford and Bucks Light Infantry
Died on Saturday 25th September 1915, aged 17
Commemorated on Panel 39.

Arthur was born at home, eldest son of George and Clara Sadler, of Chimney-on-Thames, Bampton, Oxfordshire.

He volunteered in Oxford and went out to France on Friday 16th July 1915 to join the Battalion shortly before the horrors of the liquid fire attack at Hooge. He remained on tours of duty in the sector, however, his next major action, part of the diversionary attack for The Battle of Loos made at Bellewaarde, on Saturday 25th September would be his last. Arthur was killed during the attack.

S/10340 RIFLEMAN THOMAS SAMPSON
9th Battalion Rifle Brigade
Died on Monday 4th January 1916, aged 17
Commemorated on Panel 48.

Thomas' signature

Thomas was born in Lees, Lancashire, son of Thomas and Jane Alice Sampson, of Irk Bank, Luzley Brook, Royton, Oldham, Lancashire. He had a brother, Arthur, and two sisters, Rose and May. Thomas was educated locally.

He volunteered on Monday 3rd May 1915 in Ashton-under-Lyne, Lancashire, where he claimed to be 19 years and 4 months old and worked as a weaver. Thomas was 5ft 5in tall, with a 33in chest and weighed 118lbs. He was sent to train in Winchester on Wednesday 5th.

Thomas left to join the Battalion on Thursday 7th October with a draft. He received fourteen days Field Punishment No 2 on Tuesday 12th. For the story of Thomas' involvement at the front and the history of the Battalion, see Rifleman William Bird above. Sadly for his parents none of Thomas' personal possessions were ever sent to them as they were lost in the system.

22982 PRIVATE HERBERT SANGSTER
11th Battalion Royal Scots
Died on Sunday 14th November 1915, aged 16
Commemorated on Panel 11.

Herbert's signature

Herbert was born in Coupar Angus, Forfarshire, sister of Elizabeth Sangster, of 40 Prior Road, Forfar, both of his parents had predeceased him.

He enlisted in Blairgowrie, Perthshire, on Wednesday 26th May 1915 when he claimed to by 19 years old and worked as a grocer's assistant. Herbert was 5ft 4in tall, with a 32½in chest, weighed 110lbs and had a brown birthmark on the upper part of his right forearm.

He was sent for training where Herbert received a number of punishments for minor misdemeanours:
* Tuesday 20th July three days close confinement;
* Thursday 22nd three days close confinement for offences during inspections;
* Wednesday 11th August five days close confinement on for having dirty ammunition on parade and inattention to orders;
* Thursday 2nd September seven days close confinement for having dirty equipment during an inspection.

In early October 1915 Herbert left for France and joined the Battalion in the field on Tuesday 5th October following the Battalion's service at the Battle of Loos. He began tours of duty in the southern sector of the Salient, perhaps the one of the worst front lines on the Western Front. The trenches collapsed by themselves even without the assistance of German artillery so Herbert was constantly rebuilding them whilst at the front: *"It required an effort to rise above the depression caused by the evidences of decay that seemed to brood over*

Ypres and its surroundings, and it was possibly a blessing in disguise that the sodden ditches, which passed for trenches, necessitated unflagging labour on the part of the Royal Scots to prevent them from tumbling in." After the casualties at the Battle of Loos, and before new drafts of officers arrived in the line, many of Herbert's officers were little older than him. He continued to undertake a series of tours of duty but was not involved in any particular action until he was killed. After surviving the horrors of Loos Herbert was killed in the daily exchange of fire between the lines.

His sister was sent Herbert's personal possessions that included the New Testament, a purse, letter, photographs, purse and mirror and after the war she received his medals.

41530 PRIVATE
GEORGE ARTHUR SAUNDERS
2nd Battalion Cameronians (Scottish Rifles)
Died on Wednesday 1st August 1917, aged 17
Commemorated on Panel 22.

George was born at home, son of Edward and Jane Saunders, of 2 Crownland Cottage, Eastgate, Moffat, Dumfriesshire.

He volunteered in Berwick-on-Tweed and was posted to the King's Own Scottish Borderers with service number 25780 before transferring to the Cameronians. George went out to France on Thursday 7th October 1915 and joined the Battalion in northern France. He remained on tours of duty in the Bois Grenier sector until mid-March 1916 when he moved to Flesselles, north of Amiens, for a week of training. George was sent to serve between Thiepval and La Boisselle on the Somme, as yet to gain the infamy it would during the summer campaign.

George remained on the Somme and witnessed over the weeks the increase in activity that culminated in The Battle of the Somme that was launched on Saturday 1st July.

He went into his allotted reserve position late on Thursday 29th June. At 9.00am on Saturday 1st July George had been moved forward to the assembly trenches. A further barrage was laid down at 9.15am before he could be deployed. The Division made little progress and took heavy casualties, however, the attitude of the men was described: *"The men went in in high spirits, and came out with regret; they are only waiting for our next chance."* George was relieved late in the evening and sent to the rear before entraining at Dernancourt and finally arrived in the Bruay area. He spent a week training and was then sent to serve in the Givenchy sector and the old Loos battlefield.

... an attack on Zenith Trench

George returned to the Somme in October that had changed considerably over the ten weeks since he left it. He took part in an attack against *'Zenith Trench'* and *'Orion Trench'* during the afternoon of Monday 23rd October. It was a fierce action that was initially held up by machine gun fire but the Battalion captured their allotted objective at *'Zenith'* then moved on to capture *'Orion'*. The enemy mounted two weak counter-attacks that were repulsed. George remained serving on the Somme until mid-January 1917 when he was moved to the Vaux area to undertake fatigues for two weeks before returning to the front in the Bouchavesnes sector. George was serving at Rancourt when The Retreat to the Hindenburg Line began and moved forward into the new acquired but devastated area. His next action was at Gouzeaucourt at 7.45pm on Thursday 12th April and he had to advance through thick snow in a blizzard, it was a difficult assault but eventually successful.

George was part of the assault on La Vacquerie at 11.00pm on Saturday 5th May. He charged across the open ground with freezing rain driving into his face. His officers, and those of the supporting Battalions, got lost in the pitch black of a moonless night in dreadful weather. The raid was not a great success as a result. At the end of May George was relieved and sent for rest and training in Flanders around Merris and Caëstre. The next battlefield George would experience would be his last, the Ypres Salient. He was sent to Ypres and was billeted in the ramparts before marching along the Menin Road into the trenches in front of Hooge from mid-June. The Battle of Messines had been a great success and it was hoped that the next, and main, offensive at Passchendaele would equal or surpass it. George and his comrades were allocated the sector as it would be where they would attack when the forthcoming offensive began so they would know the ground. The whole area was like an ever-increasing ants nest from behind the lines to the firing trenches. Men and material were arriving, marching backwards and forwards, the Royal Engineers, pioneers and men from all battalions on fatigues were constructing new light railways, roads, laying miles of cable, miles of duckboards, constructing or improving trenches and dugouts et al. Guns were being hauled into position with ammunition dumps being established ready to supply the hungry guns, mortars, rifles and machine guns, together with incredible supplies of stores to sustain the men at the front.

Whilst George undertook tours of duty and fatigues the enemy introduced a new form of deadly gas, mustard gas that was more frightening and vile than any other yet deployed. Across the whole sector raids were made against the enemy to gain information and to confuse them as to when the real offensive was to begin. George was withdrawn from front line duties on Tuesday 10th July to Bomy, south of Hazebrouck, to undertake specially prepared training for ten days over exact models of the ground that he and the Battalion would attack. Whilst training HM King George, accompanied by Field Marshal Sir Douglas Haig, visited the training grounds to observe the men. George returned to the trenches at Hooge in anticipation for the offensive to begin on Friday 27th July, however, it was postponed. Lieutenant Colonel Colin Robert Hoste

King George and Sir Douglas Haig

Stirling, led his men forward in the attack on Tuesday 31st and was wounded (he was mortally wounded in action on Sunday 24th March 1918 and died on Wednesday 29th and is buried in St Sever Cemetery, Rouen). George reached the first main objective at *'Jaffa Trench'* but heavy machine gun fire was placed on the Battalion from *'Kit and Kat'*. He battled on and whilst consolidating the position during the early hours of the next morning George was killed by shell fire.

445138 PRIVATE FRANCIS SAVOIE
42nd Battalion Canadian Infantry (Quebec Regiment)
Died on Friday 2nd June 1916, aged 16
Commemorated on Panel 24.

Frank, or Francis', signature

Francis or Frank was the son of Henri and Marie Obeline Savoie, of Paquetville, New Brunswick.

He was educated locally.

He enlisted aged only 15 years old, at Sussex, New Brunswick, on Wednesday 30th June 1915, where Francis claimed to have been born in Bathurst, New Brunswick, on Tuesday 15th September 1896, therefore aged 18 years and 10 months, and employed as a farmer. Francis was 5ft 7in tall, with a 36in chest, a medium complexion, brown eyes and hair, with a large birth mark on his torso. He completed his enlistment papers with an English bent using the name 'Frank Savoy'.

Frank was sent to England from where he crossed to France on Saturday 9th October 1915. He entrained for northern France and was billeted in Flêtre. On Friday 15th he paraded for an inspection by General Sir Edwin Alderson following which he marched across the Belgian border to *'Aldershot Huts'*. For the following eight days Frank was sent into the front line attached to experienced troops for practical training. On Tuesday 2nd November he moved to billets along the Neuve Eglise to Romarin road in heavy rain. He was sent on fatigues re-digging the trenches. Fatigues continued until Saturday 8th January 1916 when he was sent into the front line with the Battalion relieving the 3rd Battalion. On Tuesday 11th January they came under grenade fire: *"Shortly before eight o'clock this morning, the enemy opened rifle grenade fire of twelve or fifteen rifle rounds on trenches 14-A and 15-A. The officer in charge of the latter asked O.C. Mortar Battery to reply and 8 rounds were fired with apparent effect a breach being noticed in the front line German trench.*

After an interval of about twenty five minutes rifle grenade fire was resumed on our right sector. One fell outside dugout in the right of D-4 where the parapet is revetted with corrugated iron which threw the charge into the dugout and 6 men sleeping there were all wounded. The other men were wounded at various points along D-4 including some of the men carrying out the wounded at the top of communication trench D-4. In all, 2 men were killed and nineteen wounded, four of the latter seriously. Owing to the congestion of telephone line there was some delay in getting artillery retaliation. The battery responded promptly as soon as communication was obtained and only 2 or 3 rifle grenades were fired after the battery opened. Our rifle grenades fired about 70 rounds. The enemy's fire activity extended over a period of about 35 minutes including the lapse of 25 minutes referred to."

Frank remained in the line until the end of the month when he moved to billets in Dranouter. General Currie sent the following message to the Colonel of the Battalion: *"It gives me a great deal of pleasure to inform you that during the stay of the 7th Infantry Brigade in the 1st Brigade area, they behaved at all times most gallantly. Besides, they did a great deal of very necessary and useful work.*

At the time they took over the line, the trenches, owing to the very bad weather, were not in the best of shape but your fellows have made a great difference. I went over the line last Saturday morning and was delighted with what I saw had been done and so expressed myself to the Brigadier General MacDonnell. I asked him to convey my thanks to all ranks of his Brigade: I know he will, but I want you to know as well how I have appreciated them. They were active in their patrolling, did a lot of wiring, greatly improved the front trenches, worked hard on supporting points and were aggressive always, while I deeply regret their casualties I do not think they were excessive.

Brigadier General Hughes has written me in warm terms of praise of what has been accomplished by MacDonnell's Brigade."

Frank spent nine days in training before returning to reserve in Loker on Wednesday 8th March. On Saturday 11th he returned to the front line where his line was raided at 5.10am on Wednesday 15th, which was repulsed. He continued to serve in the southern sector around Kemmel until Monday 20th when he moved to Poperinghe. Frank was billeted in a convent on the rue de Boeschepe for thirty-six hours. He was able to enjoy the safety of town with its wide variety of bars, cafés and entertainment. During the night of Tuesday 21st Frank marched to a train that quietly moved to

the Asylum in Ypres from where he marched into the line and the Battalion relieved the 8th Buffs. During the night of Friday 24th a patrol went out to reconnoitre a new German line that was described by Sergeant Jones: *"The new trench of the enemy is abut 3 ft deep with 1½ ft of earth thrown up to the front and rear. It is 2 ft wide at the bottom and 3 ft wide at the top. It is not revetted in any way. It has no bath mats. It is not full of water, but*

soggy. It is of recent construction. It has been continued on to the right of the hedge and runs in rear thereof. It has no dugouts. It has no regular sentries. It is not garrisoned. It is connected with the wood behind by a shallow trench. It is sufficiently far advanced to admit of being worked on in the day time. It has no M.G. emplacement. No sap-head is under construction. No gas cylinders are installed. No sandbag work was noted." The German artillery bombarded their line and badly damaged it and until he was relieved Frank worked on rebuilding the line. When relieved he had a long and tiring march to 'Camp F' on the Reninghelst to Vlamertinghe road, arriving at 5.00am. General Frederick Loomis, DSO, inspected the Battalion in their camp on Friday 31st.

The Battalion was sent to 'Zillebeke Dugouts' on Tuesday 4th April from where they were sent into the line the next day. Their eight day tour of duty was spent in the pouring rain and under continuous artillery bombardment. The Battalion was sent to 'Camp B' near Poperinghe where all the men were inoculated against typhoid and paratyphoid. Frank was sent out on nightly work parties to the front line and on Friday 28th General Sir Douglas Haig visited them and undertook an inspection. The weather improved during May which made strengthening the front line easier and more sustainable. After a series of duties Frank was relieved and sent to the Ramparts at Ypres. On Friday 2nd June the Battalion was attacked in force and Frank was sent into the line to support position. During the defence and counter-attack Frank was killed.

7156 PRIVATE DENNIS SCOTT
2nd Battalion East Surrey Regiment
Died on Sunday 9th May 1915, aged 16
Commemorated on Panel 34.

Dennis was born at home, eighth son of Charles and Ellen Scott, of 18 Orcus Street, Lisson Grove, St Marylebone, London. He was educated locally.

He enlisted in Marylebone and was sent for training before embarking to France and onward to Belgium. Dennis joined the Battalion whilst in bivouac in Brielen on Tuesday 27th April 1915 five days after the opening of the Second Battle of Ypres and soon went into the front line. He had the opportunity of a hot bath then paraded for an inspection by General Edward Bulfin on Wednesday 5th May and the next day by General Sir Herbert Plumer. The Germans launched an attack on Saturday 8th and at

Edward Bulfin

11.00am orders were received to march into the line between Potijze and Wieltje. Over the next two days the Battalion held steadily onto the line but were not ordered to advance. They were continuously shelled and during a bombardment Dennis was killed.

SECOND LIEUTENANT
JOHN HARRISON SELLERS
3rd Battalion, attached 'A' Company,
2nd Battalion Northumberland Fusiliers
Died on Monday 24th May 1915, aged 17
Commemorated on Panel 12.

John was the son of William Arthur and Gertrude Helena Sellers, of Seaward, The Links, Whitley Bay, Northumberland. He had an older sister, Dorothy Lilian, and a younger brother, Warren. John was educated at Royal Lancaster Grammar School, Newcastle-upon-Tyne, from 1909. John received a scholarship at Armstrong College and was a member of Durham University OTC.

He volunteered on Saturday 15th August 1914 and sent for officer training being commissioned on Wednesday 28th April 1915. John left for France on Thursday 13th May where he joined the 2nd Battalion whilst they were serving in the Second Battle of Ypres. The Battalion had taken severe losses and were in much need of reinforcements of officers and men.

John was soon deployed to the trenches in the Hooge sector. He was in camp in Vlamertinghe when at dawn on Monday 24th (Whit Monday) the enemy launched a gas attack that was followed by an infantry attack. John marched with his men at noon towards the battlefield to take part in a counter-attack. They went around to the south of Ypres and via 'Hell Fire Corner' into the trenches. Captain H C Stephen, his Company Commander, moved the men into the assault trenches from where he led the Battalion over the top at 2.45pm. They did not get far until Captain Stephen was wounded and John was killed, together with many of the Battalion.

17387 PRIVATE HAROLD SHAW
1st Battalion East Yorkshire Regiment
Died on Monday 9th August 1915, aged 17
Commemorated on Panel 31.

Harold was born at home, son of Joseph and Edith Elizabeth Shaw, of 15 Chapel Lane, Salter Hebble, Halifax, Yorkshire. He had two older and one younger brother and a younger sister. Harold was educated locally and was then employed as a doffer in a local worsted mill.

He volunteered in York and went out to France on Wednesday 7th July 1915 to join the Battalion on the Ypres Salient after they had suffered their first gas attack whilst serving between 'Irish Farm' and La Brique. Harold began serving in the trenches and with chatting to his new comrades soon discovered the realities of war.

Harold was relieved late on Monday 2nd August and marched to billets in Poperinghe. Whilst he relaxed and enjoyed the bustling town the next day Colonel Clarke and senior officers were visiting the area around 'Maple Copse'. Colonel Clarke inspected his new Headquarters and he described the situation: "Two very small cellar rooms, with fairly solid roof, and remains of a wall between them gave shelter to the officers and signallers respectively, whilst outside a quadrangle trench (revetted with bricks and sandbags) gave good all-round defence which, with a few dug-outs therein, provided accommodation of a sort for a weak platoon. The Company Commanders went off with their guides to see the trenches while soon after Major Rigg (C.O. 6th K.O.Y.L.I.) took Willis (A/Adjutant) and myself round the greater part of the line, which ran in a rough semicircle from the left-hand edge of Zouave Wood along its eastern fringe, forming a deep re-entrant, and thence into Sanctuary Wood, where it joined on to that of the next battalion. The line, only having been held for a few days, was barely defensible: the parapets were not high enough and the trenches not deep enough; water lay in many places, dug-outs were few and flimsy, and the few communication trenches were shallow and unrevetted. It was, indeed, a depressing prospect, and we returned to Poperinghe in the late afternoon with very mixed feelings." General Walter Congreve visited Harold's billets and chatted to the men during the morning of Thursday 5th wishing them well for their forthcoming tour. In the early afternoon Harold paraded then marched along the pavé to 'Zouave Wood' where he arrived at 10.00pm, however, the relief took three and a half hours to complete. It did not take until dawn for Harold and his comrades to realise what lay ahead of them as the smell of decomposing bodies, or parts thereof, that had been lying there for nearly a week blew into trenches. It was a grim and shocking sight, not only for the recently arrived young Harold but for many of his older and experienced comrades. From 2.45am until 3.30am the next morning the night was pierced with the shattering noise of the artillery as the shells whistled above Harold that crashed into the German line the short distance ahead of him. Unfortunately for Harold the bombardment brought a reply in kind from the German artillery. Just as the shells stopped pouring down the rain came by way of a huge thunderstorm. A further heavy bombardment fell across the sector on Saturday 7th that cost the Battalion thirty-six casualties. Late in the evening Chaplain Neville

Talbot arrived at Headquarters seeking permission and assistance in searching for the body of his brother, Gilbert. Luckily for him Sergeant Shepherd thought he knew where the body lay and with three stretcher-bearers took Chaplain Talbot out into No Man's Land. Gilbert's body was found and recovered, he now lies in Sanctuary Wood Cemetery and 'Talbot House' the home of TOC H in Poperinghe was named after him. (Gilbert Talbot's letters and his story is reproduced in the companion series to this publication, 'I Was There', details of which can be found at the end of the book.) The enemy continued to shell the area and casualties mounted all through until the point the Battalion began its attack that was described: *"The ultimate objective of our operations is to recover the high ground north of the Crater in the direction of A.19-P.7 and to establish ourselves on a line through the Stables and Q.14 towards A.19. The G.O.C. considers that our best chance of success is to reduce the men in the front line to a minimum, hold important points with machine guns, establish communications, and relieve men in the front line as opportunity offers."* At 2.45am on Monday 9th the preliminary bombardment was laid down with, as would have been expected, the compliment returned in short measure. As the whistles blew, that could hardly be heard above the noise, as the bombardment ended ahead of Harold was a scene from Dante's 'Inferno'. The night sky was lit by a range of different colours from shells, machine guns, rifles and flares, smoke billowed across No Man's Land, earth was moving in every direction from the shelling with enormous plumes shooting into the sky and shrapnel flying all about. How anyone could move forward into such a scene is now incomprehensible. Harold charged forward with fixed bayonet following the bombing parties that added to the general mêlée. It will never be known exactly how far Harold managed to get towards the German trenches or if he managed to put his bayonet training to the test. All that we do know is that Harold gave his young life during a grim, close fought battle.

10097 PRIVATE JAMES SHEEHY
2nd Battalion Royal Munster Fusiliers
Died on Tuesday 10th November 1914, aged 17
Commemorated on Panel 44.

James was born in St Ann's, Cork, son of Mr and Mrs Mary Sheehy, of 2 Upper Quarry Lane, Blackpool, Cork. He enlisted in Cork and went out to France on Friday 28th August 1914. The Battalion had suffered badly in action at Etreux on Thursday 27th that left it with only five officers and one hundred and ninety-six men. They continued to march south but shortly afterward those left, and drafts that arrived including those with James,

were split up and joined the Corps Headquarters to undertake a wide range of fatigues.

Lieutenant Colonel Arthur Bent took command of the Battalion on Sunday 4th October but they remained as a Corps unit for the time being. They moved to the Ypres Salient in early November but it was not until Friday 9th that Colonel Bent had a whole Battalion to command in the field. They were deployed to Bellewaarde Farm and it was the first experience for James, and many of the men, of the battlefield. The next day he marched to Klein Zillebeke where the Battalion came under shell fire. One burst close to James and he was killed, one of very few casualties. Although James had been in France for six weeks he never had the opportunity to serve in the front line or engage the enemy.

He is commemorated on the South Mall War Memorial, Cork.

3/10700 PRIVATE
ERNEST JOHN SLATER
2nd Battalion Duke of Wellington's
(West Riding Regiment)
Died on Thursday 21st January 1915, aged 17
Commemorated on Panel 20.

Ernest was born in Battersea, London, second son of Robert Darnell Slater and Emily Charlotte Slater, of 85 Priory Road, West Croydon, Surrey. He had an older and a younger brother and two younger sisters.

He volunteered in Halifax and went out to France on Saturday 5th December 1914. For Ernest's story and that of the Battalion see Private George Robertshaw, above.

S/10683 PRIVATE
HAROLD WILFRED SLATTERY
2nd Battalion The Buffs (East Kent Regiment)
Died on Thursday 27th May 1915, aged 17
Commemorated on Panel 12.

Harold Wilfred Slattery
Harold's signature

Harold was born in Lewisham, London, on Saturday 24th July 1897, the second son of George and Alice Slattery, of 9 Sangley Road, Catford, London. He had three brothers, Daniel, Patrick and Frank and two sisters, Alice and Ivy. Harold was educated locally and was then employed as a motor omnibus cleaner. He enlisted in Woolwich, London, on Saturday 25th July 1914 for six years service, the day after his 17th birthday and despite war clouds gathering in Europe there appeared to be little likelihood of a European war within ten days. Harold was a Roman Catholic, 5ft 5¼in tall, with a 33in chest, weighed 117lbs, had hazel eyes, fair coloured hair and a scar on his right cheek. He was described as *"A steady and reliable man"*. Thomas Greenacre, on behalf of his employer, described him to be sober and honest and that he had left their employment of his own free will to enlist.

He remained in England training when the Battalion left for the Western Front on Saturday 16th January 1915. Harold went out to France on Thursday 11th March and joined the Battalion whilst they were serving in the Kemmel sector with billets in Loker. At the end of the month Harold began to serve in the St Eloi sector until Saturday 10th April when he was relieved and sent to serve close to the Broodseinde crossroads. It was a difficult area to serve in as some of the German trenches were only a matter of feet ahead and where they were plagued by a heavy trench mortar. It accurately targeted the Battalion's trenches and the force of each shell destroyed the trenches and during the four-day tour one officer and twenty-two men were killed, with four officers and sixty-two men wounded.

Harold was in a bivouac at St Jan on Wednesday 21st as the German bombardment of Ypres was increasing in intensity with smoke and flames rising high into the air. The German fire was so intense that even in St Jan, supposedly safe, machine-gun bullets flew about. At 3.30am on Friday 23rd the Battalion was ordered to Wieltje, taking the line some eight hundred yards to the north. They took part in the counter-attack and served in the line until Tuesday 27th when they were relieved to St Jan; the village came under heavy shell fire, and late on Wednesday 28th Harold was sent to Verlorenhoek. Initially the line was relatively quiet, but on Monday 3rd May the Germans commenced a bombardment at dawn which was followed by an attack as described in the Battalion Diary: *"The Germans now occupied the woods behind D.5, a movement which made D.4 quite untenable; they were held up, however, by a small part of Buffs under 2nd Lieut. Backhouse and a company of Royal Fusiliers under Captain Ford, who gallantly held on to the new support trench despite fearsome enfilade fire from heavy howitzers and other artillery. Captain Houblon and Lieut. Sharp and remainder of D Company who were still holding D.4, were now being enfiladed by Germans from D.5 and taken in reverse from the wood. Captain Houblon, therefore, was compelled to retire along the trench line, a movement which was carried out steadily. The Germans were still pressing forward and soon occupied a portion of the new support trench where it joined D.4. Our men and the enemy were now only a few yards apart, unfortunately the enemy were in greater numbers and a far stronger situation. Many of the enemy were shot, especially when they filed out of the wood in front of D.5. In the retirement we also lost heavily."*

Harold was finally relieved from the line and sent to bivouac in a wood near Poperinghe, arriving in the early hours of Wednesday 5th May. When the roll was called it was depressing, as they had lost their Colonel, Augustus Geddes (who is buried in Ypres Reservoir Cemetery), and five officers killed, nine wounded and two missing. The number of men lost was difficult to calculate as so many of the drafts that had arrived on Friday 30th April and Saturday 1st May had been deployed to the front before their names had been recorded.

It was estimated that over seven hundred were killed, wounded or were missing.

Harold returned to the line on Saturday 8th May for a four-day tour of duty before being sent to a camp near Poperinghe. The Battalion had seen considerable service during the Second Battle of Ypres and on Saturday 20th May Field Marshal Sir John French addressed the men: *"I came over to say a few words to you and to tell you how much I, as Commander-in-Chief of this Army, appreciate the splendid work that you have all done during the recent fighting. You have fought the Second Battle of Ypres, which will rank amongst the most desperate and hardest fights of the war. You may have thought because you were not attacking the enemy that you were not helping to shorten the war. On the contrary, by your splendid endurance and bravery, you have done a great deal to shorten it. In this, the Second Battle of Ypres, the Germans tried by every means in their power to get possession of that unfortunate town. They concentrated large forces of troops and artillery, and further than that they had recourse to that mean and dastardly practice, hitherto unheard of in civilized warfare, namely, the use of asphyxiating gases. You have performed the most difficult, arduous and terrific task of withstanding a stupendous bombardment by heavy artillery, probably the fiercest artillery fire ever directed against troops, and warded off the enemy's attacks with magnificent bravery. By your steadiness and devotion, both the German plans were frustrated. He was unable to get possession of Ypres — if he had done this he would probably have succeeded in preventing neutral Powers from intervening—and he was also unable to distract us from delivering our attack in conjunction with the French in the Arras-Armentières district. Had you failed to repulse his attacks, and made it necessary for more troops to be sent to your assistance, our operations in the south might not have been able to take place, and would certainly not have been so successful as they have been. Your Colours have many famous names emblazoned on them, but none rill be more famous or more well-deserved than that of the Second Battle of Ypres. I want you one and all to understand how thoroughly I realize and appreciate what you have done. I wish to thank you, each officer, non-commissioned officer and man, for the services you have rendered by doing your duty so magnificently, and I am sure that your Country will thank you too."*

The Germans mounted an attack at Hooge on Monday 24th and the Battalion was sent forward to reinforce the 3rd Battalion Royal Fusiliers who had been driven from their line. Harold remained in the line under heavy shell fire until one burst close to him and he was killed.

G/6410 PRIVATE HENRY GERALD SMITH
3rd Battalion Middlesex Regiment
Died on Saturday 24th April 1915, aged 15
Commemorated on Panel 51.

Henry was born at home, sixth son and tenth child of John and Emily Smith, of 63 Victor Road, College Park, Willesden, London.

He volunteered in Willesden, and following a short period of training Henry was sent out to join the Battalion with a draft, arriving just before the beginning of the Second Battle of Ypres. He went up to the Salient and into reserve at St Jan where he was serving when the Germans launched the first gas attack on Thursday 22nd April 1915. The Battalion was immediately ordered to take position astride the crossroads and entrench. Under the command of Colonel Augustus Geddes combined force, Henry was sent to help the Canadians at St Julien. During the first counter-attack against the German line Henry was cut down and killed. (Colonel Geddes died on Wednesday 28th April 1915 and is buried in Ypres Reservoir Cemetery.)

... attacking the German line

4030 PRIVATE JAMES SMITH
1st/6th Battalion Northumberland Fusiliers
Died on Thursday 2nd March 1916, aged 17
Commemorated on Panel 8.

James was the son of the late John and Jane Smith. He enlisted in Newcastle-upon-Tyne and following training went out to France. He entrained to Belgium and marched to join the Battalion whilst they were serving in the St Eloi sector in early 1916.

Apart from having to contend with the privations of service on the Western Front and the dangers of the front line, all ranks had to contend with trench foot and other medical problems. A Medical Officer wrote: *"The men, on the whole are of good physique, but many turn up in a dirty condition suffering from lousiness and scabies. In one draft of one hundred and fifty men, twenty-three were found with scabies. It has been proved that practically every man in the front line suffers from some degree of lousiness, and that the extent depends a good deal on the personal element. Disinfection, even for thirty or forty minutes, does not in every case destroy the lice, and though their destruction would be helped by subsequent washing in water to which creosol had been added, the washer women strongly object to creosol as it affects their hands."*

General Sir Douglas Haig accurately recorded the problems of the front line during the winter: *"The maintenance and repair of our defences alone, especially in winter, entails constant heavy work. Bad weather and the enemy combine to flood and destroy trenches, dug-outs and communications; all such damages must be repaired promptly, under fire, and almost entirely by night.*

Artillery and snipers are practically never silent, patrols are out in front of the lines every night, and heavy bombardments by the artillery of one or both sides take place daily in various parts of the line. Below ground there is continual mining and counter-mining, which, by the ever-present threat of sudden explosion and the uncertainty as to when and where it will take place, causes perhaps a more constant strain than any other form of warfare. In the air there is seldom a day, however bad the weather, when aircraft are not busy reconnoitring, photographing, and observing fire. All this is taking place constantly at any hour of the day or night, and in any part of the line. ...

One form of minor activity deserves special mention, namely, the raids or 'cutting-out parties' which are made at least twice or three times a week against the enemy's line. They consist of a brief attack, with some special object, on a section of the opposing trenches, usually carried out at night by a small body of men. The character of these operations like the preparation of a road through our own and the enemy's wire the crossing of the open ground unseen the penetration of the enemy's trenches the hand-to-hand fighting in the darkness and the uncertainty as to the strength of the opposing force gives peculiar scope to the gallantry, dash and quickness of decision of the troops engaged; and much skill and daring are frequently displayed in these operations. The initiative in these minor operations was taken, and on the whole has been held, by us; but the Germans have recently attempted some bold and well-conceived raids against our lines, many of which have been driven back, although some have succeeded in penetrating, as has been reported by me from time to time."

'The Bluff' had been captured by the enemy and the High Command was determined to recapture it. It would be a difficult task and in the hope to fool the Germans a number of raids were made in advance of the substantive attack. James took part in one such raid on Thursday 2nd March and was killed in the process.

889787 PRIVATE JOHN ISAAC SMITH
14th Battalion Canadian Infantry (Quebec Regiment)
Died on Wednesday 7th November 1917, aged 15
Commemorated on Panel 24.

John Smith
John's signature

John was the son of Sarah McWhirter (formerly Smith, née Long), and the late Nicholas Smith, of New Richmond, Province of Quebec. He volunteered in Richmond on Friday 7th April 1916 when he claimed to have been born on Saturday 5th March 1898 and worked as a farmer. John was 5ft 9½in tall, with a 36½in chest, a clear complexion, grey eyes, light brown hair, a cyst on his left cheek and one on his left groin.

John was sent for training before being sent to England where training continued until embarking to France. He joined the Battalion in the field. The Battalion was serving in the Calonne sector in February 1917 undertaking fatigues and serving in the front line. They were relieved on Monday 5th March and marched to Bully Grenay where they rested before continuing to Hallicourt where billets were provided in the various houses in the village. They began training for two weeks before beginning fatigues, repairing communication trenches and dugouts. They moved into the trenches in the Thélus sector from Saturday 24th for a tour of duty and returned to training whilst camped in 'Lependu Huts'. In preparation for the forthcoming offensive the Battalion relieved the 4th Battalion at 'Maison Blanche', Thélus. Each man of the Battalion was carrying a rifle, one hundred and twenty rounds of ammunition, five sandbags, forty-eight hours of rations, a waterproof sheet, a box respirator worn in the alert position, a smoke helmet, goggles, a ground flare and a full water bottle. At

5.30am on Monday 9th April the attack began where they came under heavy rifle and machine gun fire from the Bavarian troops they were advancing upon. With expert use of Mills grenades two machine guns were put out of action and the crew were shot dead. The advance went well and all the objectives set the Battalion were achieved. They continued to serve in the sector until moving to the Arleux sector at the end of the month. In early May the Battalion was sent into reserve where the men were able to clean up, have a hot bath and received a fresh issue of underclothes and uniform. Now clean and smart, the Battalion marched to Château de la Haie on Wednesday 9th May for an inspection by General Arthur William Currie, and the next day by General Sir Julian Byng who took the salute as they marched passed the dais.

... Château de la Haie

The Battalion returned to fatigues when they moved to the lower slopes of Vimy Ridge on Friday 1st June. They took over the front line at 'Quebec Trench' on Wednesday 6th, following a tour of duty, followed by a period in reserve, they removed to a hutted camp near Mont St Eloy. At the end of the month they marched to 'Thélus Cave' and began fatigues but it was not until Thursday 5th July did they go back into the front line once more. It was relatively quiet except for intermittent shelling and trench mortars that kept everyone on their toes. After a week they were relieved to Bracquemont for training followed by Ruitz on Sunday 22nd.

The next sector where the Battalion served was on the old Loos battlefield from the beginning of August. They were sent to billets in Mazingarbe before going into the front line. Tours of duty and training continued, Field Marshal Sir Douglas Haig inspected the Brigade outside Marles-les-Mines where the Battalion was billeted. In early October they returned to Gauchin Légal before moving to Staples on Thursday 23rd August for training for the forthcoming work on the Salient. The basic daily routine was:

6.30am	Reveille
6.54am	Sick Parade
7.00am	Breakfast
8.00am-8.45am	Physical Training
8.45am-9.00am	Bayonet Fighting
9.00am-12.30pm	Morning Parade

10.00am-10.30am	*Lecture*
1.00pm	*Dinner*
2.30pm	*Orderly Room*
2.30pm-5.00pm	*Sports*
5.30pm	*Tea*
7.00pm	*Retreat*
9.00pm	*First Post*
9.30pm	*Last Post*
9.45pm	*Lights Out*

A fleet of lorries collected the Battalion on Wednesday 31st October and drove them to Ebblinghem where they entrained to Ypres. They arrived at 11.45am then marched by platoon to 'Camp A' that were a series of old trenches and pill boxes at Wieltje. During the night the sky was alive with German aircraft being chased by the Royal Flying Corps and coming under anti-aircraft fire. When the Battalion moved forward the Battalion's Headquarters were established at 'Kronprinz Farm'. A German raiding party were fired upon at 1.40am on Saturday 3rd November that sent them running. A heavy and sustained barrage was laid on the line at 4.45am that cut off communication between Headquarters and the front. The next day the Germans continued to heavily shell the sector to the right of the trenches occupied by the Battalion whilst a number of men were out repairing the wire. When relieved they returned to 'Camp A' that also came under heavy shell fire. At 5.00am on Tuesday 6th a further bombardment fell on the camp and John was badly wounded. Despite the best efforts of the Royal Army Medical Corps John died the next morning.

10399 PRIVATE
LEONARD VICTOR SMITH
1st Battalion Cheshire Regiment
Died on Monday 16th November 1914, aged 17
Commemorated on Panel 19.

Leonard was born at home, fourth son of Joseph and Clara Smith, of 32 Bentinck Street, Birkenhead, Cheshire. In addition to his brothers, he had a younger sister. Leonard was educated locally.

He volunteered in Birkenhead and went out to France on Wednesday 7th October 1914. Leonard joined the Battalion after they had served on the Aisne and met them with a draft when they arrived in Béthune. He marched off from his billet on Monday 12th into the line for the first time at Festubert. The next morning Leonard took part in his first attack against the German lines. As he advanced heavy fire came from a large farm that fell shortly afterwards and was converted into a Casualty Clearing Station until it was surrounded by the enemy. With the wounded in danger of being burnt

alive and without an escape route there was little option other than to surrender. The fighting continued and on Friday 16th the Battalion's objective of Rue d'Ouvert was captured. Leonard was ordered to press on and in the early evening of Saturday 17th Violaines was taken. The momentum was lost and little further progress was made to push the enemy back. Leonard was in the line in front of Violaines on Thursday 22nd when the enemy attacked in force and caught the Battalion in enfilade fire. The Brigadier wrote: *"The surprise was obviously due to the insufficient covering parties, not far enough out. But it is probable that, in any case, the large number of the enemy would eventually have compelled retirement."*

The desperate fighting since Leonard joined had decimated the Battalion, and he was very lucky to have survived. From Wednesday 28th he was sent to Neuve Chapelle that was under attack. The service in northern France drew to a close and the Battalion was sent to serve in Ypres where they arrived on Saturday 7th November.

Leonard marched down the Menin Road to take up position and participate in the First Battle of Ypres. He took part in the fierce battle at Nonne Boschen on Wednesday 11th November and remained in the line until he was killed. Although he had only served for a month Leonard had seen considerable service and fought hard in a number of battles.

Leonard is commemorated on the Birkenhead War Memorial.

113558 PRIVATE
ROBERT BALLANTYNE SMITH
4th Canadian Mounted Rifles Battalion
(Central Ontario Regiment)
Died on Friday 2nd June 1916, aged 17
Commemorated on Panel 32.

Robert's signature

Robert was the fourth son of William and Isabella McDonald Smith, of 128 Great Hamilton Street, Glasgow, Scotland. He had older siblings James, Mary, Thomas, William, Margaret, Janet and a younger sister, Rachael.

He volunteered on Thursday 19th August 1915 when he claimed to have been born in Duntocher, Dunbartonshire, on Monday 14th December 1896, was working as an office clerk and had served with the 57th Regiment (Militia). Robert gave his mother as his next of kin, living at 585 Chamberlain Street, Peterborough, Cambridgeshire. Robert was a Presbyterian, 5ft 3in tall, with a 34½in chest, a fair complexion, blue eyes and auburn hair.

For his story see Private John Kennedy, above, who enlisted the day after Robert but they died together.

2027 PRIVATE WILLIAM SMITH
Leicestershire Yeomanry
Died on Thursday 13th May 1915, aged 17
Commemorated on Panel 5.

William was born in Leamington Spa son of James Basil and Elizabeth Martha Smith, of Baker Street, Lutterworth, Rugby.
He volunteered in Lutterworth and went out to France on Tuesday 16th February 1915. For William's brief story, see Private Thomas Maddock above.

5606 PRIVATE JOHN SMULLEN
'B' Company, 2nd Battalion Royal Dublin Fusiliers
Died on Monday 24th May 1915, aged 17
Commemorated on Panel 46.

John was born at home, son of Charles and Maggie Smullen, of Church Street, Leighlinbridge, County Carlow.
He enlisted in Carlow and went out to France on Monday 18th January 1915. John joined the Battalion whilst they were billeted in Nieppe. He began tours of duty in the sector where he served until Saturday 20th March when the Battalion was sent to the Messines area — between the River Douve and the Wulverghem to Messines road. It was a difficult first tour as the trenches were below those of the Germans who could see quite clearly observe all movements. He was relieved to Bailleul on Monday 12th April and whilst there General William Pulteney inspected the Battalion. At 7.30pm on Friday 23rd John moved via Westoutre, Ouderdom, Vlamertinghe to Ypres, where everyone discarded their packs, then on to St Jan, arriving at midnight on Saturday 24th. He went into the line at 4.00am from where he took part in an advance, at 6.30am, on St Julien where the Canadians were still holding part of the village despite the appalling gas attack. Progress was difficult, no artillery cover could be provided as they were advancing into a 'friendly' village where the wire remained uncut. German machine gun and rifle fire was heavy and the Fusiliers took very heavy casualties. By the end of the day John and the men had dug themselves in a quarter-mile from the village. He remained there under heavy shell fire until Friday 30th. The Germans launched a gas attack along the line on Sunday 2nd May, however their advance made little headway. During the evening of Monday 3rd John was relieved and went into bivouac at La Brique, arriving at 2.00am, only to have two bombs dropped on the camp from a German aeroplane causing two casualties, both wounded.

... German bombers

From the evening of the Wednesday 5th until 1.30pm on Saturday 8th, John was relieved to Château des Trois Tours from where he was sent to the woods by Potijze Château. The Battalion took part in the attack on Frezenberg which was repulsed and by the end of the next day they were out close to 'Shell Trap Farm'. John was relieved to the grounds of Vlamertinghe Château on Wednesday 12th, which today remains much as it was during the war. At 2.45am on Monday 24th May the Germans sent over gas that drifted slowly towards the line occupied by John and comrades. It

... the author took WWI veteran Laurie Bristow's first visit to Vlamertinghe Château seventy-five years after being stationed there. It was exactly as he remembered and where he enjoyed playing football in the grounds in front of the house.

was more than three miles wide and forty feet in depth — the Germans then laid down an artillery barrage. Thankfully orders had been issued to all the men to prepare their respirators in anticipation of the attack. The Germans took 'Shell Trap Farm' and orders were given to counter-attack and retake it. The heavy shell fire cut off effective communication: messengers were either killed or wounded taking messages to and from Headquarters. Orders got through to the artillery to shell the Farm with extreme accuracy, because the trenches surrounding it were still held by the British. Their work was effective and the shrapnel shells rained down on the Farm. The German shell fire and gas assaults forced some men to retire. During the close fire fight, John was killed.

He is commemorated on Leighlinbridge War Memorial.

A/1667 LANCE SERJEANT
HENRY JOHN SPEER
9th Battalion King's Royal Rifle Corps
Died on Monday 22nd November 1915, aged 16
Commemorated on Panel 53.

Henry was born in Holloway, son of Edith Dora Speer, of 35 Glentan Road, Lee, London, and the late Charles Henry Speer. He was educated locally.

He enlisted in London and was sent for training in Petworth, West Sussex, and Aldershot, Hampshire, from where he left for France, arriving in Boulogne on Wednesday 21st July 1915. Henry entrained for northern France and was sent to Belgium. Whilst training for the front he heard the sound of battle and met with battle-hardened men who had been serving at the front for some time. Henry undertook a series of tours to the front which brought him face to face with the enemy, but he was not involved in any particular action until the end of July.

A large mine was blown at Hooge on Thursday 22nd July and a week later he marched into the line close to the crater and 'Sanctuary Wood': "The crater itself was untenable, owing to constant trench-mortaring and 'straffing', and the trenches, dry but the crest dilapidated beyond measure, ran up to the lip on either side, with no definite connection round the crater. The sector had an evil reputation for being subject to incessant sniping and bombing, besides trench-mortaring and shell fire: but on the night of 29th/30th, when the two battalions took over from the very tired and worn out 7th Rifle Brigade and the 8th K.R.R.C., there was ominous silence. No notice was taken by the enemy of the noise inseparable from a relief, and even a few bombs thrown by the new-comers into the German trenches — in places only 15 feet away — provoked no reply. Half an hour before dawn the trench garrison stood to arms, and there was a still complete quiet. Then at 3.15 a.m., with dramatic suddenness, came the carefully planned German stroke. The site of the stables of the château was blow up, whilst a sudden hissing sound was heard by the two companies of the 8th Rifle Brigade on either side of the crater, and a bright crimson glare over the crater turned the whole scene red. Jets of flame, as if from a line of powerful hoses, spraying fire instead of water, shot across the front trenches of the Rifle Brigade, and a thick black cloud formed. It was the first attack on the British with liquid fire. At the same time fire of every other kind was opened: trench-mortar bombs and hand-grenades deluged the front trenches, machine-gun and shrapnel bullets swept the two communications trenches the 300 yards of open ground between the front and support lines in Sanctuary and Zouave Woods; high-explosive shells rained on these Woods, whilst the ramparts of Ypres and all exits from the town were bombarded anew.

The surprise was complete, and would probably have led to an entry even at the strongest part of the line. Most of the 8th Rifle Brigade in the front trenches were overwhelmed, the rest fell back gradually over the fire-swept open ground to the support line. The enemy did not follow: he at once set about consolidating the trenches he had secured, and trying to increase his gain by attacking the 7th K.R.R.C. in front, flank, and rear. There was desperate trench fighting, in which parties again brought up Flammenwerfer, but rapid fire was turned on to them at 20 yards range, and the attempt to use them broke down. In the end, however, after several counter-attacks, all but a small sector of the K.R.R.C. trenches were lost."

Henry was relieved from the line on Saturday 31st, lucky to have survived when so many of his friends and comrades were left on the battlefield.

His next major action was in the same area, at Bellewaarde. Henry went into the line on Friday 24th September ready to support the attack the next day which was a diversionary attack for the Battle of Loos. At 4.19am a mine was blown under the German lines and a fierce battle took place. Attack followed by counter-attack. It was the fiercest battle so far witnessed by Henry and the Battalion.

Henry continued to serve in the sector until he was killed in the front during a tour of duty.

26837 PRIVATE
HARRY RUDKIN SPENCE
142nd Company Machine Gun Corps (Infantry)
Died on Saturday 9th June 1917, aged 17
Commemorated on Panel 56.

Harry was born in Boroughbridge, Yorkshire, the only child of James Edward and Kate Spence, of 14 Brookeville Avenue, Hipperholme, Halifax, Yorkshire. He was educated locally.

He volunteered in Lancaster in the Royal Lancashire Regiment with service number 20961 before transferring to the Machine Gun Corps.

Harry went to joint his Company in the field. He served on the Ypres Salient before preparing for The Battle

... a depiction of Harry's situation on the battlefield

of Messines where not only were the mines of vital importance but so was the support from the Machine Gun Corps. Nineteen mines were blown along the Messines Ridge at 3.10am on Thursday 7th June that was the signal for the attack. Harry poured fire on a number of predetermined targets, some of which had already been blown off the face of the earth. He kept moving forward with the infantry to support them and help pin down the enemy. Harry managed to fight on for over forty-eight hours before his position was hit by shell fire and he was killed.

7308 PRIVATE
STANLEY WADE SPENCER
2nd Battalion East Surrey Regiment
Died on Sunday 9th May 1915, aged 16
Commemorated on Panel 34.

Stanley was born at Hendon, third son of Edwin and Mary Louisa Spencer, of Oak Cottage, Chavey Down, Ascot, Berkshire. He was educated locally.
He enlisted at Mill Hill and was sent for training before being sent out to France and thence to the Salient, joining the Battalion with a draft. Stanley gained some horrific experiences for a boy of sixteen, including witnessing the results of the first gas attack.
The Battalion had been due to leave the line and go for some rest but this was cancelled as a result of the gas

attack that had commenced at 5.00pm on Thursday 22nd April 1915. They were ordered to remain in position and that evening gas shells exploded near his trench and the fumes gradually drifted towards him; thankfully, at this stage, no-one was badly effected. The next day the shelling became heavier and at 1.00pm the field grey uniforms of the German infantry were seen advancing on their whole line. 'Trench 23' was lost to the Germans as the defenders had been overcome by gas — a party of fifty German infantrymen occupied the captured trench. A counter-attack was mounted and they were driven out, the Battalion taking eight prisoners. Shortly afterwards the remainder were attacked by 'A' Company and an officer and twenty-eight men were captured: the rest were killed. The Germans continued to press hard on their lines and 'Trench 25' was captured but they were able to consolidate the position despite gallant counter-attacks. Stanley was relieved from the line on Monday 3rd May, via Frezenberg, to Poperinghe where he was in reserve. Later in the evening he was sent to bivouac at Brielen. Here, for the first time since Thursday 15th April, the Battalion had the opportunity of resting, bathing and generally cleaning up. They were inspected by General Edward Bulfin on Wednesday 5th May and the next day by General Sir Herbert Plumer. In the morning of Saturday 8th Stanley paraded with his comrades and at 11.00am marched to Frezenberg and took position on the Ypres to Zonnebeke road to assist in a counter-attack to retake some captured trenches. The attack was not able to move forward far due to heavy artillery fire and withering machine-gun fire. The major attack was postponed and then cancelled and the men remained in the line to await further orders. Throughout Saturday 8th and Sunday 9th the line was accurately targeted by the German artillery and Stanley was killed, one of ninety-six of the ranks killed over the three day period, with forty-eight missing and one hundred twenty-nine wounded; four officers were killed and five wounded.

3119 RIFLEMAN
ARTHUR EDWARD EMMANUEL STAINER
'B' Company, 1st Battalion Rifle Brigade
Died on Thursday 13th May 1915, aged 17
Commemorated on Panel 50.

Arthur was born in Alverstoke, Hampshire, eldest son of George and Sarah Ann Stainer, of 11 Holley Street, Stoke Road, Gosport, Hampshire.
He volunteered in Gosport and was sent for training. Arthur went out to France on Saturday 1st May 1915 with a draft that joined the Battalion two days later in

Elverdinghe. Arthur was allocated to a platoon and the next day the Battalion was sent into reserve. He went into the front line for the first time on Saturday 8th near *'Mousetrap Farm'*. The German artillery began shelling the sector and was targeting the remnants of the farm buildings. Arthur continued to fight on against heavy odds until he was killed.

2354 PRIVATE
EDWARD THOMAS STEEL
3rd Battalion Royal Fusiliers
Died on Saturday 8th May 1915, aged 17
Commemorated on Panel 6.

Edward was born in Lambeth, the only son of Mrs Mary Elizabeth Steel, of 15 Waterfall Cottages, Waterfall Road, Wimbledon, London.
He enlisted at Blanconway and was sent for training. For Edward's story, see Private Edward Oven, above.

5451 RIFLEMAN THOMAS STEWART
2nd Battalion Royal Irish Rifles
Died on Saturday 25th September 1915, aged 17
Commemorated on Panel 40.

Thomas was born at home, son of Mrs Louisa Stewart, of 65 Brownlow Street, Shankhill Road, Belfast, and the late James Stewart.
He went out to France on Thursday 13th May 1915 with a draft. For Thomas' story, and that of the Battalion, see Lance Corporal James Connolly, above.

488410 PRIVATE
WILLIAM DAVID STEWART
Royal Canadian Regiment
Died on Wednesday 31st October 1917, aged 17
Commemorated on Panel 10.

William's signature

William was born at Georgetown, Colorado, USA, the son of William David and Susan A Stewart (née Cairns), of Londonderry, Nova Scotia.
He volunteered on Saturday 4th March 1916 in Halifax, Nova Scotia, where he claimed to have been born on Saturday 10th September 1898 and was working as a labourer. He was sent for training with a composite battalion but unable to go overseas. He re-volunteered on Tuesday 12th December when he claimed to have been born on Monday 26th September 1898. William was 5ft 4½in tall, weighed 111lbs, had a 33in chest, a medium complexion, blue eyes, dark brown hair, had scars on his left shoulder and on his right leg.
William joined the Battalion whilst they were in camp at Château de la Haie in July 1917, then moved into the Souchez Valley sector for further training, followed by Lapugnoy from Thursday 27th.
The extended period of training ended on Saturday 19th August when William marched out of the town for Nœux-les-Mines where he was billeted. The Regiment relieved the 22nd and 25th Battalions in the front line at Les Brebis, in the Lens sector. William served in the sector until Tuesday 5th September when he moved to Petit Servins where he was able to clean up throughout the next day. He marched to *'Lependu Camp'* on Thursday 7th for training until going into the relatively quite sector at Méricourt then back to Neuville St Vaast at the end of the month. William returned to Méricourt on Sunday 1st October where he came under light shelling. The next day the bombardment increased in intensity until on Wednesday 4th a number of raids were made on the Regiment's position that were successfully repulsed. The next day William was relieved and sent to a bivouac at Ecurie from where he marched to billets in Bailleul, arriving early on Saturday 7th. Training for taking part in The Third Battle of Ypres began and he marched to a camp in Pradelles on Monday 16th. THT The Duke of Connaught and Prince Arthur of Connaught inspected the Regiment in Borre on Sunday 22nd. At 2.15am the next morning William entrained at Caëstre for Ypres, arriving at 6.30am. He marched out to St Jan then onward to *'Camp C'* in Wieltje. The next morning a number of enemy bombers flew over the camp and dropped a cluster of bombs. William was sent on fatigues carrying ammunition to the Gravenstafel sector then assisted in evacuating the wounded. William was killed when a shell burst close to where he was working.

... rescuing the wounded

2606 PRIVATE
CLARENCE WILFRED STIFF
2nd Battalion Monmouthshire Regiment
Died on Thursday 6th May 1915, aged 17
Commemorated on Panel 50.

Clarence was born at home in 1898, the second son of James John and Mary Stiff, of York House, Cwmbran, Newport, Monmouthshire. He was a scholar at the Cwmbran Wesleyan Sunday School. Clarence was a member of Cwmbran Cricket Club and the bugle band. He volunteered in Pontypool, Monmouthshire, in October 1914 when he was described a large boy being over 6ft tall. He continued training until leaving for France with a draft on Wednesday 17th February 1915 with his friend John Mogford. They died within twenty-fours hours of each other. For Clarence's story, see Private John Mogford above.

Clarence is commemorated on the Cwmbran Park and on the British Legion Memorial, St Gabriel's Church.

Clarence the proud young soldier and the 'Death Penny' that was sent to his parents in the 1920s

1975 PRIVATE MATTHEW STOBBART
1st/4th Battalion Northumberland Fusiliers
Died on Wednesday 16th June 1915, aged 17
Commemorated on Panel 8.

Matthew was born in Bardon Mill, Northumberland, son of Joseph Stobbart, of Stublic Bog, Langley-on-Tyne, Northumberland.

He volunteered in Hexham, Northumberland, and was sent for training with Battalion, leaving with them for France on Tuesday 20th April 1915. Matthew entrained to the Steenvoorde sector, however, instead of having a period of training, including practical experience in the trenches, the Battalion had to be deployed to the Ypres Salient. The Germans had launched a gas attack at 5.00pm on Thursday 22nd that began the Second Battle of Ypres. Matthew marched nearly fifteen miles to reach Brandhoek. He marched along the pavé to Ypres and rested in the Market Square, with much of the town in flames or smouldering from the constant shell fire over the previous few days. Matthew marched out of the town and to the front; initially he was moved hither and thither but not deployed. Matthew was in the line on the afternoon of Monday 26th when he took part in an attack. The Brigade recorded: *"Although the task set to the Brigade had been impossible and its losses devastating, it had not hesitated to obey. Having arrived at a line beyond which no one might pass and live, the men got shelter where they could, but there was no thought of retiring."* Early the next morning Matthew was relieved and marched to Wieltje. Matthew continued to fight through the difficult actions on the Frezenberg Ridge then at Bellewaarde. He finally received a little rest at the end of May. In the early evening of Sunday 6th June Matthew once again returned to the trenches: *"Marched 6 p.m. Guides at Kruisstraat at 8.45 p.m. Cross Canal 9.15 p.m. delayed by battalion in front and forms of transport. Two wagons overturned in the road. Very muddy. Bad marching. Sanctuary Wood at midnight. One relieved guides lost his way, and one company and the Machine Gun Company did not get on that night."* One of the NCOs recorded: *"It was an awful distance and the trenches were in a pitch-dark wood. We were lost once or twice, and what with slipping about and falling down, and the pace that was set, everybody was 'fed up'. It was turned 2 a.m. when we manned the trench."* During a further attack on Bellewaarde Matthew was killed.

... marching to the front

110535 PRIVATE
WILLIAM ARTHUR STODDART
5th Canadian Mounted Rifles Battalion
(Quebec Regiment)
Died on Friday 2nd June 1916, aged 17
Commemorated on Panel 32.

William was the only son of Mrs N H Petrie (formerly Stoddart), of 8 Fourth Street South, St Petersburg, Florida, USA, and the late Mr William George Stoddart. He was educated locally and was attending Cornwall Commercial College.

He volunteered in Montreal, Province of Quebec, on Monday 10th May 1915 when he claimed to have been born in Thorold, Ontario, on Tuesday 25th August 1896, and was a student. He gave his father, living in Cornwall, Ontario, as his next of kin. William was a Presbyterian, 5ft 5½in tall, with a 34½in chest, a fair complexion, grey eyes, fair hair and a vaccination mark on his left arm.

For William's story, and that of the Battalion, see Private John Carr above. William's body was found by, amongst others, Private John Ferguson who was on his way to the front. With his comrades John buried William on the field where they found him.

304053 GUNNER
GUY REGINALD STRATTON
2nd Division Ammunition Column
Canadian Field Artillery
Died on Saturday 3rd June 1916, aged 17
Commemorated on Panel 10.

Guy's signature

Guy was the son of Walter C Stratton, of 24 Ritson Road, Oshawa, Ontario, and the late Emma Ester Stratton.

He volunteered in Kingston on Monday 1st November 1915 when he claimed to have been born on Wednesday 21st April 1897 and was a student. Guy was a Methodist, 5ft 8in tall, with a 36in chest, a dark complexion, brown eyes and dark coloured hair.

Guy trained in Canada before sailing to continue training in England before joining his comrades in the field with a draft. He arrived in Boeschepe in late April whilst the Division Ammunition Column was being reorganised. He moved to a camp in Ouderdom where his work began supplying the front line. Whilst supporting the action near Mount Sorrel he was killed by shell fire.

6855 PRIVATE
VICTOR MARWOOD STRINGFELLOW
13th Battalion Australian Infantry, AIF
Died on Thursday 27th September 1917, aged 17
Commemorated on Panel 17.

Victor's signature

Victor was born in Petersham, New South Wales, son of Ethel Mary Stringfellow, of 25 Laura Street, Newtown, New South Wales, and the late Charles William Stringfellow. His mother divorced Charles Stringfellow for bigamy in 1923, she remarried to become Mrs Ethel Gibbs and continued to bring up her remaining five sons.

He volunteered on Thursday 14th September 1916 when he claimed to be 18 years old and working as a postal assistant. Victor was 5ft 6¾in tall, with a 30in chest, weighed 120lbs, had a hard complexion, hazel eyes, brown hair and a mole on his left groin. Both of Victor's parents signed his consent to enlist.

He embarked on *SS Port Nicholson* in Sydney on Wednesday 8th November 1916 and disembarked in Devonport on Wednesday 10th January 1917. Victor was sent for training in Codford, Wiltshire, where on Wednesday 14th February he was admitted to hospital with influenza for two weeks. On Wednesday 30th May, whilst training, he was punished with one hour of extra rifle drill for failing to keep his rifle in a clean and proper condition.

Victor left for France on Monday 23rd July and arrived in Le Havre the next day. He joined the Battalion in the field on Saturday 11th August whilst they were serving in the Messines to Ploegsteert sector. Victor had been with them for less than a day when he accompanied the Battalion for training. He marched back to the sector on Sunday 19th and went into the front line for the first time. Victor was attached to other members of his platoon who gave him instruction in what to do when on duty in the trenches, how to do it and most importantly how to take care. Both the Royal Flying Corps and the Luftstreitkräfte were patrolling the sky above the trenches and engaging each other in dog fights with an enemy machine being brought down at 10.00am. The enemy artillery was undertaking a heavier than normal bombardment of the sector with a variety of high explosive. Throughout the tour, that lasted until late on Wednesday 29th, there was almost a constant artillery duel. Victor marched to Neuve Eglise where on Thursday 30th he spent the day resting and cleaning himself and his equipment. The next morning he was able to get a hot bath and was issued with clean clothing. In the afternoon Victor moved to the Bomy area and began training that followed the syllabus below that was considered to be elementary:

Monday 3rd

7.15-7.30am	Foot inspection
9.00-9.25am	Falling in and inspection of platoons
9.30-10.00am	Bayonet fighting & muscle exercises
10.05-10.20am	Lecturette - cause and prevention of trench feet
10.20-10.35am	Inspection of box respirators
10.35-11.30am	Specialist training:
	- Lewis gunners
	- Wiring squad
	- Riflemen
	- Bombers
11.35-12.00noon	Close order drill - 5 minutes saluting
2.30pm	Company cricket matches

Tuesday 4th

7.15-7.30am	Organised games
9.00-9.25am	C.O.'s parade
9.30-10.00am	Guards and sentries
10.05-10.20am	Lecturette - march discipline
10.20-10.35am	Muscle exercises
10.35-11.30am	Specialist training
11.35-12.00noon	Close order drill - 5 minutes saluting
2.30-4.00pm	'A' Coy's Lewis gunners on 25 yard range

Wednesday 5th

9.30am	Battalion route march - not less than 10 miles - dress, marching order, mid-day meal to be carried. Transport to parade. Route to be notified later. Foot inspection immediately on return to billets.

Thursday 6th

7.15-7.30am	Physical drill and organised games
9.00-9.15am	Falling in and inspection of platoon
9.15-9.25am	Gas helmet drill
9.25-9.45am	Bayonet fighting & muscle exercises
9.50-10.05am	Lecturette - range finding & judging distance
10.05-10.35am	Musketry for all section of the platoon
10.35-11.30am	Specialist training
11.35-12.00noon	Close order drill - 5 minutes saluting
2.30-4.00pm	'B' Coy's Lewis gunners on 25 yard range
8.30-9.00pm	Marching on a compass bearing in the dark with box respirators on

Friday 7th

7.15-7.30am	Physical drill and organised games
9.00-9.20am	C.O.'s parade
9.20-9.40am	Rapid manipulation of bolt & rapid aiming
9.45-10.05am	Lecturette - fire direction and fire control
10.05-10.35am	Bayonet fighting & muscle exercises
10.35-11.30am	Specialist training
11.35-12.00noon	Company drill
2.30-4.00pm	'C' Coy's Lewis gunners on 25 yard range
2.30pm	Cricket matches

Saturday 8th

7.15-7.30am	Physical drill and organised games
9.00-9.15am	Falling in and inspection of platoon
9.15-9.45am	Bomb throwing from cover to cover
9.45-10.05am	Lecturette - demonstration of bomb tactics
10.10-10.30am	Lecturette on the history of the Bn. and Esprit de Corps
10.30-12.00noon	A simple outpost scheme
2.30-4.00pm	'D' Coy's Lewis gunners on 25 yard range

Sunday 9th   Church Parade

A second specially designed programme followed for the second week and to build on the previous week. The specialist training *"will be even more vigorous than last week"*.

Monday 10th

7.15-7.30am	Physical drill and organised games
9.00-9.15am	Falling in and inspection of platoons
9.15-9.30am	Rapid load with ball ammunition - against a high bank
9.30-11.00am	Further exemplification of Friday's exercises on platoon in the attack. Use of Lewis Gun, Rifle Grenadier, Bombing Section and Rifleman.
11.10-11.20am	Lecturette - Artillery Formations
11.20-12.00noon	Company deploying from Column of Route to Artillery Formations (casualties to occur amongst Platoon and Section Commanders). Rallying.
2.00-3.30pm	Specialist training
8.00-9.30pm	Companies marching to a point of assembly in Artillery Formation in the dark with box respirators on

Tuesday 11th

7.15-7.30am	Physical drill and organised games
9.00-9.10am	Falling in and inspection of platoons
9.10-9.50am	Lecturette on points to be observed during the attack:-

1 Role of: Lewis Gunners
               Riflemen
               Bombers
               Rifle-bombers
               Moppers-up
               Carrying parties
               Scouts
               Runners

2 Formations in attack

3 Artillery section. Action of Stoke Mortars & Vickers Guns

4 Development of the attack

5 Consolidation

6 Role of: Rapid wiring parties
               Patrols
               Covering parties

	7 Information - collection & transmission of
	8 Hostile counter attack
9.50-10.05am	Rapid fire
10.15-12.00noon	Company attacking on a narrow point assuming other companies on flanks:
	a Artillery Formations
	b Deployment into waves (of varying strengths)
	c Waves to halt on prearranged lines & reorganise under covering parties
	d Leap-frogging
2.00-3.30pm	Specialist training
Wednesday 12th	Battalion Tactical Exercise
Thursday 13th	
7.15-7.30am	Physical training and organised games
9.00-9.20am	A disposal of platoon commanders
9.20-9.40am	Trigger pressing and rapid aiming
9.40-10.15am	Bomb throwing for Lewis Gunners and Riflemen
10.15-10.45am	Lecturette on new Hun system of defence
10.50-12.00noon	Coy. Tactical Exercises. Platoon Cmdrs. to solve problems set by the O's C.
2.00-4.00pm	Special training
Friday 14th	
9.00-9.30am	At disposal of Platoon Cmdrs. recapitulation or organisation
9.30-10.00am	Lecturette - 'Consolidation'
10.00-12.00noon	Specialist training
8.00-10.00pm	Battalion in attack.
Saturday 15th	Brigade Tactical Scheme.
Sunday 16th	Divine Service

Victor continued to train in the camp until moving to Steenvoorde on Thursday 20th to complete the training. Victor was collected by omnibus and driven to the canal bank north of Ypres from where he went into the trenches for the second and last time. He was ready to take part in an attack that commenced at 5.30am on Wednesday 26th. Victor was led forward under a creeping barrage, by 7.30am the Red Line was captured and consolidation was under way. Attacks continued that were followed by consolidation and in the early hours of the next morning Victor was hit by a shell splinter and killed.

His mother received a package of Victor's possessions that included a wallet, photographs, cards and badges he had collected. She was sent his British War Medal no 52114, Victory Medal no 51499 and Memorial Plaque and Scroll no 332456.

His mother wrote on Thursday 3rd July 1930 requesting information relating to the location of Victor's grave as she had sent money for a gravestone inscription but had heard nothing. She received a reply that confirmed Victor was commemorated on the Menin Gate and that she should apply for a refund of monies for the gravestone inscription.

S/10883 PRIVATE
JOHN ALFRED STURMAN
1st Battalion The Buffs (East Kent Regiment)
Died on Friday 31st December 1915, aged 17
Commemorated on Panel 12.

John Alfred Sturman
John's signature

John was born at home, the only child of Noah Sturman and the late Mrs Sturman, of Lewisham, London. Following his elementary education he worked as a farm labourer.

He volunteered on Monday 10th August 1914 in Lewisham and was sent for training with the 3rd Battalion in Dover, Kent. John was 5ft 5¼in tall, with a 36½in chest, grey eyes, brown hair, weighed 130lbs and had a scar under his right knee.

John received the following punishments whilst he was training:

* Wednesday 23rd December 1914 — three days confined to barracks for overstaying his pass;
* Friday 7th May 1915 — four days confined to barracks for being absent from a tattoo;
* Friday 21st May — five days confined to barracks for not complying with an order and being rude to an NCO;
* Monday 5th July — seven days confined to barracks for being absent from a parade;
* Friday 30th July — ten days confined to barracks and forfeit of pay.

John went out to France on Wednesday 18th August 1915 and joined the Battalion whilst they were in barracks in Poperinghe. He undertook tours of duty on the Salient, mainly around La Brique until he was killed on New's Year's Eve.

In June 1928 his father wrote to the authorities: *"I believe this was my boy John, I do not know what the records say about his father or who his nearest relatives were, but I did not know till 10 years after in March, I thought he was in Australia all the time and was looking for him through the papers, he was like lots of boys full of life & fun, perhaps I did not know how much I cared for him, I have been thinking of trying to find out where he is buried and visiting it.*
I have no picture of him.
Would you please help me. I was in the navy in the Red Sea."
John is commemorated on Lewisham War Memorial.

3/7694 PRIVATE
COLIN ALISTER SUTHERLAND
1st Battalion Argyll and Sutherland Highlanders
Died on Sunday 9th May 1915, aged 17
Commemorated on Panel 44.

Colin's signature

Colin was born in Wimbledon, Surrey, oldest son of William Colin Sutherland, MA, and Daisy Gwendlyn Bloomfield Sutherland, of Green Brae, Colehill, Wimborne, Dorset. He had three younger brothers, Ian Hamish Bloomfield, Neil Pulsford and Bruce Donald.

Colin left school to volunteer on Tuesday 1st September 1914 in Woolwich, London, where he claimed to have been born in Wimbledon, London, aged 19 years and 38 days and was unemployed as he had just left school. Colin was 5ft 8in tall, with a 36¼in chest, weighed 154lbs, and had a small mole in the lumbar region.

He sailed from Southampton to Le Havre on Thursday 1st April 1915 and joined the Battalion in the field on Wednesday 7th. Colin was promoted to Acting Corporal shortly after he arrived in Flanders. He was allocated to a platoon and began work at the front, however, 'normal duties' did not last long. At the commencement of the Second Battle of Ypres Colin served at Polygon Wood before moving to Hooge where, on Monday 10th May, a fierce battle broke out. After surviving the first horrific day Colin was killed the next day after being in the line almost constantly for more than three weeks.

11137 PRIVATE
FORREST SOMERSET SUTHERLAND
'C' Company, 4th Regiment South African Infantry
Died on Thursday 20th September 1917, aged 16
Commemorated on Panel 16A.

Forrest was the only son of Forrest and Margaret Somerset Sutherland, of Pretoria, Transvaal.

Forrest volunteered and was sent for training before joining the Regiment in the field with a draft whilst they were serving on the Somme that helped replenish the Regiment following the Battle of Arras.

He was sent north to Belgium, arriving in Brandhoek on Friday 14th September. Training commenced, with an emphasis on how to clear each pill-box, trench or dug-outs and how to move the captured German prisoners to the rear. After three days of training he was sent into the line to the north of the Ypres to Roeselare railway. Final preparations for the attack were made that were made more difficult when at 10.00pm on

Wednesday 19th heavy rain poured down until dawn. The battlefield was already a quagmire and the rain made it even worse. At 5.40am the British artillery laid down a significant high-explosive barrage with the intention of smashing the German pill boxes. Forrest was led forward to capture 'Beck House' and 'Borry Farm'. Their next objective was 'Mitchell's Farm' — still under artillery fire — that was also captured. By 7.00pm Forrest was consolidating his position before moving forward against the second objective of the Langemarck to Gheluvelt line. During the advance Forrest was killed, his body was not recovered.

76083 PRIVATE
KEITH WAVERLEY SUTTIE
29th Battalion Canadian Infantry
(British Columbia Regiment)
Died on Wednesday 19th April 1916, aged 17
Commemorated on Panel 28.

Keith's signature

Keith was the eldest child of David Alison and Bertha Eva Suttie, of 841 Howe Street, Vancouver, British Columbia, previously of Tomb Street, St Anne's, County Antrim, Northern Ireland.

He volunteered in Vancouver on Monday 9th November 1914 when he claimed to have been born on Thursday 9th July 1896 in Belfast, Ireland, and was working as a florist. Keith was a Baptist, 5ft 9in tall, with a 34½in chest, a dark complexion, brown eyes and black hair. He came to England with the Second Canadian Contingent and sent for training at Otterpool, Kent, before leaving for France on Friday 17th September 1915. He embarked on *SS St Seriol* in Folkestone, Kent, bound for Boulogne that was reached at midnight. He entrained to Cassel then marched to billets in St Sylvestre where on Tuesday 21st Generals Plumer, Alderson and Turner inspected the Battalion. The next day Keith marched to 'Aldershot Camp', near 'Westhof Farm', where on Monday 27th his comrade, Private Colin McDonald, was the first man from the Battalion to be killed (he is commemorated on the Menin Gate). Shortly afterwards Generals Sir Edwin Alderson and Huntly Ketchen visited the front line. The tour of duty lasted until Wednesday 13th October when the Battalion was relieved to billets in Loker. Keith remained in the trenches between Kemmel and Lindenhoek, with billets in Loker, until Sunday 6th February 1916.

Keith marched to Méteren, via Bailleul, where good billets were provided in the local farms. He undertook training until being taken by motor lorry to La Clytte on Wednesday 16th February and returned to the trenches at Kemmel. After a four-day tour Keith was relieved to 'Scherpenberg Huts' where he rested overnight before returning to his previous billets in Loker. The Battalion marched to Bailleul on Thursday 24th to attend a concert during the afternoon followed by a few days rest then returned to the trenches at Kemmel on Tuesday 29th where he remained until Saturday 1st April. Keith was again sent to Méteren then moved to 'Camp J'.

Early on Monday 3rd he marched to Reninghelst where hot baths awaited him before another inspection at noon by Generals Alderson and Ketchen. At 4.45pm Keith marched to Dickebusch where he was issued with materials to take to the Voormezeele sector and began fatigues. The Battalion undertook a bombing raid on the craters on Thursday 6th but lost a number of men due to heavy German shelling of the sector. Late on Friday 7th the Battalion was relieved from 'Scottish Wood' to 'Camp D' in Dickebusch where the exhausted men got some well-deserved rest. Keith was provided with a hot bath then began training and undertook fatigues. During the evening of Monday 17th Keith marched to Voormezeele where at 2.30am the next morning he assisted in repulsing an attack on the craters. Keith was killed in action during the morning of Wednesday 19th.

1769 RIFLEMAN
FRANCIS CYRIL TAYLOR
1st Battalion Monmouthshire Regiment
Died on Saturday 8th May 1915, aged 17
Commemorated on Panel 50.

Francis was born in Craig, Newport, son of David John and Annie Taylor, of 52 Tredegar Street, Rhiwderin, Newport, Monmouthshire. He volunteered in Rogerstone, Monmouthshire, and was sent for training in Bury St Edmunds, Suffolk, followed by Cambridge.

Francis Taylor

Francis left with the Battalion from Southampton for Le Havre on Saturday 13th February 1915. He entrained for final training in northern France near Bailleul.

Francis began tours of duty without being involved in any particular action until the opening of The Second Battle of Ypres on Thursday 22nd April. Francis saw action on the Frezenberg Ridge; when the British line was straightened and withdrew closer to Ypres he

was in the trenches at Brielen. The enemy laid down a particularly heavy bombardment across the sector on Tuesday 4th May that heralded the next stage in the German offensive. Francis went with his platoon into the line for the last time on Thursday 6th but it was a difficult relief. He arrived in the trenches early the next morning and was immediately ordered to repair them as they had been badly damaged by shell fire. The enemy continued to shell the area in preparation for an attack that finally was launched on Saturday 8th. The British artillery did all they could to reply but it did not match the intensity of the Germans. The infantry came forward in superior numbers and despite a desperate defence of the line the enemy was able to push the line back. In the closely fought battle Francis was killed.

246278 PRIVATE NELSON TAYLOR
38th Battalion Canadian Infantry
(Eastern Ontario Regiment)
Died on Thursday 15th November 1917, aged 17
Commemorated on Panel 28.

Nelson was the brother of Jennie Taylor, of 552 Mclaren Street, Ottawa, Ontario, whom he gave as his next of kin when volunteering in Ottawa on Thursday 13th May 1915. He gave his date of birth as Friday 11th February 1898 and was working on a ranch as a driver. Nelson was a Roman Catholic, 5ft 3in tall, with a 34in chest, a fair complexion, blue eyes and brown hair.

Nelson sailed with the Battalion to England, as a bugler, where training continued. He marched from 'Bramshott Camp', Hampshire, to Liphook Station on Sunday 13th August 1916 and entrained to Southampton. He arrived at 3.30pm and paraded on the dock until embarking on SS Archangel two hours later that sailed to La Havre, arriving at 7.30pm. After a particularly rough crossing he arrived and disembarked at 7.30am then marched to a rest camp. With some delight everyone was promised a swim in the sea the next day but that was postponed as the sea remained rough and it was therefore dangerous. However, on Wednesday 16th the majority of the Battalion took the opportunity for a skinny dip. Suitably dry and re-clothed Nelson marched to the station in the afternoon to entrain to northern France. A route march took him to 'St Lawrence Camp' near

Reninghelst from where practical experience in the trenches began in front of Kemmel. He returned to 'St Lawrence Camp', followed by 'Devonshire Camp', and finally to 'Quebec Camp', where he continued to train until beginning his first tour of duty in the front line on Friday 1st September in the Kemmel sector. After three weeks in the sector he marched to Hazebrouck, arriving on Sunday 24th, where he was billeted for the night. The march continued the next morning to Gandspette where training began that continued in Fieffes-Montrelet and Warloy-Baillon.

Nelson marched through Albert and arrived at 'Tara Camp' at noon on Thursday 12th October where he was issued with a new set of badges to sew onto his uniform. His first work was to help bury the dead, a grim task of recovering decomposing and mutilated bodies — enough to turn the strongest of stomachs. He continued with this work and more 'pleasant' fatigues until 2.30pm on Thursday 26th when he went into the front line for the first time on the Somme. He then worked on fatigues in 'The Chalk Pits' until being relieved. Nelson was sent to Albert for a hot bath and was issued with clean clothing. He completed another tour of duty before moving via Bouzincourt, Varennes, Rubempré, Beauval, Diéval to Bruay. In each village he stopped for a couple of days and in Bruay the Battalion was reorganised whilst he trained. Nelson moved to Cambligneul then went into the line at Vimy Ridge on Saturday 30th December to begin tours of duty. When out of the line he spent time in Villers-au-Bois (in the 'Bijoli Line') and Cambligneul during January 1917. 'The Calgary Herald' sent a gift of cigarettes and tobacco to the Battalion that Major Parkinson distributed amongst the men. In March Nelson remained in the trenches at Vimy but when out of the line he switched from Cambligneul for Coupigny followed by Château de la Haie. Whilst Nelson was not involved in any particular action at Vimy during the first three months of the year, it was never a quiet sector. There was constant sniping, artillery bombardments, and raids made on the enemy

... a naval gun in action on Vimy Ridge

trenches — it was never a safe or pleasant place to be. From Monday 26th March the artillery increased the intensity of the bombardment of the enemy lines. At 7.00pm the next evening the Tunnellers fired a camouflet close to 'Montreal Crater'. A huge plume of gas shot fifty feet into the air and a crater of over twenty-five feet was left as a reminder.

At 5.30am on Monday 9th April Nelson was led over the top and charged the enemy with the first objectives quickly captured. He continued on to 'Clutch Trench' where he helped consolidate the position. Nelson remained on the battlefield until being relieved to Château de la Haie on Saturday 14th where he rested over@night then marched to 'Coupigny Huts'. The Battalion was reorganised whilst Nelson and his comrades trained. Nelson left the camp on Tuesday 24th and marched to 'Zouave Valley' then went into reserve at 'Hospital Ridge'. He moved into the front line late on Wednesday 2nd May for two weeks including being in reserve to undertake fatigues. Nelson marched to Bethonval Wood on Wednesday 16th for three days then returned to the support line. He marched to 'Canada Camp' at Château de la Haie at the end of the month where he got some much-needed rest, enjoyed a range of sporting events and undertook training. Nelson returned to 'Zouave Valley' during the afternoon of Friday 8th June for three days then was sent to Bethonval Wood for three days training that included working with aeroplane support. The transport section took part in a Brigade Competition and they won first place with their horse 'Big Nigger' that cheered up the whole Battalion. Nelson returned to the trenches where as usual a constant artillery duel was maintained.

A period of three weeks extended training in Villers-au-Bois began on Monday 2nd July and when complete Nelson once again returned to the support lines at Bethonval Wood. He went into the trenches on Tuesday 31st at 'Avion Mill' to serve in the front line, support and reserve trenches. Nelson remained in the sector until Thursday 20th September when he was sent for training at Gouy Servins for a week, then moved to 'Souchez Camp' that signalled the end of Nelson's service in the area. Months of hard work in the chalk and mud in the trenches of Vimy that were never quiet made Nelson a battle-hardened soldier. He had experienced and seen more in a year in his short life than most of us would wish to see today.

A series of moves by train, omnibus and marching took Nelson to Staples on Sunday 14th October for ten days of training in preparation for the next offensive at Passchendaele. The Third Battle of Ypres had been fought for eleven weeks, the battlefield was a dangerous swampy morass, front line trenches had long disappeared to be replaced by water-filled shell holes that occasionally were joined together. It was clear that the offensive was over and little more would be achieved by continuing but with the attitudes of the day (without the benefit of rose-tinted hindsight) it was worth continuing in the hope of breaking the German resolve, if not their front line.

Nelson arrived in Brandhoek at 8.15am on Tuesday 23rd October and marched to 'Erie Camp', settling into his hut in the early afternoon. HRH Field Marshal The Duke of Connaught inspected the Battalion the next day who expressed himself delighted with them and wished them well for their forthcoming service on the Salient. Nelson was able to have a hot bath in Poperinghe then visit its bustling cafés and other distractions before moving via Ypres to Potijze on Sunday 28th. Late in the evening he marched out towards Zonnebeke to take the line near 'Augustus Farm' and 'Hillside Farm'. Throughout the next day he was prepared for the move into the front line. Nelson took part in the attack that began at 5.40am on Tuesday 30th and the objectives were quickly achieved and he busily assisted in consolidating the position.

Nelson is recorded as dying on Thursday 15th November, however, the Battalion was training in Hondinghem in northern France on that date. There is no record of him as an accidental casualty on that date. It can only be assumed he had been badly wounded in the field during the last attack he took part in. It is odd, therefore, that if he died two weeks later in a hospital that he did not have a marked grave but of course, not impossible.

10075 PRIVATE
HAROLD CHARLES THOMSON
3rd Battalion Canadian Infantry
(Central Ontario Regiment)
Died on Sunday 2nd May 1915, aged 17
Commemorated on Panel 18.

Harold's signature

Harold was the son of Bessie Thomson, of 3030A Dundas Street West, Toronto, Ontario, and the late Charles James Thomson.

He volunteered in Valcartier, Province of Quebec, on Tuesday 22nd September 1914 when he claimed to have been born on Sunday 1st September 1895 and was working on the railroad. Harold was 5ft 11in tall, with a 36in chest, a dark complexion, brown hair and eyes, and had a T-shaped scar on the back of his head. Harold arrived at Devonport on *SS Tunisian* on Monday 19th October 1914 and marched to Friary Station where he entrained for Amesbury, Wiltshire. He was sent to 'Bustard Camp', passing Stonehenge *en route* where the next day the Battalion was addressed

by General Sir Edwin Alderson. (Stonehenge was owned at the time by Sir Edmund Antrobus, Bt, father of Lieutenant Edmund Antrobus who died on Saturday 24th October 1914 and is commemorated on Panel 9 of the Menin Gate.)

Field Marshal Lord Roberts inspected the Battalion on Saturday 24th then training commenced. A continuous parade of visitors arrived and on Wednesday 4th November HM King George V and HM Queen Mary, accompanied by HRH Princess Mary, Field Marshals Roberts and Kitchener. He spent Christmas in the camp where a special dinner, attended by General Malcolm Mercer, was provided by Toronto City Council.

... a Royal Inspection on Salisbury Plain

Harold completed his training in England and marched to Amesbury where he entrained for Avonmouth and sailed to St Nazaire at 3.00am on Tuesday 9th February 1915 on *SS City of Edinburgh*. He entrained for northern

SS City of Edinburgh

France and was sent to billets in Merris where one of his men, Private Horne, died of pneumonia.

Harold marched to Armentières on Wednesday 17th February where all ranks were given front line practical experience. Brigadier General Walter Congreve, VC, came to visit the men whilst training in the front line on Friday 19th. The Battalion was considered ready to take the line in its own right at the end of the month and moved to Bac St Maur from where they took the line then served in northern France until the end of the month.

Following a period of training in Winnezeele from Wednesday 7th April Harold moved to billets in Poperinghe on Sunday 18th. He marched along the pavé to Vlamertinghe on Wednesday 21st and began training. Harold was in camp when the first gas attack was launched at 5.00pm on Thursday 22nd April. He was sent to Brielen, where he arrived at

1.15am the next morning. At 5.00am the Battalion began to move forward to support the counter-attack against 'Kitchener Wood' and St Julien. The Germans mounted a further attack at 4.30am on Saturday 24th then continued to press home attacks at St Julien. Throughout the time Harold was serving at the front he was under a constant bombardment and remained in the line until Tuesday 27th when he was relieved and returned to Vlamertinghe. He was able to rest all day but at 11.00pm he marched to a bivouac behind the line where he waited for orders. At 7.30pm on Wednesday 28th Harold went to dig a line of trenches in the area held by the Lahore Division until 4.30am when he marched to a bivouac for some rest. Harold paraded for Divine Service conducted by Chaplains Beattie and Gordon on Sunday 2nd May that was attended by General Malcolm Mercer. At 8.00pm he was ordered to the front line and entrenched with the expectation to take part in either an attack or a defence of the line. The Battalion was not deployed but whilst at the front Harold as killed by shell fire.

1626 PRIVATE
GEORGE THOMAS THORPE
5th Battalion Yorkshire Regiment
Died on Monday 26th April 1915, aged 17
Commemorated on Panel 33.

George was born in Hull, son of Louisa Thorpe, of 4 Sails Yard, Oxford Street, Scarborough, Yorkshire. Following his elementary education he worked in a bottling store then in the Whitby Brewery Company, Yorkshire.

At the outbreak of war George was at Annual Camp at Dagenwy, Wales, when he was ordered to pack up his kit and prepare to return to Scarborough. Upon arrival orders were received for the Battalion to mobilise. George trained in Newcastle before entraining for Folkestone, Kent, on Saturday 17th April 1915 where he sent a postcard home:

"Dearest Mother,

Arrived at Folkestone but don't know when we go across the Channel, but will write again as soon as I can, so this is all. So keep smiling as I am well and in the best of spirits. Your loving son, George."

George sailed on *SS Onward* to Boulogne where he arrived in the early hours of Sunday 18th April then had an arduous march to *'St Martin's Camp'*, high above the town. The next day entrained to Cassel then marched to billets near Steenvoorde. The Second Battle of Ypres began at 5.00pm on Thursday 22nd and the sound of the guns could be clearly heard. Orders were received for the Battalion to prepare their kit and embus to Poperinghe from where they marched via

Vlamertinghe to the Yser Canal, arriving on Saturday 24th. George was then marched to Potijze from where he took the line to support the defence of Ypres. The fighting was fierce and often at close quarters with the use of bayonet and bomb. Attack and counter-attack followed with monotonous regularity. George was in the thick of the fighting until he was killed, his body was left, then lost, on the battlefield.

The *'Scarborough Mercury'* published on Friday 4th June: *"Anxiety for Private Thorpe — Mrs. Thorpe, 4, Sails-Yard, Oxford Street, has received news that her son Private Geo. T. Thorpe, 5th Yorks, has been wounded. Several letters which she has sent have been returned marked 'wounded' and also bearing a note that the locality of the hospital is not known. The fact that a registered letter sent just after the 5th Yorks went to France was returned in this way, leads to the supposition that Private Thorpe was wounded some time ago. Mrs Thorpe received official notification that her son had been wounded last week, and that if he became worse she should be informed. The number of the hospital was, in this case, also missing. Mrs. Thorpe is very anxious to hear more definite news."*

Sadly it was not long before the dreadful news of George's death reached his mother.

He is commemorated on the Scarborough War Memorial.

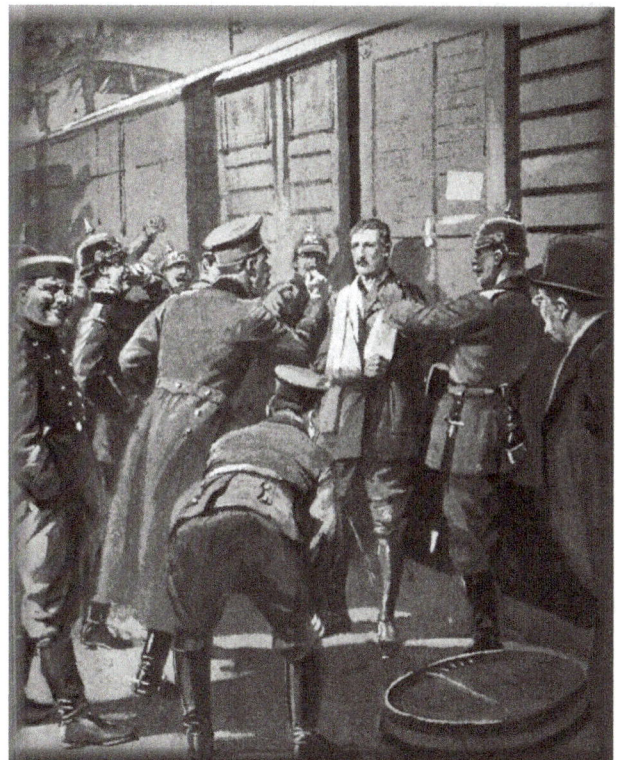

... propaganda illustration to show a wounded prisoner of war being maltreated by the Germans

1594 Trooper
Sidney Charles Thurston
Royal Horse Guards
Died on Thursday 13th May 1915, aged 17
Commemorated on Panel 3.

Sidney Thurston
Photograph courtesy of
Norfolk County Council, image NP00010765.

Sidney was born in Towcester, eldest son of Robert Joseph and Mary Thurston, of 3 Melton Cottages, Melton Road, Wymondham, Norfolk.

He volunteered in Norwich, Norfolk, and went out to France on Wednesday 11th November 1914. As Sidney was travelling across the Channel and entraining to Ypres his colleagues were fighting hard in the final action of the First Battle of Ypres at Nonne Boschen. He was made most welcome when he arrived with a draft that helped to begin to bring the Guards back up to strength.

Sidney served through the winter and spring with his troop undertaking training and a range of tasks, including fatigues.

With the opening of The Second Battle of Ypres Sidney was made ready to support the line. General Henry de Lisle deployed the Horse Guards to Hooge on Tuesday 11th May. Arthur Conan Doyle wrote in 'The British Campaign in France and Flanders': "Their presence in the front firing line was a sign of British weakness, but, on the other hand, it was certain that the Germans had lost enormously, that they were becoming exhausted, and that they were likely to wear out the rifling of their cannon before they broke the line of defence. A few more days would save the situation, and it was hoped that the inclusion of the cavalry would win them.

They took over the lines just in time to meet the brunt of what may have been the most severe attack of all. The shelling upon May 12 can only be described as terrific. The Germans appeared to have an inexhaustible supply of munitions, and from morning to night they blew to pieces the trenches in front and the shelters behind which might screen the supports. It was a day of tempestuous weather, and the howling wind, the driving rain, and the pitiless fire made a Dantesque nightmare of the combat. The attack on the right fell upon the Third Cavalry Division. [The Royal Horse Guards were part of the Division.] … This Division was exposed all morning to a perfectly hellish fire, which was especially murderous to the north of the Ypres-Roulers road. At this point the 1st Royals, 3rd Dragoon Guards, and Somerset Yeomanry were stationed, and were blown, with their trenches into the air by a bombardment which continued for fourteen hours. A single sentence may be extracted from the report of the Commander-in-Chief, which the Somersets should have printed in gold round the walls of their headquarters. 'The North Somerset Yeomanry on the right side of the brigade' says the General, 'although suffering severely, hung on to their trenches throughout the day and actually advanced and attacked the enemy with the bayonet.'

The Royals came up in support, and the brigade held its own. On one occasion the enemy actually got round the left of the 3rd Dragoon Guards, who were the flank regiments, upon which Captain Neville, who was killed later upon the same day, gave the order, 'Even numbers deal with the enemy in the rear, odd numbers carry on!' which was calmly obeyed with complete success. … (Captain Thomas Villiers Tuthill Thacker Neville is buried in Bedford House Cemetery.) All the infantry losses, heavy as they were, are eclipsed by those of the Third Cavalry Division, which bore the full blast of the final whirlwind, and was practically destroyed in holding it back from Ypres. This splendid division, to whom, from first to last, the country owes as much as to any body of troops in the field, was only engaged in the fighting for one clear day, and yet lost nearly as heavily in proportion as either of the infantry divisions which had been in the firing line for a week. Their casualties were 91 officers and 1050 men. This will give some idea of the concentrated force of the storm which broke upon them on May 12. It was a most murderous affair, and they were only driven from their trenches when the trenches themselves had been blasted to pieces. It is doubtful whether any regiments have endured more in so short of time. These three brigades were formed of corps d'élites, and they showed that day that the blue blood of the land was not yet losing its iron. The casualty lists and the succeeded action of the 24th read like a society function."

Sidney is commemorated on Hingham War Memorial.

1024315 Private
William Edward Tricker
3rd Battalion Canadian Infantry
(Central Ontario Regiment)
Died on Tuesday 6th November 1917, aged 17
Commemorated on Panel 18.

William's signature

William was born in Ipswich, eldest son of Edgar William and S Elizabeth Tricker, of 2 Coe's Cottages, Bramford Lane, Ipswich. He was educated in the

Workhouse School, Ipswich. William left for Canada as a youngster to seek work and a new life.

He volunteered in Toronto, Ontario, on Wednesday 6th September 1916 when he claimed to have been born on Tuesday 18th January 1898. William was a Presbyterian, worked on a farm and was 5ft 5in tall, had a 37½in chest, a fair complexion, hazel eyes, light brown hair, and four vaccination marks on his left arm.

William was sent for training before leaving for England to continue his training. He went out to France to join the Battalion with a draft. At the end of May the Battalion was training in Petit Servins where on Thursday 3rd and Friday 4th June enemy aeroplanes dropped bombs on their camp. William moved to the trenches at 'Mont Forêt Quarries' on Friday 11th for a three-day tour. From Saturday 19th he undertook fatigues on the 'Ridge Line'. He moved to 'Winnipeg Huts' on Sunday 1st July then went into the front line, the Battalion occupying 'New Brunswick Trench', 'New Brunswick Road', 'Quebec Trench' and 'Canada Trench'. William remained in the sector until moving to Nœux-les-Mines in early August where he undertook training whilst a number of Court Martials were held. A number of William's comrades were organised by Lieutenant Scott into a concert party who gave a performance on Tuesday 7th August that followed a football match. Two days later William marched back to serve at the front line. It was a difficult relief as the Battalion came under sustained shell fire and Private George Ballinger was mortally wounded (he is buried in Bully-Grenay Communal Cemetery, British Extension). Private Ballinger's 17 year old son, William, was hospitalised gun shot wounds ten months later (he had enlisted as a 16 year old). After an active tour of duty where a number of patrols were sent out that encountered enemy patrols the Battalion was relieved to Mazingarbe where breakfast was waiting for him. The next day the Battalion was taken for a hot bath and clean lice-free clothing was issued. William paraded in his tin hat and full kit on Monday 27th and marched in battle order to Berthonsart for an inspection by Field Marshal Sir Douglas Haig. Training and sporting events then continued at Orlencourt followed by Monchy-Breton.

William marched to Hersin in the early hours of Monday 3rd September, a tiring march over the pavé that took over six hours in the stifling heat. Billets were provided in a convent that was devoid of the devout! The next afternoon the YMCA gave a concert that was followed by a series of games. William returned to the business of war on Wednesday 5th when he was sent into the support trenches at Cité St Pierre. It was an active sector, where in addition to the normal shelling, trench mortars poured forth their fire from one side to another causing considerable damage to the parapets and trenches. William worked hard on repairing the trenches and improving them as German aircraft were on constant patrol over his line. He was in the line when the Royal Engineers launched over four hundred gas drums on the German positions at Lens at 3.20am on Thursday 13th. It drew an immediate response from the enemy artillery who bombarded the sector in retaliation. Fatigues, training, rest and taking part in sporting events continued until moving into the front line on Tuesday 18th. At 4.50am the next morning a party of Germans raided an advanced post at 'Nabob Valley' who were repulsed by effective Lewis Gun fire. A number of the Battalion went out into No Man's Land to retrieve the German dead and to ascertain any information that could be gained from their bodies. Two of his comrades were in the Divisional boxing competition, Private Taylor won but Private Marks lost (he would be killed on Friday 30th August 1918 and is buried in Quebec Cemetery, Cherisy). The enemy, supported by their artillery, mounted a raid on Thursday 20th and during a close-fought fight, Major Herbert Gourlay Wickens was killed (he is buried in Fosse No 10 Communal Cemetery Extension, Sains-en-Gohelle), three officers were wounded, ten men were killed and twenty wounded (most of the dead are buried in Aix-Noulette Communal Cemetery Extension). The Germans launched a gas attack on Friday 21st with over three hundred shells landing across the area. A heavy barrage was laid down at 8.00am the next morning for nearly two hours. William was relieved and arrived in Fosse 10 at 4.00am on Sunday 23rd when a hot meal was provided. After some sleep he was able to enjoy a good hot soak and then had the rest of the day to relax. The next morning he paraded and a number of gallantry awards were announced before marching off to Bruay for training. As usual the training was punctured by sporting events, bath parades, concerts and time for relaxing. At 7.20am on Sunday 7th October William paraded on the market square then marched via Ruitz, Barlin, Hersin, to Aix-Noulette, arriving at 11.20am. Unfortunately William and his comrades were provided with somewhat leaky accommodation at 'Noulette Huts', not helped by the very heavy rain. He soon was back in training or taking part in sports. William moved to Hallicourt on Friday 12th and on Tuesday 16th General Sir Henry Sinclair Horne inspected the Battalion at Fosse 7.

With their training for service on the grim battlefield of Passchendaele at an end for the time being, the Battalion began its move towards Belgium on Saturday 20th. William finally arrived in the Terdeghem area to complete his training. General Sir Arthur Currie inspected the Battalion at St Marie Cappel on Saturday 27th, accompanied by General Archibald Cameron MacDonnel. A long and tiring march took William to Staple on 30th for a hot bath, the last real clean up William would ever have.

William paraded early on Friday 2nd November and marched to Bavinchove Station at 5.40am. An hour later the train pulled out and trundled via Steenvoorde and Poperinghe to Ypres. He then marched slowly along the clogged roads to a muddy bivouac at Wieltje where he attempted to get some rest to the sound of battle being fought close by. Late on Saturday 3rd William had been lead forward to the 'Wurst' area and the Battalion Headquarters were established at 'Kronprinz Farm' before it was split and moved to 'Bellevue Farm' and 'Waterloo Farm' on Monday 5th. 'A' Company came under heavy shell fire with Lieutenant Richard Darryl Garrett and ten of his men were killed (Lieutenant Garrett is buried in Vlamertinghe New Military Cemetery). Major Harry Hutchison was badly wounded and subsequently died in a field hospital and is buried in Lijssenthoek Military Cemetery. Whilst William waited orders on the muddy, water-logged battlefield orders were being sent continuously to the Battalion Headquarters that had to be sent onto the companies. At 1.13am on Tuesday 6th Lieutenant Colonel McLaughlin synchronised watches and the wait continued. At 6.00am precisely the preliminary barrage began that was soon answered by the enemy. Shells began to rain down around 'Waterloo Farm' that wounded a number of men in a stretcher party as William and his comrades began their advance to wards Passchendaele. A number of German prisoners were pressed into stretcher bearer service who replaced the injured Canadians. The objectives set the Battalion began to be achieved despite the rain turning the battlefield into a quagmire ably assisted by the German artillery! It was heavy going and a difficult fight during which William was hit. He would not have survived long as the mud soon consumed his body.

1908 RIFLEMAN
FRANCIS PHILIP TURNER
1st/12th Battalion London Regiment (The Rangers)
Died on Saturday 8th May 1915, aged 17
Commemorated on Panel 54.

Francis was born in Wandsworth, oldest son of Philip John Henry and Cecilia Florence Turner, of 13 Dunvegan Road, Eltham, London. He had a younger brother, Henry.
He went out to France on Sunday 18th April 1915. For Francis' story see Rifleman William Klagge, above.

S/12011 RIFLEMAN
LOSCOMBE TURNER
9th Battalion Rifle Brigade
Died on Friday 30th July 1915, aged 17
Commemorated on Panel 50.

Loscombe was born in Lenham, Kent, third son of Henry and Laura Turner, of Whybanks, Otterden, Faversham, Kent. He was educated locally.
He enlisted in Canterbury, Kent, and was sent for training. Loscombe went out to France on Tuesday 29th June 1915 and joined the Battalion in the field. For his service in the field and that of the Battalion see Rifleman David Ross, above.

2156 PRIVATE PERCY TURNER
1st Battalion Welsh Regiment
Died on Tuesday 25th May 1915, aged 17
Commemorated on Panel 37.

Percy was born at home, the fourth son of Elizabeth Jane Turner, of 5 Emlyn Avenue, Ebbw Vale, Monmouthshire, and the late Herbert Harry Turner. Percy was educated locally and then went to work in the local colliery.
He volunteered in Cardiff and went out to France on Wednesday 17th March 1915. For Percy's story see Private Edmund Jones above.

TF/2796 PRIVATE WILLIAM TURNER
1st/8th Battalion Middlesex Regiment
Died on Sunday 25th April 1915, aged 17
Commemorated on Panel 51.

William was born in Hammersmith, son of Elizabeth Turner, of 30 Leffer Road, Shepherd's Bush, London. He was educated locally and was then employed as a telegraph messenger boy.
He volunteered in Stamford Brook, Middlesex, and left for France on Monday 8th March 1915. For William's story, and that of the Battalion, see Private Owen Rose, above.

1687 RIFLEMAN
WILLIAM ERNEST TAYLOR UGLOW
1st/9th Battalion London Regiment
(Queen Victoria's Rifles)
Died on Friday 1st January 1915, aged 17
Commemorated on Panel 54.

William was born at home, eldest son of William Ernest and Florence Annie Uglow, of Beaumont View,

Cheshunt, Hertfordshire. He had three elder sisters and four younger brothers. Following his elementary education he was employed by Messrs Marks and Clark of Lincoln Inn Fields, London.

At the outbreak of war he volunteered in London and was sent for training until leaving on Wednesday 4th November 1914 for Southampton. He embarked on *SS Oxonian* for Le Havre then marched to *'No 1 Rest Camp'*. The next day William entrained for a twenty-six hour rail journey to St Omer. The Battalion undertook training in northern France: on Thursday 19th William marched to Hazebrouck and after a night of rest continued to Bailleul. Two days later a Taube bombed the area close to his billet near a hospital that took the brunt of the attack. William marched across the border into Belgium and was billeted in Neuve Eglise on Friday 27th before taking the line at Wulverghem. William undertook a series of duties in the area without being involved in any particular action. Christmas was spent out of the line and a good time was had by all in the Battalion. New Year was spent in the line and all was relatively quiet until early on New Year's Day when the Germans commenced shelling them, a barn where a good number of men were resting was hit and eleven men were killed and thirty-six wounded, one of those being William.

Captain Woodruff Cox wrote: *"'B' Company's sector was situated in front of a semi-ruined farmhouse known as the Petite Douvre Farm, and the actual trench of which I had command was close to the Douvre River. The trench consisted of a high command parapet of very indifferent construction and in a bad state of repair and in only a few places raised to the height of a man's shoulder. One of our machine-guns under Lieut. Fargus was placed near the centre. The trench at that time was in a very muddy state and most of the men were squatting on the fire-step or on wooden boxes, sheltering behind the parapet. I was seated on one of these boxes just below the parapet near the Douvre River end of the trench. I noticed Brian Fargus inspecting the gun position, and with his usual disregard for personal safety he exposed himself once or twice and a sniper hidden in the Petite Douvre Farm had one or two shots at him. When Fargus had finished his inspection he came along the trench in my direction, the sniper potting at him from time to time as his head showed over the parapet. On reaching me I warned him that he had been spotted and got him to sit beside me on the box, and we discussed the situation generally. At the end of five minutes' conversation Fargus found his position somewhat cramped and shifted slightly. At that moment I raised myself so as to see over the parapet from behind some sandbags. Brian Fargus put his hand on my shoulder saying something about getting along and raised himself to practically a standing position. Almost at once a shot was heard from the direction of the farm and*

poor Fargus dropped dead behind me shot right through the centre of the forehead. He was buried at night close behind the trench he was in when he was hit, at a place called 'the willows,' it being practically impossible in those days to carry the body to the rear owing to the awful condition of the track across the fields."

337 LANCE CORPORAL FRANK GILBERT USHER
21st Company Australian Machine Gun Corps
Died on Thursday 20th September 1917, aged 17
Commemorated on Panel 31.

Frank's signature

Frank was born at home, son of Richard and Annie Mary Usher, of Hidden Vale, Oakey, Toowoomba, Queensland.

He volunteered in Brisbane, Queensland, on Saturday 18th March 1916 when he claimed to be 18 years and 2 months old and was employed as a woodcutter. Frank was a Congregationalist; 5ft 9½in tall, with a 33in chest, weighed 124lbs, had a dark complexion, brown eyes, dark colour hair, and had scars on his left shin, on the back and front of his head and under his right jawbone. He embarked on *SS Orontes* in Melbourne on

SS Orontes

Wednesday 16th August 1916 and disembarked in Plymouth on Monday 2nd October. He was sent for training in Bulford followed by Grantham — Frank sailed from Southampton to France on Saturday 17th March 1917. Frank entrained to the Somme where final training began. He then began to serve in the front line near *'Delsaux Farm'* near Beugny.

Frank's first experience of an enemy attack was on Sunday 15th April when he was in the trenches between Hermies, Demicourt, Lagnicourt and Morchies. The Germans were able to capture Lagnicourt and pushed forward in many sectors although taking heavy losses. The War Diary records: *"Chief lessons from a Machine Gunners point of view is that the ideal outpost weapon is the Lewis gun which the machine gun has once more proved that, in capable hands, the most effective weapon in support reserve line, for smashing an attack in force."* Frank was ordered to a position in front of Lagnicourt on

Monday 16th where he remained until being relieved on Tuesday 24th. The next day Frank was given some proper rest and ANZAC Day was celebrated. He was taken to Riencourt on Saturday 28th when he was provided with a hot bath, clean clothes and his bedding was aired. Frank paraded early on Tuesday 1st May when it was announced that he had been promoted to Lance Corporal. He undertook a route march to Gueudecourt in the morning of Wednesday 2nd and inspected the old front line, during the afternoon two football matches were played against the 3rd Company Australian Machine Gun Corps. In the evening an urgent order was received to send the Company into the line at Lagnicourt that was reached by 4.00am; over the next couple of days they came under heavy shell fire. The Germans launched a heavy gas attack on Monday 14th sending over thousands of shells until 3.45am the next morning. They followed it up with an attack that was repulsed by the good work of Frank and his team supporting the infantry who poured rapid fire on the advancing enemy. During the night further gas shells rained down and a 5-inch high velocity gun kept up a constant fire that was described in the War Diary as: "… extremely annoying in this neighbourhood". Frank was not relieved until Saturday 19th when at last he could escape the constant gas attacks. He helped organise his platoon to pack the limbers early on Tuesday 22nd then marched out of camp at 2.45pm. He arrived in Bazentin at 6.30pm where good billets were provided over night and the next day marched to Dernancourt. Frank was able to have another hot bath at Vivier Mill on Thursday 24th and in the afternoon he washed down the limbers. Training began on Monday 28th coupled with fatigues. Frank left from Albert on Friday 27th July bound for Steenbecque where he arrived at 9.30pm then marched to a prisoner of war camp north of Hazebrouck. Further training was provided until Wednesday 8th August when the equipment was packed up ready to move off to Vieux Berquin the next day. Frank was sent out on a series of tiring route marches and part of the training he undertook was rectifying gun stoppages whilst blindfolded.

Frank marched across the border into Belgium and was sent to 'Château Segard' where he prepared his gun to go back into the front line. Late on Wednesday 19th September he moved forward slowly along the roads toward the front. The traffic was heavy and the roads were badly congested. Finally Frank arrived in his allotted position and immediately came under heavy shell fire. At 5.40am on Thursday 20th the preliminary bombardment fell on the German lines and the infantry went forward and captured the first and second objectives. In the early afternoon Frank was mortally wounded during a German counter-attack. He was taken to a Casualty Clearing Station where he died. Frank is recorded as being buried in Belgian Battery Military Cemetery with reference number 31129 Sheet G, however, on Friday 30th December 1921 the Australian Graves Services wrote to confirm that Frank's remains had not been found or identified. In the CWGC description and history of the Belgian Battery Military Cemetery it states: "Seven of the burials are unidentified and special memorials commemorate three casualties known to have been buried in the cemetery, but whose graves could not be located." It can be assumed that young Frank is one of the burials.

His parents were sent his British War Medal no 45598, Victory Medal no 45076 and Memorial Plaque and Scroll no 3328815.

2004 PRIVATE
GEORGE WALTER VICKERY
1st/2nd Battalion London Regiment (Royal Fusiliers)
Died on Tuesday 16th February 1916, aged 17
Commemorated on Panel 52.

George was born in St Pancras, London, only son and younger child of Florence Louise Vickery, of 18 Hilldrop Road, London, and the late George Vickery, FNCA (his father had worked as a political agent).
He enlisted before the war and following mobilisation was sent to guard the Southampton to Amesbury railway station until sailing to Malta on Friday 4th September 1914. A ten-day journey brought George to Valletta where he served until Saturday 2nd January 1915 when he embarked for Marseilles. The port was reached on Wednesday 6th. George entrained to northern France and began to train with experienced troops before undertaking tours of duty in the front line.
George's first and only major action was at Hooge in July 1915 when flammenwerfer was used for the first time. George continued to serve on tours of duty on the Salient until he was killed by a shell bursting close to him.

2878 PRIVATE ROBERT PERCY WALLER
'D' Company,
1st/5th Battalion Durham Light Infantry
Died on Sunday 16th May 1915, aged 16
Commemorated on Panel 38.

Robert was born in Thonaby-on-Tees, eldest son of Thomas and Jane Ann Waller, of 85 Windsor Road, Stockton-on-Tees. He was educated locally.
Robert volunteered and was sent for training before

leaving for France with the Battalion, arriving in Boulogne on Sunday 18th April 1915 under the command of Lieutenant Colonel G O Spence. He entrained to northern France, arriving on Wednesday 21st and was billeted in the area of Cassel. Robert had only settled in for a day when he was ordered to parade in preparation for the move to the front. From the heights of Cassel the opposing artillery blasting and booming away on the Salient could be clearly heard and their flashes visible. Late on Friday 23rd a fleet of London buses, complete with their advertising hoardings, arrived to collect the Battalion. The buses rattled their way along the cobbled roads to Poperinghe and onward to Vlamertinghe where they were dropped off. Robert and the Battalion formed up to march along the tree lined cobbled road to camp at Brielen and they could clearly see the town of Ypres being bombarded and on fire. The Germans had launched the first gas attack at 5.00pm on Thursday 22nd and the line was under great pressure; the Battalion was sent to help support the position. Their hutted camp came under heavy fire but thankfully no casualties were suffered. After twelve hours in camp they were ordered to move forward via St Jan to Wieltje and take part in a counter-attack. Robert marched at 'double quick time' to Fortuin to take the line for the first time and helped repulse an attack. Robert survived his first tour, and action, in the front line. He continued to serve in and out of the line during the fierce action of The Second Battle of Ypres until Robert was killed on Sunday 16th May.

He is commemorated on the Stockton-on-Tees War Memorial.

14715 PRIVATE
CHARLES WILLIAM 'CHAS' WALTON
1st Battalion Lincolnshire Regiment
Died on Wednesday 16th June 1915, aged 17
Commemorated on Panel 21.

Chas was born in Sudbrook, Grantham, Lincolnshire, second son of Eliza Marshal (formerly Walton), of Wilsford Lane, Ancaster, Grantham, and the late Henry Walton, he had a twin sister, Nellie. Following his education he worked on a farm.
He volunteered in Bourne, Lincolnshire, and went out to France on Wednesday 12th May 1915. For Chas' story, see Private Levi Coles, see above.
Chas is commemorated on Ancaster War Memorial. His elder brother, Private Thomas Richard Walton, died on Monday 3rd July 1916 and is commemorated on the Thiepval Memorial.

1621 PRIVATE LOUIS WARWICK
1st/5th Battalion King's Own
(Royal Lancaster Regiment)
Died on Saturday 8th May 1915, aged 17
Commemorated on Panel 12.

Louis was born in Horwich, Lancashire, eldest son of George Albert and Annie Jane Warwick, of 29 Connie Street, Openshaw, Manchester. He had two younger sisters and a younger brother.
He enlisted in Lancaster on Friday 4th September 1914 and was sent for training in Didcot, Oxfordshire, and Sevenoaks, Kent. He entrained with the Battalion in Sevenoaks on Sunday 14th February 1915 for Southampton on an old cattle boat and sailed to Le Havre at 7.00am, arriving twenty-four hours later.
For Louis' story and that of the Battalion until Tuesday 4th May, see Private James Cathcart, above. Late on Tuesday 4th May Louis was relieved from the front line to dug-outs in the rear and returned to the line on Friday 7th. Louis took part in a counter-attack on Saturday 8th when he was killed.

7970 PRIVATE GEORGE WATT
1st Battalion Highland Light Infantry
Died on Tuesday 27th April 1915, aged 17
Commemorated on Panel 38.

George was born at home, son of Mrs Cumming (formerly Watt), of 18 Amos Close, Dalkeith.
He volunteered in Edinburgh and went out to France on Tuesday 5th January 1915 to join the Battalion in the field with a draft whilst they were serving in Rue de Bois sector. George served through the difficult Battle of Neuve Chapelle then returned to general tours of duty. After serving in the sector the Battalion was sent to serve on the Ypres Salient.
George was killed by shell fire during the opening stages of the Second Battle of Ypres.

2253 PRIVATE WALTER DAVID WEBB
3rd Battalion Royal Fusiliers
Died on Monday 26th April 1915, aged 15
Commemorated on Panel 6.

Walter was born in Oxford, son of Walter and Priscilla Webb, of 39 Wilmington Square, Spa Fields, London. He was educated locally.
He enlisted in Marylebone, London, and after training Walter went out to France with a draft, entrained for northern France then went to Belgium to join his Battalion in the field on Sunday 7th March 1915. After a short period

of training he commenced tours of duty in the front line. Walter had the opportunity of seeing Ypres before it was completely destroyed. Many shells and bombs had already landed on the town, but it remained relatively intact. It was a vibrant and quite exciting place for most soldiers, particularly for one so young. The shops remained open around the market square selling a wide range of souvenirs that were in particular demand. The cafés continued to ply their trade and expanded their pavement tables into the street that hindered many a marching soldier going into or out of the line.

At the outbreak of the Second Battle of Ypres Walter was back in the line at Gravenstafel. When the Battalion arrived in the trenches it was clear to all the men (and boys) that a German attack was about to commence. Walter had already had the misfortune to witness the first gas attack a couple of days before. At 3.30am on Saturday 24th the Germans launched their second gas attack, Walter and his comrades had little effective defence against gas, the equipment had not yet been invented, nor did they have much conception of the power and affects the gas could have. This was followed up by an enormous artillery barrage by the British to counter the German attacks. Attack and counter-attack followed and during the latter part of Monday 26th Walter was killed: his young body was not recovered and lies to this day unidentified on the battlefield.

15894 PRIVATE ARTHUR WEDGWOOD
1st Battalion Royal Scots Fusiliers
Died on Saturday 25th September 1915, aged 17
Commemorated on Panel 19.

Arthur was born on Wednesday 23rd March 1898 at Barrow Hill, Derbyshire, fourth child of William and Emma Wedgwood, of 222 South Street, New Whittington, Chesterfield, Derbyshire. He was educated locally then was employed in the foundry at the Staveley Coal and Iron Company Limited.

He volunteered in November 1914 in Chesterfield and was sent to train in Scotland. Arthur went out to France on Wednesday 12th May 1915 to join the Battalion whilst they were serving on the Salient. They had fought through the Second Battle of Ypres where they had taken considerable losses. Arthur settled down to tours of duty, mainly in the

Arthur Wedgwood

Hooge sector. He would take part in only one action that would cost him his life. For the Battle of Loos that would open a few miles to the south on Saturday 25th September a series of diversionary attacks were planned to distract the enemy. One took place at Bellewaarde: Arthur moved into the assembly trenches and waited for orders to attack. At 3.50am on Saturday 25th a preliminary bombardment began and half an hour later a mine was blown north of the Menin Road. The officers blew their whistles and clambered into No Man's Land followed by their men. The Battalion's objective was a German strong point north of *'Sanctuary Wood'*. The enemy defended their position well with devastating power. Arthur was mown down in a hail of bullets, with many of his comrades, as he charged to attack the enemy at the point of the bayonet. Arthur is commemorated on the War Memorial in St Barnabas Church, New Whittington.

9821 PRIVATE
HAROLD CHARLES WELLBELOVE
'B' Company,
1st Battalion Gloucestershire Regiment
Died on Saturday 7th November 1914, aged 16
Commemorated on Panel 34.

Harold was born in Kingston-upon-Thames, Surrey, son of Mrs Amelia E Turner, of 19 Bessborough Gardens, Westminster, London. He was educated locally.

He enlisted in Bristol and following the outbreak of war the Battalion mobilised. Harold sailed from Southampton to Le Havre on board the *SS Gloucester Castle* on Wednesday 12th August 1914. He, with the Battalion, were sent to Rouen and from there to Le Nouvion, a long and tiring train journey. They marched to Mons, the Brigade Diary recorded: *"The Gloucesters are pretty strong, but the whole position is very extended and not at all ideal for the defence (not half so good as the line we were on last evening)."*

At 3.00am on Monday 24th orders were sent to the Colonel that the Battalion should hold on at all costs and fresh supplies would be sent up but within two hours the order to commence the retirement was received, with a further order delaying the retirement! RQMS Brasington wrote: *"This order was received with great disappointment by all ranks, as they had so eagerly looked forward to a fight and showed the dissatisfaction usually shown by a British soldier at anything in the nature of retirement."* The first night was spent under the guns by one of Maubeuge's forts. The march then continued south. The Brigade Diary recorded: *"We were nearly blocked on the way by motor lorries which had dumped supplies for to-day (preserved meat, biscuits, jam, Oxo cubes* for iron rations) on the roadside. We picked these up as we passed." By 11.00am on Tuesday 1st September they had arrived in Villers-Cotterêts where artillery fire could be clearly heard but by the time they had rested and eaten the artillery was lessening in intensity and they continued to march southward. Captain Grazebrook recorded: *"We seemed to go miles in the dark, up hills and down valley, but always on. Distances always seem greater in the dark, but judging from the halts it couldn't have been more than 15 miles. At dawn we were told we were going to take up a defensive position, and even marched back a short distance, but nothing came of it and on we went again, on, on, on, always on."* Harold's march ended at Rozoy-en-Brie on Saturday 5th September — he had marched two hundred miles:

August	To	Miles
Monday 24th	Neuf Mesnil	17
Tuesday 25th	La Grand Fayt	15½
Wednesday 26th	Oisy	15
Thursday 27th	Bernot	23
Friday 28th	Bertaucourt	21
Saturday 29th	(Resting)	
Sunday 30th	Brandcourt	10
Monday 31st	Missy-aux-Bois	18
September		
Tuesday 1st	Mareuil	19
Wednesday 2nd	Crégy	18½
Thursday 3rd	Signy Signets	16½
Friday 4th	Moroux	11½
Saturday 5th	Rozoy	15

Harold now started to march northward, crossing the Petit Morin and onward to the Marne but fresh food was in short supply. Captain Grazebrook wrote: *"We got our first issue of fresh meat today, but by the time the cooks had a chance of stewing it, it was no longer fresh and had to be thrown away. Hard luck!"* Harold was not engaged in any action on the Marne as the Battalion pressed on to the Aisne. As they went through the village of Priez the results of battle could be seen. Captain Grazebrook wrote: *"Along the road on the other side of the village we pass for a mile or so the results: on either side of the road the remains of rifles, equipment and ammunition, graves of various men killed in action, spots where German shells had burst on horses and wagons, fearful messes in places, broken telegraph poles, dead horses and further piles of German equipment, etc. equally spread about. … This was most certainly the coldest night we had, the only protection we could get was from a wall built up of bundles of straw from a rick in the fields."* By Friday 11th the continuous hard marching, the weather conditions and poor food was having an effect on the Battalion as one of the officers recalled: *"Up to now we had not had many cases of dysentery or other sickness but the cold of the nights after day's heat, together with the wet, the repetition of tinned meats and insufficiently cooked food and the large quantity of only half-ripe apples and pears, were beginning to affect everyone."* Harold was ordered to dig in and over the ensuing weeks he was heavily engaged in action before being sent to Moulins until Friday 16th October when the move to Flanders commenced.

Harold arrived in Poperinghe on Tuesday 20th October. At 1.45am on Wednesday 21st he marched via Elverdinghe to Langemarck and immediately came under artillery fire. After being relieved he was sent via Wieltje to Hooge on Monday 26th where he took a position and began to dig in. At 5.30am on Thursday 29th the Germans attacked Gheluvelt. At 7.00am Harold and the Battalion was sent into support at Veldhoek. Gheluvelt, the village, was lost but the Germans were unable to break through to Ypres. Harold helped build a barricade at the Veldhoek crossroads; the German attack started to falter and the Battalion took a heavy toll of the advancing German infantry. Despite the end of the main attack Harold remained under attack until Monday 2nd November 1914 when he was sent to 'Sanctuary Wood' for rest. Early the next morning Harold heard the pounding of the guns bombarding Gheluvelt. He paraded and marched down the Menin Road where the Battalion came under heavy fire from 'coal-boxes'. From Veldhoek a Belgian armoured car was moving down the road pouring machine-gun fire at the advancing German infantry. Harold, under Captain Blunt, advanced through the woods towards Château Harenthage where his Captain was shot by a sniper in the shoulder. By 6.00pm Harold was entrenching his position and awaiting orders. Later in the evening an attack by the Battalion was made on the German lines, but their cheering and shouting as they advanced alerted the enemy to the attack. They rained fire on the advancing troops who were forced to retire but during the attack his Company Commander, Captain Blunt was killed. The Battalion was eventually relieved to 'Sanctuary Wood'.

Early on Tuesday 3rd Harold moved into the support trenches at Harenthage Château, however, the Battalion was not required and they were returned to their bivouac. Over a period of a few days the Battalion took the opportunity of re-organising themselves near Bellewaarde Farm after the heavy fighting of previous days. At 4.00pm on Friday 6th November Harold marched to the area west of Zillebeke, arriving in the dark to relieve the cavalry to the north of Zwarteleen. The next morning was misty and whilst orders were received to make an attack, conditions were not right and the attack was cancelled. Later in the day an attack was led by Captain Rising and Major Ingram towards Zwarteleen but as they were very much out in the open with very little cover they suffered heavily, with forty-three killed, including Harold. In addition forty-seven men were wounded and eight listed as missing.

R/8301 RIFLEMAN GEORGE WESTON
18th Battalion King's Royal Rifle Corps
Died on Monday 21st May 1917, aged 17
Commemorated on Panel 53.

George was born in Litchborough, Northamptonshire, eldest son of Mr J George and Mrs Sarah Weston, of 6 Browning Street, Salford, Manchester.

He volunteered in Manchester and went out to France on Wednesday 19th May 1915. George arrived on the Salient and was immediately sent into the line. He had only been serving in the trenches for a matter of a few hours before he was killed.

George is commemorated on Salford War Memorial.

10248 PRIVATE
EDWIN GEORGE WHITE
1st Battalion Wiltshire Regiment
Died on Friday 12th March 1915, aged 17
Commemorated on Panel 53.

Edwin was born in Lambeth, London, son of Arthur and Ada White, of 25 Dragon Road, Peckham, London.
Edwin went out to France on Tuesday 26th January 1915 to join the Battalion whilst they were serving in the Kemmel to St Eloi sector with billets in Loker. At 2.45am on Friday 12th March he marched through the ruins of Kemmel out to the line at the Spanbroekmolen, arriving at 5.30am. Edwin waited in the watery trenches until 2.30pm when a preliminary bombardment began. At 4.10pm the whistles were blown and Edwin went over the top and charged towards the German lines. The bombardment had not cut or obliterated the enemy barbed wire so little progress could be made. German machine gunners had a range of easy targets and in the mêlée Edwin was shot dead.

467096 PRIVATE
LEONARD CHARLES WHITE
42nd Battalion Canadian Infantry (Quebec Regiment)
Died on Friday 2nd June 1916, aged 17
Commemorated on Panel 28.

Leonard's signature

Leonard was the fifth son of Edward and Alice White, of 3116, 42nd Avenue West, Kerrisdale,

Vancouver, British Columbia. He had older siblings, Lionel, Frank, Gertrude, Stanley and Harold.

He volunteered in Calgary, Alberta, on Monday 26th July 1915, where he claimed to have been born on Wednesday 7th April 1897, in Croydon, Surrey, and was working as a farm hand. Leonard was a Presbyterian, 5ft 7in tall, with a 34½in chest, a fair complexion, brown eyes and hair.

For Leonard's story and that of the Battalion, see Private Francis Savoie, above.

9795 PRIVATE ERIC WIDMER
1st Battalion Dorsetshire Regiment
Died on Sunday 2nd May 1915, aged 16
Commemorated on Panel 37.

Eric was born in Manchester, Lancashire, third son of Emil and Henrietta Widmer, of 48 Canning Road, Walthamstow, London. He was educated locally.

He enlisted in Stratford, London, and was sent for training before leaving for France with a large draft of men, joining the Battalion in Le Touret on Tuesday 27th October 1914. Eric's first few days in northern France were spent marching with the Battalion, finally arriving in Strazeele on Saturday 31st. At 7.00am the next morning he prepared his kit then paraded ready to be taken across the border into Belgium. A fleet of London buses arrived, still bedecked with their pre-war advertisements, to take the Battalion to Neuve Eglise where they were billeted. No time was given to train for the front line. Over three hundred men who had arrived only a week earlier took the line for a sixteen day tour of duty in Ploegsteert Wood from Monday 2nd November. The trenches were shallow and when Eric and his comrades dug two feet down into the mud they hit water. No dug-outs existed and cover from the intense artillery was nonexistent.

On New Year's Day 1915 Eric was sent with the Battalion to billets in Bailleul, a busy bustling town that provided a wide range of entertainments and amusements for the troops, a welcome diversion from the front line. During early January he was given training by the Royal Engineers in bomb throwing as well as how to make hurdles and fascines. Until Tuesday 2nd March 1915 Eric served in the Wulverghem sector.

Eric marched from Bailleul to an unpleasant camp between Ouderdom and Vlamertinghe where he remained for two days before continuing his march northeastward into Ypres town and out to the front along the Ypres to Comines Canal, close to 'The Bluff'. Ypres was still very much the medieval town and not yet destroyed. Lieutenant Colonel Ransome wrote: *"The town of Ypres was at this time quite habitable. Only* the portion round the square in which the Cloth Hall stood, and the neighbourhood of the station, had been shelled badly. Many cafés and shops were open. A large market was held regularly, when the streets were thronged with peasants from the neighbouring villages. Any hostile shelling that took place was directed on the Cloth Hall and the Menin Gate."

Eric continued to serve in the sector for some time, Lieutenant Colonel Ransome wrote: "The Dorsets at this time completely dominated the Germans opposite them. Enemy sniping was reduced to a minimum, and any German sniper who became a nuisance was marked down and invariably dealt with successfully. A careful programme of machine-gun harassing fire was carried out every night, and a number of contrivances, calculated to annoy the enemy and reduce his moral, were invented and put into practice by Lieut. F. J. Morley.

These were the days before the Stokes mortar and the Mills bomb, but Lieut. Morley used an improvised mortar — in reality a stove pipe, and even filled bottles with powder and nails and employed them as hand-grenades." Whilst on 'The Bluff' the British mines were blown on Hill 60 and in the ensuing battle was captured. Eric and the Battalion kept up a continuous fire on the German lines opposite them to keep them occupied as Hill 60 was taken. The Germans were keen on retaking the Hill and punishing the British for its capture, and Eric came under sustained withering fire.

The Germans launched the first gas attack on Thursday 22nd April against the French Colonial troops in the northern sector of the Salient. Major Cowie, Officer Commanding the Battalion, made arrangements for the Battalion to withdraw if necessary. Major Cowie took his men to bivouac at Kruisstraat on Sunday 25th from where Eric was sent forward to assist in digging the 'Hooge Switch'. He marched to Hill 60 on Thursday 29th to relieve the 1st Battalion Devonshire Regiment. Lieutenant Colonel Ransome wrote: "The approach to the front line was an unpleasant experience. The Germans were employing a thorough programme of harassing fire. The canal bridge, all roads and tracks, and finally the railway cutting leading to Hill 60, were under incessant shell fire. The support position consisted of shelters dug into the hill-side and covered with corrugated iron and sand-bags."

The Germans counter-attacked against Hill 60 using gas on Sunday 2nd May; Lieutenant Colonel Ransome wrote: "The first news of the presence of gas was a telephonic message from Captain Hawkins, whose company, 'D', was holding the left portion of the front, known as the Zwarteleen salient. He described the situation as serious and expressed a doubt as to his ability to hold his trenches, owing to gas. It appeared that the enemy had discharged gas from at least five points in their front line — three opposite the right trench, No. 38, and two in front of Zwarteleen Salient. The breeze carried the gas to the left of No. 38, garrisoned by 'A' Company, but Hill 60 trench and the salient were seriously affected.

Major Cowie, accompanied by the Adjutant, proceeded to the Hill and assumed command there. He found that Captain Batten had made excellent dispositions and that the situation was quiet, except for intermittent bombing. He then went to the Salient, now garrisoned by the Devons, and found the deep and narrow trenches blocked with dead, with many others dying in terrible agony. It was a deplorable sight and one which no eyewitness can ever forget."

There was little defence from the effects of gas as little was known about how to combat it at the time. Eric's young life ended due to the effects of gas and his body was not recovered from the field.

A junior officer wrote an article for a Dorset newspaper: "I expect you have heard how the Germans on this 'Hill 60' played us the dirtiest trick that any British regiment has yet had to put up with. The Canadians did not have it like we did, they had it from four hundred to five hundred yards away, whereas our trenches are at the most forty yards from the Germans. I saw more of the affair than anyone else, so I can tell you exactly what happened. At about seven o'clock I came out of my dugout and saw a hose sticking over the German parapet, which was just starting to spout out a thick yellow cloud with a tinge of green in it. The gas came out with a hiss that you could hear quite plainly. I at once shouted to my men to put on respirators (bits of flannel), then I got mine and went and warned my Captain, who did not know yet. Then the Huns began a terrible bombardment, not so much at us, but at our supports and our dressing station.

Now, either they had miscalculated the direction of the wind or else it had changed, for the gas did not come directly towards us but went slantwise, then our trench being so close the gas went into part of the German trenches as well as ours. They bolted from theirs when they got a whiff of the filthy stuff, a few of our men staggered away down the hill, some got into a wood behind it and died there, as the ground was low and the gas followed them, others only got as far as the mine head and communication trenches. The Company in support on my left moved into the firing line, as did also half of my platoon, consequently, I was left with a few men to do all the rescue work. My men were splendid; they all came with me into the gas, except the ones I ordered to stay behind, and we must have saved scores of lives. The men in most cases were lying insensible in the bottom of the trenches, and quite a number were in the mine head, which was the worst possible place. The best place after the first rush of gas was the firing line, being the highest point.

I was the only officer not in the firing line, and I should think quite two hundred men passed through my hands, some died with me and some died on the way down. The Battalion had, I believe, three hundred and thirty-seven casualties. I can't understand how it was I was not knocked out; it must have been the work I had to do. I was simply mad with rage, seeing strong men drop to the ground and die in this way. They were *in agonies. I had to argue with many of them as to whether they were dead or not. Why we got it so hot was because of the closeness of our trenches to the Germans, and this affair does away with the idea that it is not deadly. I saw two men staggering over a field in our rear last night, and when I went and looked for them this morning they were both dead. Altogether, I suppose, one hundred or two hundred men and two or three officers are dead or will die of the stuff. I am absolutely sickened. Clean killing is at least comprehensive, but this murder by slow agony absolutely knocks me. The whole civilian world ought to rise up and exterminate those swine across the hill."*

10966 PRIVATE
CHARLES FREDERICK WILLIAMS
1st Battalion Wiltshire Regiment
Died on Tuesday 22nd June 1915, aged 17
Commemorated on Panel 53.

Charles was born at home, oldest son of Frederick Charles and Mary Ann Williams, of 5 Market Place, Melksham, Wiltshire. He was educated locally.
He volunteered in Devizes, Wiltshire, and went out to France on Tuesday 4th May 1915. Charles was sent to join the Battalion with a draft whilst they were serving between Hooge and *'Sanctuary Wood'*. The Second Battle of Ypres had run its course and the area was relatively quiet.

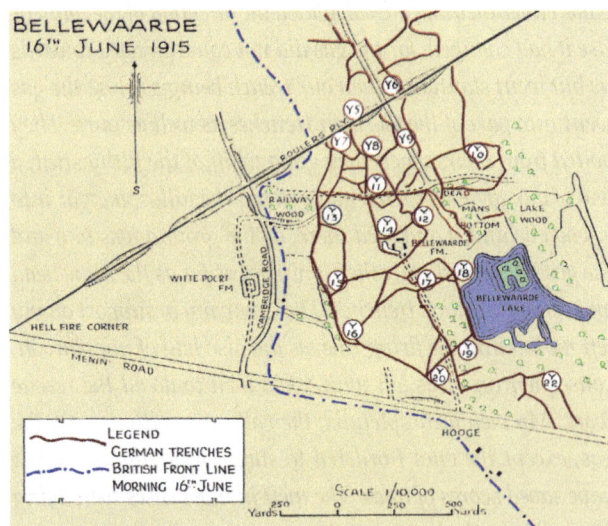

Charles took part in a significant and carefully planned action in the early hours of Wednesday 16th June. The objectives around Bellewaarde were captured but as the position was being consolidated the enemy began a counter-attack. The Germans came forward in significant numbers and as the bombs ran out to halt their advance the Battalion was forced to retire. It was a costly action with over two hundred officers and men killed, wounded or listed as missing. Charles was to make a further attack on the same position six

days later. The German machine gunners remained untouched by the preliminary bombardment so were able to pour heavy fire on the attackers. Charles was cut down and killed instantaneously.
He is commemorated on Melksham War Memorial.

9049 PRIVATE
FREDERICK PHILIP WILLIAMS
4th Battalion The King's (Liverpool Regiment)
Died on Tuesday 27th April 1915, aged 17
Commemorated on Panel 4.

Frederick was born in Exeter, Devon, son of Mrs Susan Jane O'Brien, of 60 Arlington Street, Liverpool.
He volunteered in Liverpool and was sent for training in Edinburgh. Frederick left with the Battalion, under the command of Lieutenant Colonel John Woolley Allen, from Southampton and sailed to Le Havre where he disembarked on Saturday 6th March 1915. Frederick entrained to Lillers, via Hazebrouck, for final training. Following a night in the town he marched to a billet in a farm at Robecq. The onward move toward the battlefield continued on Wednesday 10th arriving in Vieille Chapelle where the Battle of Neuve Chapelle could be clearly heard. Frederick did not serve in the action and after undertaking practical training in the trenches he transferred to Calonne where from Saturday 10th to Friday 23rd April was instructed in attacking tactics.
Late on Friday 23rd Frederick began a series of moves that would take him to the Ypres Salient. He reached La Brique at 5.00pm on Monday 26th. At 3.00am the next morning he marched to St Jan where at noon Frederick took part in his only attack. It was recorded: *"The King's, splendidly led by their officers, advanced in short rushes, with the enemy pumping lead into them and men falling in heaps. A number, under Major E. M. Beall, succeeded in getting to within two hundred yards of the enemy's line, but it was evident that the wire in front of the German trench was untouched, and it was impossible to push on further. This spirited dash enable a number of the 1/4th Gurkhas to join the small party which was holding on to the farm."*

414441 PRIVATE
HAROLD EMMERSON WILSON
8th Company Canadian Machine Gun Corps
Died on Friday 2nd June 1916, aged 17
Commemorated on Panel 32.

Harold's signature

Harold was the son of the late W S and Jane Wilson, of New Waterford, Cape Breton, Nova Scotia.

He volunteered on Monday 9th August 1915 in Sydney, Nova Scotia, where he claimed to have been born on Wednesday 17th February 1897 and was working as a druggist (working for a pharmacist). Harold was 5ft 7in tall, with a 33in chest, a dark complexion, brown eyes, dark brown hair, and had a small scar on his right foot. After training in Canada Harold was sent to England to continue his training before joining the Company in the field whilst they were serving on the Salient.

Harold's first experience of the front line began on Monday 24th April 1916 for a four-day tour of duty. His next tour in early May took him to the Hooge sector where he served until being sent to billets near Poperinghe from Monday 22nd May. After a week Harold marched along the pavé towards Ypres and throughout the march the enemy was shelling the road and its immediate vicinity. He carefully made his way around Ypres and out to the trenches in front of 'Maple Copse' arriving shortly before midnight on Wednesday 31st. Throughout the warm and breezy Thursday 1st June the German artillery shelled the sector heavily directed by several observation balloons. At 8.30am the next morning an intense bombardment began directed by German aeroplanes flying low over the sector. The enemy infantry attacked in force that overwhelmed the defending Canadian forces. Harold, together with many of his comrades, died on that terrible day. His body was lost as the battle raged on.

3412 PRIVATE RALPH CECIL WILSON
1st/2nd Battalion London Regiment (Royal Fusiliers)
Died on Friday 11th June 1915, aged 17
Commemorated on Panel 52.

Ralph was the son of Leonora Wilson, of 89 Coleshill Buildings, Pimlico Road, London, and the late Arthur James Wilson.

He went out to France on Sunday 9th May 1915 to join the Battalion with a draft. Ralph undertook three weeks of tours of duty without being involved in any particular action when he was killed by a shrapnel shell bursting close to him.

3389 PRIVATE JOHN WINN
1st/8th Battalion Durham Light Infantry
Died on Monday 26th April 1915, aged 16
Commemorated on Panel 38.

John was the son of Joseph Winn, of 9 Dale Street, Ushaw Moor, County Durham. He was educated locally.

He enlisted in Durham and was sent for training. John arrived in Boulogne on Saturday 17th April

1915 from where he was sent to northern France to continue training for the front line. At 2.00pm on Friday 23rd he paraded at Le Riveld near Cassel, then marched to Steenvoorde where the Battalion was met by a fleet of omnibuses and driven via Poperinghe to Vlamertinghe. John marched towards Ypres and the sound of battle, continuing to Verlorenhoek, and during the march came under shell fire for the first time. The Battalion moved onward to Frezenberg arriving on the Gravenstafel Ridge, 'Boetleer's Farm', at 3.00am on Sunday 25th where the Battalion supported the 8th Canadian Battalion. The Germans commenced an artillery barrage on their line from 9.00am until 2.00pm when their infantry attacked. The first attack was repulsed; train loads of reinforcements were seen arriving and further attacks ensued. By 4.00am on Monday 26th the Battalion was forced back to the Hannebeek and John was killed during one of the many attacks, his body was not recovered.

He is commemorated on Ushaw Moor War Memorial.

12901 PRIVATE
JOHN HUTLEY WINNAN
2nd Battalion Duke of Cornwall's Light Infantry
Died on Friday 23rd April 1915, aged 17
Commemorated on Panel 20.

John was born at home, third son of Edward and Eliza Ann Winnan, of 64 Killigrew Street, Falmouth, Cornwall. He had older siblings, Edward, Holly, Sidney and Felicitra and younger siblings Bertie, Christopher and Carrie. He was educated locally.

He volunteered in Falmouth and went out to France on Thursday 1st April 1915.

For John's story, and that of the Battalion, see Private George Hood.

144969 PRIVATE ERNEST WOOD
4th Canadian Mounted Rifles
(Central Ontario Regiment)
Died on Friday 2nd June 1916, aged 16
Commemorated on Panel 32.

Ernest's signature

Ernest was born in Kentish Town, London, son of Frederick Peace Wood and Louisa Mary Ann Wood, of 177 Gowan Avenue, Todmorden, Toronto, Ontario. Ernest had elder sister, Mary.

He volunteered on Monday 23rd August 1915 in Smith Falls where he claimed to have been born on Friday 19th March 1897 in Chelsea, London, and was working as a labourer. Ernest was 5ft 3in tall, with a 32½in chest, a ruddy complexion, grey eyes, light coloured hair and four vaccination marks on his left arm. He was considered to be a little under developed but it was expected that Ernest would soon come up to the required standard.

Ernest joined the Battalion in the line on Thursday 16th March 1916 just as they moved to Zillebeke where they remained until mid-May when they were relieved until the end of the month and undertook training.

Ernest was ordered to parade in full pack ready to return to the line on Wednesday 31st May. He collected his gas mask and iron rations before the Battalion left by train for Ypres Asylum, to the west of the town. They marched to 'Transport Farm' from where they took over the line at Mount Sorrel. At 6.00am their commander, Lieutenant Colonel Ussher visited each Company to ensure all was prepared and ready for a visit by Major General Malcolm Mercer later that morning (General Mercer was killed on Saturday 3rd and buried in Lijssenthoek Military Cemetery). As the General and his party were being led forward for the visit the Germans launched an artillery barrage which lasted four and a half hours. The moment the barrage relented a mine was blown and the infantry charged forward in large numbers. The artillery and the mine had been particularly effective and destroyed the front line, many of the defenders were buried alive or blown to pieces. Ernest was killed: over ninety per cent of the Battalion were killed, wounded or listed missing in the action.

3613 PRIVATE JACK WOODCOCK
1st/5th Battalion Duke of Wellington's
(West Riding Regiment)
Died on Tuesday 9th November 1915, aged 16
Commemorated on Panel 20.

Jack was born in Collingham, Yorkshire, son of John and Kate Woodcock, of Malling's Cottages, Ampthill Road, Bedford. He was educated locally.

He enlisted in Mirfield, Yorkshire, and was sent for training. Jack's comrades from the Battalion embarked in Folkestone, Kent, for Boulogne on Wednesday 14th April 1915 whilst Jack remained in England training. Jack left with a draft to join the Battalion in the field on Tuesday 29th June. He soon got into training with his experienced comrades who taught him as well as possible to keep safe whilst in the line. Jack undertook tours of duty that were interspersed with rest and training until he was killed in the front line on the Salient.

414927 PRIVATE
PERCY ARNOLD WRIGHT
13th Battalion Canadian Infantry (Quebec Regiment)
Died on Tuesday 13th June 1916, aged 17
Commemorated on Panel 24.

Percy's signature

Percy was the adopted son of Mrs Roland Wright, his aunt, of 10 Doyle Street, Truro, Nova Scotia.

He volunteered on Tuesday 10th August 1915 in Aldershot, Hampshire, where he claimed to have been born on Wednesday 21st July 1897, and was working as a pipe fitter. Percy was 5ft 7¼in tall, with a 36in chest, a fair complexion, blue eyes, fair coloured hair, and a vaccination mark on his left arm.

He trained in Canada and England before joining the Battalion with a draft in Belgium.

Percy marched to billets near 'Red Lodge' in the Ploegsteert sector on Friday 17th March 1916 and after some rest began fatigues. A week later he paraded in the field next to 'Underhill Farm' then marched off to Méteren. Percy undertook some training but most of the time was given to rest and recreation. At 4.00am on Tuesday 28th Percy got up to pack his kit and clean up the billets until 8.00am when the Battalion paraded on the Méteren to Schaexhen road. The Pipe Band led the way to 'Dickebusch Huts', via Bailleul and Loker. Throughout the morning of Thursday 30th enemy aeroplanes buzzed the camp and shortly afterwards a number of 'whizz-bangs' fell around the area without causing much damage. Late in the evening Percy went to the front line at 'Glasgow Cross Roads'. During the five-day tour the Battalion took a number of casualties, mainly from rifle fire or rifle grenades that exploded in the trenches — those who were killed were buried in 'Railway Dugouts'. After three days in Dickebusch Percy was taken to the 'Hop Factory' in Poperinghe for training. Early on Friday 15th April Percy was issued with three days worth of rations then boarded an omnibus that took him to 'Bedford House' from where he marched to 'Woodcote House' and into the trenches between 'Lovers Lane' and 'New Years Trench', with Colonel Buchanan establishing his Headquarters in 'Gordon Terrace'. The enemy artillery targeted Percy's line that caused considerable damage to the parapet and inflicted seven casualties. During Tuesday 18th and Wednesday 19th a large number of casualties were sustained from shellfire and everyone was pleased to be relieved to Dickebusch on Sunday 23rd but sad to leave so many comrades buried in the field. Percy moved to 'Dominion Lines' on Tuesday 2nd May for a week of training. He returned to the front for a sixteen-day tour then entrained to *'Patricia Lines'* for rest and was able to have a hot bath. He visited Poperinghe with his mates to enjoy all that the town had to offer, with its bustling cafés, shops, brothels and other entertainments.

During the morning of Friday 2nd June Percy paraded and after PT went on a route march then returned to the camp for training. After lunch he enjoyed a Battalion sports afternoon. At the front the Germans had launched a significant attack at Mount Sorrel and the line was under threat of being broken. At 7.30pm Colonel Buchanan received orders for the Battalion to stand to. Shortly afterwards he led them towards Zillebeke but, due to the terrible congestion on the roads that were also under artillery fire, it took until 2.00am to reach their position. Before the Battalion could be deployed they lost eight men killed, a further ten died from their wounds with another thirty hospitalised, all from shellfire. Throughout the day Percy remained under fire until the early evening when he moved forward to *'Maple Copse'* where he dug in to consolidate the new position that was made more difficult as the rain began to fall heavily. Percy was relieved on Wednesday 7th to *'Café Belge'* then onto Dickebusch where he was collected by an omnibus and driven to

...the Café Belge

'Camp I' beyond Reninghelst. The next morning, when the roll was called, it revealed that over one hundred and twenty were killed, wounded or missing. Percy spent the morning cleaning his rifle and kit followed by himself. He was then given training for a forthcoming attack at *'Observation Ridge'* and *'Vigo Street'*.

Percy paraded on Sunday 11th June and marched via Reninghelst, Ouderdom, Dickebusch to *'Woodcote House'* then onto *'Railway Dugouts'*. During the afternoon General Currie visited the Battalion and congratulated all ranks on the good work they had undertaken the week before. He returned to the front line where a heavy bombardment began late on Monday 12th and at 1.30am Percy was led forward into No Man's Land. The enemy had a good field of fire and took account of a large number of the Battalion, including Percy, they were buried where the fell, where possible. The enemy also lost heavily and a number of prisoners were taken who were passed back to be sent to the cage. The Battalion had lost twelve officers and two hundred and ninety-two men were killed, wounded or listed as missing.

23345 PRIVATE
ARTHUR JAMES YEOMAN
3rd Battalion Worcestershire Regiment
Died on Tuesday 21st September 1915, aged 17
Commemorated on Panel 34.

Arthur was born at home, second son of Isaac Henry Lea and Edith Mary Yeoman, of 85 Mary Street, Balsall Heath, Birmingham. He had an elder and a younger brother, and two younger sisters. Arthur was educated locally.

He volunteered in Birmingham and went out to France on Sunday 11th July 1915. Arthur entrained with other members of the draft to Poperinghe to join the Battalion whilst they were in bivouac just outside the town at Busseboom.

Arthur had his first experience of the front line at St Eloi on Wednesday 21st July. During the week-long tour of duty both the enemy and the British blew mines and there was a constant artillery duel. He spent a large amount of time reconstructing or repairing the trenches. As soon as his work was complete a bombardment would wreck the trench and he would have to start over again. Late on Wednesday 28th Arthur marched to a bivouac at Dickebusch where he rested then trained until Tuesday 3rd August. His next tour of duty was at La Brique that was somewhat quieter in comparison to St Eloi. Following the tour he was sent to rest at Ouderdom and on Friday 27th went into the line at Hooge. He remained on tours of duty in the sector until he was killed. Arthur returned to the trenches for the last time on Sunday 19th September where the enemy were pounding the line, almost non-stop. A shell burst close to him and he was killed.

432719 PRIVATE
ARTHUR WESLEY YOUNG
49th Battalion Canadian Infantry (Alberta Regiment)
Died on Friday 2nd June 1916, aged 16
Commemorated on Panel 30.

Arthur's signature

Arthur was the son of Mr and Mrs George R Young, of Picton, Ontario.

He volunteered in Edmonton, Alberta, on Tuesday 12th January 1915 when he claimed to have been born on Thursday 30th November 1893 and worked as a butter maker. Arthur was a Methodist, 5ft 4in tall, with a 35in chest, a fair complexion, grey eyes and fair coloured hair.

For Arthur's story, see Private John Dunlop, above.

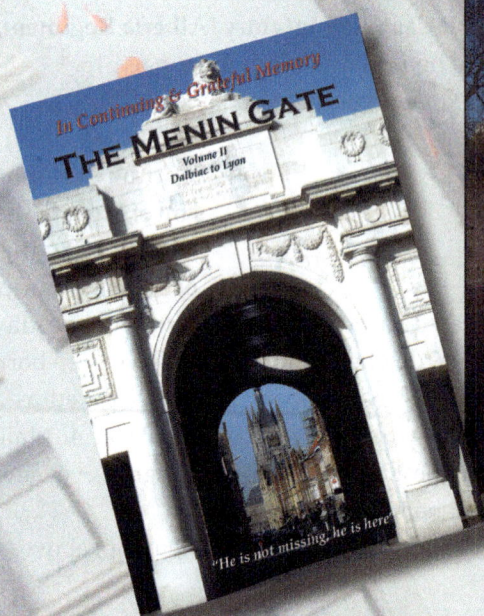

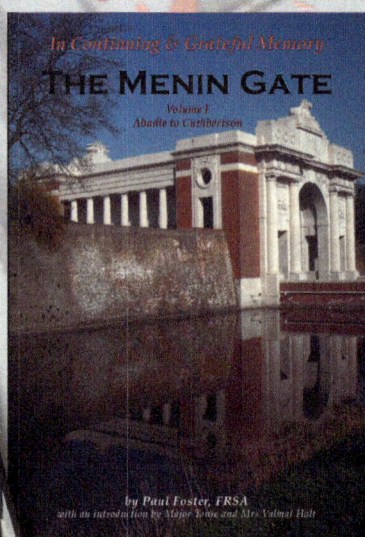

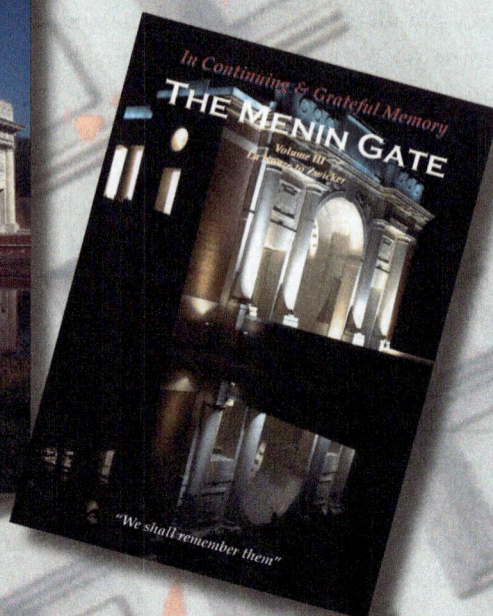

'In Continuing & Grateful Memory'
THE PLOEGSTEERT SECTOR

This 502 page book includes profusely illustrated cameos on five hundred individuals who are commemorated on the Ploegsteert Memorial or buried in the surrounding twelve cemeteries, together with a detailed tour of the sector to accompany the text (and a photographic tour of the inaccessible parts of Ploegsteert Wood); the history of the Christmas Truce; General Erich Ludendorff's history of the German Spring Offensive; and general tourist information to assist the visitor.

The Ploegsteert sector is a fascinating area to visit. It first came to public prominence as the centre of the Christmas Truce in December 1914 but the desperate fighting that took place prior is often overlooked as most concentrate on the First Battle of Ypres that raged only a few miles to the north. The sector was active throughout the war although it was not involved in a major action until 1917 during the Battle of Messines and again during the German Spring Offensive in April 1918.

Order on line visit: www.remembering1418.com
or send a cheque payable to 'W P Foster'
for £25.00 to: IC&G, 15 Cress Way, Faversham, Kent ME13 7NH.

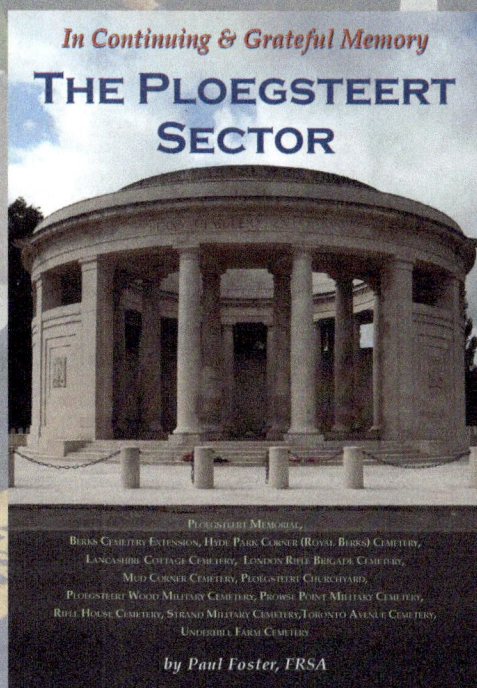

In Continuing & Grateful Memory
THE PLOEGSTEERT SECTOR

PLOEGSTEERT MEMORIAL,
BERKS CEMETERY EXTENSION, HYDE PARK CORNER (ROYAL BERKS) CEMETERY,
LANCASHIRE COTTAGE CEMETERY, LONDON RIFLE BRIGADE CEMETERY,
MUD CORNER CEMETERY, PLOEGSTEERT CHURCHYARD,
PLOEGSTEERT WOOD MILITARY CEMETERY, PROWSE POINT MILITARY CEMETERY,
RIFLE HOUSE CEMETERY, STRAND MILITARY CEMETERY, TORONTO AVENUE CEMETERY,
UNDERHILL FARM CEMETERY.

by Paul Foster, FRSA

'In Continuing & Grateful Memory'
FROM YPRES TO ZILLEBEKE VIA HOOGE

This 550 page book includes cameos on nearly 500 hundred individuals who are buried in twelve cemeteries. It is illustrated throughout with photographs of the men, contemporary photographs and illustrations in black and white (although many in colour), with the majority of the maps and diagrams in colour. Of the individuals included in the publication are: six Victoria Cross winners, ten who were Shot At Dawn, fifteen Olympians and international sportsmen, a wide range of the 'establishment', including HH Prince Maurice of Battenberg, and eight sets of brothers who lie buried together — these are only a few of the fascinating tales that are related in the book. I am particularly delighted to have been able to include a page dedicated to my good friends John Giles, the Founder of The Western Front Association, and his wife Margery, with a lovely tribute written by their son, Howard.

Nigel Buckle wrote: "The book is an essential when visiting the Ypres Salient. It was a revelation to read the fascinating stories of so many soldiers who lie buried in the cemeteries. For me, it brought the Salient alive once more."

In Continuing & Grateful Memory

FROM YPRES TO ZILLEBEKE VIA HOOGE

by Paul Foster, FRSA

Order on line visit:
www.remembering1418.com
or send a cheque payable to 'W P Foster'
for £32.99 to: IC&G, 15 Cress Way,
Faversham, Kent ME13 7NH.

BIRR CROSS ROADS CEMETERY
HOOGE CRATER CEMETERY
MAPLE COPSE CEMETERY
MENIN ROAD SOUTH MILITARY CEMETERY
PERTH CEMETERY (CHINA WALL)
RAMPARTS CEMETERY, LILLE GATE
RE GRAVE, RAILWAY WOOD
SANCTUARY WOOD CEMETERY
TUILERIES BRITISH CEMETERY
YPRES RESERVOIR CEMETERY
YPRES TOWN CEMETERY & EXTENSION
ZILLEBEKE CHURCHYARD

'In Continuing & Grateful Memory'
BOY SOLDIERS KILLED IN BELGIUM 1

This 442 page book provides 450 cameos of young boys aged between 14 and 17 who gave their lives during the First World War. It is a companion to Volume 2 that covers those commemorated on the Menin Gate only.

The boy soldiers are buried in all parts of Belgium in nearly 100 cemeteries. As with Volume 2 I have included some stories of 18 year old officers to illustrate how young so many of the officers were who came straight from school to command troops on the Western Front.

In addition there is a wealth of additional information that includes lengthy cameos on Jack Cornwell, the youngest Victoria Cross winner, Lieutenant Geoffrey Ottley who was only 18 when he was awarded the Distinguished Service Order and the story of Boys Bradford, VC, MC, who was the youngest British General at 25. All three gave their lives during the First World War.

The book is profusely illustrated with colour maps, contemporary photographs and illustrations.

In Continuing & Grateful Memory

BOY SOLDIERS KILLED IN BELGIUM 1

Over 400 individual stories of the young men aged 14, 15, 16 and 17 who died fighting in the trenches of Belgium during the Great War

"He was too young to fight and too young to die"

BY PAUL FOSTER, FRSA

Order on line visit:
www.remembering1418.com
or send a cheque payable to 'W P Foster'
for £28.99 to: IC&G, 15 Cress Way, Faversham, Kent ME13 7NH.

"I Was There!"

During the First World War and in its immediate aftermath a large number of books based on letter and diaries of those who were killed were published. Many of them were private publications compiled by their immediate family and are no longer available. After some consideration I selected a series of such books and faithfully reproduced the original. Where appropriate, I have added contemporary illustrations and photographs. In each publication an additional section has been added that provides a series of cameos on a selection of those mentioned in the text that significantly adds to the appreciation of events discussed in the letters and diaries.

The books are filled with fascinating details often missing from other publications and puts you in the front line with the troops looking at the war through their eyes and recorded at the time.

THE BOOKS CAN BE ORDERED FROM

www.remembering1418.com

or by post from 15 Cress Way, Faversham, Kent ME13 7NH

(cheques payable to Paul Foster)

THE LETTERS OF ARTHUR GEORGE HEATH
6th Battalion Queen's Own (Royal West Kent Regiment)

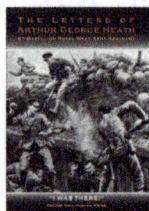

Lieutenant Arthur Heath volunteered on Thursday 20th August 1914 and his letters home and to his friends begin from that date. They chart his training in England, leaving for France and then serving in northern France in the trenches. His letters reflect the optimism felt by so many men and then the reality of life at the front. Lieutenant Heath was killed in action Friday 8th October 1915 at Loos. The original book was published by his family in 1917. In Part II there are cameos on thirty-four personalities mentioned in his letters.

162 pages — £7.99

ACTIVE-SERVICE DIARY
1st Battalion Irish Guards

The letters of Lieutenant Teddy Shears cover the period from Monday 22nd January 1917 to Wednesday 4th July 1917 when he finally was able to serve in France. Teddy left with a draft and you follow him into the front line where his optimistic and cheery letters provided a detailed experience of an officer and his men. Teddy served on the Somme and on the Salient where he was killed when hit by a shell splinter. The original book was published by his parents in 1919. In Part II there are cameos on twenty personalities mentioned in his letters.

104 pages — £7.99

DENIS OLIVER BARNETT, IN HAPPY MEMORY
Artists Rifles and Leinster Regiment

Denis Barnett volunteered and enlisted in the Artists Rifles. He left for France on Monday 26th October 1914 and served with them until he was commissioned on Saturday 9th January 1915 to the Leinsters. Denis served in northern France and on the Ypres Salient where he was mortally wounded and taken to Poperinghe where he died on Monday 16th August 1915. The original book was produced by his family shortly after his death. In Part II there are cameos on over twenty personalities and events mentioned in his letters.

220 pages — £9.45

A MEMOIR,
EDWARD WYNDHAM TENNANT
4th Battalion Grenadier Guards

Edward 'Bim' Tennant was the son of Edward, Baron Glenconner and Lady Pamela. The family was part of 'the establishment' and very well connected. He was much loved by his mother who produced the original book in his memory and traces his life from a baby, his school life and then as a soldier in France. It also contains many of his poems including those written in the trenches. The book is highly detailed and provides a fascinating insight into the attitudes of society in Edwardian Britain, Bim's family life and friends (many of whom were killed in the war), his schooling and the excitement of a newly commissioned officer going to war. Bim was killed on Friday 22nd September 1916 on the Somme and he is buried in Guillemont Road Cemetery together with many of his friends and contemporaries. In Part II there are cameos on fifty-eight personalities mentioned in his letters.
358 pages — £11.99

GILBERT WALTER LYTTELTON TALBOT
7th Battalion Rifle Brigade

The story and letters of Gilbert Talbot, in whose memory 'Talbot House' was named in Poperinghe, is fascinating. Many visit both 'TOC H' and Gilbert's grave in Sanctuary Wood but know little about the man himself. His family were aristocratic and he had a traditional upbringing for a boy of his background. He became President of the Oxford Union and a glittering career in politics beckoned but his life ended at Hooge on Friday 30th July 1915. The letters and well written commentary are exemplary that any student of the First World War should not miss. The original book was produced by his father in 1917. In Part II there are cameos on thirty-one personalities mentioned in his letters and much more.
132 pages — £7.99

SOLDIER AND DRAMATIST, BEING THE
LETTERS OF HAROLD CHAPIN
Royal Army Medical Corps

This book of letters from Harold Chapin to his mother, wife and son provide an interesting slant on the First World War. He was an American, a well-known actor, an author and a playwright. At the outbreak of war he volunteered and enlisted in the Royal Army Medical Corps serving in France from March 1915. Although not in the front line manning the parapet Harold undertook dangerous and important work at the front. His cheerful 'newsy' letters are full of fascinating details that fill in many gaps when learning of life on the Western Front in northern France. Harold's service was cut short when he was killed during the Battle of Loos and is now commemorated on the Loos Memorial. In addition to Harold's letters in Part II provides information on four of his plays and an appreciation by E B Osborn.
186 pages — £7.99

LETTERS OF
CAPTAIN SIR EDWARD HULSE
1st and 2nd Battalion Scots Guards

Edward Hulse became the 7th Baronet on the death of his father in 1903 at the age of thirteen. He was educated at Eton College and went up to Balliol. Apart from running his estates Edward was an officer in the Coldstream Guards from 1912 before transferring to the Scots Guards the next year. He went out to France with the BEF at the outbreak of war and served with the 1st Battalion until November 1914 when he transferred to the 2nd Battalion Scots Guards. His account of the 'Christmas Truce' at Ploegsteert is often quoted and referred to — his original letter forms part of the book. It is a fascinating history that traces the many actions from Mons to Neuve Chapelle where he was killed on Friday 12th March 1915. In Part II there are cameos on fifty-eight personalities mentioned in his letters.
170 pages — £8.45

LETTERS FROM FRANCE –
A D GILLESPIE
Argyll & Sutherland Highlanders

Douglas Gillespie was an intelligent young man who was educated at Winchester and New College, Oxford. He was well travelled and but for the First World War he was expected to become an accomplished lawyer. He was commissioned and left for France in February 1915. He served on the Ypres Salient and in northern France being killed on Sunday 26th September 1915 during the Battle of Loos. His long and detailed letters provide an intimate view about life in the trenches. The original book was published by his family in 1916. In Part II there are cameos on twenty-eight personalities mentioned in his letters.
228 pages — £9.45

THE LETTERS OF GEORGE BRENTON LAURIE
1st Battalion Royal Irish Rifles

Lieutenant Colonel George Laurie born in Canada who became a professional soldier. He was gazetted to the Royal Irish Rifles in September 1885, the last officer to be commissioned in the Army with the rank of Lieutenant. He served with them in Gibraltar, Egypt, Sudan, Malta, South Africa, Ireland, India and Aden before the First World War. He was appointed to command the 1st Battalion in 1912 and took them to France in November 1914. He was in the front line and participated in the 'Christmas Truce'. He was killed on Friday 12th March 1915 during the Battle of Neuve Chapelle. His fascinating letters from a senior front line officer are packed with information and cheery news from the trenches. The original book was compiled by his wife in May 1921 and dedicated to his three children. In Part II there are cameos on sixty-two personalities mentioned in his letters and notes on some of the events.
214 pages — **£8.45**

LETTERS TO HIS WIFE, WAR POEMS AND OTHER VERSES – ROBERT ERNEST VERNÈDE
12th Battalion Rifle Brigade

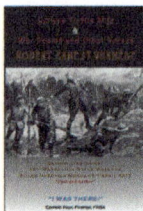

In this publication I have combined two of Ernest's books, *'Letters To His Wife'* that was published in 1917 and covers his life in the First World War, and *'Poems and Other Verses'* that were written during war were published in 1920. Ernest was a popular author who published his first novel, *'The Pursuit of Mr Faviel'*, in 1905.
Ernest was keen to play his part in the war but due to his age he had been turned down several times. Eventually he was able to enlist in the Public School Battalion, Royal Fusiliers, and whilst training was sent for officer training. In November 1915 Ernest left for France and he served in northern France, the Ypres Salient, the Somme and was killed on the opening day of the Battle of Arras.
His wonderfully individually styled letters, coupled with his poems, makes a terrific read. In Part II there are cameos on twenty-eight personalities plus notes on events mentioned in his letters coupled with information on his novels.
232 pages — **£8.45**

RICHARD VINCENT SUTTON, A RECORD OF HIS LIFE
1st Life Guards
attached Guards Machine Gun Regiment and Staff

Sir Richard Sutton, 6th Baronet, or 'Dick' as he was known to his family and friends, inherited his title at a very young age. This wonderfully produced book was shortly after his death that covers his life from birth. His first letters are from Ludgrove Preparatory School and contain some of his little sketches he sent home. Dick went out to Belgium in October 1914 and soon saw service at the First Battle of Ypres. He continued to serve with the Life Guards until he joined General Sir Henry Rawlinson and served on his staff until at his own request he returned to the front with the Guards Machine Gun Regiment. Dick survived the war only to succumb to influenza and died on Friday 29th November 1918. In Part II there are cameos on eighty-five personalities plus extensive notes on events mentioned in his letters.
318 pages — **£10.99**

A MEMOIR – JULIAN & BILLY GRENFELL AND FRANCIS & RIVERSDALE GRENFELL

The book amalgamates two publications on the Grenfell cousins, Julian and Billy, Francis and Riversdale. The four of them would give their lives for King and Country during the first year of the First World War with Francis winning the Victoria Cross and Julian the Distinguished Service Order. Julian was a poet who wrote the well-known poem *'Into Battle'* amongst many others.
Julian, 3rd Baron Grenfell, who was named after his illustrious relation, has kindly written a fascinating introduction to the publication, that provides a contemporary and valuable insight to the family.
Their separate but intertwined lives prior to and during the war provide a fascinating insight into the attitudes of society, the language and a way of life that vanished at the conclusion of the war.
Within ten months the four of them had been killed after seeing the horrors of the First World War from the beginning. Riversdale was the first to die on Friday 4th September 1914 and in 1915 Francis died on Monday 24th May, two days later Julian succumbed to his wounds on Wednesday 26th and finally Billy who was killed on Friday 30th July 1915. We will never know

what contribution they would have made to society, like so many their promising futures were cut short.

In Part III there are cameos on eighty-six personalities plus extensive notes on events mentioned in his letters.

322 pages — **£11.99**

CHARLES LISTER, LETTERS AND RECOLLECTIONS
Royal Marines,
Hood Battalion Royal Naval Division

Charles Lister was the second son of Thomas, Baron Ribblesdale and Lady Charlotte. He had a typical upbringing for a member of the aristocracy and was educated at Eton College before going up to Balliol College, Oxford.

A highly intelligent young man Charles decided to make his life as a diplomat. He passed the Civil Service examinations then served in Rome and Constantinople. Through his family and friends he was also able to spend considerable time in India and Europe. His knowledge of the diplomatic situation and personal insight during the build up to and outbreak of the First World War is fascinating.

As soon as it was possible Charles volunteered and joined the army. He first worked as an interpreter before joining the Royal Naval Division and being sent to serve at Gallipoli. During the voyage he was with his great friend, Rupert Brooke, who died *en route* and Charles was responsible for the burial party. He was wounded shortly after arriving on the beaches but refused the offer to return to a desk job in the Foreign Office. Charles rejoined his men at the front where he was slightly wounded however he made light of it in his letters. Charles was wounded for the third time and he died on board the hospital ship, the *SS Gascon*. He now lies in East Mudros Military Cemetery.

Lord Ribblesdale published *'Letters and Recollections'* a year after Charles' death. I have re-set the original book and, where appropriate, added contemporary illustrations to compliment the text.

Part III of this publication contains additional information and over eighty cameos of those who were mentioned in the original publication.

392 pages — **£12.49**

In Continuing & Grateful Memory
Specialised Battlefield Tours

I began organising battlefield tours to the Western Front in 1981. In the early years I enjoyed taking veterans back to where they had served on the battlefields, from Ypres to the Somme. Many of them had never previously returned to the battlefields they had left at the end of the First World War — sadly those opportunities no longer exist.

The fully-guided specialised tours normally are for four or five days starting in Dover. We stay in a high standard of hotels (based in central locations), with all meals, museum entrances *et al* included. (The only additional costs are for additional personal drinks not already provided with meals etc and single room supplements.) The tours welcome everyone and we provide time to accommodate individual requests and visits. We cater for all levels of knowledge — from the expert to the first-time visitor.

The main aim is that you enjoy your trip; also that you will improve your knowledge, visit new places, return feeling you have received good value for money — then come back again on another tour!

My tour each year to Ypres for 11th November that has become an institution includes, in addition to tour of the Salient and the ceremonies in the town, a Remembrance Day Reception and Dinner with an after-dinner speech. The tours throughout the rest of the year are based on specific battles, places and personalities, with new tours added each year. A full information pack, with notes and maps, support the tour.

If you would be interested in joining a forthcoming tour and would like further information please contact me:

visit: www.remembering1418.com

email: remembering@btinternet.com

post: c/o 15 Cress Way, Faversham, Kent ME13 7NH

I look forward to the opportunity of meeting you on a tour.

Paul Foster

Paul Foster, FRSA

Lightning Source UK Ltd.
Milton Keynes UK
UKOW06f1617121014

239990UK00005B/29/P